"Kracht has accomplished excellent, dedicated work in providing his assessment of these incredibly important fieldnotes from, it should be recognized, an exceptionally special group of honored elders."

—INÉS HERNÁNDEZ-ÁVILA, *Reading Religion*

"Benjamin Kracht provides keen insight into the belief system and worldview of the Kiowa people. This ethnographic window reveals what is sacred, powerful, and spiritual among this warrior people of the southern plains. Kracht's scholarship advances our understanding of the true reality of the Kiowas."

—DONALD L. FIXICO, Distinguished Foundation Professor of History at Arizona State University and author of *Call for Change: The Medicine Way of American Indian History, Ethos, and Reality*

"*Kiowa Belief and Ritual* offers a meticulously researched and richly detailed account of pre-reservation Kiowa religious life. Benjamin Kracht makes extensive use of interviews conducted with Kiowa elders in 1935, and their recollections and experiences make for compelling reading. This is a significant contribution to the literature on Native North America."

—MICHAEL PAUL JORDAN, assistant professor of ethnology at Texas Tech University

"[An] encyclopedic and yet still surprisingly personalized . . . rendition of Kiowa religion. The result is what could hardly be imagined as a more complete summary of a people's beliefs and rituals at a particular moment in time—a moment that had just ended when the data were collected and that, despite all of the tribulations and losses faced by the Kiowa, continues not only to be remembered but to reverberate through their culture."

—JACK DAVID ELLER, *Anthropology Review Database*

KIOWA BELIEF AND RITUAL

Studies in the
Anthropology of
North American
Indians Series

EDITORS

Raymond J. DeMallie
Douglas R. Parks

KIOWA BELIEF AND RITUAL

Benjamin R. Kracht

Published by the University of Nebraska Press,
Lincoln, in cooperation with the
American Indian Studies Research Institute,
Indiana University, Bloomington

The University of Nebraska Press is part of a land-grant institution with campuses and programs on the past, present, and future homelands of the Pawnee, Ponca, Otoe-Missouria, Omaha, Dakota, Lakota, Kaw, Cheyenne, and Arapaho Peoples, as well as those of the relocated Ho-Chunk, Sac and Fox, and Iowa Peoples.

First Nebraska paperback printing: 2022

Library of Congress Cataloging-in-Publication Data
Names: Kracht, Benjamin R., 1955– author.
Title: Kiowa belief and ritual / Benjamin R. Kracht.
Description: Lincoln: University of Nebraska Press, in cooperation with the American Indian Studies Research Institute, Indiana University, Bloomington, [2017] | Series: Studies in the anthropology of North American Indians | Includes bibliographical references and index.
Identifiers: LCCN 2016039778 (print)
LCCN 2016040279 (ebook)
ISBN 9781496200532 (cloth: alk. paper)
ISBN 9781496232656 (paperback)
ISBN 9781496201461 (pdf)
Subjects: LCSH: Kiowa Indians—Religion. | Kiowa Indians—Rites and ceremonies. | Indiana University, Bloomington. American Indian Studies Research Institute, issuing body.
Classification: LCC E99.K5 K73 2017 (print) | LCC E99.K5 (ebook) | DDC 978.004/97492—dc23
LC record available at
https://lccn.loc.gov/2016039778

Set in Merope by Rachel Gould.

For B. Harold Kracht
and Clifton Tongkeamah,
my fathers. And my
children, Elena and Robert.

Contents

Illustrations

Kiowa Pronunciations

Though some scholars today use the Parker McKenzie system for rendering Kiowa language terms (Palmer 2003; Meadows 1999, 2008, 2010), I prefer the system utilized by Laurel Watkins (1984).

Kiowa phonemes are as follows:

CONSONANTS (WATKINS 1984, 7)

p'	Ejective labial stop; articulated forcefully.[1]
t'	Ejective dental stop; articulated forcefully.
k'	Ejective velar stop; articulated forcefully.
p^h	Aspirated labial stop; articulated forcefully.[2]
t^h	Aspirated dental stop; articulated forcefully.
k^h	Aspirated velar stop; articulated forcefully.
p	Voiceless labial stop; as in pat.
t	Voiceless dental stop; as in tag.
k	Voiceless velar stop; as in cone.
$?$	Voiceless laryngeal stop; glottal stop.
b	Voiced labial stop; as in boat.
d	Voiced dental stop; as in dog.
g	Voiced velar stop; as in goat.
ts'	Ejective alveolar affricate; hissing noise.
ts	Voiceless alveolar affricate; as in soap.
s	Voiceless alveolar fricative; as in sit.
h	Voiceless laryngeal fricative; as in hide.
z	Voiced alveolar fricative; as in zebra.
m	Labial nasal; as in mine.
n	Dental nasal; as in nice.

l	Dental liquid; as in leaf.[3]
y	Palatal glide; acts as a diphthong with back vowels *u'*, *o'*, and *w'* and with low front vowel *a*.
i	High front vowel; as in he.[4]

VOWELS (WATKINS 1984, 9)

e	Mid front vowel; as in hay.
a	Low front vowel; as in law.
u	High back vowel; as in you.
o	Mid back vowel; as in toe.
ɔ	Low back vowel; as in caught.

Precisely following the Watkins orthography, however, is somewhat problematic since it was published later than most sources on Kiowa culture and religion; hence variant spellings of names appear throughout published and unpublished sources. Kiowa names appearing in this work are spelled according to cited sources. As the majority of the 1935 fieldnotes are typewritten, the limited number of keys representing international phonetic alphabet, tone, nasal, and stress markers, as well as variant spellings, make orthography somewhat inconsistent. In some cases, the students rendered words phonetically or added diacritical markers in pencil, so I tried to follow the handwritten spellings whenever possible. Because 1935-era typewriters did not have a key for low back vowel /ɔ/, /w/ was used instead. Because word-processing tools allow for the use of IPA characters, I substituted /ɔ/ for /w/ whenever possible. For instance, the word for power, which appears as *dwdw* in the fieldnotes, is rendered as *dɔdɔ* in the text. Otherwise I have maintained the integrity of the original spellings. I also adopted the spellings used by each student, regardless of inconsistencies. Variant spellings of names also were cross-checked using the "List of Persons" published by Merrill et al. (1997, 335–438).

Notably, scholarly works on the Kiowas by William C. Meadows (1999, 2008, 2010) have modified the original orthography from the 1935 fieldnotes into the Parker McKenzie system, potentially changing the pronunciation and meaning of the firsthand spellings. In addition, such modifications do not account for the presence of four Kiowa dialects associated with the modern communities near Anadarko, Carnegie, Hobart, and Meers, Oklahoma.

Regarding different orthographies, it should be pointed out that within the Kiowa community, there is no single system that has widespread usage. For instance, I attended a conversational Kiowa class in Anadarko on May 23, 1994, taught by David L. Paddlety and have a copy of the work sheet that was distributed that day. The orthography employed by Paddlety is somewhat similar to the style used in the photocopied Kiowa hymnals available in some of the Baptist and Methodist churches. Nevertheless, Paddlety commented that the language classes taught in Carnegie use a different orthography.

Preface

Unfinished Business: The 1935 Santa Fe
Laboratory of Anthropology Expedition

Given the grim economic depression of the 1930s, it is truly remarkable that the Laboratory of Anthropology in Santa Fe, New Mexico, sponsored two ethnographic field schools in the Southern Plains (Ewers 1992, x), an area typically overlooked by researchers favoring the indigenous cultures of the Southwest or the Northern and Central Plains. In 1933, the first field school, directed by Ralph Linton (University of Wisconsin), was conducted in southwestern Oklahoma among the Comanches, and the second field school, directed by Alexander Lesser (Columbia University) in 1935, focused on the neighboring Kiowas. Both field schools compiled massive data resulting in a number of publications on these formerly nomadic Plains tribes (Hoebel 1941, 1960; Linton 1935; Wallace and Hoebel 1952; Mishkin 1940; Richardson 1940; Collier 1944), though the planned collaborative ethnographies never materialized (DeMallie and Ewers 2001, 37). Recently, the collective Comanche fieldnotes were compiled and edited by Thomas W. Kavanagh (2008), but the much more extensive Kiowa fieldnotes, which contain invaluable information about the prereservation-period horse and buffalo culture, remain largely unpublished.[1]

Due to budget cuts in 1935, the Santa Fe Laboratory of Anthropology was compelled to eliminate funding for archaeology, so that year fellowships were available to students only for the ethnographic field study among the Kiowas. Applications were due by April 5, and scholarship recipients were to be notified by director Jesse L. Nusbaum in early

June. Successful candidates would receive round-trip transportation to the field site—Anadarko, Oklahoma—in addition to subsistence costs during the nine-week period.[2] The Kiowa field party was one of the final Rockefeller Foundation–funded ethnographic field expeditions sponsored by the Laboratory of Anthropology.[3]

Alexander Lesser arrived in Anadarko on June 19 to establish "living quarters" for the students and then spent the next four days traveling "many hundreds of miles visiting the old men and women of the tribe and explaining our purposes and plans. Thus, informants and interpreters were available before the group assembled."[4] On June 24, 1935, five anthropology graduate students converged in Anadarko for their first official meeting with Professor Lesser: Donald Collier (University of Chicago), R. Weston LaBarre (Yale University), Jane Richardson (University of California), William R. Bascom (University of Wisconsin), and Bernard Mishkin (Columbia University). By the time they departed on August 28, they had compiled over thirteen hundred pages of single-spaced fieldnotes derived from cross-interviewing thirty-five Kiowas employing as many as twelve interpreters.[5]

In his final report, Lesser noted that the students had gathered "ample, perhaps exceptional, material on Kiowa economics, political organization, authority, law, rank, kinship, family life, warfare, societies (men's and women's), religious conceptions, the vision complex, medicine men and sorcery, the Sun Dance, the Ten Medicine complex, cult movements, etc."[6] However, only three publications resulted from this extensive data base (Mishkin 1940; Richardson 1940; Collier 1944), so the bulk of the 1935 Santa Fe Laboratory of Anthropology Kiowa fieldnotes remain unpublished. Hence a wealth of information pertaining to nineteenth-century Kiowa culture is available in these materials, today housed in the National Anthropological Archives.[7] Of special importance are the data pertaining to indigenous Kiowa belief systems, since there is scant literature covering indigenous Southern Plains religions.

Significantly, the 1935 Santa Fe Laboratory of Anthropology field school provided the graduate students an opportunity to interview the survivors of the prereservation horse and buffalo culture, which ended abruptly in May 1875, after which the Kiowas were forced to reside within boundaries set forth by the October 1867 Medicine Lodge Treaty. Collecting memory ethnographies typified early twentieth-century anthropological fieldwork, whose practitioners feared that indigenous lifeways and knowledge systems would disappear in a rapidly changing world. These eyewitness and first-generation reflections on the horse and buffalo days are undoubtedly the best materials available for reconstructing preservation Kiowa beliefs and rituals.

Concomitantly, Alice Marriott—the first woman to receive an anthropology degree from the University of Oklahoma—conducted ethnographic fieldwork with the Kiowas in the summers of 1935 and 1936 and maintained contact with her Kiowa friends until her death in 1992. Marriott's paid interpreter was Ioleta Hunt MacElhaney, daughter of George Hunt of Mountain View, Oklahoma, who served as Marriott's principal informant (Marriott 1952, 54, 58; Marriott 1945, x). Hunt (Set-maun-te, or Bear Paw) spent his youth living with his uncle Tah-bone-mah, or I-see-o, who was an army scout for Fort Sill's Indian Troop L. Playing with the soldiers' children and attending their schools, Hunt learned English, which made him a valuable interpreter and informant for James Mooney, Hugh L. Scott, Wilbur S. Nye, and Marriott. Hunt's first wife was Odletay-di (Spliced Hair), who was known as Julia Given after attending Carlisle Indian Industrial School (Marriott knew Hunt's second wife, Lillie Goombi). Ioleta, their youngest daughter, obtained a sociology degree from Keuka College, a Baptist women's college, and subsequently worked as a teacher, social worker, and missionary. Marriott became an adopted member of the Hunt family, a relationship that enabled her to work with members of the extended family (Loughlin 2005, 132).

Marriott wrote about the Kiowas in *The Ten Grandmothers* (1945) and in *Greener Fields* (1952), an anecdotal account of her early fieldwork in southwestern Oklahoma and later fieldwork in New Mexico among the Pueblos. She also published a children's book, *The Black Stone Knife* (1957), and *Kiowa Years: A Study in Culture Impact* (1968), written for public schools through the auspices of the Anthropology Curriculum Study Project, sponsored by the American Anthropological Association. *The Ten Grandmothers*, undoubtedly her most popular book, offers useful information about indigenous Kiowa culture, though historical events, chronologies, and personal identities are distorted in this semifictional account following the lives of Hunting Horse's two wives from the mid-nineteenth century to World War II. For instance, in the first story, "The Bear," Marriott describes the death of Comanche warrior Red Sleeve in the summer of 1847. However, she embellishes the story by intertwining details concerning the death of bundle keeper Heap O' Bears in the summer of 1868 (Marriott 1945, 3–14). Although Marriott provides useful information throughout *The Ten Grandmothers*, particularly from a woman's perspective, for historical purposes the stories should be carefully scrutinized by comparing them to other sources — in this instance, James Mooney's *Calendar History of the Kiowa Indians* (1898, 286–87, 322–25).

Why did Marriott fictionalize stories about the Kiowas in *The Ten Grandmothers*? According to Patricia Loughlin, one of her biographers, Marriott "distanced herself from professional anthropologists, preferring to call herself an ethnologist who wrote for the general public" (Loughlin 2005, 127). Marriott's decision to present the Kiowas to a lay audience in lieu of the anthropological community makes her fieldnotes especially important. Typed copies of her fieldnotes, housed in the Western History Collections at the University of Oklahoma, contain valuable information about Kiowa culture. Marriott described the importance of her fieldnotes:

> Field notes are an anthropologist's investment in the future. Each time they are reviewed, different facts emerge, and differing relationships are established among them. If the same field notes could not supply information for more than one book, the anthropologist would have failed in his work or would not have matured as a person. (Marriott 1952, 119)

That Marriott fictionalized events and changed names in her publications enhances the value of her fieldnotes — now available to scholars — in comparison to the voluminous Santa Fe fieldnotes.

An interesting backstory relates to the coexistence of Marriott and the Santa Fe field party in Kiowa country during the summer of 1935. Significantly, there seems to have been little, if any, interaction between Marriott and the other students. LaBarre wrote Marriott's home address and phone number in the last page of his third spiral notebook, but there is no other mention of her in the Santa Fe fieldnotes.[8] In *Greener Fields*, Marriott alludes to an unnamed student — presumably LaBarre — as a rival from an "important university" who stole one of her informants in the summer of 1936. She accuses him of being "worse than unethical" in his elicitation of data pertaining to religion and claimed that he published an article—though its existence is unknown—about a Beowulf-like story among North American Indians, a story she previously had told to one of her collaborators (Marriott 1952, 90–95). An indirect reference to Marriott (and possibly to Carol K. Rachlin) appears in the introduction to LaBarre's (1957) unpublished autobiography of Charley Apekaum (Charcoal). LaBarre relates that the manuscript is a verbatim rendering except for the omission of several names, including those of "two ethnographers from the University of Oklahoma, of whom Apekaum was critical." LaBarre remarked that he had "no way of checking the justice of his [Charley's] comments" (LaBarre 1957, 1a), but this is undoubtedly a reference to Marriott and her advisor, Forrest E. Clements, head of the anthropology department. Obviously Marriott and LaBarre did not communicate, and it is doubtful that she had any connection to the Santa Fe field party, though both often worked independently with the same collaborators.

Marriott has been lauded as a female ethnographer who worked with women interpreters and collaborators to capture the feminist voice in ethnographic writing, something largely absent in early twentieth-century American anthropology, an era dominated by male anthropologists working mostly with men (Loughlin 2005, 128, 149). Indeed, Marriott brought more gender balance into ethnographic reporting, though it should be emphasized that Jane Richardson, the lone woman in the Santa Fe field party, interviewed Kiowa women in addition to men. Moreover, LaBarre, Collier, Mishkin, and Bascom also worked with women. Hence the Santa Fe fieldnotes represent a wealth of information solicited from men and women.

After the Santa Fe field school and Marriott's research ended, another twenty to forty years would pass before serious efforts were made to interview Kiowa elders, most of whom were at least two generations removed from prereservation times (Greene 2001, 29; Boyd 1981, xvii–xx). Publishing materials gleaned from the Santa Fe fieldnotes, augmented by Marriott's fieldnotes, will significantly enhance the existing literature concerning Plains religions.

Acknowledgments

Research for this book started in 1983 when I first met Betty Tanedooah, who was a student in introduction to cultural anthropology taught by Thomas M. Johnson at Southern Methodist University. I was Tom's teaching assistant. Betty introduced me to her husband, Clifton Tongkeamah (1932–1993), and both introduced me to Kiowa culture. Within several years, I had shifted my dissertation topic from urban Indian health to Kiowa belief systems. Over thirty years later, I still maintain close relationships with the remaining members of the Tongkeamah (also spelled Tongkeamha) family, including Raymond Tongkeamha, Prenella Tongkeamha, and Melissa Tongkeamha Kaulity (d. 2016). It's impossible to list all the Kiowas who have helped me over the years, though several deserve recognition, including Dorothy Tsatoke Gray, Gus Palmer Sr., Lavena Tongkeamha Pewo, Weiser and Henrietta Tongkeamha, Amos Aitson, Evalu Ware Russell, Patricia Ware, Richard and Trina Stumbling-bear, Ernest "Iron" Toppah, Hess Bointy, Bryan "Jake" Chanate, Roderick "Smokey" Gwoompi, and Ira Kaulay. During early days of fieldwork, Johnny and Marcia Davilla were instrumental in introducing me to Kiowas in the Anadarko area. Special thanks to Ray C. Doyah for reading earlier drafts of this manuscript.

Funding for ethnographic fieldwork and archival research came from various sources, including the Institute for the Study of Earth and Man, Graduate Council, and David J. Webber Anthropology Fellowship, Southern Methodist University; Smithsonian Institution Ten-Week Graduate Student Fellowship; Short-Term Fellowship, the D'Arcy McNickle Center for the Study of the American Indian, Newberry Library; Jacobs Research Funds, Whatcom Museum of History and Art; American Philosophical

Society, Phillips Fund for Native American Research and Faculty Research Committee grants, Northeastern State University.

The staff at the National Anthropological Archives deserves much credit for helping locate archival materials during my ten-week residency at the Smithsonian Institution during the summer of 1987, especially Vyrtis Thomas, Paula Fleming (the "Fairy Godmother"), and Kathleen Baxter. Ives Goddard was my advisor, and Marion Kaulaity Hansson, a fellow-in-residence, graciously shared her Kiowa perspective about the Santa Fe Laboratory of Anthropology fieldnotes. While at the Smithsonian, I spent evenings in the U.S. National Archives across the street, and hanging out with Leonard R. Bruguier (1944–2009), also a graduate student fellow. Those were extraordinary times.

Completion of this manuscript could not have occurred without the guidance and editorial assistance of Raymond J. DeMallie, teacher, mentor, and friend since my undergraduate days at Indiana University. His patience and support will always be appreciated. Thanks also go to Raymond A. Bucko and Daniel C. Swan for their thoughtful critiques of the manuscript. As always, I accept full responsibility for any errors contained within.

KIOWA BELIEF AND RITUAL

Introduction

Ethnographic Studies of Plains Indian Religions

Numerous books and articles describe the nomadic horse and buffalo and semisedentary village tribes of the Great Plains, but scholarly sources covering indigenous religious beliefs and practices are scant. Few monographs are solely devoted to tribal religions, and material on religion is scattered piecemeal or restricted to a single chapter in many historical and ethnographic accounts. Nevertheless, it is possible to contextualize the studies of Plains Indian religions into (1) eyewitness accounts; (2) compilations of folklore and mythology; (3) comprehensive studies of the Sun Dance and societies; (4) standalone monographs, dissertations, and articles; and (5) Native and collaborative accounts. A cursory examination of the literature will demonstrate the importance of the Santa Fe Kiowa fieldnotes and the need to publish more tribally specific accounts of indigenous Plains religions.

Eyewitness Accounts

Notable written accounts by explorers, traders, artists, photographers, missionaries, and military personnel describing Plains Indian cultures date back to the early nineteenth century. Though numerous publications resulted from their endeavors (DeMallie and Ewers 2001, 24–28), several works reporting on religious beliefs and practices merit mentioning. Between 1833 and 1856, American Fur Company trader Edward T. Denig lived in the Northern Plains and wrote about the Teton Sioux, Assiniboines, Plains Crees, Arikaras, and Crows (1930, 1961). Married to an Assiniboine woman, Denig (1930) wrote extensively on Assiniboine religion. In 1833, travelers in the Central and Northern Plains witnessed waning ceremonies, including one of the last Skiri Pawnee Morning Star ceremonies, observed in 1833 by naturalist Washington Irving (1868) and his nephew John Treat Irving (1835), and the Mandan Okipa ceremony, described and depicted by artist George Catlin that July (Catlin 1973, 1:155–84; Catlin 1967). After Catlin, Prince Maximilian of Wied-Neuwied, accompanied by Swiss artist Karl Bodmer, ascended the Upper Missouri River via steamboat and wintered at Fort Clark (1833–34), where they visited nearby Mandan and Hidatsa villages, documenting their rituals and belief systems before they were decimated by the 1837 smallpox epidemic (Maximilian 2008–12).

Other notable nineteenth-century studies include essays by R. S. Neighbors (1852) on the Comanches and Gideon Pond on the Dakotas (1854) in Henry Rowe Schoolcraft's six-volume encyclopedia on American Indian cultures. Pond published on the Dakota through the Minnesota Historical Society (G. Pond 1867), as did Samuel W. Pond (1908). What little is known about Tonkawa beliefs was collected by Albert Gatschet at Fort Griffin, Texas, in the 1880s (Gatschet 1884).

Folklore and Mythology

Two individuals at the turn of the last century stand out among independent researchers for ethnographic coverage of Plains cultures and religions: George Bird Grinnell and Edward S. Curtis. After graduating from Yale University in 1870, Grinnell, a naturalist and conservationist, made his first journey to the Great Plains. During his sojourns to the Plains from his home in New York City, Grinnell befriended many Plains Indians, eventually publishing Pawnee (1889, 1890) and Blackfoot (1892) folklore. Most of his publications, however, were devoted to Cheyenne culture, folklore, warfare, and religion (Grinnell 1910, 1914, 1915, 1923, 1926; Wishart 2004, 303–4; DeMallie and Ewers 2001, 32). Besides using Curtis's skills as a photographer, he and his collaborators conducted in-depth linguistic and ethnographic research on more than eighty tribes, including Plains cultures, culminating in an underutilized twenty-volume work, *The North American Indian* (1907–30), which includes materials on folklore, ceremonies, and mortuary practices (DeMallie and Ewers 2001, 33).

Besides documenting the Sun Dance, Dorsey published on the folklore of the Osages, Cheyennes, and Caddos (1904d, 1905b, 1905d); coauthored a volume of Arapaho oral traditions with Alfred L. Kroeber (Dorsey 1903a; Dorsey and Kroeber 1903); and through collaboration with Pawnee ethnographer James Murie produced collections of Arikara oral traditions (1904), Wichita mythology (1904b), and Skiri Pawnee oral traditions (1904c; Dorsey and Murie 1907; DeMallie and Ewers 2001, 35). Elsie Clews Parsons, a sociologist influenced by anthropologist Franz Boas, conducted most of her ethnographic fieldwork in the American Southwest but published a treatise on Kiowa folklore (Parsons 1929). Other students of Boas recording Plains folklore include Alfred L. Kroeber for the Gros Ventres (Kroeber 1907), Robert H. Lowie for the Crows (Lowie 1918), and Clark Wissler, who with a Native collaborator coauthored a collection of Blackfoot myths (Wissler and Duvall 1908).

Alice Marriott published a volume of Kiowa folklore (1963) and later collaborated with Carol K. Rachlin on a collection of Plains mythology (Marriott and Rachlin 1975). Another University of Oklahoma alumnus, Gilbert McAllister, recorded Plains Apache mythology (McAllister 1949). During this era, Richard W. Randolph befriended Oneha, the ninety-year-old daughter of storyteller Twenty Man, who taught him about Sweet Medicine and Northern Cheyenne folklore (Randolph 1937). In the 1980s, William T. Waters conducted fieldwork among the Chiewere Siouan–speaking Oto/Missourias and wrote a master's thesis on folklore (Waters 1984) and Douglas R. Parks published on Arikara folklore (Parks 1984, 1991).

Sun Dance and Societies

At the turn of the last century, museum anthropology—devoted to collecting and preserving the material and "mental" culture of American Indians—was at its zenith (Bucko 2004, 188). In 1905 Clark Wissler assumed responsibility for overseeing comparative studies of Plains cultures at the American Museum of Natural History and eventually produced two important anthologies, devoted to the diffusion of the Sun Dance and to societies and ceremonies (DeMallie and Ewers 2001, 34). Contributions to the Sun Dance volume (Wissler 1915–21) include descriptions of the ceremony as practiced by the Crows (Lowie 1915a), Oglalas (Walker 1917), Blackfoot (Wissler 1918), Hidatsas (Lowie 1919a), Shoshonis,

Utes, and Hidatsas (Lowie 1919a), Wind River Shoshonis and Utes (Lowie 1919d), Sarcees (Goddard 1919a), Plains Crees (Goddard 1919b; Skinner 1919a), Sissetons (Skinner 1919c), Plains Ojibwas (Goddard 1919c; Skinner 1919b), Canadian Dakotas (Wallis 1919), and Kiowas (Spier 1921a). Leslie Spier also contributed a summary essay that attempted to reconstruct the history of the ceremony as it spread from tribe to tribe (Spier 1921b).

Research conducted by Dorsey between 1900 and 1907 resulted in several Sun Dance monographs, including descriptions of the Arapaho (1903a), Cheyenne (1905c), and Ponca (1905a) ceremonies. Around the same time, Hugh L. Scott, stationed at Fort Sill, gathered information about the Kiowa Sun Dance, which had ended in 1890 (Scott 1911). Ralph Linton, director of the 1933 Santa Fe Laboratory of Anthropology field school, published an account of the Comanche Sun Dance (Linton 1935). A firsthand account of the Oglala Sun Dance written by a Native author was translated and edited by Ella C. Deloria, herself a Dakota (Deloria 1929). A classic among acculturation/culture change studies of the mid-twentieth century, Fred Voget's work documented the diffusion of the Wind River Shoshoni Sun Dance to the Crows (Voget 1950, 1984). Through her 1954–58 teaching position at the Lame Deer agency BIA school, Margot Liberty learned about the Northern Cheyenne Sun Dance (Liberty 1965, 1967, 1980). Fr. Peter J. Powell began working with Cheyennes in Montana at the same time and then eventually gathered data among Oklahoma Cheyennes. Coverage of the Sun Dance is found in volume 2 of his classic work *Sweet Medicine* (Powell 1969, 2:611–855), which includes photographs and color plates of Sun Dance paints. In a piece privately published the same year, independent scholar Edward A. Milligan (1969) describes a Teton and Yanktonai Sun Dance at Standing Rock Reservation.

Summary articles in Wissler's societies and ceremonies volume (Wissler 1912–1916) cover age grades (Lowie 1916a) and dancing and shamanistic societies (Wissler 1916). Tribal essays cover the Oglalas (Wissler 1912a), Blackfoot (Wissler 1913), Eastern Dakotas (Lowie 1913a), Crows, Hidatsas, and Mandans (Lowie 1913b), Crows (Lowie 1913c), Plains Crees (Skinner 1914a), Plains Ojibwas (Skinner 1914b), Iowas, Kansa, and Poncas (Skinner 1915a), Poncas (Skinner 1915b), Arikaras (Lowie 1915b), Plains Shoshonis (Lowie 1915c), and Kiowas (Lowie 1916a). Reo Fortune and

Margaret Mead spent the summer of 1930 in Nebraska with the Omahas, resulting in Fortune's study of secret societies (Fortune 1932).

Several firsthand accounts of the Sun Dance have been published. In 1881 John G. Bourke (1894) observed a Sun Dance at Pine Ridge Agency. Alice C. Fletcher of Harvard University's Peabody Museum witnessed Sioux (1883, 1887a, 1887b, 1887c) and Omaha rituals (1885, 1887d, 1892, 1896). Assisted by professional photographers, George A. Dorsey, curator of anthropology at Chicago's Field Columbian Museum, observed and recorded Arapaho and Cheyenne Sun Dances in the early twentieth century (1903a, 1905c). More recently Fr. Peter J. Powell recorded five Cheyenne Sun Dance ceremonies between 1959 and 1964 (Powell 1969, 611) and Thomas H. Lewis attended several Sun Dances on Pine Ridge Reservation in the 1960s (Lewis 1968, 1972).

Monographs, Dissertations, and Articles

Inspired by the theory of cultural evolution—that world cultures had progressed from stages of savagery to barbarism to civilization—John Wesley Powell, founder and first director of the Bureau of American Ethnology (BAE), founded in 1879, dispatched field workers to document the allegedly vanishing lifeways of American Indians. Many BAE ethnographies actually provide descriptive linguistic and cultural descriptions that are useful today to interpret indigenous belief systems if one overlooks the limitations of the evolutionary model imposed by Powell and other anthropologists of the late nineteenth century (DeMallie and Ewers 2001, 29–30; Bucko 2004, 188–89). Notable BAE scientists covering Plains religion were James Owen Dorsey, James Mooney, and Frances Densmore. Dorsey, formerly a missionary among the Omahas and Poncas, published the exceptional *Omaha Sociology* (1884), as well as works on Siouan religions (1885a, 1894) and Kansa mourning customs (1885b). Mooney (1896) documented and photographed the 1890–91 Ghost Dance movement. Although her studies focused primarily on music, Frances Densmore (1918) also thoroughly documented Lakota religion.

In 1899, Franz Boas was appointed professor of anthropology at Columbia University, and from there he dispatched the first generation of doctoral students to record cultural data from Plains tribes. Among his earliest students, Alfred L. Kroeber and Clark Wissler conducted fieldwork on the Northern Plains, resulting in monographs on the Arapaho (Kroeber 1902–7) and on Blackfoot bundles (Wissler 1912b). Part 2 of Kroeber's book covers Arapaho ceremonial organization, and part 3 describes religion. Wissler's position at the American Museum of Natural History enabled him to train and collaborate with independent field researchers who contributed several AMNH publications, enabling him to coauthor an article with archaeologist Herbert J. Spinden on the Skiri Pawnee Morning Star Ceremony (Wissler and Spinden 1916). Gilbert Wilson, employed by the American Museum from 1908 to 1918, coauthored an article on Hidatsa beliefs with George Pepper (Pepper and Wilson 1908).

Another student of Boas, Robert H. Lowie, engaged in fieldwork among the Assiniboines (1909) and the Comanches (1912; Kavanagh 2008) and wrote extensively about Crow religion (1914, 1922, 1924); the last seven chapters of his Crow monograph (1935) are devoted to religion, societies, and the Sun Dance. Before retiring from Columbia University in 1936, Boas sent some of his last students to the Plains to document languages and cultures, and to trace the diffusion of cultural traits, as in Ruth Benedict's classic study of the vision quest and guardian spirits (Benedict 1922, 1938). Between 1928 and 1936, Gene Weltfish spent time in Pawnee, Oklahoma, learning the language as a tool for understanding Pawnee lifeways and belief systems (Weltfish 1965). During their brief marriage, Alexander Lesser collaborated with Weltfish documenting the Caddoan languages but also wrote an important monograph about the Pawnee Ghost Dance and how the older hand game fused into this revitalization movement (Lesser 1933a).

During the Boasian era, several publications on Plains Indian religions originated from individuals not directly affiliated with Boas. Foremost was anti-Boasian Ralph Linton, who worked at the Field Museum from 1922 to 1927 (Bohannan and Glazer 1988, 183) and used manuscripts from Dorsey and Murie to produce several articles on Skiri Pawnee bundles and ceremonies, including the Morning Star Ceremony (Linton 1922a, 1922c, 1923a, 1923b, 1926). Joab Spencer, a missionary in Kansas, wrote about Kansa customs, including the Calumet Dance (Spencer 1908). Melvin Gilmore, a University of Nebraska graduate who spent his early professional career at the Nebraska and North Dakota state historical societies, published on Hidatsa and Arikara beliefs and bundles (Gilmore

1926, 1932). Students at the University of Chicago during the tenure of A. R. Radcliffe-Brown (1931–37) were encouraged to study kinship and social organization; some of Radcliffe-Brown's students merged British social anthropology with the American Boasian tradition, resulting in studies of kinship and social organization by Fred Eggan, as well as in-depth cultural studies (DeMallie 1994, 5–7; DeMallie and Ewers 2001, 37–38), including books on Mandan and Hidatsa kinship and ceremonial organization by Alfred Bowers (1950, 1965) and studies of Plains Apache bundles and shamanism by Gilbert McAllister (1965, 1970).

By the mid-twentieth century, monographs on Plains Indian cultures included scant information from elderly survivors of the horse and buffalo era, as the majority of them had passed away. Ethnographic data collecting now depended on oral traditions passed down from the parental and grandparental generations, increasing the chronological gap from firsthand information about prereservation lifeways and belief systems. Nevertheless, numerous historical ethnographies as well as synchronic studies focusing on contemporary issues were being published. Most scholars, however, favored reservation communities, resulting in more publications about Northern Plains tribes, especially the Lakotas and Cheyennes. Perhaps the desire to study seemingly less acculturated groups (Bucko 2004, 190) created a bias against fieldwork in the Central and Southern Plains, especially postallotment Oklahoma (after 1901).

John C. Ewers, a student of Clark Wissler at Yale University, began fieldwork with the Blackfoot in 1941 after becoming the first museum curator on the Blackfeet Reservation in northwestern Montana. Some of the elders born in the mid-nineteenth century contributed information to *The Blackfeet*, which includes a chapter on indigenous belief systems (Ewers 1958). Linguistically related to the Cheyennes, Arapahos, and Blackfoot, the Algonkian-speaking Gros Ventres (Atsinas) were the subject of a monograph on religion by Fr. John M. Cooper (1957), edited posthumously by his student Regina Flannery. In another Northern Plains study, folklorist Thomas Vennum (1982) traced the diffusion of the Dakota Drum, or Dream Dance, to the Plains Ojibwas. E. Adamson Hoebel—a participant in the 1933 Comanche field school—trekked to the Lame Deer Agency in Montana during the summers of 1935 and 1936 and eventually published a succinct historical ethnography (Hoebel 1960) that includes chapters on Cheyenne ceremonies, worldviews, and personality. More recent historical ethnographies with chapters covering religion were written by John H. Moore (1987, 1996), who began working with the Cheyennes in 1970 and wrote his dissertation on religion (Moore 1974), though he spent more time with the Southern Cheyennes after he moved to Oklahoma in 1977. After Mari Sandoz introduced him to Northern Cheyennes in 1956, Fr. Peter Powell began working with elders born as early as the 1860s and has written about the Sacred Arrows, the Medicine Hat, and the Sun Dance (Powell 1958, 1960, 1969 [vol. 2]).

Besides heavily including the Cheyennes, the Northern Plains literature is also dominated by the Sioux, especially the Lakotas. The Yuwipi rite, a divinatory ceremony performed at Pine Ridge Reservation, is the subject of Luis S. Kemnitzer's doctoral thesis and two articles (1968, 1970, 1976). Likewise, Yuwipi is the central theme in a monograph by William K. Powers (1982), who also wrote a historical ethnography that reconstructs early eighteenth-century Oglala beliefs and rituals and then moves into the twentieth century with an examination of the seven rites through social structure and social relations (Powers 1977). Raymond J. DeMallie provides an overview of nineteenth-century Lakota religious beliefs (DeMallie 1987) in an edited volume delineating indigenous beliefs, the advent of Christianity, and traditions in the contemporary context (DeMallie and Parks et al. 1987). More recently, Fr. Raymond A. Bucko published a comprehensive history of the Lakota sweat lodge ritual based on his Pine Ridge fieldwork (Bucko 1998).

The religious beliefs and rituals of other Northern Plains Siouan groups have received some attention in the literature. In his article on Dakota "tree dweller cults" James H. Howard (1955) describes the forest sprite in Santee, Yankton, and Yanktonai mythology as a typically malevolent being who lured hunters deep into the forest but could bestow upon selected individuals healing powers, hunting success, or even clairvoyance. Ethnographic accounts of the Canadian Sioux (Howard 1984) and the Stoneys (Snow 1977) describe belief and ritual, and Rodney Frey's (1987) monograph provides a brief historical sketch of the Crows and then examines modern-day worldviews and sacred rites. Northern Plains Village Tradition cultures—the Mandans, Hidatsas, and Arikaras—were studied in the early to mid-twentieth century, though more recent research by

Caddoan specialist Douglas R. Parks has shed light on Arikara beliefs. Working with some of the last fluent Arikara speakers, Parks collected and edited stories pertaining to mythology and concepts of power (Parks 1991). The sacred and political geography of the linguistically related Pawnees, formerly of Nebraska, is described by Parks and Waldo R. Wedel (1985). Other Central Plains tribes, the Dhegiha Siouan–speaking Omahas and Poncas as well as the Chiewere Siouan–speaking Oto/Missourias have received some coverage in Howard's (1965) Ponca monograph, and the religious beliefs of the Quapaws, Dhegiha speakers of the Southern Plains, have been described by historian David Baird (1980) and Ottawa County, Oklahoma, historian Velma S. Nieberding (1976).

Compared to the Northern Cheyennes, the Southern Cheyennes of western Oklahoma have received little coverage. Created by culture hero Sweet Medicine, Cheyenne warrior societies, as described by Karen Daniels Peterson (1964), played important roles in ceremonials like the Sun Dance and Sacred Arrows renewal ceremonies. Harold N. Ottaway (1970) wrote a short treatise on the Sacred Arrow ceremony derived from his master's thesis, and more recently Karl H. Schlesier (1987) published a speculative reconstruction of late nineteenth-century Cheyenne ceremonialism and shamanism. Among works focusing on Southern Plains groups, several specifically describe Plains Apache mourning and death practices (Opler and Bittle 1961; Sanford 1971). An independent researcher, Kay Parker Schweinfurth (2002), delineates Plains Apache spirituality utilizing William E. Bittle's Plains Apache fieldnotes, particularly the transcribed stories of seven elders born between 1876 and 1903. Bittle, and students from the University of Oklahoma's anthropological field school, worked with the Plains Apaches from 1952 into the late 1960s. Two doctoral dissertations are the sole ethnographic/historic works regarding Comanche (Gelo 1986) and Kiowa (Kracht 1989) belief systems.

Drawing largely upon twentieth-century ethnographies, religious studies professors Howard L. Harrod and Lee Irwin have nicely summarized nineteenth-century Plains Indian belief and ritual in several monographs. Three books by Harrod examine Northern Plains religions. *Renewing the World* (1987) compares ritual and symbolic forms in Crow, Cheyenne, Arapaho, and Blackfoot cultures to ascertain the relationship between symbolic forms enacted in ritual and "the shape of religious and moral attitudes, dispositions, and sensibilities among peoples of the Northwestern Plains" (Harrod 1987, 1). Cultural and religious identity among the Mandans, Hidatsas, Cheyennes, and Crows are examined in light of cultural transformation during the prereservation era in *Becoming and Remaining a People* (1995). In his final book, *The Animals Came Dancing: Native American Sacred Ecology and Animal Kinship* (2000), Harrod expands his comparative database to include the Atsinas, Western Crees, Lakotas, Assiniboines, Arikaras, and Central Plains Pawnees. Based on his comparative study of the twelve Plains cultures, Harrod identifies cultural patterns embodied in shared symbols and religious beliefs reflecting the kinship between animals and hunting cultures. Finally, through examination of over 350 "dream accounts" representing twenty-three Plains tribes, Lee Irwin (1994) has constructed a "visionary epistemé," the shared characteristics of the Plains vision quest.

Native and Collaborative Accounts

Most scholarly studies of Plains Indian religions could not occur without bilingual Native collaborators assisting and translating for non-Indian researchers; oftentimes collaborators receive little recognition for their contributions. Moreover, Native voices typically are filtered through the lenses of anthropology, history, religious studies, literature, and other academic and nonacademic viewpoints, resulting in one-sided analyses. Despite the fact that the literature covering Plains religions is written primarily by non-Indians, individuals from various Plains tribes have made significant contributions that have offered a better understanding of indigenous belief systems.

At the turn of the last century, important contributions to Central Plains studies of religion were made by Francis La Flesche and James Murie. Of mixed Omaha/Ponca and French descent, La Flesche, a chief's son, grew up on the Omaha Reservation in Nebraska, received a master's degree in law in Washington DC, and eventually worked for the BAE. He assisted and interpreted for Alice C. Fletcher, who guided his anthropological education. Together, they authored a comprehensive Omaha ethnography in which one chapter covers religion (Fletcher and La Flesche 1911). On his own, La Flesche published several articles on Omaha religion (1889, 1890) and later conducted extensive research on Osage religion (La

Flesche 1919, 1920, 1921, 1930, 1939, 1995). Also born in Nebraska, James Murie, of mixed Pawnee descent, received a four-year education at Hampton Institute and was taught anthropology through collaborative work with Alice C. Fletcher, George A. Dorsey, and Clark Wissler. Murie's work with Dorsey resulted in collections of Arikara (Dorsey 1904a), Wichita (Dorsey 1904b), and Skiri Pawnee oral traditions (Dorsey 1904c; Dorsey and Murie 1907; DeMallie and Ewers 2001, 35). From Murie's collaboration with Fletcher came an important study of the Pawnee Hako ceremony (Fletcher and Murie 1904) and shorter accounts of other Pawnee ceremonies (Fletcher 1899, 1900, 1902, 1903). Murie's work under Wissler's supervision produced studies of men's societies and ceremonies (Murie 1914, 1981). More recently, professional astronomer Von Del Chamberlain (1982) based his treatise on Pawnee cosmology and ethnoastronomy on the publications of Murie, Fletcher, Dorsey, and Weltfish.

Independent field researchers who collaborated with Wissler contributed several American Museum of Natural History publications. Notable works were produced on Blackfoot mythology from data gathered by David C. Duvall, a Blackfoot (Wissler and Duvall 1908), and texts dictated or written by Lakota holy men collected by James R. Walker—a physician at Pine Ridge Agency—produced a thorough study of Lakota belief and ritual (Walker 1917, 1980). Also connected to museum studies, National Museum of the American Indian deputy assistant director George P. Horse Capture (Gros Ventre) published Fred Gone's account of the seven visions of Bull Lodge (Horse Capture 1980). Northern Cheyenne historian John Stands in Timber taught Margot Liberty about the Sun Dance and the sacred Medicine Hat bundle (Liberty 1965, 1967, 1968). Stands in Timber has also worked with Fr. Powell. A collaborative ethnography by Robin Ridington and Denis Hastings (Omaha) describes the Omaha Sacred Pole and its repatriation by Harvard University's Peabody Museum (Ridington and Hastings 1997).

Beginning in the late 1920s, a myriad of biographies and autobiographies about American Indians were published, many by non-anthropologists. Although these are too numerous to name them all, several monographs in particular merit attention due to partial coverage of prereservation belief and ritual. Undoubtedly the most famous works cover the Oglalas, including Luther Standing Bear's (1928) autobiographical account of his youth at the Great Sioux Reservation, travels with Buffalo Bill's Wild West show, education at Carlisle Indian School, and eyewitness observations of events surrounding the Ghost Dance movement. *Land of the Spotted Eagle* (Standing Bear 1933) is more important for the study of religion. Considered an American classic, *Black Elk Speaks* (Neihardt 1932) resulted from John Neihardt's 1930 interviews with holy man Black Elk, who recounted his power vision and experiences with the Wild West show and the Ghost Dance, or "messiah craze," at Pine Ridge. Inspired by Black Elk's revelations to John Neihardt, Joseph Epes Brown went searching for the elderly sage and spent the winter of 1947–48 learning about the sacred pipe and the affiliated seven sacred ceremonies (Brown 1953). Working with transcriptions of Neihardt's 1931 and 1944 interview data, DeMallie (1984) has provided detailed biographical information about holy man Black Elk in *The Sixth Grandfather*.

Mari Sandoz's (1942) biography of Crazy Horse was based in part on stories she heard from Oglala elders visiting her childhood home on the upper Niobrara River and from later interviews with those who had known Crazy Horse. Other notable ethnographic portraits provide good coverage of Plains Apache Jim Whitewolf (Brant 1969), Crow chief Plenty-Coups (Linderman 1930), Northern Cheyenne Wooden Leg (1931), and Comanche medicine woman Sanapia (Jones 1972). Unfortunately, Weston LaBarre's autobiography of his Kiowa friend and interpreter Charles Apekaum (Charley Charcoal) remains unpublished (LaBarre 1957). All of these sources have pertinent information regarding belief systems.

Sources on Kiowa Culture and Religion

Published sources on Kiowa religion date back to the early 1870s. Thomas C. Battey, a Quaker missionary and schoolteacher, was probably the first Euro-American to witness and write about Kiowa religious ceremonies. Friend Battey, who traveled with Kicking Bird's band during the summer of 1873, attended the "Maggot Creek Sun Dance" on Sweetwater Creek, a tributary of the North Fork of the Red River in the Texas Panhandle. Although he understood very little of Kiowa beliefs and rituals, Friend Battey noted some personal rituals connected to medicine shields, curing, and mourning, and he recorded Kicking Bird's interpretation of the cosmos and afterlife (Battey 1968, 166–84, 208–10, 147–49, 243–45, 106–

11). James Mooney later praised Battey's account, initially published in 1875, despite some inaccuracies resulting from interpreters inadequately versed in the Kiowa version of Plains sign language (Mooney 1898, 440).

James Mooney, the first ethnologist to conduct ethnographic fieldwork with the Kiowas, is still favorably remembered by Kiowa elders. In fact, elderly collaborators have pulled old, dusty copies of his masterful *Calendar History of the Kiowa Indians* (1898) off their shelves in response to some of my questions, a phenomenon that Marriott also experienced (Marriott 1952, 36). A newspaper journalist from Richmond, Indiana, Mooney was hired in 1885 by BAE director John Wesley Powell in recognition of Mooney's eagerness to accumulate American Indian ethnographic data. During the last week of December 1890, Mooney was en route to Indian Territory to work with the Western Cherokees—he planned to travel farther west afterward to study the Kiowa language— when he learned of the December 29, 1890, tragedy at Wounded Knee, South Dakota, which compelled him to spend the next few years investigating the Ghost Dance religion among Great Plains and Great Basin tribes (Merrill et al. 1997, 2). While visiting present-day southwestern Oklahoma in early 1891, Mooney first met the Kiowas, who became his favorite tribe (Ewers 1979, vii–viii). Twelve years later, in 1903, Mooney described why he chose the Kiowas for a major research project: "Now I am most of my time with the Kiowas. I hope to work them up as a complete tribal study. I picked them out about twelve years ago, after having seen a great many tribes, as being the best study tribe upon the Plains, and the most conservative—as being the most Indian" (Mooney, quoted in Hinsley 1981, 221).

For almost thirty years, Mooney intermittently worked with the Kiowas, having established many lifelong friends among them before his death in 1921. Mooney spent the majority of his research time with the Kiowas between 1893 and 1903, living with them and interviewing Kiowa elders (Hinsley 1981, 219): T'ébodal (One Who Carries a Buffalo's Lower Leg), the oldest member of the tribe at age eighty; Setĭmkía (Stumbling Bear); Setk'opte, or Paul Saitkopeta (Mountain Bear); Gaápiatañ (Feathered Lance) and Â'dal-pepte (Frizzlehead), two of the last medicine shield keepers; Sett'an (Little Bear); Anko (In the Middle of Many Tracks); Zoñtam, or Paul Zotom; and Ohettoint (Buffalo, or Charley Buffalo). Using a pictographic buffalo-hide calendar given to him in 1892 by Sett'an, Mooney interviewed these men to reconstruct Kiowa culture dating back to 1832. Mooney was especially interested in Kiowa heraldry, as represented by medicine shield and painted tipi societies (Mooney 1898, 146–47; Ewers 1979, x; Ewers 1978, 8–12; Merrill et al. 1997, 2–3).

Notably ahead of the times, Mooney was an exceptional ethnographer. During his first ten years' residence with the Kiowas he astutely observed the rapid culture change in Kiowa society in conjunction with the disso-lution of the KCA (Kiowa, Comanche, and [Plains] Apache) Reservation. An eyewitness to the Kiowa transition from tipis to houses, Mooney strongly felt that Kiowa traditions needed to be written down and pre-served. Years later, the methods used to collect data for *Calendar History of the Kiowa Indians* would be standard ethnohistorical procedures (Ewers 1979, xiii; Hinsley 1981, 221). Always the complete researcher, Mooney also interviewed non-Indians who intimately knew the Kiowas and obtained copies of their journals and notes. Noteworthy non-Indians included Captain (later General) Hugh L. Scott, Seventh Cavalry, Fort Sill, who commanded Indian troops in the 1890s; Quakers Lawrie Tatum (Kiowa agent from 1869 to 1873) and Thomas C. Battey; and Father Isidore Rick-lin of Anadarko, Oklahoma (Mooney 1898, 147).

Only small portions of Mooney's Kiowa field materials were used in *Cal-endar History*, his only major Kiowa work (Ewers 1979, xi). Mooney's field-notes on Kiowa heraldry (Mooney 1891–1904) have never been published, although they were utilized, along with the miniature tipis whose man-ufacture he commissioned, for John C. Ewers's short treatise on painted tipis (Ewers 1978). The heraldry fieldnotes are housed in the National Anthropological Archives at the Smithsonian Institution, where they are waiting for a patient ethnohistorian to decipher Mooney's difficult-to-read cryptic handwriting and idiosyncratic shorthand. Mooney himself admitted that his fieldnotes would be difficult for others to interpret (Hinsley 1981, 221). Despite these obstacles, Mooney's fieldnotes are crit-ical because he reconstructed the history of the Kiowa Sun Dance and associated warrior and shield societies back to the late eighteenth cen-tury, emphasizing the principal family lines connected with Kiowa reli-gious ceremonies. Mooney's heraldry notebook also contains readable information on Buffalo Society medicine shields.

Hugh L. Scott, stationed at Fort Sill between 1889 and 1897 as commander of Fort Sill's Indian Troop L, made many Kiowa, Comanche, and Plains Apache friends and became fluent in the Kiowa version of Plains sign language (Merrill et al. 1997, 3), which he eventually used to interview T'ébodal, Frizzlehead, Feathered Lance, and I-see-o (Tahbonemah) about the Kiowa Sun Dance (Scott 1911). In 1892, the elderly Dohásän II (Little Bluff), who would die within a year, presented his friend Captain Scott a color pencil sketch on manila paper, not an ordinary drawing but a reproduction of the oldest known pictographic calendar among the Kiowas, the calendar of Dohásän, principal Kiowa chief from 1833 until his death in 1866. Dohásän II (aka Pakonkya or Black Buffalo) knew Scott would preserve the final revision of the calendar he had maintained for twenty-seven years following his uncle's death. Scott shared the calendar and his research notes with Mooney, who collected three other calendars. Collectively, the four calendars were the basis for Mooney's reconstruction of the summer and winter counts and Sun Dance chronologies used in *Calendar History* (Mooney 1898, 143, 146). Mooney's and Scott's accounts are similar except that Mooney's narrative presents more of an anthropological perspective.

Andres Martinez, called Andele by the Kiowas, was a Mexican boy captured by Mescalero Apache raiders near present-day Las Vegas, New Mexico, and sold to the Kiowas in 1866. Raised Kiowa, Martinez became a popular "Kiowa" interpreter and informant in the 1890s (Mooney 1898, 147). Martinez had learned about the Kiowa Sun Dance through his adopted Kiowa father, Sét-dayâ'-ite (Many Bears, or Heap O' Bears), and then Napawat, who inherited the Taime bundle and guardianship of Martinez after Many Bears was killed in 1868 (Methvin 1899, 87; Methvin n.d., 83). Methodist missionary John Jasper Methvin met Martinez in the late 1880s, converted him to Christianity, and subsequently wrote Andele's life story (Methvin 1899; Forbes 1985, 41–73). Methvin wrote about Martinez's role in the Sun Dance, but his bias against non-Christian practices tainted his interpretations (Methvin 1927, 177). Others working with Martinez to reconstruct the extinct Sun Dance included Robert H. Lowie, who interviewed him in June 1915 about the involvement of Kiowa military societies in the Sun Dance (Lowie 1916b, 1923, 279), and Leslie Spier, who worked with Martinez in August 1919 (Spier 1921b,

437). Their Sun Dance accounts rely principally on the previous works of Battey, Scott, and Mooney, and Spier even cites Lowie throughout his article (Spier 1921b).

In April 1896, Isabel A. H. Crawford, a graduate of the Baptist Missionary Training School, Chicago, left the Elk Creek Kiowa mission at the western edge of the KCA Reservation where she had been working for three years and traveled forty miles southeast, where she established residence in the Saddle Mountain Kiowa community nestled in the Slick Hills, north of the Wichita Mountains. Ten years later, Crawford departed Kiowa country after successfully establishing a permanent church at Saddle Mountain. Her devotion to the Kiowas is evidenced by her desire to be interred there. She died in 1960. The epitaph on her tombstone in the Saddle Mountain cemetery reads: "I dwell among my people." Crawford, well liked by the Kiowas, fondly remembered by Saddle Mountain elders, witnessed firsthand and wrote about the post-1894 Ghost Dance and the peyote religion at Saddle Mountain at the turn of the last century. Her two books, *Kiowa: The History of a Blanket Indian Mission* (1915) and *From Tent to Chapel at Saddle Mountain* (n.d. [ca. 1909]), offer rich eyewitness accounts of missionary efforts and religious diversity on the KCA Reservation in the 1890s.

In 1933, the U.S. Army transferred Wilbur S. Nye to Fort Sill, north of Lawton, Oklahoma. Shortly after his arrival, Nye, a student at Fort Sill's Field Artillery School, was assigned to research the history of the military post, established in 1869. Nye immediately sought the services of Hugh L. Scott, who introduced him to an old Kiowa friend, George Hunt, nephew of former Troop L scout I-see-o. For the next four years, Hunt introduced Nye to Kiowa and Comanche elders, many of whom he interviewed (Nye 1937, xvii–xviii). Hunt had been instructed in the Sun Dance religion by Mo-keen, a dark-complexioned Mexican captive who eventually became the assistant to the keeper of the Sun Dance–related Taime bundle and also had participated in the 1887 "Oak Creek Sun Dance," the last complete Kiowa Sun Dance ceremony ever performed (Corwin 1958a, 73–82). Nye's (1934) account of the Sun Dance was narrated to him by George Hunt, but since Nye was untrained in anthropology, he did not fully understand some of the information Hunt shared. Consequently, Nye misrepresented some major concepts of Kiowa belief systems. For instance, he assumed that the Sun Dance was in some way the worship of the sun or of a "supernatural being who lived beyond the sun," and he referred to the ten sacred medicine bundles as the "Grandmother gods" (Nye 1937, 341), a misnomer.

In her 1945 publication, *The Ten Grandmothers*, Alice Marriott perpetuated the "grandmother" bundle misnomer. Marriott obtained the information for her book during the summers of 1935 and 1936 through the assistance of George Hunt and his daughters, Ioleta Hunt MacElhaney and Margaret Hunt Tsoodle, Marriott's principal collaborators (Marriott 1945, viii–xi). Because Marriott and Nye both relied on George Hunt during the same time period, it is possible that the concept of the "Ten Grandmothers" derived from him. Many contemporary Kiowas knowledgeable about the bundles do not accept this name (Boyd 1981, 8; Mikkanen 1987). According to Kiowa legends, the culture hero Half Boy transformed himself into the Ten Medicines bundles, known today as the *talyi-da-i* (Boy Medicine) bundles (Mooney 1898, 239; Momaday 1969, 35; Denton 1987, 71). Some say that the problem resulted from interpreting the Kiowa word *talyi* (boy) as "grandmother" (Harrington 1928, 209, 217; Meadows 1999, 37), since grandmothers and grandsons use *talyi* as a reciprocal kin term.

George Hunt's affiliation with anthropologists continued through his nephew, Adolph Goombi, who served as Mildred P. Mayhall's principal collaborator during the late 1950s. In her book *The Kiowas* (1984), descriptions of Kiowa religion, including coverage of the Sun Dance and sweat lodge rituals, reiterate previous accounts by Battey, Mooney, Spier, and Scott. Moreover, Mayhall also perpetuated the Ten Grandmothers misnomer (Mayhall 1984, 122, 147).

Kiowa belief systems and the Sun Dance are described in W. W. Newcomb's book *The Indians of Texas* (1978), an account relying on the previous works of Battey, Mooney, Methvin, Scott, and Marriott. Newcomb also refers to the Ten Grandmothers bundles (1978, 210–21). Perpetuation of this stereotype helps me to understand why many Kiowa elders complain that most scholars do not understand the intricacies of Kiowa culture (Boyd 1981; Mikkanen 1987).

In the late 1950s, Hugh D. Corwin, a retired businessman from Lawton, Oklahoma, and director of the Comanche County Historical Society, published several articles and two books regarding turn-of-the-century Kiowa history and culture, based on interviews with numerous Kiowa and non-Kiowa elders (Corwin 1958a, 1958a, 1959, 1961–62, 1968). His accounts are valuable due to his focus on the transition from the Sun Dance and bundle complexes to Christianity. An unpublished manuscript, "50 Years with the Kiowa Indians, 1850–1900," is housed in the D'Arcy McNickle Center for the History of the American Indian at the Newberry Library in Chicago. Typewritten in 1962, the manuscript is based on interviews with between twenty-five and thirty Kiowa elders over seventy-five years of age. Corwin's motivation was to reconstruct the last half of the nineteenth century before information was lost given the high death rate of elders who were born before 1900.

An attempt to correctly inscribe Kiowa culture in the 1970s through an oral history project was funded by the National Endowment for the Arts and Texas Christian University. The project was designed to salvage information dating back to the nineteenth century before it was lost, so elders were sought for interviews and some archival research was conducted in Oklahoma, Texas, and Washington DC. Maurice Boyd's *Kiowa Voices* volume 1 (1981) and volume 2 (1983) resulted from the research. In the first book, subtitled *Ceremonial Dance, Ritual and Song*, Boyd fails to offer new interpretations of Kiowa religion and the Sun Dance, despite the abundance of written and oral sources. Moreover, the elders interviewed were never active participants in the Sun Dance, since the last complete ceremony was conducted in 1887, so they could only relate what they had been told by their parents and grandparents. Therefore, their accounts do not necessarily reflect the deepest levels of meaning of the symbols representing nineteenth-century Kiowa beliefs and rituals, and the first volume is replete with ethnographic detail errors.

To commemorate the one-hundredth anniversary of the 1887 Oak Creek Sun Dance, the last ever held, a Kiowa, Arvo Quoetone Mikkanen, wrote an account of the Sun Dance primarily based on Boyd and Mooney, adding nothing new to what is already known about historical Kiowa religious beliefs and practices (Mikkanen 1987). Further details concerning Kiowa belief systems and the Sun Dance are found in books lavishly illustrated with the pictographic calendar records of Silver Horn (Greene 2001, 109–37; 2009).

The 1935 Santa Fe Field Party

Largely overlooked but undoubtedly the best source on nineteenth-century Kiowa religious practices are the ethnographic fieldnotes compiled by the 1935 Santa Fe Laboratory of Anthropology summer field party. Financially supported by the Rockefeller Foundation and guided by Professor Lesser, Weston LaBarre, William Bascom, Jane Richardson, Bernard Mishkin, and Donald Collier spent the summer interviewing Kiowa elders, including those who had participated in the extinct Sun Dance or had been involved with the Taime and ten *talyi-da-i* bundles. At the end of each day of interviewing, the students typed their hand-written fieldnotes, their collaborative efforts resulting in 1,314 pages of single-spaced notes (LaBarre et al. 1935).

Recent critiques of early twentieth-century ethnographic fieldwork in Native North America necessitate a careful examination of the methodologies employed by the 1935 field party. As noted by Howard L. Harrod (2000, xix–xx, 141–42n) and Raymond Bucko (2004, 179, 188–89), salvage ethnography was conducted during an era of colonial oppression, when American Indian cultures, languages, and religions were under constant attack, especially between 1883 and 1933, when certain dances and ceremonies were deemed immoral. Consequently, having learned to distrust outsiders, Indians typically were leery toward those asking questions about religious beliefs and practices. When utilizing materials from this era, today's researcher must ascertain whether or not such data were obtained through the willingness of collaborators to cooperate. Quality data collection ultimately depended on rapport between anthropologists and the elderly consultants and interpreters, which brings into question what was lost through translation and rendering oral traditions into textual form. Moreover, ethnographic studies focusing on the past heavily relied on the memory of elderly collaborators more so than on participant-observation; reconstructing the "ethnographic present" of a bygone era without witnessing the events related by elders potentially tainted interpretations of the past as unchangeable until disrupted by the dominant Euro-American culture. That American Indians had always innovated religious traditions in response to continuously changing sociocultural and environmental conditions often was overlooked by ethnographers focusing on "pristine" cultures of the past.

Harrod (2000, 142n) also suggested that the "academic perspectives, cultural prejudices, and human weaknesses of the anthropologists" conducting fieldwork are embedded in their field records. Hence biographical information about Lesser and the members of the 1935 field party, and about Marriott, should illuminate the paradigms shaping their field methods. In 1929, Alexander Lesser finished his graduate studies at Columbia University upon completion of his dissertation, a historical reconstruction of Siouan kinship systems based on comparative kinship terminology. Lesser married fellow graduate student Gene Weltfish in 1925, and until their divorce in 1940 they often worked together among the Pawnees, as suggested by Franz Boas, their mentor (Parks 1985, 65–66, 68). A critic of Radcliffe-Brown's "nonhistorical functionalism," Lesser believed that synchronic data capturing "a single moment in the stream of time" had to be analyzed together with diachronic, or historical information, since cultures are not frozen in time (Lesser 1933a, xxii–xxiii). Lesser utilized this methodology in *The Pawnee Ghost Dance Hand Game* (1933), based on his fieldwork in Oklahoma between 1928 and 1931. Theoretically, Lesser's emphasis on combining diachronic and synchronic data coalesced Boas's historical particularism with functionalism (Parks 1985, 69).

During the 1935 field season, Weltfish worked with the Pawnees while Lesser directed the Kiowa field party. Lesser originally selected the Plains Apaches for study until he learned that Gilbert McAllister (University of Chicago) had been working with them for several years. Lesser then moved on to the neighboring Kiowas for the field study, and McAllister graciously offered to share any Kiowa data he recorded while working with the Plains Apaches. McAllister also informed Lesser that Dr. Forrest E. Clements (University of Oklahoma) considered conducting fieldwork with the Kiowas in the near future, but it is doubtful that Lesser contacted Clements — Marriott's academic advisor.[1] Territoriality marked this era of ethnographic fieldwork.

When the students arrived in Anadarko on June 24, Lesser held a meeting in the evening to discuss methods and group objectives. The next day was spent discussing "problems of Kiowa ethnology based on the available sources" followed by "several hours of introductory work with our main interpreter [Charley Apekaum] on kinship problems." Obviously, Lesser wanted the students to have background information on Kiowa social organization before conducting interviews. On June 26, the students worked collectively with "a major informant and our main interpreter," which was followed by individual work with primary collaborators and interpreters—as needed—the next day. Afterward, Lesser spent a day with each student and then left them on their own to conduct interviews, except when he was needed. Initial interviews were conducted to determine "the subjects on which the informants could speak with authority" to establish an inventory of collaborators and their areas of expertise. At the end of each day, fieldnotes were typed and a "reference copy of all notes was made available to all students." Seminars were then conducted to identify particular subjects, and after "five or six weeks," two-day conferences attended by the "two best interpreters" were held to discuss ethnological and personal problems. Since the students shared copies of typed fieldnotes and worked with the same collaborators, Lesser believed they all developed a basic understanding of Kiowa culture that would enable each to contribute specific chapters for a collaborative monograph.[2]

Bernard Mishkin, also affiliated with Columbia University, had completed his master's degree the previous year and was mentored by Boas and Ruth Benedict. During her undergraduate career at the University of California, Jane Richardson studied under Alfred L. Kroeber, Robert H. Lowie, and Paul Radin before entering the anthropology graduate program in 1933. A student of Edward Sapir and John Dollard at the Yale Institute of Human Relations, Weston LaBarre was influenced by the writings of Hungarian psychoanalyst and anthropologist Géza Róheim (LaBarre 1980, 166–71). Like Richardson, Donald Collier received his undergraduate degree from the University of California and then in 1933 began doctoral work at the University of Chicago as a student of A. R. Radcliffe-Brown and Fay-Cooper Cole. Across town, William Bascom studied under Melville Herskovits at Northwestern University. All together, the senior graduate students who participated in the field school represented a wide range of interests and training, including historical particularism, functionalism, culture and personality, and culture change. Regardless of their theoretical backgrounds, the 1935 Kiowa fieldnotes produced by the students are largely descriptive, with little if any analysis.

Upon conclusion of the field school, Donald Collier wrote that the Santa Fe Laboratory field party fared well among the Kiowas and claimed that the best way to establish rapport with collaborators was to inform them "that we are doing the same work that Mooney did and that we want to complete his work. All the older people remember him and their response to a reference to Mooney is amazing."[3] Ledger statements indicate that collaborators and interpreters were paid two dollars a day and one dollar for a half day's work, which was good pay during the Great Depression.[4] Undoubtedly, working for the field party at least brought temporary financial relief to those who participated. In his final report, Lesser emphasized the "lasting friendships with informants and interpreters and with many Kiowa men and women with whom we did not work," that group members "were cordially welcomed at a peyote meeting," and that the students cooperated nicely with one another and with him.[5]

During the field school, Weston LaBarre developed a strong friendship with principal interpreter Charley Apekaum, worked with him the following summer, and eventually wrote his autobiography, which remains in manuscript form (LaBarre 1957). Apekaum's autobiography provides further insight into the field school. According to Charley, Enoch Smokey and Jim Waldo (Kogaitadl, or Lean Elk), members of the Native American Church, objected to the field school and the next year were outspoken against LaBarre's collaborative study of the peyote religion with Richard Evans Schultes. By this time, the Kiowas were divided into two religious factions—Christianity and the Native American Church. Because there were some animosities between members of these religions—exacerbated by missionaries who preached against peyote and tribal religions—members of the Native American Church, many of whom owned personal or tribal medicine bundles, were reticent to talk to outsiders about religion. Smokey, president of the local Native American Church chapter, claimed he did not trust the students because of the "bad record" of a certain university-based anthropologist (the names are deleted). Apekaum, a self-identified conservative who believed in the "old Indian customs," supported the students because they helped preserve important cultural knowledge beneficial to the enlightenment of non-Indians. Moreover, he believed that anthropologists living among Indians to learn about history and tribal customs gained the confidence and cooperation of elderly collaborators, resulting in good data (LaBarre 1957, 130, 49–50, 54).

Through Charley's support, the field school students established rapport with members of the Native American Church, who provided valuable information that summer. Jim Waldo even helped LaBarre with his peyote studies the following year. Perhaps the students gained the trust of Native American Church adherents because they opposed anti-peyote legislation. In 1937, Collier and LaBarre submitted written statements defending the peyote religion in response to Senate bill 1399, which threatened to restrict interstate shipment of peyote harvested from the peyote gardens near Laredo, Texas. John Collier, Donald's father and Indian commissioner 1933–45, helped lobby against the proposed bill, which failed.[6] Collier and LaBarre obviously maintained good relationships with their Indian friends.

At first, Alice Marriott's relationships with members of the Native American Church were not as positive. In *Greener Fields*, she discusses her relationship with An-pay-kau-te, or Aukaunt, better known as Frank Given (1853–1939), the maternal uncle of Ioleta Hunt MacElhaney and Margaret Hunt Tsoodle. Given, a Ten Medicines bundle keeper, lived near Tsoodle (Packing Stone, or Little Henry), another sacred bundle keeper. At first, Given offered to talk to Marriott about his bundle but changed his mind after being threatened by Tsoodle and the other keepers. His reticence might have been conditioned by Marriott's affiliation with Ioleta, an ardent Christian who often tried to proselytize collaborators, thus hindering attempts to obtain detailed information about indigenous Kiowa beliefs. In the summer of 1936, Alice and Ioleta stayed in a spare room in the Tsoodle household, which consisted of Tsoodle, his oldest wife, and Margaret and her husband, one of Tsoodle's sons. Tsoodle would not speak directly to Marriott, because she assumed daughter-in-law status due to her relationship to Margaret. Like others in his cohort, Tsoodle maintained avoidance relationships with opposite-sex affines, but he established stronger relations with the Santa Fe field party students, possibly because there were fewer restrictions. Moreover, the field party students could ask direct questions using structured interview techniques, whereas Marriott utilized an indirect approach employing semistructured techniques. However, Margaret and her husband took

Marriott to peyote meetings that summer, and Frank Given and Tsoodle became more cooperative. Marriott and Given became close friends (Marriott 1952, 74–75, 80–87, 110; Loughlin 2005, 149–51).

Political divisions might have had some influence on the Santa Fe field school, as noted in an annotated reference by LaBarre in the Apekaum autobiography: "I recall some politically-fomented opposition to the Santa Fe Laboratory party of last year" (LaBarre 1957, 129). During the early twentieth century, those Kiowas deemed citizens registered as Republicans due to the popularity of President Theodore Roosevelt, and then more joined the GOP after passage of the 1924 Snyder Act that extended blanket citizenship to American Indians. By the 1930s, most Kiowas who were Republicans were elderly, belonged to the Native American Church, owned medicine bundles, and were disinclined to speak English; meanwhile, those registered as Democrats typically were younger, more likely to have attended school, and spoke English. Initially a Republican, Charley Apekaum switched to the Democratic Party because he felt it would do more for Indians. Notably, Charley's choice of political affiliation was based on his membership in the American Legion, which connected him to politicians campaigning in Indian country who needed interpreters when visiting powwows. Republicans did not trust younger Democrats like Charley, who was perceived as a supporter of Commissioner Collier's Wheeler-Howard Bill, which became law in 1934 as the Indian Reorganization Act. As a result, Democrats began joining the Republican Party, and those holding political offices lost their positions. Apekaum served on the KCA Business Committee for two years but was voted out of office in 1934 (LaBarre 1957, 129–30). Based on tribal politics, it is not surprising that Enoch Smokey, a staunch Republican, opposed the 1935 field party, because Charley Apekaum was their principal interpreter and contact person.

Enoch Smokey's opposition to the field party might have stemmed more from economic reasons than from religious or political differences. In 1918 Smokey, James Waldo, Parker McKenzie, and several others worked as language informants for John P. Harrington, who noted that Smokey enthusiastically worked extra hours to finance fixing up his car so he could travel to Taos Pueblo (Harrington 1928, 1n). Perhaps Smokey was outspoken against the students' presence because he wasn't a paid consultant. Paying small stipends to Native collaborators was standard practice at the time, so individuals not getting paid might have harbored hard feelings toward individuals like Charley who were paid consultants. At the same time, Marriott paid Frank Given fifty cents an hour and was upset upon learning that LaBarre had visited the elderly bundle keeper. In *Greener Fields*, Marriott claimed to have avoided LaBarre, whom she thought was unethical for stealing her informant and who had been seen drinking beer with Charley Apekaum, which she perceived was unethical and illegal. Given promised Marriott that he wouldn't tell LaBarre the same stories he told her (Marriott 1952, 83, 90–91, 94). That Marriott wanted nothing to do with LaBarre is probably related to Apekaum's criticism of Marriott (LaBarre 1957, 1a). Importantly, the obvious factional conflicts between anthropologists and the interpreters and elderly collaborators with whom they worked does not lessen the importance of both sets of fieldnotes.

That Marriott and the field school students obtained quality data was perhaps tempered by earlier friendships forged between James Mooney, Hugh L. Scott, and Wilbur S. Nye and some of their elderly collaborators. In the 1890s, Mooney and Scott worked closely with the same Kiowas, and because of Scott's connection to Indian Troop L, they were assisted by I-see-o and his nephew, George Hunt. In 1933, Scott solicited Hunt to serve as Scott's interpreter, and the two worked closely together until Hunt's death. In addition to working with Mooney, Scott, and Nye, Hunt served as an interpreter and liaison for Marriott, and to a lesser extent for the Santa Fe field party students. Enthusiastic about researching Kiowa culture, Hunt connected these scholars with Kiowa informants. In fact, some of the Kiowas whom Hunt introduced to Nye also worked with the field party, including Jimmy Quoetone, Hodltagudlma (Red Dress), Mary Buffalo, Heap O' Bears, Hunting Horse, and Andrew Stumbling Bear. Senko, or Sanko (Prickly Pear), worked with both Marriott and LaBarre. Undoubtedly the rapport established between Mooney, Scott, and Nye and the Kiowas was transferred to the field party students and to Marriott.

Kiowa Interpreters and Collaborators

By the summer of 1882, Kiowa families related by blood and marriage had established ten distinct reservation encampments named after such geographical landmarks as mountains and creeks: (1) Mount Scott—

originally settled by families of the "peace chiefs" Kicking Bird and Stumbling Bear; (2) Saddle Mountain—an area about ten miles northwest of
Mount Scott; (3) Sugar Creek—ten miles west of Saddle Mountain; (4)
Cedar Creek—east of present-day Carnegie; (5) Stinking Creek—south
of Carnegie; (6) Samone Camp—west of Carnegie; (7) Elk Creek—near
modern Hobart, Lone Wolf, and Gotebo; (8) Rainy Mountain Creek—
southwest of contemporary Mountain View; (9) Hog Creek—several
miles west of the agency in Anadarko; and (10) Red Stone—several miles
northwest of Hog Creek. Of the ten encampments, the largest enclaves
were at Rainy Mountain, Mount Scott, Saddle Mountain, and Hog Creek.[7]
Finally, some students returning from Carlisle Indian Industrial School
settled near the agency in Anadarko (Levy 1959, 83–86).[8] By 1935, survivors
of the prereservation horse and buffalo culture and their descendants
were living in houses on allotments near their former encampments.
The Santa Fe field party worked mostly with Kiowas living in the Mount
Scott, Hog Creek/Red Stone, and Carnegie communities.

After 1875, members of the Stumbling Bear/Kicking Bird band settled
north of Mount Scott in the Canyon Creek and Medicine Creek valleys
(Twohatchet 1996, 8–9) near modern Meers and westward toward Saddle
Mountain and Sugar Creek. Since principal interpreter Charley Apekaum
was born and raised in the vicinity of Mount Scott it is not surprising that
numerous collaborators were from his community. Major collaborators
included Charley's father, Old Man Apekaum, and his cousin, Sankadota, or Old Man Sankadota (Medicine Feather), both affiliated with the
peyote religion, and Jimmy Quoetone (Wolf Tail), who worked closely
with Bernard Mishkin. Guy Quoetone (1885–1975) and George Hunt,
Jimmy's sons through different wives, were interpreters. Quoetone, a
Christian convert, helped establish the Mt. Scott Kiowa Indian Methodist
Church and became a Methodist minister. Quoetone's good friend and
fellow convert, the famed cavalry scout Hunting Horse (Old Man Horse
[1850–1953]) and his younger wife, Pitma, lived along Frizzle Head Creek,
northwest of Meers. Noted artist Monroe Tsatoke, Horse's son through
his older wife, Pitoma, also served as interpreter. Also from the Meers
area was Luther Sahmaunt (1860–1958), who was married to Virginia
Stumbling Bear (Corwin 1958a, 31, 42, 105–12, 193; Nye 1937, 193). Both
were Christians. Max Frizzlehead (Frizzlehead II, or Frizzlehead the

Younger), whose father had worked with Mooney, also collaborated with the field party and belonged to the Native American Church. Sadly, he passed away toward the end of the field school on August 15. Recently, Raymond Tongkeamha reminded me that even today the Mount Scott Kiowas are referred to as "progressives" because they were the first Kiowas to adopt Christianity and the peyote religion.[9]

Reflecting his commitment to the culture and personality approach, Weston LaBarre compiled a photograph album, "Kiowa Indian Snapshots," which includes short biographies of eighteen of the interpreters and collaborators who aided members of the field party. Insights into the personalities of the collaborators and the utility of the data they provided are helpful in evaluating the quality of the fieldnotes.[10] LaBarre depicted the Mount Scott/Meers collaborators as follows:

Monroe Huntinghorse [Tsatoke], a young Kiowa artist, whose paintings have had exhibition all over the country, including New York. We used to "play hookey" from work on hot days and go swimming.

Old Man Horse [Hunting Horse], Monroe's father, a man of personal speculative bent. He is "the Kiowa philosopher," if anyone is.

Jimmy Gueton [Quoetone, Wolf Tail, or Wolf Den Digger], a grave courteous old man with a remarkable memory. He was Bernard's chief informant.[11]

Undoubtedly the best-known of the field party collaborators was Haungooah, or Silver Horn (1860–1940), the talented artist and calendar keeper who had worked with Mooney at the turn of the century (Greene 2001, 2008). Silver Horn, the maternal nephew of Dohásän—the last undisputed chief of all the Kiowas before his death in 1866—also served as keeper of one of the Ten Medicines bundles. In 1901, Silver Horn moved to his wife's allotment near Stecker, approximately ten miles south of Anadarko and closer to the Red Stone community inhabited by his brothers White Buffalo Konad and Ohettoint, or Charley Buffalo (Greene 2009, 16). Charley Buffalo—also a Ten Medicines keeper—died the year before the arrival of the field party, but his widow, Mary Buffalo, worked closely with LaBarre, assisted by her son Homer, an interpreter, and Homer's wife, Alice Take It Out. Kintadl, or Moth Woman, Silver Horn's sister, was Jane Richardson's principal collaborator. David Paddlety, a Baptist minister and Red Stone resident, provided his services as an interpreter. Most everyone else followed the peyote religion.

Those living in the Hog Creek community between Red Stone and Anadarko who collaborated with the field party included White Horse II, Bert Geikauma (Crow Lance), and Lynn Ware. Although Charley Apekaum was born near Mount Scott, he was living in the Red Stone community in 1935. LaBarre provided the following biographies of Red Stone/ Hog Creek Kiowas:

Charley Apekaum [underline mine], chief interpreter and contact man. An unusually intelligent Indian, he had been in the U.S. Navy in the first World War. He was known as a Lothario also. Like his grandfather and great-grandfather, he has had over ten wives—but in these degenerate times he had them successively, not simultaneously. "Apekaum" means "charcoal" & he was so named because his father (an informant) killed a white man hauling charcoal in Texas in the old days. Charley went on dates with us, once with a Delaware woman, Bernard with a Comanche, and I with a Caddo girl. Charley was our chief interpreter, and second only to Mary Buffalo my closest friend among the Kiowa Indians.

Mary Buffalo, my chief informant in the Kiowa tribe, a fine old woman and a natural aristocrat. Her husband [Ohettoint, or Charlie Buffalo, who died in 1934] was a keeper of one of the "Ten Medicines" and as such a member of a kind of priestly Supreme Court. Her grandfather was the famous Onsokyapta, owner of the Sun-dance image (taimé) and thus the supreme pontiff of the whole tribe. Mary was 88 [b. 1847] when this photo was taken in 1935 and her lifetime extends back to the old war & buffalo-hunting days. An intimate friend, Mary told me everything from the contents of the sacrosanct Ten Medicines to Kiowa practices in childbirth.

Old Lady Kintadl [Moth Woman], Jane's chief informant, a sweet-tempered old woman with a remarkably detailed memory of the old days. But her daughter-in-law teased her unmercifully because she had not been bought in marriage the type conferring the most prestige upon the woman.

Bert Crow-Lance [Geigomah, or Geikauma], an implicit believer in Kiowa ways, told me he was going on a four-day fasting vision-quest, to discover from the spirits where he could find gold or diamonds (in Oklahoma), or lacking that, oil, so he could support his large family. He flew in the air over a field of snakes, then his mother appeared in his vision and told him to go back because he had forgotten his pipe.

Lynn Ware (part Yaqui, from Mexico), teller of Sindi [Saynday] stories. Sindi is the Kiowa supernatural trickster, who regularly does all the sinful things prohibited by the culture, such as speaking to one's mother in law and other nameless crimes. Such stories are a valuable safety-valve in a culture as fantasied escapes from its restrictions. Corset human nature in one spot and it bulges out in another!

David Paddlety . . . David is a Baptist minister, but during a recent lunar eclipse he ran out and shot a shotgun at the evil spirits troubling the moon. . . .

Alice-Take-it-Out (referring to the care of the Ten Medicines?) . . . Alice made me a bead belt to illustrate aboriginal pattern of the "tipi" and the "dragonfly" etc. . . . She is Homer Buffalo's wife.

Homer Buffalo, Mary's only living son. He is part Comanche. He & his wife put on the first peyote meeting any of us had ever attended for my benefit. An interpreter.[12]

Nestled along the southern banks of the Washita River twenty-six miles west of Anadarko, Carnegie—an old railroad and farming community—is considered the epicenter of Kiowa culture (Meadows 2008, 137), especially since the Kiowa Tribal Complex is located west of town along Highway 9. When Carnegie was established in 1901, Kiowa families were living on nearby allotments bordering the numerous creeks feeding the Washita

River from the south. Kiowa allotments southeast of Carnegie adjacent to Gawky and Cedar creeks were inhabited by Lone Bear; Sanko (Senko, or Sainko), a shaman; and Gontahap (Mrs. Bluejay), whose husband was a well-known shaman. Living farther south in the vicinity of Cat Springs, near Boone, was Albert Cat (Oyebi). To the southwest of Carnegie were those living near Zodletone, or Stinking Creek, including Heap O' Bears; Jim Ahtone (Aton, or Wooden Club), a peyote doctor, also lived southwest of Carnegie. Immediately west of Carnegie, and just south of the Washita River, an area noted for Ghost Dance encampments and keepers of tribal medicines, were the allotments of White Fox and Little Henry (Tsoodle, or Packing Stone). Ned and Luther Brace, interpreters for the field party, lived in the former Samone community located at the modern junction of Highway 9 and Feather Dance Road, between Carnegie and Mountain View. Southwest of Mountain View lived Belo Kozad, or Cozad (Bedaltena, They Caught Him By The Bridle). Finally, Haumpo lived near Gotebo, southwest of Mountain View. With few exceptions, all were adherents of the peyote religion. LaBarre provided several brief biographies of individuals from these communities:

Belo Kozad [Cozad], an engaging and intelligent informant. He carries the older man's usual feather fan. The following year, 1936, he led a peyote meeting for me at Stecker. [He was LaBarre's chief peyote contact.]

Heap o' Bears, owner of a famous name, a great old liar and buffalo hunter, and despite his look a jolly old fellow and good informant.

White Fox, the Kiowa chief pontiff, head of the Ten Medicine Keepers, a kind of priestly supreme court, is the native equivalent of the Chief Justice. These medicines are extremely sacred, even today, and in theory date back to the beginning of the world; they are used judicially and legally to stop fights, to confer tribal victory in war, etc. White Fox has a personal dignity remarkable even in a plains Indian, but is very reserved.

Little Henry (or "Packing Stone") [Tsoodle], a Big Man of the Kiowa. One of the Ten-Medicine Keepers, and his second wife. The missionaries oppose polygyny, so Little Henry solves the problem by having separate domiciles for each, one on each side of a creek—which with a little linguistic ambiguity confuses the missionaries. . . .

Ned Brace, formerly state head of the Native American Church (peyote) until successive jailings for alcoholism ousted him. But judge him leniently!—Indian susceptibility to intoxicants has a long psychological-cultural history behind it. (And we use coffee and tobacco but eschew opium just as irrationally as the Indians eat peyote but condemn alcohol. We officially abhor cannibalism, but it is the central sacrament of our religion, symbolically.)

Lone Bear, a medicine man and one of the phoniest characters I ever met. He was a born Tory and reactionary, was one of the "Sons-of-the-Sun," an anti–Ghost Dance, anti-peyote group. He is said to be able to vomit small turtles, which he places in a bowl of water. He is the only Kiowa who deliberately tried to misinform me; his Sundance information, when checked with about a dozen other informants was sheer blather. He was an "ah-day," a product of the Kiowa institution of ritually and painstakingly spoiled son. Friend Lone-Bear once demonstrated his power to vomit red-paint to Bill [Bascom] who was driving the car with Lone Bear beside him. Suddenly he spit and splattered Bill all over with red clay and saliva. Unfortunately for the trick, Bill had unsuspectingly seen Lone Bear surreptitiously put something into his mouth a few minutes before.

Senko, a very lovely old informant. He demonstrated a medicine-cure on me, somewhat startling in nature until I realized what it was. The Kiowa cure disease by shamanistic sucking out of foreign objects, toads, snakes, beetles, stones, arrow points, etc.[13]

Though Sanko (Prickly Pear) was a practicing shaman, he informed Marriott that he had converted to Christianity forty-two years earlier, which would have been 1893.[14] Both Marriott (1945, 173–87) and Nye (1962, 267–75) related how Sanko received death threats from Tonakɔt (Snapping Turtle) shortly after his conversion. Accordingly, Tonakɔt, a peyotist and greatly feared shaman and sorcerer, was angry with Prickly Pear for abandoning the peyote religion. Nye's version of the story occurred around 1895, whereas Marriott's dated it in 1888. Although the details of the story vary slightly—George Hunt was Nye's informant and Sanko told his version to Marriott—once again Marriott changed the dates to mesh with the ordering of the other stories in *The Ten Grandmothers*. Again, her fieldnotes provide more accurate information.

Since beginning ethnographic fieldwork in Kiowa country in January 1987, I have worked with descendants of several of the 1935 collaborators. Without exception, I have found them wonderful collaborators and have developed long-lasting friendships with some of them. Of those from the Mount Scott/Meers community I have worked with descendants of Stumbling Bear, Jimmy Quoetone, and Hunting Horse. Of those representing the Hog Creek/Red Stone communities, I have worked with descendants of White Buffalo Konad, Bert Geikauma, and Lynn Ware. And of those from the Carnegie area I have spent time with descendants of White Fox, Jim Ahtone, and Little Henry Tsoodle. Most of these individuals were raised by parents and grandparents who had converted to Christianity at the turn of the last century, though theirs was an indigenized form melded with Kiowa culture. Perhaps because their ancestors had not completely eschewed their culture after choosing the Jesus road, the majority of the individuals I interviewed did not view their past lifeways negatively. Indeed, most were willing to share insights into Kiowa history and culture because they are proud of their heritage. Over the years, several Kiowas have indicated to me that they cooperate with anthropologists, historians, and other scholars because outsiders consider the Sioux to be the archetypical Plains Indians, and they believe that the Kiowas deserve more attention! My positive experiences with the descendants of those assisting the field party members bolsters my confidence in the overall quality of the data contained in the 1935 fieldnotes. Marriott's fieldnotes also provide valuable information she collected from Frank Given, Tsoodle, George Hunt, and others.

Characteristics of Plains Religions in Kiowa Belief Systems

The Kiowas share several traits in common with other North American tribes, and more specifically Plains tribes in regard to indigenous religious beliefs and practices, including: (1) concepts of power (Grim 2005a, 759–65; Irwin 1994) and places of spiritual power, or "cosmography" (Irwin 1994, 26), also referred to as "geosacred sites" (Meadows 2008, 28; Gulliford 2005, 945–50); (2) a plethora of guardian spirits, or "dream-spirits" (Irwin 1994, 31), capable of bestowing power upon individuals through spontaneous dreams and visions, or through formalized vision quests (Irwin 1994, 2005, 1127–33); (3) the manifestation of power through medicine bundles (Harrod 2005, 93–101) owned by spiritual and ceremonial practitioners (Kracht 2005a, 1025–35) and by members of sacred societies (Kracht 2005b, 974–84); (4) ceremonial song and dance (Kracht 2005c, 206–13), especially the Sun Dance (Archambault 2001, 983–95; Brown 1989, 193–99; Liberty 1980, 164–78; Grim 2005b, 1051–59); and (5) common symbolism, including sacred numbers and directions, mythology and oral traditions, sacred pipes and tobacco, and an emphasis on eagles, buffalo, and bears as the most important power animals (Powers 1989, 19–33; Stover 2005, 1085–92; Kracht 2005b, 978). Absent in Kiowa cosmology is the belief in a creator, as found among the Sarcees, Comanches, Blackfoot, Plains Crees, Gros Ventres, Cheyennes, and Arapahos. Indeed, Kiowa beliefs in power forces more closely parallel Siouan beliefs (Kracht 2005a, 1025).

1

Kiowa History, 1832–1868

Kiowas interviewed in 1935 who were born during the prereservation period described religious beliefs and practices that developed after the Kiowas migrated from Western Montana to the Northwestern Plains toward the end of the seventeenth century. Kiowa migrations were concurrent with the movements of other peoples to the Northwestern and Northern Plains from peripheral regions of the Plateau, Great Basin, Subarctic, and Northeast culture areas in response to the horse and bison robe trade. During the eighteenth century, "the culture of the horse-using buffalo hunters became the dominant culture of the Great Plains" (Ewers 1980, 334).

Horses had been extinct in the Western Hemisphere for over ten thousand years until they were reintroduced to the New Mexican frontier by Spanish settlers in the seventeenth century. Though Spanish law prohibited the sale of horses and firearms to Indians, Pueblos living in the Rio Grande Valley gained access to horses owned by ranchers and traded them to Apaches, who became fully equestrian by the 1630s. Apache raiders began stealing horses from Spanish settlements, or obtained them by trading captives to the Pueblos. Utes and Navajos also acquired horses, and in 1659 mounted Navajo marauders were reported northwest of Santa Fe. During the seventeenth century, Pecos Pueblo, the crossroads between the Pueblos and the Plains, became the focal point for the diffusion of horses to Plains Indians. In the wake of the 1680 Pueblo Revolt, at least ten thousand horses fell into Indian hands; afterward, trading and raiding became the primary means for acquiring horses. For instance, LaSalle reported in 1682 that Kiowas and Plains Apaches had recently traded horses stolen from New Mexico to Pawnees or Wichitas. By the end of the eighteenth century, Comanches and Utes left the Great Basin and began attacking Apaches and Pueblos for horses and plunder (Haines 1976, 63–79; Ewers 1980, 3–4, 332; Swagerty 1988, 355).

Comanche and Ute horse herds increased from raiding into New Mexico, though Comanche herds propagated through selective breeding made possible by the mild winters in the Southwestern Plains and adjacent regions of New Mexico, Northern Mexico, and coastal Texas. In the Southwestern Plains, horses were acquired from raids into Texas, New Mexico, and Mexico, captured from the feral herds ranging from Eastern Colorado to Western Nebraska or through selective breeding. Other tribes migrating to the Plains, especially the Cheyennes and Lakotas, had horses by 1760, but the scarcity of horses in the Northern Plains resulted in Cheyenne migrations south to raid Comanche and Kiowa herds (Secoy 1953, 3; Klein 1993, 144; Moore 1996, 85–86).

Groups migrating to the Plains proper during the eighteenth century—the emergent horse and buffalo culture—began organizing into tribal nations as they transformed into equestrian bison hunters dependent on horses. Increased mobility allowed for the formation of flexible social groups that mirrored the formation of the migratory bison herds that aggregated for the mating season between July and September, and during the winter, but dispersed into smaller herds the rest of the year. The addition of horses allowed for different hunting bands to coalesce into larger communities for communal hunts during the summer and winter; individual bands could then disperse following the seasonal hunts (Secoy 1953, 24–25; Moore 1987, 53–55).

Toward the end of the eighteenth century, several developing nations inhabited contiguous territories around the Black Hills, including Kiowas, Plains Apaches, Cheyennes, Arapahos, and Lakotas, as reported by Lewis and Clark during their 1803–5 expedition through the Middle Missouri region (Moore 1987, 61–66). By this time, horse raiding largely replaced trading, and a three-tiered class system emerged based on individual ownership of horses: a horse-rich upper class, a middle class, and a horse-poor lower class dependent on the upper classes (Ewers 1980, 338–39; Klein 1993, 139, 142). Other contributing factors to the development of "rank" societies in the Plains included access to supernatural power and the accumulation of war honors, as among the Comanches

(Kavanagh 1996, 28). Religious traditions also began transforming into distinctive tribal and individual identities as the new emigrants reformulated their cultures in response to changing social and physical environments (Harrod 1995, 3–4). John C. Ewers describes the period from 1800 until the demise of the bison herds as the "heyday of Plains Indian Horse Culture" in which the "traits of the horse complex" crystalized and persisted (Ewers 1980, 335).

According to Alan M. Klein (1993), the "buffalo culture" developed between 1850 and 1880 based on the Plains Indian production of bison robes and meat in exchange for firearms and metal goods peddled by Euro-American traders. Ultimately, the supply of bison was a critical economic variable, as were the relations and forces of production, the availability of horses and ample pasturage, encampment size, and the presence of enemies. Although symbiosis existed between the groups, Indians became dependent on European-manufactured items by the 1860s when Americans dominated the hide trade. By this time, intertribal warfare related to controlling hunting territories, and stealing horses was exacerbated by the arrival of Anglo settlers, the construction of railroads, the influx of white hide hunters, and the inevitable demise of the bison herds by the early 1870s (Klein 1993, 137–56).

Kiowa transformations into the horse and buffalo culture paralleled the social and religious development of other emergent Plains nations. Oral traditions assert that the Kiowas acquired the cultural characteristics of mounted equestrians after trekking to the Plains in search of horses. As the Kiowas developed the trappings of the horse and buffalo culture, encounters with other tribal groups resulted in conflicts, alliances, or both that undoubtedly shaped Kiowa beliefs and kinship. The horse and buffalo culture briefly reached its apex by the mid-nineteenth century before waning at the onset of the reservation period in the late 1860s. By this time, contact with Euro-Americans brought about further changes that influenced Kiowa culture and religion.

Linguistic Classification and Early Migrations before 1832

Kiowa, classified in the Kiowa-Tanoan branch of the Uto-Aztecan language family, is distantly related to the Tiwa, Tewa, and Towa languages spoken in ten of the Eastern, or Rio Grande Pueblos of New Mexico (Watkins 1984, 1–2). It has been postulated that the Kiowas separated from the Pueblos in pre-Columbian times and migrated north, suggesting that they were once sedentary horticulturalists (Levy 2001, 907), although the Kiowas have no memories of horticultural traditions (Mooney 1898, 153). Cultural affiliation with the Pueblos has been suggested on the basis of similarities in clothing decoration, an emergence creation myth, and culture heroes Spider Grandmother and the War Twins (Marriott and Rachlin 1975, 35, 39–40). Kiowa oral traditions identify the mountainous Yellowstone River region of Western Montana as ancestral homelands, which the Kiowas left sometime in the late seventeenth century in an eastward migration that brought them into Crow country, where the two tribes became lasting allies (Mooney 1898, 153–55).

Accompanied by the smaller Plains Apache tribe, the Kiowas migrated farther southeast, obtained horses, and then reached the Black Hills of South Dakota/Wyoming by 1775. Lewis and Clark reported that during the winter of 1804–5, Kiowa encampments were situated along the north fork of the Platte River, south of the Black Hills (Moore 1987, 61). While living near the Black Hills, the Kiowas established trading relations with the Mandans and Arikaras, semisedentary horticulturalists of the Middle Missouri River region. They also encountered and fought the enemies of the Crows—the Lakotas and Cheyennes, who drove the Kiowas south of the Black Hills toward the Arkansas River (Mooney 1898, 155–57). Concomitant to being pushed south, the Kiowas began raiding Spanish settlements south of the Red River and skirmishing with the more populous Comanches, who dominated the territory south of the Arkansas River in present-day western Kansas and Oklahoma, western Texas, southeastern Colorado, and northeastern New Mexico. Mild winters, ample grazing, and close proximity to the Spanish settlements of New Mexico made the Southwestern Plains a horse-rich area coveted by northern tribes (Fowler 1996, 11; Ewers 1980, 22–23, 45n; Osborn 1983, 566). Caught between the Lakotas and Cheyennes to the north and the Comanches to the south, the Kiowas and Plains Apaches negotiated peaceful relations with the Comanches sometime between 1790 and 1806, creating a Kiowa-Comanche-(Plains) Apache (KCA) alliance against northern tribes, particularly Lakotas, Cheyennes, and Pawnees (Mooney 1898, 161–64;

Kavanagh 1996, 146; Levy 2001, 908). In order to control trade with the Arikaras and other Northern and Central Plains tribes, allied Cheyenne and Arapaho bands successfully kept the Kiowas and Comanches south of the Arkansas River between 1790 and 1840 (Moore 1996, 90–92).

Following the alliance, the early nineteenth-century KCA tribes dominated the Southwestern Plains: the Kiowas and Plains Apaches occupied the northern region adjacent to the Arkansas River, and to the south the Comanches roamed the Staked Plains of the Texas Panhandle (Levy 2001, 908). Among the Kiowas interviewed in 1935, Moth Woman and Luther Sahmaunt acknowledged that the Kiowas obtained horses from the Comanches and by capturing wild mustangs in the Staked Plains through methods such as driving them into corrals with fire and chasing down pregnant mares in late March prior to the foaling season.[1] As with other tribes migrating to the Plains toward the end of the late seventeenth century, the acquisition of horses transformed the pedestrian Kiowas into equestrian hunter-gatherers who trained their mounts for specialized uses in transportation, hunting, and warfare; the emergent horse and buffalo culture produced social differentiation based on wealth in horses and plunder (Fowler 1996, 8–11; Levy 2001, 908).

Kiowa Social Organization
Kinship

On August 25, their first full day in the field, the Santa Fe field party students sat down with Charley Apekaum, their principal interpreter, to learn about Kiowa culture, starting with kinship. Over the course of the summer, a number of elderly Kiowas described Kiowa kinship and social organization dating back to the horse and buffalo days of the nineteenth century. Besides Charley Apekaum, those sharing information about Kiowa social organization included Hunting Horse, Lone Bear, Belo Cozad, Mrs. Hokeah, Jimmy Quoetone, and Luther Sahmaunt.

Similar to other Great Plains tribes that pursued the migratory bison herds—Cheyennes, Arapahos, Plains Apaches, Lakotas, and Plains Crees—Kiowas employed a generational kin, or Hawaiian type of kinship system in which relatives are identified according to gender and generation. Hawaiian systems restrict the number of kin categories. Thus, collateral kin in the grandparents' generation are called grandparents, those in the parents' generation are parents, relatives in ego's generation are called siblings, and so on. Hawaiian systems are typical in societies characterized by bilateral kinship and kindreds (Keesing 1975, 104; Eggan 1955, 89, table 2; Holder 1974, vii). LaBarre's interpretation of nineteenth-century Kiowa kinship (fig. 1 in this volume) is based on information gathered from Apekaum.[2]

As depicted in figure 1, collateral kin in the grandparents', parents', ego's, and ego's children's generations were addressed as grandparents, parents (except for opposite-sex siblings), siblings, and children. Not depicted are the grandparents' siblings, who were addressed and respected as grandparents. Great-grandparents and great-grandchildren had a special relationship based on using reciprocal sibling terms of address. Apekaum related that the Kiowa system had a slight variation in that the father's sister and mother's brother were called "aunt" and "uncle" as opposed to "mother" and "father."[3] Ray C. Doyah recently commented that

> great-grandmothers and great-granddaughters are referred to as sisters while the male side are referred to as brothers, beyond this, as explained by my mother, Beatrice Ahpeatone Smith, and several of my deceased relatives, the kinship markers ceased to exist because "We didn't live long in those days to recognize or have a name for relationships beyond the third generation." In today's society it is customary for my grandchildren to call my mother big sister. I have never heard the males referred to as big brother by great-grandsons.[4]

Fred Eggan (1955, 93) identified the Kiowa system as a Kiowa-Apache (Plains Apache) subtype, similar to the generational Kiowa-Apache and Jicarilla Apache (a transitional system) systems and possibly related to the classification systems of the Lipan Apaches, Caddos, and Wichitas.

Other unique characteristics of Kiowa kinship were described in 1935 by various elders. According to Hunting Horse, a sister's son addressed his mother's brother as *tsegi* (uncle). This special relationship, marked by lavishing the boy with gifts and almost never denying his requests, also involved a joking relationship concerning sexuality. As the boy developed into adulthood, the role reversed, and he was expected to care for his maternal uncle. Relationships between the mother's brother and sister's daughter were similar. Likewise, a boy or young man could consult his father's sister about sexual matters that he never mentioned to his "sisters" or "mothers."[5] Lone Bear added that ego's cousins were addressed as brothers and sisters, whereas brothers and sisters called each other *da* (siblings of opposite sex). Sisters addressed each other as *na·bi*, and brothers called one another *ba·bi*.[6] Hunting Horse and Belo Cozad pointed out that Kiowa brothers and sisters followed strict avoidance/respect relationships at age ten, after which they spent little time together, especially alone, which was considered highly improper. Brothers refrained from using profane language around their sisters, nor could they embrace except in greeting after a long absence.[7] A man was very close with his sister's husband, treating his brother-in-law with the same respect as his sister, as noted by Hunting Horse, who said that in similar fashion, sisters-in-law were close, like sisters.[8] Apekaum stated that nieces and nephews were referred to as *go·dl* (son) and *i·ta* (daughter). Not depicted in figure 1 is the generation of ego's grandnephews, grandnieces, and grandchildren, who were called *k'o* (grandson) and *ta·ki* (granddaughter).[9]

Group Formation and Bands

During the horse and buffalo days, Richardson learned that extended family groups, or kindreds, the building blocks of Kiowa society, typically led by the oldest brother of a family, were composed of "his own brothers, his sisters and their spouses, his parents, his mother's and father's brothers, and his sons and daughters with their families" (Richardson 1940, 6). According to Lone Bear, these people were the nucleus of the kindred.[10]

Mrs. Hokeah, Hunting Horse, and Jimmy Quoetone discussed stratification induced by the horse and buffalo culture, which created an upper echelon of *ondedɔ* (rich) kindreds representing principal families called *do'oi* (family of many tipis), a term alluding to the large size of wealthy kindreds. Brothers in these prominent families camped together, each nuclear family occupying a tipi, whereas the young unmarried men stayed together in their own tipi. Patrilocal postmarital residence was ideal for the sons and daughters of wealthy families, for custom preferred ambilocal residence with the richer of the two families exchanging spouses based on relative wealth in horses and other goods, along with the war record and reputation of the family leader.[11] Lone Bear told Richardson that rich families often preferred their children to marry less wealthy individuals, prompting Alexander Lesser to suggest that these marriages provided stronger bonding within the kindred, instead of weakening it by intermarriage with a rival *ondedɔ* family.[12]

Hunting Horse and Lone Bear said that wealthy, prominent kindreds often had several socially insignificant, unrelated *kɔɔn* (poor people) in their camps. These poor families, lacking horses, property, or highly ranked kin, attached themselves to wealthy kindreds for protection and the benefits of cooperative hunting. The most prominent Kiowa kindreds attracted large numbers of lower status non-kin; coalesced bands hunted and conducted raids together.[13] Below the *ondedɔ* families (10 percent of tribal population) in rank were the *ondegupa* (second-rank) families (30–50 percent of tribal population), whose leaders did not possess the same war honors as the *ondedɔ* warriors. *Kɔɔn*, or poor people, constituted anywhere from 10–50 percent of the tribal population, and below them were the *dapom* (bums, or no-accounts) and *go·bop* (captives), composing 10 percent of the total population. Band leaders were from the top two social ranks (Richardson 1940, 15). It is notable that these percentage ranges are reflective of the oftentimes conflicting data regarding band formation and social classes obtained by members of the field party. Mishkin attributed these discrepancies to the rapid collapse of the Kiowa war complex during the 1870s (Mishkin 1940, 37). Nevertheless, at the height of the horse and buffalo culture, ca. 1832 to 1875, there were between ten and twenty prominent kindreds to which the rest of the tribe was affiliated. Richardson identified these "primary political unit[s]" as bands (Richardson 1940, 6). The Kiowa word for band, *topadoga*, is derived from the word *dopadok'i* (camp command, or main chief). According to Lone Bear, the ten to twenty *topadoga*, loosely organized, flexible bands, were led by the ten to twenty most important Kiowa men, or camp chiefs.[14]

Mishkin (1940, 26n) observed that the bands were social groups not to be confused with the five Kiowa "bands" (Ewers 1978, 11, fig. 3), or "subtribes" (Mooney 1898, 227), of the aggregated Sun Dance encampment, or with geographical residence groups (see fig. 14, this volume). Instead, the bands were defined by Lone Bear as fluid, amorphous residence groups that camped together in the Sun Dance circle.[15] For example, the Kiñep

(Big Shields) section of the encampment was occupied by four *topadoga* led by four high-ranking camp chiefs. Following the conclusion of the Sun Dance, each band experienced fission and fusion as each band leader trekked to predetermined locations for the fall buffalo hunt. Richardson estimated that the Kiowa prereservation population of approximately sixteen hundred, subdivided into ten to twenty bands, had an average band size ranging between twelve to fifty tipis at any given time (Richardson 1940, 6). Band size was largely determined by the popularity of the camp chiefs, or band leaders, and it was common for families to move between several bands due to quarrels or the desire to visit other relatives, as related by Jimmy Quoetone, Hunting Horse, and Mrs. Hokeah.[16]

Similar to other Plains societies, Kiowa bands included non-Kiowas, including members of other tribes and non-Indian captives taken during raids into Texas and Mexico. For instance, Feathered Lance, Pá-tadal, and Sitting Bear were of Sarcee descent (Mooney 1898, 160), Mo-keen was a Mexican who voluntarily joined the Kiowas sometime between 1840 and 1850, when he was ten years old, and Andres Martinez, or Andele, was given to Heap O' Bears by Mescalero Apaches sometime after his capture near Las Vegas, New Mexico, in 1866 (Mooney 1898, 160, 173–74, 181, 234–36; Corwin 1959, 73, 129–42). John H. Moore has illustrated how multiethnic, multilingual bands developed in Cheyenne society resulting from intermarriage to traders or members of "foreign" bands to form trade and military alliances; rules of exogamy also contributed to marriage outside the band. Likewise, bands in other Plains societies were composed of kin groups and individuals recruited through capture or marriage. Bands affiliated with a tribal nation observed the same traditions and came together in the Sun Dance circle, a symbol of their "national identity." Despite coalescence into tribal encampments for ceremonies, bands "were the most significant units of social and political structure on the Plains" (Moore 1987, 318–20, 11).

Leadership abilities and charisma were identified by Collier as essential personality traits for band leaders, as were other attributes—being honorable, peaceable, just, kind, courteous, generous, and helpful. Luther Sahmaunt said that ideally, the camp chief was the greatest warrior in his band, had fought numerous battles, obtained many war honors, and survived to be forty or fifty years old. Prior to his death, the *dopa-*

dok'i appointed a successor, usually a favorite son.[17] An important role of the *dopadok'i* noted by Lone Bear was to select camp locations for his band. Upon conclusion of the Sun Dance, the camp chiefs met to discuss where each planned to travel for the fall hunt, then camp criers went throughout the Sun Dance encampment to announce which direction each *dopadok'i* was headed. Families and individuals chose which leader to follow, departed from the aggregated community, and then traveled slowly while hunting bison en route to the predetermined location, usually a favorite camp site along a cottonwood-lined waterway. While traveling, the band leader was called *hobatsat* (traveling leader). If several bands camped together, the most distinguished camp chief was recognized as the leader.[18]

Although the Kiowas were subdivided into ten to twenty bands, Mooney identified two geographical divisions: the T'ó-k'íñähyup (cold men; or men of the cold, or northern, country) and the Gwá-halégo, derived from the Comanche word *Kwáhadi*, or *Kwáhari* (white-tailed deer). During the prereservation era, the northern group ranged along the Arkansas River in Kansas, and the southern group inhabited the Staked Plains with the Kwahada Comanches (Mooney 1898, 227).[19] Moth Woman remembered the prereservation divisions, which she called *t'o·kyahu* (cold people) and *tsadlk'ihu* (hot people). She also mentioned a third, or middle division.[20] During the Southern Plains wars between 1867 and 1875, the southern division was identified as a hostile Kiowa faction, the Guhale band that was allied with the Kwahada Comanches.

As in other Plains tribes, political, economic, and religious variables affected Kiowa social organization—warfare and trade with other tribal nations; raiding for horses, plunder, and captives; and aggregating for the Sun Dance (Klein 1993; 139–41; Moore 1987, 318–20)—though ecological factors also determined group formation on a seasonal basis. Analogous to bison herd aggregation after mid-June for the rutting season, the Kiowa and Plains Apache Sun Dance bands formed the Sun Dance circle. Afterward, the people fragmented into *topadoga* groups that followed the mating herds until their dispersal. Winter brought about the separation of nuclear and extended family groups from the bands to hunt the scattered herds that had broken up into small male and female groups. Early spring marked the coming of the foaling season, and, in several months, the herds would again aggregate for the rut, beginning another annual cycle (McHugh 1972, 156–57, 192–93; Levy 1961). Jimmy Quoetone, Hunting Horse, and Red Dress described how the bands aggregated and dispersed throughout the year. Coalescence of the ceremonial bands into the four-to-six-week Sun Dance encampments paralleled the height of the summer rut. Breaking camp and the departure of the different *topadoga* mirrored the dispersal of the herds, which stampeded after each hunt and then re-formed. Likewise, *topadoga* were flexible entities characterized by interband movement, because it was not unusual for several bands to camp in the same general territory, no more than two or three days apart. Jimmy Quoetone recalled that every evening in the band camps, the older men visited and smoked, discussing the best time to move camp. The *dopadok'i* made decisions to move based on their wisdom. Movements after the re-formed herds largely were contingent on the amount of time necessary for the women to butcher the carcasses and sun-dry the meat, as well as the availability of adequate forage for the immense Kiowa horse herds. These late-summer-to-early-fall band camps stayed in one location for no more than two weeks. Each band encampment was composed of small family group clusters strewn along both banks of a watercourse, sometimes extending for several miles. Breaking camp was not a unified effort as families departed on an individual basis and headed for the next arranged location. Since this was a popular time for inter-family visiting, relocating camps had many stragglers.[21]

The Prereservation Kiowas

Reconstructing Kiowa history prior to the onset of the reservation period requires an examination of Mooney's *Calendar History of the Kiowa Indians* (1898), which is based largely on oral histories associated with the pictographic calendars of Sett'an (Little Bear), Ankopaá-iñgyadéte, or Anko (In-The-Middle-Of-Many-Tracks), and Dohásän II, nephew of the famed head chief. Stories related by Mountain Bear, Stumbling Bear T'ebodal, Frizzlehead, Feathered Lance, Paul Zotom, and Charley Buffalo dating back to the winter of 1832–33 were always correlated to winter and summer counts. Tribal migrations, Sun Dances, and conflicts with Mexicans, Texans, and other tribes were among the first- and second-hand tales Mooney collected. Over thirty years later, Nye interviewed elders born in the mid-nineteenth century who remembered the pre-reservation era: Hunting Horse (b. 1847); his second wife, Pitoma; Mary Buffalo (b. 1847); Botadli; Frank Given (b. 1853); and Jimmy Quoetone (b. 1855). Nye also interviewed those who were born during the reservation period, including Andrew Stumbling Bear (b. 1874) and George Hunt (b. 1881), his interpreter. Memories of prereservation times can be found in *Carbine and Lance* (1937) and *Bad Medicine and Good* (1962). In 1962, Corwin became alarmed that many Kiowa elders were dying, so he set out to interview as many as possible of the approximately twenty-five elders over the age of seventy-four. Information in the unpublished manuscript "50 Years with the Kiowa Indians, 1850–1900" was obtained from Rev. Albert Horse, Hunting Horse's son, Robert Onco, the son of Anko, Helen Quoetone Curley, the granddaughter of Jimmy Quoetone, Charley Redbird, Luther Sahmaunt, and Isaac Tsone-to-koy. Relations with Cheyennes and Arapahos can be found in Moore's *The Cheyennes* (1996) and Grinnell's *The Cheyenne Indians* (1923) and *The Fighting Cheyennes* (1915), and with the Comanches in Kavanagh's *The Comanches: A History, 1706–1875* (1996).

By the early 1830s Kiowas and Plains Apaches occupied lands bounded by the Arkansas and Red Rivers in southwestern Kansas, western Oklahoma, southeastern Colorado, and the Texas Panhandle. Bordered on the north and northwest by the Southern Cheyennes, Southern Arapahos, and Lakotas, who had pushed them south, other enemies included Pawnees to the north and Osages and Caddos to the east. Allies included the confederated Wichita tribes to the southeast and the Comanches to the south and southwest. Kiowa war expeditions frequently raided south into Texas and Mexico and traveled west to fight Navajos and Utes or to conduct friendly trade with the Pueblos. The relocation of eastern tribes into present-day Eastern Kansas and Oklahoma in the 1820s and 1830s exacerbated Southern Plains intertribal warfare. Increased conflict compelled the Kiowa *topadoga* to aggregate in large winter and summer encampments.

Coalescence undoubtedly was motivated by the westward push of Osages as well as on the near-annihilation of a Kiowa village on the west fork of Otter Creek in the Wichita Mountains in the early spring of 1833, when a pedestrian Osage war party descended on the encampment that was devoid of most of its warriors—who were away on a war expedition against Utes—killed many women and children, and then placed their severed heads into brass buckets, where they were discovered by those who had escaped the massacre. Moreover, the attackers seized the sacred Taime bundle, preventing the Kiowas from conducting the Sun Dance that summer. Following the massacre near K'ódaltä K'op (Beheading Mountain), the Kiowa leader A'dáte (Island-man) was deposed in favor of Dohásän, who served as principal Kiowa chief until his death in 1866.

Without the Taime bundle, there was no Sun Dance in 1834. That summer, Kiowa, Comanche, and Wichita villages located at the western edge of the Wichita Mountains were visited by a dragoon expedition from Fort Gibson, Indian Territory, accompanied by an Osage-Cherokee-Delaware-Seneca peace delegation. Convinced of their peaceful intent, the allied tribes agreed to send leaders to Fort Gibson, where negotiations resulted in promises of peace between Osages and Kiowas, who also agreed to maintain amiable relations with the American soldiers. On May 26, 1837, Kiowa, Plains Apache, and Tawakoni leaders met with government officials at Fort Gibson to sign a treaty agreeing to peaceful relations with Osages and immigrant Creeks and Cherokees, and with all United States citizens who trekked the Southern Plains en route to Texas and Mexico. Dohásän was one of ten prominent Kiowa leaders who signed the Treaty of 1837. By this time, Kiowa and Comanche skirmishes with the Cheyennes and Arapahos had intensified.

Elderly Cheyennes interviewed in the early twentieth century by Grinnell remembered skirmishes with Kiowas dating back to the mid-1820s when Cheyenne warriors journeyed south of the Arkansas River to steal horses. Clashes with the KCA alliance were also related to the diminishing bison herds. By the 1830s, bison were increasingly scarce between the Platte and Arkansas River Valleys, largely due to commerce along the Santa Fe Trail, migration across the immigrant trails, the relocation of eastern tribes to the Indian Territory, and the bison robe trade. Cheyenne aggression climaxed during attacks on Kiowa villages in the summers of 1836, 1837, and 1838. Peace was finally established between the two alliances in the summer of 1840, possibly prompted by vast depopulation incurred by the winter of 1839–40 smallpox epidemic that swept the Southern Plains.

For the next thirty years, the Kiowas inhabited the lands between the Arkansas and Red Rivers. Coalesced summer and winter camps were often located at the confluence of Wolf Creek and the North Canadian River in northwestern Oklahoma, in Kansas along Medicine Lodge Creek and Mule Creek, tributaries of the Arkansas River, and along the Arkansas west of the Great Bend. Adhering to the terms of the Fort Gibson Treaty, they maintained peaceful relations with the few Americans they met along the Santa Fe Trail or at Bent's Old Fort—in southeastern Colorado—although any group south of the Arkansas River perceived to be Texan or Mexican was targeted by raiding or revenge war parties. Interactions with Texans and Mexicans were typically violent. Helen Quoetone Curley told Corwin that Kiowa war parties usually targeted San Luis Potosi, though the Kiowas "considered the Mexican men cowardly" as opposed to Texans, who "would fight to the last breath in defense of their homes and families."

Like Cheyennes, the Pawnees sought Southern Plains horses concomitant to the Lakotas driving them south. By the 1840s, Pawnee raiding parties in the vicinity of the Arkansas River stole horses from Indian villages and Santa Fe Trail travelers. Back north in the Central Plains, overland traffic across the Oregon Trail had incessantly scattered Platte River bison herds, so the Pawnees also desired to utilize the richer hunting grounds between the Arkansas and Red Rivers. The earliest conflicts with Pawnees recorded by the Kiowa calendars occurred in the winter of 1846–47. For the next ten years, the Cheyenne-Arapaho-KCA alliance waged war against the Pawnees and several immigrant tribes in Indian Territory. Despite vast depopulation caused by the 1849 cholera outbreak that swept through the Plains—which reduced Kiowa population by at least one-half—the Southern Plains alliance tenaciously fought to defend their horses and buffalo hunting lands south of the Arkansas. Skirmishes with the Pawnees were noted by the Kiowa calendars for the winter of 1849–50; the summers of 1851 and 1852; and the winters of 1854–55, 1855–56, and 1857–58. Kiowas blamed the Pawnees, Potawatomis, and the Sac and Fox for the dwindling bison populations and attacked them to disrupt their hunting whenever possible. Amiable Kiowa-American relations were solidified by the July 1853 Fort Atkinson Treaty, negotiated at the military post located on the Arkansas River in present-day Kansas. Because the treaty was designed to protect the ever-expanding Southern Plains settlements and Santa Fe Trail merchants, the fifteen KCA representatives signing the treaty promised to maintain friendly relationships with the United States and permit safe passage of overland travelers, though they reluctantly agreed to allow the construction of roads and military posts in their territory. Convincing the leaders to cease raids into Mexico was another point of contention, although the treaty-signers promised to release any Mexican captives taken in the future and to refrain from sending war parties into Mexico. Shortly after the treaty sessions, raiding parties headed toward Mexico anyway. From the KCA point of view, Mexicans and Texans were natural enemies possessing livestock and potential captives, so halting raids into their lands was unthinkable. Mexico was particularly attractive for plunder, horses, and captives, the latter taken to replace their own children who died from the epidemics that swept through the Southern Plains. Clifton Tongkeamah used to joke that every family has some Mexican blood due to the large number of captives taken in the mid-nineteenth century (see Corwin 1959).[22] The Kiowa calendars document raids into Mexico in the winter of 1855–56, and the summers of 1857, 1858, and 1861.

Between 1857 and 1864, Kiowa country was centered more in southwestern Kansas, partially because of the trading alliance with the Cheyennes but primarily due to the expansion of Texas settlements, which forced them farther north from their southern territories. Northward expansion was also caused by the increasing scarcity of bison in the Southern Plains. Further population pressures occurred in the wake of the 1858 Pike's Peak gold rush, the founding of Denver, and the flux of fortune-seekers across the Southern Plains. Given the high volume of adventurers and immigrants who drove away the buffalo, it is not surprising that the Southern Plains war parties raided their caravans and communities.

By late summer 1860, Fort Larned was established at the confluence of Pawnee Fork and the Arkansas River, and Fort Wise (later Fort Lyon) was built near Bent's New Fort based on the belief that the Kiowas and Comanches posed the most serious threat to the Santa Fe Trail. The previous year, an Indian agency and adobe-picket military post had been established east of contemporary Fort Cobb, Oklahoma, overlooking the Washita River. Fort Cobb served as the new agency for the confederated Wichitas, Caddos, Tonkawas, and Penateka Comanches, and as a point of departure for forthcoming attempts to pacify the Kiowas and Comanches. Secession and the outbreak of the civil war, however, led to the withdrawal of federal troops from Fort Cobb, Fort Arbuckle, Fort Wichita, and Texas outposts. Jacksboro, Texas, became the northwestern edge of the frontier, guarded only by Texas Rangers and local militia that were largely ineffective against Kiowa-Comanche raiding parties. Comforted that Texans were enemies of the United States, the Kiowas launched numerous raids into Texas, as noted by winter counts in 1860–61, 1862–63, 1863–64, and 1866–67. Kansas military posts also incurred manpower shortages as regular troops were removed and replaced by volunteers whose ominous assignment was to provide protection for the hordes of travelers subject to raids as they traversed the Santa Fe Trail. Fort Larned, originally established to guard the Pawnee Fork sector of the well-used trail, became the agency for the Cheyennes and Arapahos in 1862 and the KCA tribes the following year; the latter received their annuities from this location until the reestablishment of Fort Cobb in 1868. The presence of these tribes in southwestern Kansas in the early 1860s coincided with the shrinkage of the upper Arkansas River hunting grounds triggered by the swelling population of Eastern Colorado following the 1858 gold rush. Settlements now bordered them on the west, south, and east. Contact with Americans was inevitable, as evidenced by the smallpox epidemic that struck Southern Plains villages during the winter of 1861–62, further reducing their numbers. Depopulation, however, did not deter Kiowa raiding parties.

By 1862–63, population pressures, intertribal warfare, and incessant raids south into Texas and Mexico caused great consternation among agency and post personnel at Fort Larned. Indian sightings along the Santa Fe Trail in the vicinity of the fort continuously incited rumors of Indian insurgency. Despite rumors of a general Indian "uprising" in the Colorado Territory, the Kiowas honored their treaty commitments and avowed peaceful feelings toward Americans in Kansas and in southeastern Colorado. However, by the summer of 1864, clashes between Colorado volunteers and the Cheyennes, Arapahos, and Lakotas in the undulating terrain bounded by the Platte and Arkansas Rivers affected the Southern Plains tribes. Since the KCA tribes were part of the Cheyenne-Arapaho-Lakota alliance, they invariably were drawn into the war. Late in the fall, Kiowas and Plains Apaches fled the Fort Larned area, traveled west, and relocated near a Comanche winter encampment in the Texas Panhandle on the South Canadian River, between Mustang Creek and the wreckage of Bent's abandoned trading post at Adobe Walls. At this location, in the early morning hours of November 25, 1864, the Kiowa encampment, numbering about 175 lodges, was attacked by 335 volunteers and 72 Ute and Jicarilla Apache scouts led by Colonel Kit Carson. In the aftermath of the battle, the Kiowa village and provisions were burned by Carson's men. Four days later, Colonel John M. Chivington's Colorado volunteers assaulted Black Kettle's Cheyenne winter village at Sand Creek, just below Fort Lyon.

The atrocities committed at the Sand Creek Massacre generated public outrage that prompted the formation of a federal treaty commission to negotiate with the Plains tribes recently pushed into conflicts precipitated by the presence of settlers, traders, and immigrants who scattered the wildlife between the Platte and Canadian Rivers. In mid-October, the confederated Cheyenne-Arapaho and KCA tribes assembled at the mouth of the Little Arkansas River to sign the Little Arkansas Treaty: the Kiowas and Comanches agreed to withdraw south of the Arkansas River, away from the Santa Fe Trail, and agreed to reside on a reservation in the near future. In January 1866, Dohásän tragically passed away in an encampment along the South Canadian River. Leadership allegedly passed to Gúi-pägo (Lone Wolf), although Te'né-angópte (Kicking Bird) and Set'aide led rival factions until the end of the Southern Plains wars in May 1875. Corwin asserts that Zépko-eétte (Big Bow), Stumbling Bear, and Paí-tälyí (Sun Boy) also contended for leadership.

Steadfast in their promise to maintain peace in Kansas and to avoid the Santa Fe Trail, Kiowa war parties instead struck south into Mexico and Texas, recently restored to the union. Raids into Texas continued unabated through the fall of 1866 because the Kiowas and Comanches failed to recognize that Texans, enemies of the Americans for four years, were now to be treated as Americans. Criticism of Kiowa-Comanche raids into Texas and the incessant warfare between the army and the Cheyennes north of the Arkansas led to congressional authorization in July 1867 of a peace treaty commission to negotiate with the various Plains tribes. The commission arrived at Fort Larned that fall and sent out liaisons to summon the Southern Plains tribes to rendezvous at Medicine Lodge Creek, where on October 21, KCA leaders signed a treaty that identified them as confederated tribes. They agreed to eventually settle on a reservation between the Washita and Red Rivers in present-day southwestern Oklahoma, though treaty provisions permitted them to hunt the nearly extinct buffalo as far north as the Arkansas River provided they avoided Kansas settlements. Kiowa concepts of time and boundary stipulations, however, differed from those of the government officials, so their days of free range in Kansas were almost over.

The summer 1868 Sun Dance was held on Medicine Lodge Creek, close to the location of the treaty-signing. After completion of the dance, a Kiowa-Comanche war party over two hundred strong headed west following the South Canadian River seeking to avenge Navajos they had fought the previous summer. Bad omens along the way greatly diminished the size of the force, except for the organizer who had "sent the pipe," and Heap O' Bears, who brought along two miniature replicas of the sacred Taime image. Disaster struck the remaining Kiowa warriors, who encountered and were defeated by a contingent of Ute warriors, who killed seven Kiowas, including Heap O' Bears, and captured the Taime facsimiles. News of the tragedy reached the Kiowa villages assembled near Fort Larned that fall to receive their annuities. Immediately withdrawing from Fort Larned, the Kiowas moved south for the winter, selecting a camping site close to Black Kettle's ill-fated Cheyenne village on the Washita River in western Oklahoma. This southward migration marked the permanent abandonment of the Arkansas River territory and coincided with the establishment of the KCA Reservation as stipulated by the Medicine Lodge Treaty and ratified by the U.S. Senate in August 1868. Despite the relocation to the new reservation, Kiowa and Comanche war parties continued raiding into Texas and Mexico for horses and captives. Aggression against Texans intensified, culminating in the Red River War, which ended in May 1875 when the last warriors surrendered. Afterward, the Kiowas and their allies were confined to their assigned lands, ushering in a new era of rapid culture change that signaled the end of the horse and buffalo culture.

2

Kiowa Beliefs and Concepts
of the Universe

The Santa Fe Laboratory of Anthropology fieldnotes contain a wealth of information about Kiowa cosmology and concepts of power as well as and its manifestations and distribution throughout the universe. Most of the information about power was related by Mary Buffalo to Weston LaBarre. Either Charley Apekaum, her nephew, or Bert Geikauma interpreted, and Geikauma provided additional information. Additional information regarding power was provided by other collaborators. Jimmy Quoetone, with the assistance of translator Ned Brace, also contributed much information to LaBarre and Donald Collier. Ned Brace also was the primary interpreter for White Fox. Besides Mary Buffalo, Apekaum also interpreted for Heap O' Bears, Sanko, Andrew Stumbling Bear, and Bagyanoi, or Recovery Many Things. LaBarre interviewed Lone Bear using Mary's son Homer as his interpreter despite his misgivings about the veracity of his information, but Collier spent more time with Lone Bear. Hunting Horse's sons Monroe Tsatoke and Albert Horse interpreted primarily for interviews conducted by William Bascom and for some by LaBarre. George Hunt interpreted for Bascom's interviews with Goomda, or Medicine Wind. Jane Richardson's entries do not list an interpreter, but she worked primarily with Moth Woman. Some data were obtained by Bernard Mishkin from Belo Cozad and Silver Horn.

Significantly, the majority of the interpreters and collaborators, with exceptions, were practicing members of the Native American Church. Jimmy Quoetone, a former peyotist, had converted to Christianity in 1887. Like Quoetone, Hunting Horse also became a Christian and had to divorce one of his wives in order to join the church. One son, Albert Horse, became a Methodist minister, whereas the other, Monroe Tsatoke, remained a member of the Native American Church. Religious differences did not influence the quality of the information obtained by the field school, as exemplified by Ned Brace, a peyotist, who was the primary interpreter for Jimmy Quoetone, as well as White Fox. Through Marriott's interviews with Tsoodle, Frank Given, and Sanko, she learned about the acquisition of power through the vision quest, the doctoring powers of shamans, the powers of Taime, and the Ten Medicines, but her fieldnotes are silent regarding the concept of power and its distribution throughout the universe.

Cosmology

Plains origin stories range from those lacking any detailed description of world origins to complex accounts of multiple creations. Genesis stories sometimes involve a creator represented by trickster or a non-personified force; variations of celestial, earth diver, and emergence motifs; or some combination thereof. Because origin myths in traditional societies are transmitted through storytelling, they constantly assume different forms due to innovation and diffusion (DeMallie and Parks 2001, 1065–66). Jimmy Quoetone recounted the creation myth to LaBarre, describing how the Kiowas emerged from the underworld when Saynday (or Sindi), the shape-shifting, part-animal, part-human culture hero, tapped on a tree or hollow log, summoning the underground-dwelling Kiowas to inhabit the earth's surface. As the people crept upward single file, a pregnant woman lodged in the narrow aperture, preventing the people below from surfacing. Only half the Kiowas made it to the world they inhabit today.[1] Belo Cozad related a similar story of creation.[2] N. Scott Momaday presented this version in *The Way to Rainy Mountain* (Momaday 1969, 16), based on Mooney's rendering (1898, 152–53). Modern accounts specify that Saynday turned the Kiowas into ants prior to their emergence (Boyd 1981, 1). Displayed in the Kiowa Tribal Complex are ten six-by-eight-foot acrylic canvas murals delineating Kiowa history; the first painting, by Parker Boyiddle, depicts Saynday transforming the people into ants, then changing them back into people as they reach the surface (Denton 1987, 71). Oftentimes the Kiowas refer to themselves as the T'epda (coming out) or Kɔuda (pulling out) people to commemorate the creation myth.

Concomitant to linguistic evidence, the Kiowa emergence myth supports an ancestral link to the peoples who emerged from Blue Lake near Taos Pueblo. Emergence themes are found throughout the Southwest among the Pueblos, and in Navajo, Yavapai, Jicarilla, and Lipan Apache mythologies; common themes include gestation, birth, fertility, and connections to the subterranean realm of the underworld (Bierhorst 1985, 82–83, 77; Witherspoon 2005, 258). In the Great Plains, the semisedentary horticultural Hidatsas, Mandans, and Arikaras have emergence myths, as well as the horse and buffalo Lakotas and Cheyennes (Bowers 1950, 117, 153–56, 183; Bowers 1965, 290, 298; Dorsey 1904a, 12–35; DeMallie 1987, 27–28; DeMallie 2001, 806; Powers 1977, 80–81; Grinnell 1923, 1:4–5; Grinnell 1926, 242–43; Bierhorst 1985, 155, map; DeMallie and Parks 2001, 1065–66), tribes that the Kiowas encountered in the late seventeenth century. The pregnant or heavy woman motif, undoubtedly a reference to fertility, also appears in Mandan, Lakota, and Cheyenne myths (Bierhorst 1985, 165–66). The Kiowa, Lakota, and Ponca myths also specify that bison emerged from the underworld to occupy the middle world of human existence. Lakota origin stories specify Wind Cave, South Dakota, as the place of emergence (Dorsey 1905a, 87–88; Irwin 1994, 41; DeMallie 1987, 27–28; DeMallie 2008, 9n10).

After the emergence event, Saynday, the Kiowa trickster, respectfully called *tsegi* (uncle) by Belo Cozad, brought order to the Kiowa universe.[3] According to White Fox, Saynday provided the first people with bison, the staff of life, by stampeding them from an underground cave.[4] Bagyanoi related that Saynday, assisted by animal helpers, stole the sun and hurled it into the sky.[5] Lone Bear identified Saynday as a paradoxical character who typically created order through disorder and was an incessant prankster constantly duping the prairie dogs, bears, and other animals that often outwitted or killed him. Nonetheless, the indestructible Saynday always was reanimated in another story to torment animals or help the Kiowas.[6]

As specified by Bert Geikauma and Lone Bear, nineteenth-century Kiowas believed Saynday was a real person and that his stories could only be narrated under certain conditions: This was, first, because some Saynday stories delineate obscene scenarios like mother-in-law/son-in-law coitus, only grandparents could tell the stories. Due to their advanced age, it was said, the elders had no shame and could make light of dreaded situations involving mother-in-law incest. Second, the stories could only be told at night, lest Saynday cut off the storyteller's nose.[7] By the 1930s, such severe sanctions were nonexistent because Saynday stories were recounted to Elsie Clews Parsons (1929), Marriott (1963), and members of the Santa Fe field party. Since then, Saynday stories have been relegated to children's folktales, although Kiowa storytellers, like the late Bryan "Jake" Chanate, employ them to impart morals to today's young people. Grandparents still tell Saynday stories to their grandchildren and jokingly blame bad luck streaks or lost articles on Saynday. Gus Palmer Sr. told me that buffoons and troublemakers often are characterized by Kiowa elders as *Saynday-dɔ*, meaning "that person is like Saynday."[8]

An important post-emergence myth is the Star Husband/Star Rope tale, a common motif among other Plains tribes, including the Cheyennes, Arapahos, Gros Ventres, Crows, Dakotas, Mandans, Hidatsas, and Pawnees (Thompson 1929, 283n, 331n; Bierhorst 1985, 159; DeMallie and Parks 2001, 1066). The story told by Jimmy Quoetone begins with a woman desiring to marry Evening Star — or Son of the Sun in Mooney's (1898, 238) version. Evening Star fulfilled the woman's wish by transforming into a beautiful porcupine and appearing before her perched in the limb of a cottonwood tree, which she ascended as it grew upward. Upon arrival at his home in the clouds, Porcupine transformed back into Evening Star and took the woman as his wife, and she soon bore a son, consummating their marriage. After some time, the woman, longing for her home and people, found a way to escape by lowering herself down a buffalo sinew rope with the infant in her arms. Angered by the sight of his fleeing wife, Evening Star cast a stone downward, which struck her forehead, killing her instantly and sending her body plummeting to the ground. Fortunately, her body absorbed the impact, sparing the infant, who clung to his dead mother while suckling her breasts.[9]

Since death cycles into life in hunter/gather mythos, the death of the mother transforms the story into the creation of the Half Boys, or Split Boys, a variant of the Star Boy epic of the Crows, Cheyennes, Arapahos, Blackfoot, Gros Ventres, Hidatsas, Mandans, Arikaras, Pawnees, and Santees (Bierhorst 1985, 158–59; Thompson 1929, 128–30). Back to Jimmy Quoetone's story, following the death of his mother, the orphaned boy began roaming the prairies until he encountered a lone tipi, which was momentarily vacant due to the absence of its occupant, Spider Woman, or Spider Old-Woman, who eventually returned and used her transformer powers to capture the boy and then put him to sleep with a lullaby: "Your mother is decomposed already, but you still nurse her." Spider Woman raised the boy, and one day presented him with a gaming wheel shaped like a spider web, along with the explicit instructions never to toss the wheel upward, a request that he ignored. Tossing the wheel up in the air, it came down with great force on his forehead, splitting him into two identical twins, the Split Boys.[10] Spider Woman and the Hero Twin motifs also exist in some Pueblo emergence myths, again supporting an ancestral Kiowa link to Taos Pueblo (Bierhorst 1985, 96; Marriott and Rachlin 1975, 35, 39–40).

Variations of this story told by Jimmy Quoetone and Heap O' Bears attribute certain exploits to the Split Boys following their appearance. One tale relates that the twins reanimated their mother, who married the younger twin, whereas the eldest wed Spider Woman: the original Kiowas descended from the two couplings.[11] A more popular story related by Quoetone indicates that the Split Boys wandered the earth, slaying monsters and overpowering evil forces, and then one day reappeared at Spider Woman's lodge, where they confronted and killed a snake, her husband. Finally, the twins separated: one traveled east and transformed into trees, mountains, and rivers, and the other journeyed west and disappeared forever.[12] In Mooney's (1898, 239) version, one twin walked into a lake, never to be seen again, whereas the other transformed himself into the ten Boy Medicines, or *zaidethali* (Split Boy) bundles. Hence the origin of the sacred *thali-da-i* (Boy Medicines), commonly referred to as the Ten Medicines.

The Concept of Power and Its Manifestations

Despite intertribal differences in belief and ritual, Plains Indian mythos share concepts of "power," a mysterious, transcendent life force with "cosmological, experiential, natural, and communal dimensions" (Grim 2005a, 760). Similar concepts are found throughout Native North America, as among California and Great Basin tribes (Bean 1977, 118; Miller 1983, 69), the Coast Salish (Amos 1977, 134), Ojibwas (Black 1977), Senecas (Isaacs 1977, 168), and Cherokees (Wahrhaftig and Wahrhaftig 1977, 231). Power is perceived as a sacred and transcendent force permeating

the universe, present in everything; this enigmatic force causes all movement, including thought, and is the source of stable, physical forms. In
Siouan cultures, the Poncas, Kansas, and Omahas call it *wakką́da* (sacred
power) (Dorsey 1894, 266–68), the Otoe/Missourias call it *wakhą́da* (Whitman 1937, 84; Waters 1984, 47–56), the Osages use variant form *wak-
ką́ta* (La Flesche 1921, 47–50; La Flesche 1930, 566–70), the Lakotas and
Assiniboines refer to *wakhą́* (Walker 1917, 152–56; Densmore 1918, 85;
DeMallie 1987, 27–28; Denig 1930, 486), whereas the Crows call it *wa·xpê·*
(Lowie 1918, 315–43), and the Mandans *xóprį* (Bowers 1950, 324–31). In
Arapaho, "sacred power" is *béétee* (Fowler 1982, 68), and in Cheyenne,
éxAhestOtse (Moore, Liberty, and Strauss 2001, 873; Moore 1996, 211–13);
these Algonkian-speaking peoples believe that power comes directly
from a creator. The Shoshonean-speaking Comanches refer to power
as *puha* (Gelo 1986, 126–27; Kavanagh 2001, 892), and the Kiowas call it
dɔdɔ (Kracht 1989, 80–81). Power is possessed by a multitude of beings
from the visible, natural world and invisible otherworlds, and it often
manifests itself through natural and supernatural phenomena. Powerful
spiritual beings that exist in trees, mountains, stars, the sun and moon,
four-legged and winged creatures, plants, whirlwinds, lightning, and
thunder can appear to humans in dream spirit form (Kracht 1989, 80–
81; Walker 1917, 153; DeMallie and Lavenda 1977, 154–63; Grim 2005a,
760–61; Irwin 1994, 151, 31).

Since power is connected to thought forms, dream spirits can confer power to humans through dreams and visions. Power is potentially
accessible to anyone intentionally seeking a vision, or to those extraordinary individuals who spontaneously receive esoteric knowledge through
life-changing events. During the visionary experience (DeMallie and
Lavenda 1977, 157, 162), or dream epistemé (Irwin 1994, 18–22), the power
recipient learns the characteristics of the spirit benefactor, as well as the
objects—feathers, birds, animal parts, plants, minerals, and so on—to
be gathered and placed in a bundle wrapped in deer or buffalo skin; the
medicine bundle embodies sacred power (Brant 1951, 38–42; Denig 1930,
483–84; Wissler 1912b). Songs learned from the dream spirits initiate
rituals of opening or manipulating the bundle to activate the life force
on behalf of others to ensure successful hunting, good fortune, or healing. Sacred powers manifested through these magical rites validate the

status of bundle owners, mostly men, who serve as leaders and healers within their communities. Sacred, mystical perceptions of power, then, should be examined in relation to the material and social realms, and how it is attainable through dreams and visions providing blueprints for respecting, harnessing, and manifesting power for the benefit of the community (DeMallie 1987, 38; DeMallie and Lavenda 1977, 157–58, 164; Grim 2005a, 761–64; Young 2001, 1032–34).

Moth Woman, Lone Bear, and Hunting Horse emphasized that the concept of *dɔdɔ* (power) was central to prereservation Kiowa beliefs.[13] Mary Buffalo and Bert Geikauma believed that this spirit force manifests itself in natural phenomena like thunder, the four directional winds, mountains, seasons, and animal, bird, or reptile guises.[14] Hunting Horse and Lone Bear concurred that these entities possess varying degrees of *dɔdɔ*. For instance, if one animal dominates another in nature, its *dɔdɔ* is stronger, and Hunting Horse stressed that "powers from above" are stronger than the powers of earthbound animals, so logically, Sun power is mightier than Buffalo power. Importantly, these powers could be good or bad since goodness and evil coexist in everything.[15] Haumpy stated that the Kiowas supplicated a multitude of these spirit powers for long and prosperous lives and offered prayers to the sun, moon, and stars, and to the plants, animals, and birds. They also believed that *dɔdɔ* could be obtained through vision quests featuring power-seekers—mostly men—offering prayers to the spirit forces. Successful vision quests, however, were rare because the spirits were not always willing to impart their powers to humans. Haumpy indicated that a few individuals did receive *dɔdɔ*, and some even accumulated different powers over the course of their lives.[16]

After listening to Moth Woman's descriptions of power, Jane Richardson likened *dɔdɔ* to a "mana-like power," and more recently, the late Kiowa linguist and historian Parker McKenzie identified *daúdaú [dɔdɔ]* as a verbal adjective meaning "possessing magical power; as medicine men were formerly regarded," or "in a state of power."[17] In abbreviated form, *dauú* translates as "supposedly possessed supernatural powers or orenda as qualities ascribed to Indian medicine men." Another derivation, the noun *daui* refers to "unit/s of medicine, pill/s, herb/s, etc.; coll., medicines."[18] The Huron word *orenda* was first utilized as a cover term by early twentieth-century ethnologist J. N. B. Hewitt to describe power as a "subsumed mystic potence in all bodies" or a "hypothetic potence or potentiality to do or effect results mystically," also found in Shoshonean *pokunt*, Siouan *wakhá*, and Algonkian *manitowi* (Hewitt 1902, 37–38; Isaacs 1977, 168). Several years later, Robert Marett used the Latin *animatism* to define an impersonal, supernatural power exemplified by *orenda*, the Cree *manitu*, Melanesian *mana*, and Siouan *wakanda* (Marett 1914, xxxii, 21, 24, 26, 109, 113). Like their predecessors James Frazer and Edward Tylor, Marett and Hewitt were cultural evolutionists who perceived tribal belief systems as vestiges of primordial religions. Marett postulated that animatism preceded *animism*, the "doctrine of souls and other spiritual beings," which Tylor had labeled the earliest stage of religious thought. According to accounts, the belief in impersonal forces preceded personalistic beliefs in spirits (Tylor, cited in Bohannan and Glazer 1988, 76; Harvey 2006, 10).

Marett and his contemporaries erroneously perceived power as an impersonal force because they overemphasized its sacred and mystical dimensions while overlooking the social and relational aspects of power. They did not fully understand that power also refers to individuals with power (as noted by McKenzie), and to the relationships or kinship between beings (Harvey 2006, 130). Moreover, comprehending power in Plains belief systems must have been a daunting task due to the Western bias of scholars, and because the "spiritualizing ideas of Christianity" had influenced Plains religious ethos since the late eighteenth century (Grim 2005a, 761–62; DeMallie and Lavenda 1977, 159). Looking beyond the limitations of early twentieth-century scholarship, however, terms like animatism and animism are useful when stripped of their evolutionary baggage. For instance, animatism could refer to a life force or power permeating the universe as represented by the Siouan *wakhá*, Huron *orenda*, and Kiowa *dɔdɔ*, specific terms that also describe persons of power. Animism, the belief in spiritual beings, or the presence of an inner soul in all things, has been reinterpreted to define relationships between humans and "other-than-human-beings" (Hallowell 1960; Harvey 2006, 17–20), the spirit helpers or dream spirits (Irwin 1994), originally identified as guardian spirits by Ruth Benedict (1922, 2–3, 13–14). Through dreams and visions, gifted individuals, particularly those who become shamans, are empowered with metaphysical powers; dream spirits are the facilitators making power available to humans. It follows, then, that Plains Indian religions variously combine animatistic and animistic beliefs representing a totality of relatedness of all powers.

In Plains cosmography, power is distributed throughout a three-layered universe consisting of upper, lower, and middle realms. Powers associated with the upper realm include the sun, moon, celestial beings, and the winged creatures of the sky; the lower realm is represented by water and underground beings, such as fish, snakes, and chthonic beings; both realms intersect with the middle realm, inhabited by humans and land animals. Visionary experiences occur in the middle realm (Irwin 1994, 26–55; Moore 1996, 203–6). Indigenous Kiowa cosmography, however, differed somewhat according to Hunting Horse, who identified three levels of the universe: sun, air (wind), and earth. Sun, moon, and stars inhabit the upper level; wind, the four directional winds, thunder, whirlwinds, tornados, and birds occupy the middle level; earth, the lowest level, is home to humans, plants, and animals, including those that live underground or underwater. The spirits spread across the cosmos are interrelated,[19] travel at night, and are potentially malevolent, according to Bert Geikauma.[20]

Upper-World Powers

Acknowledging the hierarchy of power in Kiowa cosmology, Lone Bear observed that the powers "from above" are the most powerful in the universe, followed by those of the middle world and, finally, the powers possessed by the "creatures of the earth."[21]

Sun

Early twentieth-century linguist J. P. Harrington noted that Kiowas identify Sun as the principal life force and refer to it as *da* (medicine) (Harrington 1928, 48). White Fox said that Sun is the Kiowa protector, provider, and teacher, and that Kiowas offered skin sacrifices on buffalo chips to this great power.[22] Moth Woman indicated that supplicants praying to the spiritual powers of Sun respectfully address it as *k'o* (grandfather), obviously establishing relationships with it as an other-than-human being.[23] Sun, as father of the Son of the Sun, is also connected to the creation of the Ten Medicines (Mooney 1898, 238–39) and is also the father of the bison herds according to Jimmy Quoetone.[24] Sanko acknowledged the sacred connection between Sun and bison because hunters placed fresh offerings of buffalo meat on the ground for Sun.[25] Spiritually, Sun, the greatest source of power in the upper world, nourishes all life forces in the lower world of Earth. From an ecological perspective, sunlight, nutritious grass, and fat bison are conjoined tropic levels in the Great Plains grassland food chain. Sankadota specified that Sun symbolizes an "almighty ubiquitous spirit" that was the most frequently supplicated power force on a daily basis.[26] Haumpy, White Fox, and Hunting Horse all told stories about petitions for longevity and good health, which involved lifting up a small section of skin with an awl or needle, slicing off seven strips, holding them toward Sun while praying, then placing them on a buffalo chip altar.[27] Mary Buffalo also described how fathers took their children to hilltops in the early spring to sacrifice small strips of their skin to Sun to ensure their well-being through the coming seasons.[28] Tsoodle concurred by relating how his father cut strips of skin off his chest, placing them on buffalo chips with a prayer to Sun: "I'm going to offer a piece of my son's skin that he may get well."[29] Sacrifices to Sun were very powerful prayers, especially when performed as personal healing rituals, according to Max Frizzlehead.[30] Heap O' Bears said Sun also was connected to war power, for men receiving Sun-inspired power visions typically became great warriors, a Kiowa virtue. Warriors often painted sun designs on their bodies and war shields prior to engaging in combat because sun symbols provided invulnerability. Sun symbols were also painted on the bodies of the dancers and the shields used in the Sun Dance, which was closely affiliated with Sun and war power.[31] Lone Bear pointed out that when a sun-emblazoned shield was not in use, it was placed on a tripod east of the owner's tipi, facing east toward the rising sun, like tipi entrances; throughout the day, the tripod was moved so the shield always faced the sun.[32]

Moon and Stars

The uppermost level is also inhabited by b'a (Moon), a female spirit that Mary Buffalo believed controlled women's menstrual cycles through its lunar phases.[33] Jimmy Quoetone also perceived Moon as a woman, although he was unsure whether she is the wife of Sun or mother of the stars.[34] Kiowas noted the daily revolution of the earth around the sun and that the moon sets in the east at sunrise and then rises in the west before sundown. Sanko recalled former days when elderly men recorded thirteen lunar cycles each year—six and a half-moons in the winter and six and a half-moons in the summer—by notching sticks kept in special sheaths.[35] Though not common, Hunting Horse and Mary Buffalo indicated that some people prayed to new moons for good health and general well-being,[36] even though Moon was not as powerful or as frequently supplicated as Sun according to Moth Woman.[37] Sanko described the symbolism of lunar activities as interpreted through augury: a circle around the moon portends approaching severe weather or, even worse, enemies surrounding the village; lunar eclipses signify that the moon is ill or troubled by malevolent beings.[38]

Moon coexists with stars, which Sanko called the "helpers of the moon."[39] Important stars identified by Mary Buffalo include North Star, known as the "Pawnee Star," or gu·ekyata (never-move-star), because the other stars revolve around it; and Morning Star (Venus), called da·edl (big star), is the largest, most significant star.[40] Goomda said that celestial bodies grouped into constellations form patterns such as seven men smoking, a running fox, a beaver and his den, and seven sisters chased by five stars representing Saynday; these stars had once been people.[41] Specific star clusters noted by Mary Buffalo include Pleiades, called da·mäta/n (star girls), which appeared concomitant to the creation of Devil's Tower; and the Big Dipper, known as pola/yi (rabbit), because of its big ears.[42] The colossal meteor shower witnessed on November 13, 1833, throughout the Northern Hemisphere was recorded in the Kiowa and Lakota pictographic calendars. Mooney interpreted the event to be an ominous sign (Mooney 1898, 260–61), though Sanko suggested that this natural phenomenon, called dao'gye (falling star), involved the stars assuming better positions in the sky.[43] Bagyanoi recalled stories from his childhood told by elders about the night "when the stars fell,"[44] and Mary Buffalo claimed that Zempadlte (Gnawing On A Bone) was born that night when it was "like daylight" and believed that's what gave him "strong medicine power."[45] Mary Buffalo, White Fox, and Moth Woman all identified the Milky Way Galaxy as dago·mtom (backbone of the stars).[46] According to Goomda, prayers were not offered to stars.[47]

Middle-World Powers

Winds, Thunder, Lightning, Tornados, and Whirlwinds

Sanko provided most of the information about the middle realm of the universe, air (wind), which is characterized by the winds that hold Sun, Moon, and the sky beings in place. Hunting Horse identified wind as the "authority" of the middle realm, equating it with the life principle of breathing, which ceases when people die, described as losing one's wind, or breath. Sanko went further when he said that wind combines with fire to create the warm breath of human life. Those who were sick faced the wind, opening their mouths to swallow it to restore their health. Wind is also responsible for bringing rain clouds and moving the stars.[48] Bert Geikauma provided the Kiowa names for the spirits of the winds living at the four cardinal directions: (East) the spirit of the east lives at *bai-bodebɛm* (sunrise way); (South) the spirit of the south occupies *ba·ibe·gu* (toward summer [way]); (West) the spirit of the west inhabits the *bai-yieyɛm* (sun going down [way]); (North) and the spirit of the north resides at the *ayäpegu* (toward winter [way]). Most Kiowa rituals acknowledged the four cardinal directions.[49]

Thunder, lightning, whirlwinds, and tornados that represent powerful spirits living in the middle realm of air were identified by Max Frizzle-head. Thunder, the speech of Thunderbird, is powerful because it shakes the earth and brings nourishing rains.[50] Heap O' Bears added that first Thunder in the "elm-leaf unbuttoning time" of the spring symbolizes new life.[51] According to Heap O' Bears and Max Frizzlehead, Thunder and Lightning, like Sun, are very powerful and associated with war power; warriors with Thunder power painted images of *basoguto* (thunderbird) or *bõibahétgìɛ* (lightning) on their shields and cheeks for invulnerability in combat.[52] White Fox asserted that Thunder power "in general protects man from arrows and bullets in war" because "lightning strikes things." Following the logic of sympathetic magic, where like produces like, the man with the "power of this greatest striker . . . is protected from other things that might strike him."[53]

Whirlwinds and tornados are common natural phenomena on the Great Plains, and portions of the Southwestern Plains lie within Tornado Alley, the zone with the highest frequency of violent tornados. In indigenous times, these wind powers were perceived to be very destructive, but Mary Buffalo thought they never disturbed Kiowa encampments until non-Indians upset the balance of nature.[54] Biatonma, Ioleta Hunt MacElhaney's grandmother, related to Marriott that there was "no memory for many generations of Kiowas being hurt in a windstorm" until recent times.[55] Mary Buffalo told a story about the origin of cyclones. The story begins with several shamans, or medicine men during the pre-horse era who espied a small herd of wild horses near a water hole but were unable to get close enough to observe without driving the animals away. In order to get a closer look, one of the shamans transformed himself into a mole so he could tunnel toward the water hole and then report back to the others. Since moles are blind, his descriptions lacked vital information about horse anatomy, so he had to make several trips to describe what the horses looked like. Following his instructions after the first trip, his friends used dark buff clay to mold an image to the exact dimensions of a horse, including prairie grass for the mane and tail. The horse would not move, so he made a second trip and had them cover the figure with a snake skin to give it a mottled look. Still the horse would not move, so he left, came back, and had them attach terrapin shell hooves to the figure, but the figure remained motionless. After his last trip he perceived that their breathing and snorting in the dust was caused by smoke, so he instructed them to build a fire inside the figure of the horse. When the shamans brought their creation to life, it flew into the air instead of galloping across the ground, its downward breath causing tornados. They called this monster *tseigudl* (Red Horse), which still can be seen flying through the air breathing fire, with its snake-like tail dragging the ground, causing destruction. In indigenous times the Kiowas prayed to Red Horse when they saw a tornado, in order to secure protection for their camps. They asked Red Horse to "take pity" on them while using hand motions toward it to turn it aside.[56] Biatonma also told Marriott that people sometimes prayed "that there might be no storms and sometimes it worked."[57]

Present-day Kiowas say that the old people could "talk to tornadoes," as noted by Clifton Tongkeamah, who often related how his grandmother, Fannie Tongkeamha, prayed to tornados that passed through the old homestead near Eagle Heart Springs during his youth in the 1940s. Clif remembered peering through the doorway of the tornado shelter watching her standing with outstretched arms facing the approaching storm, singing an eerie song demanding the tornado to change its course away from them; the words to the song are "Go away, we're Kiowas." Clifton's sister, Lavena Tongkeamha Pewo, told how their father, Weiser, was frequently called upon to pray in public during his later years. Once a funnel cloud was spotted heading toward the Kiowa Complex during a benefit powwow at Red Buffalo Hall. As participants fled the building, Weiser was asked to pray away the tornado. Later on, with a mischievous twinkle in his eye, he said that he began the prayer: "Oh ye of little faith." Dorothy Tsatoke Gray told a humorous story about her uncle who was very funny. One day a twister came through and everyone ran down to the storm shelter except for him. Facing the tornado, he implored it to turn south toward Lawton. Someone yelled up from the storm shelter that their kids were in school in Lawton, prompting him to say "no go north" as he pointed in the opposite direction. Unfortunately, people often die during tornados, and it's mystifying why Lone Bear did not inform the field party students about the May 1928 tornado that killed an elderly woman on his allotment; perhaps he was adhering to the tradition of not mentioning the name of a deceased relative.[58]

Ray Doyah maintains that to this day that the tornado, also called *maw-k'oun-geah* (sleeve black, or black sleeve) by his mother, Beatrice Ahpeatone Smith, and *goam-gyah haih'k'ya* (whirlwind), is feared.[59] Moth Woman said that Whirlwind originates at graves and "contains the spirit of the dead." Hence Kiowas avoid whirlwinds, but those unfortunate enough to confront them are advised to cover their heads and cross their index fingers to protect themselves "because the whirlwind has the power to twist the mouth, cross the eyes, and twist a person all up." Moth Woman stated that her husband cured twisting illnesses caused by ghosts.[60] Symptoms of facial twisting, or "ghost sickness," also found among the Lakotas, Comanches, and Plains Apaches, clinically have been identified as Bell's Palsy, or facial paralysis of unknown origin (Henderson and Adour 1981, 195–96).

Birds

Lone Bear and White Fox concurred that Eagle, the most powerful winged creature, is the father of all birds. Eagle is associated with war power through bravery and fearlessness, and its feathers adorned lances and war bonnets, a practice that continues today.[61] Lone Bear claimed that his father possessed an Eagle war shield and led war expeditions because of his war power.[62] (Marriott gathered more detailed information about these shields.) Despite Eagle's connection to war power, Hunting Horse said that Tene/taide (Bird Chief) cured fevers by fanning patients with an eagle-feather fan while blowing an eagle-bone whistle.[63] According to Mary Buffalo, certain men were known to capture eagles after spending the night in pits covered with coyote robes.[64] Hawks and falcons also symbolize prowess in combat, another virtue of the Kiowa warrior according to Lone Bear and White Fox.[65] Heap O' Bears added that Crow also possesses war power linked to its ability to successfully dodge bullets.[66] Heap O' Bears, Hunting Horse, and Haumpy all said that feathers from these birds were utilized in most healing rituals, as were those of the yellow-hammer, hummingbird, and blue darter.[67]

Thunderbird, a large eagle-like bird, was called "thunder man" by Max Frizzlehead because he communicates through thunder and lightning: *aóeta* is "distant rolling thunder with no lightning visible," and *pɔsot* is "loud thunder with lightning." Lightning occurs when Thunderbird opens his eyes and throws out light; Thunder is when the bird speaks, sometimes prompting men to say, "The bird is talking too much."[68] First thunder in the spring signifies a new year, prompting the keepers of the Ten Medicines and the Taime bundle to fill their long-stemmed pipes and pray for another year of life. Heap O' Bears referred to Thunder as the "messenger of summer."[69] Max Frizzlehead and Heap O' Bears named Crow as Thunderbird's ancient and more powerful nemesis. Crow symbolizes the cold weather of wintertime. Rare occurrences of thunder-snow during the winter signify that Thunderbird and Crow are battling, causing Crow to retaliate with a harsh blizzard. Cold spells are anticipated, and since Kiowas do not like the cold weather, no prayers were offered to winter; therefore, they prayed to the summer season.[70]

During the prereservation era, Hunting Horse said that when Thunderbird emitted thunder, children were cautioned to keep quiet "because he is talking." Once lightning struck close to an encampment and Ko/p·gotä·de "shouted out for everybody to put cedar in the fires, presumably as a sacrifice or for protection."[71] Max Frizzlehead recalled that sometime around

1870 during a tremendous thunderstorm over the Wichita Mountains, smoke was seen rising from the ground following a lightning strike. Men investigating the phenomenon stated that they saw "a large bird like an eagle outlined on the ground with some phosphorescent material." Long before that, some Kiowas "saw a thunder bird outlined on the ground when lightning struck" near the Salt Fork of the Red River.[72] According to Mary Buffalo, Basoptædlyi (Thunder Boy), who communicated with Thunder, rode into battle with lightning painted on his cheeks while wearing a war shirt adorned with a fire-belching Thunderbird. Thunderbird designs were painted on the shoulders of his war horse, with black lightning zigzags beneath each ear and on its legs. His son was painted the same way. Sometime before 1840, Thunder Boy, whose war cry rumbled like thunder, led a successful charge against the Cheyennes. Accordingly, this was one of the greatest Kiowa victories over an enemy.[73]

Like whirlwinds and ghosts, sɔpodl (Owl) — represented by the white, or snowy owl, according to Moth Woman, or the horned owl, as noted by Lone Bear — is greatly feared because owls are the spirits of recently deceased people. Lone Bear described Owl as the "reincarnation of a dead spirit," and White Fox emphasized that anyone who died could be reincarnated as an owl.[74] Jimmy Quoetone suggested that owls are "perhaps the souls of evil persons" and then told a story about events that occurred near the encampment of a war party. A man shot an owl perched in a tree, but when examining the carcass he noted that "the owl had a man's face. Just beyond the tree were the remains of some people who had been killed. The owl was the spirit of one of these."[75] Bert Geikauma and Mary Buffalo identified owls as the transmigrated souls of medicine men, and Moth Woman noted that "spirit of the dead power" obtained from Owl could be used to gain information "from the spirit of the dead in the owl."[76] Quoetone agreed that owls are spirit mediums, intermediaries between the dead and the living, so to hear the nearby hooting of this nocturnal creature signifies that someone will soon die, or that another spirit has just entered the spirit world. Hunting Horse added that owls follow people at night, inducing pok'u·n (to twist), a facial paralysis (Bell's Palsy) to those unfortunate enough to make eye contact with them.[77] Obviously, owls and ghosts are intricately related. Quoetone acknowledged that even the bravest warriors feared owls, and that when an owl dies, it reincarnates into a bear,[78] though White Fox claimed it turns into a cricket, and Laura Pedrick told stories about K'op-sau-po-dal, an owl transformed into a gigantic mountain ogre living on Mount Scott (Boyd 1983, 213).[79]

Perhaps because owls are connected to death, some men received war power from Owl. Haumpy remembered a man who carried a white owl skin as a war charm,[80] and Hunting Horse said that Tenezeptie (Bird Bow) owned an Owl battle shield.[81] However, since owls are reanimated spirits of the dead, Moth Woman said, certain men were able to obtain a·tedɔ·dɔ (spirit of dead power) allowing them to communicate with owls and ghosts during divinatory rites conducted to predict the future or to find lost objects or people.[82] Such rituals conducted by Kiowa Owl prophets are analogous to the Lakota Yuwipi rite and the Algonkian Spirit Lodge, or shaking tent ceremony (Deloria 2006, 83–106; Collier 1944).

Men with Owl power were greatly feared, in part due to their other-worldly association with owls, but largely because they could practice Owl sorcery. Hunting Horse mentioned that his father-in-law, a *sen wi*, could hoot at another person to make their face "twist all up."[83] Hunting Horse, Lone Bear and Moth Woman could identify four Owl prophets from the latter half of the nineteenth century: (1) Dɔhade (Medicine Man), also known as Mamande (Coming Up Above) (Nye 1937, 127, 234; Boyd 1983, 249–53); (2) Pɔdodl, or Pódodal (Mooney 1898, 345), who owned two live owls that forewarned him about two Navajo men who would attempt to steal his horses; (3) Pieguete, the grandfather of Kiowa Six artist Spencer Asah, who had an owl skin bundle that "was derived from dead people"; (4) and Nesonte, who received Owl power while mourning the death of her father, Gɔ/gode.[84] Gɔgode had the reputation of coughing up a tiny owl head, which was circulated among observers to rub on their bodies to "protect themselves from witches." Hunting Horse told the story about a skeptical man who laughed at this performance, provoking Gɔgode to swallow the owl head; immediately the man's face "twisted up," causing him to beg Gɔgode to reverse his sorcery. He also related that sorcerers performing shooting magic mixed a concoction of owl ashes and feathers that was thrown in the wind toward their victims, causing vision impairment.[85] Although Owl doctors were greatly feared for their capacity to practice sorcery, Lone Bear and Moth Woman said they were consulted for their ability to prophesy and to treat individuals whose faces had been twisted by whirlwinds or owls.[86] Yellow Wolf, identified by Lone Bear and Hunting Horse as one of the last Owl prophets, was interviewed in 1935.[87] Yellow Wolf made a very profound statement about his talents to William Bascom, perhaps because he thought he noted skepticism in the young anthropologist:

> You young people think that it is foolish that I can talk to the spirits. If you lived in my age I could take you and show you. I wonder if the spirits still take care of me in this new age when things are so very different.[88]

Kiowas still fear owls as harbingers of death, as exemplified by modern-day examples. For instance, in late April 1993, about a week before Clifton Tongkeamah passed away from the complications of type 2 diabetes mellitus, he and his wife, Betty Tanedooah Tongkeamah, spent the night in an Anadarko motel. In the middle of the night Betty was awakened by an owl hooting outside their window. Later she told me that was the sign Clif would not last much longer. Early in the morning of June 20, 2004, a young Kiowa girl was killed in a single-car accident on Oklahoma State Highway 58, approximately eighteen miles south of Carnegie, when she "failed to negotiate a 90-degree turn," locally known as "dead man's curve."[89] Her death was the topic of conversation the following Thursday as undergraduate students Joseph Justin Castro and Rachel Whitaker and I visited with Dorothy Tsatoke Gray and some of the ladies sewing quilts and having fellowship at Cache Creek United Methodist Church. Dorothy mentioned that one of her daughters had once seen a large white owl sitting there on the road, and that another relative saw a three-to-four-foot-tall owl wearing earrings at the same location. She mused that it could have been a medicine man, since they have the ability to shape-shift into owls. Dorothy told her daughter not to be afraid of such an animal since she is a Christian.[90]

Because all powers in the Kiowa cosmos are interrelated, certain birds and land animals are associated with the same powers, as noted by Heap O' Bears.[91] For instance, Hunting Horse said that Buffalo is connected to Hawk, Crow, and Falcon, so feathers from these birds, *bak'ase* (sacrifice feathers), were given away at the Sun Dance, which was replete with the symbols of Sun and Buffalo.[92] Mary Buffalo and White Fox described the special crow-feathered fan that rested below the Taime during the Sun Dance, and a similar fan was used during Buffalo Medicine Lodge ceremonies.[93] Heap O' Bears summarized unique power combinations as dichotomous opposites: thus, Eagle-Lightning-Fire-South opposed Crow-Snow-Cold-North.[94]

Lower-World Powers
Earth

Dom (Earth), the lowest level of the universe, was described by Jimmy Quoetone as a floating strip of land surrounded by water, with aboveground-, underground-, and underwater-dwelling powers.[95] White Fox likened Earth to the mother of all living things that provides nourishment through abundant plants and animals the same way a mother nourishes an infant.[96] According to Moth Woman and Lone Bear, Kiowas praying to Earth addressed her as "mother."[97] Anyone could pray to Earth for good health but not for personal power, though Moth Woman pointed out that Earth is less powerful than the spirits dwelling in the middle and upper worlds.[98] Hunting Horse said that people prayed more to Earth than to Moon and added that whenever his mother-in-law threw out dishwater, she prayed to Earth for the well-being of her children.[99] Since all powers can be good or bad, Bert Geikauma insisted that he never left a bucket of water out overnight lest an evil spirit traveling at night stop to "drink from it or defile it."[100] Perhaps similar logic explains why Hess Bointy was scolded by a friend's parents for throwing out the wood ashes without informing them during a visit in the mid-twentieth century.[101]

Spirits of the earth exist in plants. Bert Geikauma suggested that "maybe plants are people" that "talk and understand," which supports the notion of animistic beings as other-than-human beings.[102] Haumpy noted that sage, sweetgrass, and especially cedar are used as incense for purification and doctoring, as are certain vines and roots.[103] Earth spirits also inhabit rocks and physiographic features such as rivers and mountains, according to Mary Buffalo and Bert Geikauma.[104] White Fox pointed out that visions occur while the person experiencing them is lying on the earth, particularly on top of mountains and hills or elevated areas closer to the more powerful spirits of the middle and upper worlds.[105] Throughout Native North America, mountainous regions are sacred sites for vision quests, which probably explains why the Kiowas have lived near mountainous terrain since they left the headwaters of the Yellowstone River toward the end of the seventeenth century, migrated southeast to the Black Hills/Devil's Tower region by the end of the eighteenth century, and then were pushed south to the Wichita Mountains (Mooney 1898, 155; Gulliford 2005, 948–49; Meadows 2008, 42).[106] To this day, Kiowas acknowledge that the Wichita Mountains contain many sacred locations where vision quests occurred. In 1935, Hunting Horse identified Mt. Sheridan as a power place for visions and healing, whereas Silver Horn referred to Mt. Scott as a "vision-seeker's paradise."[107] Vision-seekers ascending its summit avoided areas marked by tobacco ashes, which identified locations used by previous aspirants. Silver Horn told a story substantiating the power of Mt. Scott, the eastern sentinel of the Wichita Mountains:

A man went up to the mountain to get a vision. On the third morning he woke up to find himself in a hollow. He went back to the mountain fell asleep and again found himself in the hollow. Again it happened. The fourth time he heard the mountain speaking—"don't get out of my sight. You will live long if you stay within range of these mountains." He went away from them and was killed.[108]

Elevated areas also were preferred locations for crevice and cave internments, though Emáa claimed that ground inhumation became more customary after the Kiowas obtained digging tools from the Mexicans.[109] Mary Buffalo and Lone Bear maintained that the dead were buried with the feet facing east and the head west, so that the spirit could travel to *komtokya*, or *gomtokya* (dead people's home), where tipis face west instead of east because the spirits are confused.[110] Emáa, the first female keeper of the Taime bundle, said that the deceased travel to the "Land of the Spirits" and then related a story about her father's encounter with a spirit village:

E's father was out hunting one day and after getting some meat he came to the place where he was to meet his relatives. He came up to what he thought was his place. His horse was shy. He saw fires blazing, heard dogs barking, and people talking. Two dark forms came in his direction. He called out asking whose camp it was. The two forms evaporated. Suddenly the whole camp faded out. He left the place and finally came to his own camp. After the people had taken the meat off his horse he found that his bridle and rope was gone. The people talked about it for a long time. They thought it was a camp of Spirits of the dead. The general opinion on this is that the dead are in this world but are invisible at will.[111]

Moth Woman, Mary Buffalo, Lone Bear, White Fox, and Heap O' Bears all agreed that recently departed spirits sometimes linger near graves or the locations where they died. Burial sites, however, were not feared unless whirlwinds were encountered, because Whirlwind originates at the grave and possesses the spirit of the dead.[112] Likewise because owls are the spirits of evil persons or shamans, people avoided going near the graves of such individuals so they would not become bewitched, as noted by Jimmy Quoetone and Mary Buffalo.[113] Nonetheless, men and even women were known to experience spontaneous visions while mourning in the vicinity of a medicine bundle keeper's grave and were bestowed powers when a spirit pitied them. White Fox, Silver Horn, Mary Buffalo, Lone Bear, Bert Geikauma, Jimmy Quoetone, Moth Woman, and Hunting Horse all confirmed this belief.[114]

Animals and Other Creatures

Kiowa traditions refer to an almost forgotten time when animals dominated the earth, and according to Mary Buffalo, they stalked and killed humans. During this mythical era, deer had extremely sharp canine teeth that they used to violently bite people until Saynday caught one and ground down its teeth with a rock.[115] In a story told by Goomda, a great race was held to determine which species would dominate the remaining animals. Humans won, and to this day, man is the "chief" of all animals.[116] According to Hunting Horse, the hierarchy of power in the spirit realm coincides with physical power in the natural world: "if in nature one animal is stronger than another, so will its power be stronger than the other's."[117] Though not as powerful as upper- and middle-world spirits, lower-world animals often bestowed power on vision-seekers who appropriated the spirit world through fasting and praying, in anticipation that one of them would take pity and imbue them with power. According to Goomda, vision quests for power were mostly conducted in the spring and summer, when animals roam the earth, as opposed to wintertime, when they hibernate.[118] White Fox described the powers of shamans: "medicine men's spirits are little animals in them," such as "a stone, or a lizard, a horned toad or a mole," miniature bison, or small pieces of buffalo hide or horn. Stronger animal spirits emerged from the shaman's mouth when he was "close to death."[119] Bison are the most powerful of the earthbound animals because they obtain their power directly from Sun, as specified by Jimmy Quoetone, who sang an old-time Kiowa song describing a buffalo standing alone on the prairie, obtaining power from Sun: "I am a buffalo, I'm standing here without water, right in the middle of the day, that's the reason I'm getting power." Furthermore, he identified Buffalo as the mediator between Sun and the Kiowa people that could impart Sun power to fortunate power-seekers. Bulls were perceived to be more powerful than cows; Buffalo power resided in the cud inside the bull's stomach, making it difficult to kill.[120] Kiowa elders acknowledged their strong connection to Buffalo and Sun, particularly because Sun helps the bison grow so the Kiowas could hunt them as their primary food source. After successful hunts, freshly cut strips of buffalo meat, called *auh-gau-peeh* (our own food) by Ray Doyah, were offered to Sun.[121] Sanko, Jimmy Quoetone, and White Fox all stated that Buffalo power was closely affiliated with warfare, so killing a buffalo bull symbolized slaying an enemy. Fathers often performed divination rites with fresh buffalo hearts to determine whether their sons would be great warriors. Buffalo was the principal symbol in Kiowa ceremonies, particularly in the Sun Dance, when a bull hide was procured to adorn the forked pole of the Sun Dance lodge. Buffalo hides and chips played important roles during renewal rites of the tribal medicine bundles.[122]

White Fox noted that bison sometimes aggregated into male herds analogous to Kiowa warrior societies, each distinguished by a hierarchy of chiefs.[123] Buffalo is more powerful than Bear and the white man's cow, for bison were known to disembowel bears and "cow" bulls in fights, as noted by Mary Buffalo, who added that Buffalo is powerful because of its great medicine powers providing great recuperative strength.[124]

White Fox and Heap O' Bears concurred that Kiowa men receiving power visions inspired by Buffalo became Buffalo doctors, or Buffalo medicine men, who frequently were requested to accompany war parties due to their ability to stop hemorrhages. Buffalo doctors collected bison hair at buffalo wallows, which they braided into bundles and wore as headgear, and they painted their bodies red and white to symbolize how bison, red in color, wore white clay paint, or the dust from rolling in the wallows.[125] Bears are still greatly feared and respected, though the nature of their power is not well recorded. In 1935, Moth Woman, Pitma, Red Dress, Gontahap (Mrs. Bluejay), and Tsoodle had vague memories of a women's secret society, the Bear Society, which was somehow related to the Ten Medicines.[126] Ambivalent feelings toward bears are noted in the Kiowa myth regarding the brother-turned-giant-bear that chased seven sisters up a huge boulder that rose toward the heavens as the bear lunged at them, inflicting scratch marks on the rock. Jimmy Quoetone's grandfather specifically referred to Devil's Tower as the location of the story, which probably originated when the Kiowas were in the northern country on their southeastward migration toward the Black Hills.[127] Jimmy Quoetone and Mary Buffalo identified the Pleiades as the constellation created by the seven siblings rising into the sky and called it *da·mät/an* (Star Girls).[128] According to Moth Woman, an old woman named Zont'ɔede conducted a healing rite called the *da·matonda* (Star Woman), or Pleiades ceremony. Somehow the vision—obtained while mourning a deceased relative— was connected with the Bear myth of the Pleiades. Since Zont'ɔede did not select an heir, her powers were not transmitted, and the ceremony became defunct.[129] Modern-day accounts of the bear story show some variation. In *The Way to Rainy Mountain*, N. Scott Momaday (1969, 8) refers to seven sisters chased up a tree stump by their brother-turned-bear, thereby becoming Ursa Minor—the Big Dipper.

Of all the animal spirit helpers that transferred power to fortunate vision seekers, *set*, or Bear, was not one of them. Haumpy and Heap O' Bears pointed out that most Kiowas, and in particular the Taime keeper and the keepers of the Ten Medicines, did not wear bear robes or eat bear meat, the latter a taboo taken seriously in 1935—and today.[130] Raymond Tongkeamha related a humorous story about a prank he pulled on a Kiowa friend several years ago at the Crow Fair in Montana. Sitting in an encampment eating dinner with their Crow hosts, Raymond's friend queried about the source of the roasted meat. Raymond said it was bear meat and his friend quickly stuck a finger down his throat to regurgitate his meal! Despite the hilarity of this story, eating bear meat results in dire consequences, as emphasized by Bagyanoi, Andrew Stumbling Bear, and White Fox. All remembered the tragedy of the summer of 1868 when several Comanche members of a combined war party against the Navajos killed and roasted a bear. Greasy bear meat smoke permeated the campsite, compelling most of the frightened Kiowa warriors to turn around and head eastward toward home, except for Heap O' Bears, keeper of two Taime effigies that were lost forever when he and the remaining Kiowas were subsequently killed by a Ute war party.[131] Mooney (1898, 322–23) and Marriott (1945, 3–14) also recounted this story, although Marriott's account is replete with inconsistencies and does not correspond to the Kiowa calendars. Notably, a number of Kiowa war chiefs were named after bears, including White Bear, Heap O' Bears, Sitting Bear, and Lone Bear.

Other animals possess varying degrees of power relating to special abilities or medicinal properties. For instance, Hunting Horse pointed out that mountain "cats" are associated with stalking and jumping powers.[132] A man with powers related to this animal can jump and attack like a cat, according to Haumpy, who also noted that Wolf has the power of prophesy; those with Wolf power were consulted regarding the outcome of war parties.[133] Wolf scouts also announced the arrival of returning war parties. Hunting Horse, Haumpy, and Mary Buffalo remembered men with Beaver power who doctored "running sores," administered vermifuges to kill parasitic worms, and had power over fish and underwater animals.[134] Mary Buffalo described tunnel-entrance tipis used for healing ceremonies performed by Beaver doctors adorned in beaver-hide shirts. Employing the sucking technique, these "old Kiowa" doctors treated sores and removed worms.[135] Hunting Horse claimed that Beaver doctors made incense from dried beaver intestines,[136] and Homer Buffalo recalled that "in [the] old days Indians made perfumes from dried testes [castoreum] of beaver."[137] Perhaps Kiowa Beaver medicine was influenced by the Comanche Beaver Ceremony, where shamans employed the sucking technique to treat tuberculosis and detect sorcery (Kavanagh 2008, 169–75, 199, 216–17, 403). Prairie dogs, often tormented by Saynday, have a highly developed social organization with leaders that bark at the edge of their holes to communicate with the community. Hunting Horse acknowledged that Prairie Dog power was used for love magic.[138] A number of animals were mentioned by Haumpy, Lone Bear, Mary Buffalo, and Moth Woman as possessing unspecified powers, including Badger, Fox, Otter, and Elk.[139] Dog power was not described, but Haumpy remembered a Buffalo medicine man who used a white dog when treating patients. He also stated that men with visions derived from horses used their powers for doctoring horses and administered a liquid medicine for urinary blockage.[140] Hunting Horse recalled a man whose power visions derived from horses and sparrow hawks who was renowned for his horse-breaking abilities. While breaking a horse he sat on its back with his arms outstretched like wings, making hawk-like noises.[141] Warriors painted their war ponies prior to engaging in combat; horse and rider as one shared war power. Horses with unusual war power were named, such as ɔdlpábai (Thick Mane), recollected by Tsoodle as a famous war pony that "understood when war was coming on" and had a no-retreat taboo once an enemy was charged. Tsoodle recounted a famous engagement against soldiers when Thick Mane was ridden in succession by White Bear, Sitting Bear, and Baitaide, each of whom killed an enemy.[142]

Moth Woman recalled five Deer doctors from her youth, including Tsontali—whose powers also were associated with the night hawk—who lived in her father's camp; and her father-in-law with Deer power obtained from a "mule-eared deer" could cure various illnesses, particularly spider bites.[143] On the same subject, White Fox remembered that during times of bison scarcity, men with Deer power were summoned into a tipi to perform all-night deer-charming rites to activate the powers of two Deer medicines—feathered arrows wrapped in deerskin—that provided the magic for deer drives. Early in the morning, two fleet-footed men departed the tipi and handed the medicines to two riders who rode with them in opposite directions, forming a large circle with a circumference of up to two miles. When they returned with the medicines, numerous men, women, and children—who had been summoned by camp criers from different encampments—retraced the path of the medicines, reforming the circle. From that position, everyone walked inward, beating the grass with sticks and pieces of wood, driving the deer inward. The deer-charming magic rendered many of the animals defenseless so they could be easily dispatched with arrows or even lassoed and led away by women. Moth Woman indicated that this practice ended by the time she was thirteen years old, sometime in the mid-nineteenth century.[144] Like deer-charming medicine, Antelope power also was used to lure antelope into hunting entrapments, according to Jimmy Quoetone, Hunting Horse, and Mary Buffalo.[145] Mooney (1898, 287–88) noted a great antelope drive near Bent's Old Fort during the winter of 1848–49, led by an "antelope medicine-man," and that the Kiowas only participated in antelope drives when bison were scarce. Kiowas also feared some creatures other than owls, including burrowing animals, like gophers and moles. People were reluctant to eat their meat, according to Lone Bear, Bert Geikauma, and Moth Woman, who believed that anyone touching dirt from their burrows would be poisoned.[146] On the positive side, Hunting Horse and Haumpy noted that men with Mole power treated skin diseases,[147] but since Mole and Gopher powers also were associated with sorcery, Moth Woman recalled a Mole doctor known to avenge women spurning his advances by causing moles to appear on their faces.[148] Coyotes howling in the distance implied that someone was sick, so Hunting Horse suggested that anyone hearing that should smear a piece of meat in ashes and throw it in their direction in order to ward off sickness.[149] Haumpy mentioned *gi/edl* ("little men [bipeds] about two feet high covered with fur, and noted for being very strong"), and Mary Buffalo told LaBarre about dwarfs living in the mountains who could "crush a person's arm if grabbed." Long ago an elderly woman had told her that dwarfs killed people by throwing rocks at them.[150] Little People, or gnomes, known for their powers to uproot trees and pull buffalo out of the mire, are still present, creating havoc in people's lives, as related to me by Hess Bointy and Patricia Ware.[151] Mary Buffalo also described ogres whose lips were "red from [the] blood of people they ate." She referred to them as *Go'sæpoDa* (mountain ogres), strong creatures with "great jaws" whose bodies were covered with black hair. She said they carried large clubs "like big rough baseball bats" and "bags for human game." Around the same time, Kiowa elder Laura Pedrick said that K'op-sau-po-dal, a transformed owl-mountain ogre, lived west of Mt. Scott (Boyd 1983, 213), and more recent Kiowa lore gathered by Russell Bates acknowledges the presence of Khot-sa-pohl, also known as Bigfoot or the Hairy Man (Bates 1987, 5–6). In 2003 and 2004, while visiting elders at Rainy Mountain Kiowa Indian Baptist Church, George Tahbone and Fred Tsoodle mused about Bigfoot sightings south of the Washita River between the communities of Washita and Fort Cobb.[152] Reptiles also possess great powers and are respected like the animals. Snapping Turtle, an aquatic reptile, possesses great healing powers associated with its dominion over fish, frogs, and other underwater beings with lesser powers, as noted by Hunting Horse, Mary Buffalo, and Bagyanoi.[153] Around 1870, a young man sleeping along a riverbank had a vision in which he traveled underwater, where he encountered fishes, underwater creatures, reptiles, amphibians, and a tipi with a door flap painted like a turtle shell. During the reservation era, Tonakɔt (Snapping Turtle) became a great healer but a feared sorcerer, according to Mary Buffalo.[154] Haumpy and Bagyanoi pointed out that Kiowas fear creatures living under rivers, streams, and small ponds, because humans and all other living beings must drink water to sustain life,[155] but Mary Buffalo was the only collaborator to make a passing reference to a "water hole monster (who controlled water animals)."[156] This is surprising considering extant Kiowa legends of an underwater monster living in the Washita River. For instance, Kiowa author Russell Bates wrote about the Tonhkyanh-hee (People Who Live Under The Water And Mud) (Bates 1987, 6–10), and Mooney even noted a painted tipi with designs of Zemoguani, a horned fish (Ewers 1978, 32).

Kiowa country is home to venomous rattlesnakes, water moccasins, copperheads, spiders, and scorpions. Snakes allegedly have power because they are without friends. Those possessing Snake or Spider power typically doctored snake, spider, and scorpion bites. Hunting Horse, Haumpy, Lone Bear and Mary Buffalo remembered that in earlier times three women and three men practiced Snake medicine, including Kiowa Charley's father, Tonsatɔma (Heating Tallow), who used the sucking method to remove venom and sometimes snake fangs from snake-bitten victims.[157] Bagyanoi told the story of how Heating Tallow once treated Red Otter, who had stepped on a rattlesnake skeleton while barefooted during a fast on Hunting Horse Hill, east of Mt. Sheridan. Within a day, Red Otter could not walk due to paralysis in his legs, so he was taken to Heating Tallow, who recommended fasting in the Wichita Mountains because his condition was incurable. Taken back into the mountains by horseback, Red Otter lay on a bed of sage for four days and nights, smoking and praying to the spirit world. Snakes appeared in a vision during the second night, informing him that the "sickness you have is very hard to cure, because [the] snake which harmed you was dead." On the third day, an enormous thunder cloud passed through the area, pelting Red Otter with rain and hail and ripping at his bison robe. Weak and dehydrated by the fourth day, Red Otter was surrounded by snakes and lizards that scurried away when a large, two-headed, snake-like bird twenty times larger than any bird he had ever seen swooped down and grabbed his legs with its talons. Red Otter felt something icy cold withdrawing from his legs and a voice saying "now you're already cured."[158] Horned toads and lizards are associated with certain powers that Jim Ahtone and Haumpy could not specify, though Sankadota claimed that in his youth he once sat under a tree when a "green lizard with black stripes" said to him, "You are a poor boy. I will take pity on you."[159] The spirit represented by the lizard became his special protector.[160]

In his autobiography, Charley Apekaum mentions that Kiowa power-seekers acquired more power from "lower animals such as owl, snake, bear, buffalo, deer, mole, beaver. . . . It's usually the animals that we see here with us—turtle too." He also indicated that power came from dogs and lizards as well. Next-most commonly, men attained power from birds like the eagle, yellowhammer, hummingbird, several types of falcons, and crows (LaBarre 1957, 100–101). By the 1930s, however, there were fewer individuals with power from these animals as indigenous religious beliefs and practices declined or were absorbed into Christianity and the Native American Church.

Kiowa Concepts of Power after 1935

During the 1935 summer field school, the anthropology students gathered ample information about Kiowa concepts of *dɔdɔ*. Christians and peyotists alike could reminisce about power, its diffusion throughout the three levels of the universe, and the birds, animals, and celestial bodies whose attributes became manifest in humans attaining their powers. Despite paradigm shifts brought about by the new religions, knowledge about older traditions was relatively intact. Native American Church members who worked with the students included Yellow Wolf, Jim Ahtone, Lone Bear, Tsoodle, and Frank Given, all peyote doctors. Other field school collaborators, notably Jimmy Quoetone, Hunting Horse, and Sanko, were former peyotists who had converted to Christianity. Charley Apekaum—chief interpreter—had followed both religions. During this era, people switched back and forth between peyotism and Christianity according to special circumstances. For instance, when LaBarre returned in the summer of 1936 to study the Native American Church, he learned that Bert Geikauma's daughter had died, compelling him to join the Baptist Church, because the peyote religion failed to save her life. David Paddlety, who also interpreted for the field school and Redstone Baptist Church, took his children to Indian doctors when they were sick (LaBarre 1957, 101–3, 164). Some older concepts of power related to shamanism and doctoring, therefore, were still intact, whereas some notions had fused into Christianity and the Native American Church; since the late nineteenth century, it was not unusual for households to be divided between the two religions. Nonetheless, worshipers in Christian churches and peyote tipis prayed to the same deity they called dɔk'i (power + man, or God), which demonstrates how indigenous concepts of power were integrated into the new religions. In 1916, Big Tree, a Christian convert, sent a letter to Secretary of the Interior Franklin K. Lane defending the Ghost Dance movement among the Kiowas, rationalizing that Indians "pray to the same God, and have many other ways of worshiping him."[161] Indeed, Yellow Wolf's reference two decades later to "this new age when things are so very different" aptly describes changes that occurred after the collapse of the horse and buffalo culture.

Jerrold Levy, a graduate student at the University of Chicago, mentored by Robert Redfield, Sol Tax, and Fred Eggan, conducted his doctoral fieldwork among the Kiowas from July 1957 to September 1958, and in June and July 1959. Influenced by the interdisciplinary focus of Redfield and the social anthropology of Tax and Eggan, and with access to Marriott's fieldnotes, Levy worked primarily in one Kiowa community with eight unnamed collaborators. In his doctoral dissertation on political organization and tribal factionalism, Levy briefly discusses power, but not in terms of dɔdɔ. Levy notes that Christian conversion "did not involve the discard of former powers if it was felt that the older power was still effective," and that several of his collaborators had participated in both Christianity and peyotism; regardless of their religious convictions, people still had "respect for those old Gods and beliefs" (Levy 1959, ii, 3–4, 16–17, 121–23).

Between January and May 1987, while collecting data for my doctoral dissertation, I spent some time interviewing Gus Palmer Sr., a Native American Church roadman—one who conducts, or "runs" peyote meetings. One afternoon Gus discussed the concept of *dɔdɔ* in reference to a peyote song called *pe·gya dɔk'i* (God that's with us [in everything]). Gus explained the song, which describes the omnipotence of God, oftentimes pointing to a picture of Jesus on the wall when he referred to God:

> I believe that . . . He [God] is everywhere in spirit. No matter. He's in the ground. He's in the air. He's in the water. He's anywhere in spirit. He's even right here [in the room where we were sitting] in spirit. A lot of people don't know that. He's there even [points to his heart]. That's what makes [the] heart tick. That's the soul. And when a person dies, He takes that. That's Him. He's there.[162]

Clearly, by the late twentieth century, vestiges of indigenous concepts of *dɔdɔ* were still present in Native American Church songs. *Dɔdɔ*, a power force permeating all levels of the universe, was now represented by an omnipotent *dɔk'i*. Christian hymns in the Kiowa language also petition and praise *dɔk'i*, the same god. Gus further explained the concept of *dɔk'i* and *dɔdɔ* in the Native American Church:

> So, by that see how the Indian has got a church? Down to earth. . . . That's far better than a building that's built with gold. God came on this earth the same way—pitiful way. We're sitting on her on this Mother Earth—pitiful way. We shed tears, we tell Him [through testimonies]. He's here. He hears it. He makes this earth; this earth *edɔdɔ* [has power or strength]. [This] means that God, they call him *dɔk'i*, "God." Everything's *dɔk'i*. . . . Everything is like "magic," *dɔ*. *Dɔk'i dɔmedɔdɔ* [earth is like magic]. The earth to the Indian, it's like things come about like magic. Come springtime, things beginning to grow, like magic, you know. He's there.[163]

Palmer's testimony reveals the merger of older Kiowa concepts related to *dɔdɔ* with the Christian concept of God. Comparing churches of gold to worshiping on the ground (Mother Earth) nicely illustrates the Kiowa sense of humility and piety; praying while sitting on the earthen floor of a peyote tipi brings the supplicants closer to God, who is magic like Mother Earth. God made the earth, so his magic and power are felt by the supplicants who offer tearful prayers. In indigenous Kiowa belief, springtime is the beginning of the new year, when the thunder and rains first appear and the ground emerges from the dormancy of winter. God's power is there, according to Gus, whose narrative nicely displays Christian and Native syncretisms in the peyote religion.

Reflecting back on this interview with Gus, I cannot remember any references to *dɔdɔ* in the Kiowa church services I've attended since then, let alone in conversations with Christian Kiowas. Over the years the only unsolicited reference to *dɔdɔ* was a comment Raymond Tongkeamha made about his open-mindedness toward anyone feeling the necessity to seek *dɔdɔ* on a vision quest. With this in mind, I thought about some of the songs performed during July 4 Kiowa Gourd Clan ceremonials at Carnegie Park. Some of the songs are dedicated to Kiowa soldiers shipping out for active duty in Afghanistan; the word *edɔdɔ* can be heard in the lyrics. Raymond and his sister Melissa Tongkeamha Kaulity both assert that references to *edɔdɔ* in a handful of the songs is a prayer that soldiers take medicine power overseas for protection. In 1959, Levy noted that power related to warfare became "ineffectual in the new situation" after their surrender in 1875 and was told that these powers had been "thrown away" (Levy 1959, 121). Had Levy looked further into religious beliefs he might have reconsidered his statement: as long as there are soldiers, war power is alive and well among the Kiowas.

3

Acquiring, Maintaining, and Manifesting Power

Among Plains tribes, power was ideally acquired through the vision quest rite by means of which a few fortuitous individuals received personal powers that protected them from enemies or gave them specific medical knowledge; a man's power became his personal guide, a spirit force to be consulted when necessary. Some men even had the ability to amass powers from a multitude of spiritual forces, and multiple individuals were known to obtain personal powers from the same source (DeMallie 1987, 34–42; DeMallie and Lavenda 1977, 157; Stewart 2001, 335; Wood and Irwin 2001, 357; Parks 2001, 383; Fowler 2001, 844; Moore 1996, 212–13; Fletcher and La Flesche 1911, 122–29; Lowie 1935, 237–51; Whitman 1937, 81–88; Cooper 1957, 264–91; Kavanagh 2001, 892; Levy 2001, 913; Foster and McCollough 2001, 932). Acknowledging their power bonds, men with similar powers formed common interest associations, or societies, connected with warfare, healing the sick and wounded, or serving the spiritual needs of the people (Dorsey 1884, 342; Wissler 1916; Lowie 1913b, 1915; Howard 1965, 114–15). In indigenous Kiowa society, individuals obtained either war power, curing power, or spiritual power through vision quests or inheritance from fathers or other elderly men. Men of power were affiliated with the principal Kiowa socio-religious institutions and participated in the Sun Dance. In this chapter, curative powers are discussed; power related to the collective Kiowa spiritual psyche and warfare is discussed in subsequent chapters.

Detailed information about vision quests, the acquisition of power, and the manifestation of power through curative rites and sorcery was recorded by the Santa Fe field party students. Working primarily with Haumpy and Hunting Horse and to a lesser extent with Botadli, Tsoodle, Goomda, and Jim Ahtone (Wooden Club), Bascom gathered the most information about vision quests and power. Next, Collier collected abundant data from Lone Bear, as did LaBarre from White Fox, Mary Buffalo, and Bert Geikauma. To a lesser extent, Sankadota, Silver Horn, and Luther Sahmaunt conveyed some knowledge about earlier times to Mishkin, and as usual Jane Richardson worked with Moth Woman. David Paddlety usually interpreted for Haumpy, as did Albert Horse for Hunting Horse and Homer Buffalo for Lone Bear. Concomitantly, Alice Marriott learned about the acquisition of power from George Hunt, Biătonmá, Kiowa George Poolaw, Tsoodle, Sanko, and Frank Given between 1935 and 1936. Her data augments the Santa Fe fieldnotes and provides additional details. Collectively, most collaborators, born between the late 1840s and the early 1870s, had vivid memories of power-seeking, a practice that was largely discontinued by the mid-1930s.

The Acquisition of Power

In indigenous Plains cultures, concepts of cosmological power were communicated to the community at large through stories connecting individuals to natural and supernatural realities that guided their daily lives. Experientially, certain individuals were known to receive sacred and mysterious powers from other-than-human persons through vision-seeking rites. Those empowered through dreams and visions were instructed by the dream spirits to assemble medicine bundles composed of various objects—animal parts, birds and feathers, plants, and minerals—related to the cosmological component of the vision. They also learned songs that activated those powers when the bundles were manipulated in public performances. Men—and sometimes women—of power possessed esoteric knowledge and extraordinary capabilities that could benefit themselves and others. Power visions validated leadership and were a ritualized means of innovation and transformation in Plains religions (Stewart 2001, 335; Bowers 1950, 335–36; Parks 2001, 383; Dorsey 1894, 413–16; Fletcher and La Flesche 1911, 221; Cooper 1957, 264–91; Lowie 1918, 315–43; DeMallie and Lavenda 1977, 157–58; Irwin 1994, 189–91; Irwin 2005, 1129; Schweinfurth 2002, 132; Grim 2005a, 762–64; Harrod

2000, 77; Harrod 2005, 96–97). As in other Plains cultures, Kiowa men acquired medicine bundles affiliated with power through visions, inheritance, and purchase (Brown and Irwin 2001, 423; Cooper 1957, 265–74; Harrod 2005, 96; Foster and McCollough 2001, 932; Schweinfurth 2002, 131). Power, a rare commodity, was largely restricted to the *ondedɔ* (rich) people, who composed approximately 10 percent of the total Kiowa population. Although *dɔdɔ* was accessible to everyone, ownership of the sacred tribal bundles resided within *ondedɔ* families that maintained possession of them through the inheritance pattern of the *ɔde* (favorite child), a practice that kept power in family lines. As specified by Lone Bear and Haumpy, a man ideally transferred his power to an oldest son, who took such matters seriously and, if not, then perhaps to another son, a daughter, or even another relative.[1] Luther Sahmaunt believed that such inheritance patterns ensured that the Kiowa upper class was structured around a group of powerful families desiring to keep their *dɔdɔ* intact.[2] According to White Fox and Jimmy Quoetone, social differentiation was also maintained by *ondedɔ*, men who typically accumulated the most distinguished war honors, whereas lesser warriors and healers typically belonged to the *ondegupa*, or "second-rank" families. Rank and status, however, were not necessarily rigid, because upward mobility was possible if lower-class men attained power visions, but this was infrequent.[3] Significantly, in his short monograph on Kiowa rank, Mishkin emphasized that the leaders of the *ondedɔ* class were outstanding warriors who had amassed numerous war honors, but he failed to mention that they also possessed warfare-related *dɔdɔ* (Mishkin 1940, 35). If a man died without transmitting his power to an heir, it shot out of his mouth and was lost forever. Sankadota related to Mishkin how the powers of Adlsedl, or Adalpepti (Bush Head, or Frizzlehead), were lost because relatives assembled at his death bed feared taking it.[4] Besides inheritance, one could "purchase" *dɔdɔ* by offering gifts of valued property—horses, bison robes, or weapons—to a man of power (see also Voget 1984, 40–41; Harrod 2005, 96–97; Parks 2001, 383; Brown and Irwin 2001, 423). For instance, Mooney noted that Buffalo medicine men possessed circular buffalo-hide war shields adorned with symbols of the healing powers bestowed by Buffalo. When the time arrived for an elderly keeper to impart his power to a son or another interested individual, that person would visit the older man, offering a lit pipe with the request, "I want your shield." After consenting to a payment of perhaps four or five horses, the young initiate was permitted to take the shield to a remote mountain peak or solitary area, where he fasted and slept with it under his head for four days in anticipation of a vision that would impart knowledge about the shield keeper's medicine.[5]

Lone Bear mentioned that, whether power was inherited or purchased, the initiate was required to endure the vision quest, a period of fasting, smoking, and praying in an isolated location up to four days at a time. A man seeking *dɔdɔ* by purchase or inheritance specifically prayed to the power of his father or sponsor, whereas lower-class men desiring power made general supplications to the spirit world.[6] Luther Sahmaunt emphasized that powers obtained through the vision quest were more powerful than those inherited or purchased.[7] Tsoodle told Marriott that dreams at home differed from power visions that occurred away from home. Sanko suggested that dreams occur "when the soul travels and won't be quiet" and could encounter bad or good spirits. Bad dreams caused by evil spirits could be sent to someone else by a shaman, or prayed away through offerings to the Ten Medicines, or by placing strips of one's own skin on buffalo chips and praying to Sun. Lone Bear told Collier that power obtained by dreaming at home—good dreams—was the same as power gained through fasting. Tsoodle also said that one could not obtain power the first time; successful power-seekers had to make between four and seven trips "to make sure of it and get the whole thing completely." He also emphasized that young boys never received visions, but if it did happen, the boy had to mature and learn how to use his power before manifesting it in front of other people. Otherwise the power would not work. Frank Given concurred and said that young men did not go on vision quests, because they were afraid of the dark! For unknown reasons, Marriott does not reference the word *dɔdɔ* throughout her fieldnotes, though Sanko told her that *käntaígi (a) anb'äde* means "he received [medicine] power."[8]

Since lofty elevations were perceived to be closest to the "spirits which travel in the air," mountains were the preferred location for vision quests according to White Fox.[9] Silver Horn identified Mount Scott, whose peak is the second-highest elevation in the Wichita Mountains at 2,467 feet, as a "vision-seeker's paradise."[10] Frank Given told Marriott that Mount Sheridan, just to the west, was where he and Hunting Horse had fasted for visions.[11] White Fox noted that if an initiate's encampment was not close to the mountains, the highest hill was sought, and since Kiowas preferred burying their dead in "high places," grave sites often were selected for vision quests, especially if the deceased had been a medicine man or keeper of a tribal or personal medicine bundle.[12] Moth Woman, White Fox, and Hunting Horse acknowledged that women normally did not engage in vision quests, but sometimes they inadvertently received power visions at grave sites resulting from their mourning practices. When close relatives or husbands died, women slashed their forearms, legs, and breasts with knives, cut their hair short, and often sliced off finger tips before mourning at grave sites of the recently deceased. Mourning women fasted and wailed in a pitiful state that often produced power visions from the sympathetic spirits of recently departed fathers, brothers, or husbands who had been medicine men.[13] Mary Buffalo noted that women having recurrent dreams about the contents of medicine bundles implied that they had been selected to inherit and care for the bundles; such occurrences were frequent.[14] Mary Buffalo's observation makes sense because women assisted their husbands in taking care of medicine bundles.

Typical vision quest rituals described by Silver Horn began with the power-seeker leaving his encampment, accompanied by a close friend or relative. Pilgrimages to the Wichita Mountains or elevated locations sometimes led the seeker and his companion twenty to thirty miles from home since band camps were not always in proximity to the mountains. Once the predetermined destination was reached, the seeker clambered toward a lofty resting place while the traveling companion departed after promising to return in four days. Clad only in a breechcloth, moccasins, and a bison robe wrapped around his shoulders, hair side out, the seeker smeared his face and arms with white clay, perhaps to symbolize the "special medicine power" of the albino buffalo. Necessary ritual paraphernalia consisted of a long-stemmed, black stone pipe, its accouterments, and a pouch of tobacco.[15]

By late evening, the seeker ascended to the highest possible location, prepared a bed of sage covered with a buffalo robe, and sat down cross-legged facing east to begin the vision rite. Before smoking, he held tobacco above his head to placate the spirits in the sky and then placed the offering on the ground. After packing his pipe bowl with tobacco, he took dry kindling from a buffalo horn and lit it by striking flint against steel. In accordance with American Indian beliefs that tobacco smoke carries prayers to the spirit world (see Paper 2005, 1101), the vision-seeker smoked and prayed the first night, crying for compassion from the spirits: "Take pity on me. I am a poor man. Give me what I ask." Then he lay down for the night. Upon awakening the next morning, the seeker smoked and prayed in the same manner, repeated the same procedure in the evening and around midnight, and any time during the night when aroused from bouts of sleep. While smoking and praying during daylight hours, the supplicant always faced Sun, and when finished, he held the pipe outward toward the sun, stem side first, recited a prayer, and then emptied the ashes on the ground as an offering. A successful vision quest was highlighted by a spirit appearing to the supplicant in a vision, bestowing him with power and its associated knowledge. If a power vision had not occurred by the fourth day of fasting, the petitioner signaled his traveling companion to return in a day or two. Following the ordeal, if the novice received a power vision, he returned home and painted a shield with symbols of his newly acquired power. Before reaching his village, the power-seeker sometimes stopped to take a sweat bath, a purification rite common to other Plains tribes before and after transcendent encounters with the supernatural (Curtis 1907–30, 6:79–81; DeMallie 1987, 34–35; DeMallie 2001, 807; Harrod 1987, 32–33, 72). When the initiate arrived at his village, no one spoke to him about his recent experiences, nor did the young man volunteer any information to let people know exactly what had happened; he did not need to say anything, for time would tell whether or not the he had received *dɔdɔ*.[16]

Silver Horn, Hunting Horse, and Lone Bear agreed that successful vision-seekers obtained either war medicine, curing power, or power to heal oneself or a sick relative. In the last instance, a sick man might travel into the mountains to fast and pray if other shamans had failed to cure him, or if he needed a vision to heal a son. Anyone obtaining power who disclosed details of the vision could cause the dream spirit to revoke his power, because newly acquired powers were believed to manifest themselves at the proper time. Thus, a man obtaining war power proved it by returning unscathed from a hard-fought battle. Someone killed shortly after returning from a vision quest obviously had not obtained war medicine. Likewise, curing powers became apparent if they effectively helped other people. Power was validated through demonstrative experiences; those who lied about having power risked facing an untimely death.[17]

Differentiating between powers obtained for warfare or for curing is somewhat confusing because Kiowa shamans carried their painted shields into battle, the same as men with war power, as noted by Mooney.[18] Haumpy said they also participated in hunting expeditions, events that often required their healing powers.[19] The primary difference between the powers is that war power represented a warrior's medicine, or protection, whereas curing power provided doctoring medicine in addition to personal protection. Both powers were considered to be mutually exclusive, for one who acquired *dɔdɔ* became either a great warrior or a healer, though Silver Horn pointed out that some shamans were also known for their fighting prowess.[20] White Fox and Silver Horn acknowledged that medicine men also had the capacity to accumulate various powers, and it was not considered unusual for powerful doctors to possess numerous powers. For instance, a shaman noted for his ability to reduce fevers could also stanch combat-inflicted wounds.[21]

Reconstructing details of the prereservation dream epistemé is somewhat problematic, which can be partially attributed to the reticence of visionaries to recount details of their visions but also to rapid culture change during the reservation and allotment eras as visionary experiences assimilated into the peyote religion, prophet movements, the Ghost Dance, and Christianity. In 1935, LaBarre learned that a handful of men still sought visions, which to him proved "the aliveness of belief even now in the efficacy of the vision-means of acquiring power and attaining desires." Bert Geikauma, his interpreter, who was poor and suffering from a debilitating disease, described a recent vision quest to "reveal to him the hiding place, in Oklahoma, of stores of diamonds and gold, or . . . of oil." After two days of fasting, Bert encountered a blinding light that rendered him unconscious. Upon regaining consciousness, he was confronted by his mother's spirit—she had died in 1902—who admonished him to abandon his quest until autumn, when cooler temperatures caused the rattlesnakes to hibernate. Then he heard distant sounds of croaking frogs that came to him "like a telephone," suggesting to him that the power had given his mother permission to visit him during his vision. LaBarre deemed the purpose of Geikauma's vision quest to be unrealistic.[22]

Botadli (Belly Boy) (b. 1852) related to Bascom details about his first vision, which probably occurred in the final days of the prereservation era. While camping on Gawky Creek west of present Fort Cobb, Botadli awakened from a nightmare shaking and trembling, symptoms that ceased the next evening after he swam in a cold spring. Incidentally, his nephew's wife had also taken sick that morning. The next night, Botadli heard people singing in a dream and perceived that the inside of his tipi was illumined by bright sunlight, which he deemed peculiar since it was nighttime. Awakening from the dream, he looked outside and observed a lunar eclipse; these strange events convinced him to fast for a vision. Early the next morning, Botadli discovered that his nephew's wife was somewhat better, so he informed her that he intended to seek a vision that might facilitate her recovery. Donning the minimal breechcloth, moccasins, and buffalo robe, and armed with a pipe and tobacco pouch, Botadli walked southwest toward Cutthroat Gap.[23]

Although Kiowas consider Cutthroat Gap haunted because it is stained with Kiowa blood, it is also a sacred site favored for its special cedar used in purification rites, as related by tribal historian Atwater Onco during a field trip in June 1993.[24] Botadli obviously felt this was an important power place for vision-seeking, and it is truly amazing that he traversed approximately thirty-five miles in one day to reach his destination. Late in the afternoon, Botadli fashioned a cedar and sage bed under a cliff on a mountain north of the gap and then proceeded to smoke and pray. Safely ensconced in the sheltered alcove, Botadli continued to pray for the recovery of the sick woman as a thunderstorm producing lightning and hail moved through the area. Later that night, in a weakened condition, Botadli heard a voice that said, "It is hard for you to get power. I can give you this: that when you walk you will stagger around," which implied that he would live to old age. For the next two days, Botadli prayed at sunrise, midday, and sunset, and three times at night, but nothing happened. After staying awake most of the third night, Botadli fell into a deep sleep and dreamed that he saw the sick woman, now recovered, working around his tipi. He thirsted greatly, but a voice instructed him not to drink until he reached a certain water hole inhabited by a small animal.[25]

On the fourth day, Botadli's brother-in-law arrived by horseback, as prearranged, to bring him back to their encampment. Riding back, they encountered the spring described in the vision, so Botadli stopped to drink. Peering into the water, he espied a strange creature that appeared to be a bull frog with a crawfish tail. Touching the creature, he prayed to it and then took four swallows of water. Now that he had fulfilled the instructions of his vision, Botadli inquired about the status of the sick woman, learning that she had made a full recovery. After arriving home, the woman told Botadli about her own vision regarding a small tree with round leaves, which she instructed him to find. Selecting the right tree from her dream, he collected some leaves and rolled them into a ball, which she wore on her belt the rest of her life. Another woman with a high fever summoned him after hearing of his experience, although Botadli claimed he was not a doctor. Nevertheless, he doctored her by touching her body all over, and her fever broke a short time afterward. According to Botadli, he gained the reputation as a doctor specializing in fevers, pneumonia, and children's stomachaches.[26] One might wonder why Botadli vividly described his vision experience to Bascom due to the belief that powers would attenuate if revealed to others. Perhaps his disclosure is connected to stories alleging that his powers waned after he failed to bring the sun down at midday during the Hot Sun Dance of 1881. Moth Woman claimed that everyone ridiculed Botadli behind his back, and that he had avoided all public gatherings since the debacle. Botadli even admitted that he had never been a very good medicine man.[27]

Haumpy told Bascom about the vision experience of Pododlte, who sought longevity, not personal power. Selecting a spot south of Rainy Mountain near Big Springs, Pododlte lay on a bed of sage with his head to the west and a buffalo skull at his feet facing east. On the third day of fasting, smoking, and praying, he saw a tipi with a white horse tethered at the front. A voice said, "If you want this power, I can give it to you. Doctor like this and charge a white horse." Peering into the tipi Pododlte saw a man doctoring a patient but refused the power because he preferred powers to live forever. Unable to grant such an impossible request, the voice instructed him to climb to the top of Rainy Mountain. Despite his weakened condition exacerbated by the oppressive midsummer heat, Pododlte gathered a fresh armful of sage and ascended the limestone knoll, where he prepared to spend the fourth night. Toward dawn, storm clouds gathered and a voice announced, "Go away from here. This is my home. I don't allow anyone here while I am at home." After he refused to leave, lightning struck and Pododlte found himself "clear off the mountain." He clambered back to the top and the same process was repeated, but the persistent Pododlte gained the summit a third time and again refused to leave. The voice, now identified as Thunderbird, offered him curing power, but Pododlte maintained that he wanted to live forever, which could not be granted. Thunderbird then instructed Pododlte to resume his quest on a hill near Rainy Mountain.[28]

Walking the short distance to the hill, Pododlte fasted a fifth night with his pipe lying at his side, waiting for the powers to take it and smoke with him, but nothing happened. On the sixth night, a voice called out, "I've got power: plenty of power. Why do you other things that have plenty of power not help this man? I'll smoke his pipe." Then a giant mountain boomer (*Crotaphytus collaris*, the collard lizard) picked up the pipe and smoked it, but upon hearing Pododlte's request for longevity, stated, "Son, you're asking the impossible. No one lives forever. I can't give you the power that you ask." At that moment an unidentified voice said, "Don't give up, son." During the seventh night, Pododlte "heard something from the west as [if] the earth were splitting," but he resisted the opportunity to flee from the frightening cacophony. A voice then identified itself: "Son, this is my home. I live here in spirit. No one before you ever came up here for anything. Why do you come here?" Listening to Pododlte's request, the voice replied, "The creator made things in this world. But death rules; all things die. Thus the creator made it. I myself have been dead for centuries, but my soul lives here." Acknowledging that Pododlte had suffered greatly in his quest for the unattainable, the voice made another offer: "You may take any of the powers that you wish to doctor with, and this may aid you in living a long time." Hence Pododlte choose powers that he used to treat pneumonia, fevers, hemorrhages, nosebleeds, and snakebite. By the time Pododlte died, he suffered greatly from rheumatism, a disease he overlooked when choosing curing powers. Later in his life, Pododlte obtained Owl power too.[29]

Haumpy's reference to a creator undoubtedly reflects Christian influences amalgamated into Kiowa belief systems and storytelling. Story forms relating conversations with transcendent beings could be another innovation in early twentieth-century Kiowa storytelling since this is a recurrent pattern in other stories collected by the field party. That Kiowa dream stories feature audio as well as visual phenomena is an unusual occurrence in the Plains dream epistemé according to Lee Irwin (1994, 242). Nevertheless, this pattern exists today in Kiowa stories about the modern-day visionary experiences of Christians and peyotists.

Maintaining Power

Power, though mysterious and sacred, was also dangerous and potentially destructive, so it demanded utmost respect. Beyond prescriptive details regarding bundle contents, body paint, and sacred songs, Plains visionaries also learned about proscriptive behaviors, or restrictions, that applied to their daily lives. Breaching these prohibitions potentially would offend the dream spirits, causing their gifts of power to attenuate (Irwin 1994, 151–52, 157–62). As noted by Hunting Horse, Silver Horn, and Tsoodle, Kiowa men acquiring healing dɔdɔ had to live according to the dictates of their spirit power. Therefore, men fasting in power places merely for self-healing often declined curing medicines offered by the spirits, primarily because they did not want to assume the responsibilities and restrictions that accompanied the powers.[30] Through Tsoodle, Marriott learned that men often refused power because they did not "like a certain part of it." In other instances, if a man went into the mountains "just to pray for long life for himself and his family," he could refuse any power offered to him since he was not seeking a vision. "Sometimes they don't want that sort of power because it's so strict." Tsoodle thought that individuals refusing power were lazy because they did not want to assume the taboos. According to Sanko men often refused curing powers because doctors had "very short lives."[31]

Lone Bear pointed out that each shaman lived according to stringent prohibitions associated with his particular medicine. Any behavioral or dietary violations would surely bring about his demise—or that of a family member—through sickness. Many medicine men had dietary restrictions and could not eat the meat of bears, moles, or fish or certain animal parts, like brains or marrow, and some could not eat their food with knives.[32] A woman identified only as Old Lady T'oyi remembered a medicine man with Snake power who could not eat *se/ko* (Kiowa bologney) or wild grapes.[33] Lone Bear identified certain behavioral taboos, such as that the medicine man could not allow people to walk behind him while he was eating, or that the shaman could not allow people in the vicinity of his patient if their feet were touching the ground.[34] Goomda said his father could not eat rabbit and had to sleep with his moccasins at the foot of the bed.[35] Beaver doctors could only treat patients in their special tipis set up a distance from any encampment, according to Moth Woman. If emergency situations occurred, another tipi was stripped clean of its contents except for the central hearth and buffalo robes on the ground.[36] Lone Bear stated that during curing episodes patients had to assume the medicine man's taboos, or his powers would be rendered ineffective.[37] He concurred with Hunting Horse that shamans could not doctor members of their own family because it was feared they would become sick themselves.[38]

Strictly adhering to taboos maintained the power of the shaman's *gietso*, identified by Haumpy as anything kept in one's body, and by White Fox as the magical powers residing in the shaman's stomach. *Gietso* could be coughed up when necessary in the form of paint (colored clays), stones, lizards, horned toads, moles, miniature bison, and pieces of horn or hide.[39] Expelling any of these substances was part of the shaman's repertoire of magical feats performed during healing episodes, founded in Kiowa disease etiology that illness was brought about through the intrusion of supernatural disease agents. Kiowa shamans who doctored employed the sucking technique somewhere on the patient's torso to extract the intruding entity, which was spit out in the form of the shaman's own medicine, according to Moth Woman.[40] Like all men with *dɔdɔ*, a shaman's *gietso* shot out of his mouth when he died and was lost forever unless a successor placed his mouth over the mouth of the dying man to catch it. Sankadota recalled cases where medicine men transferred their medicine by blowing it into the inheritor's mouth.[41]

Since men who became medicine men did so by choice, they often received instructions from older shamans in the community—usually a family member—prior to departing on vision quests, and they had probably observed curing rituals and knew something about shamanic techniques. Lone Bear, Jimmy Quoetone, Sankadota, and even Mooney knew that it was improper to discuss successful power visions, and that healing powers manifested themselves only at the proper time. Hence, before calling upon the novice's assistance, the older shamans waited for him to learn his medicine well, a process that might take several years.[42] As in other Plains cultures, older people with demonstrated powers were highly respected due to their experience, and the most powerful men had typically received multiple visions (Irwin 1994, 152–53; Irwin 2005, 244–45; DeMallie and Miller 2001, 578). Elders interviewed during the summer field school, however, did not elaborate about recurrent dreams, though Haumpy, Jim Ahtone, and Botadli recalled several men, including Pododlte, who obtained additional power through second visions.[43]

Manifesting Power

Throughout Native North America, manifesting dream powers in public performances made the animate powers of the spirit world more tangible. Empowered individuals typically manipulated their medicine bundles through song and action to activate the cosmological powers represented by the material contents of the bundles. Most important were the curative rites beneficial to those beset by illness (Grim 2005a, 763–64; Harrod 2005, 96; Irwin 2005, 244; Parks 2001, 381–83; Parks 2001a, 538; Dorsey 1894, 366–68; Whitman 1937, 180–81; Howard 1965, 99; DeMallie 1987, 33; Fowler 2001, 844; Grinnell 1923, 2:126–65; Kavanagh 2001, 892; Foster and McCollough 2001, 932; Schweinfurth 2002, 130–40). According to medical anthropologists George M. Foster and Barbara G. Anderson, public demonstrations of power, especially during healing episodes, are necessary in tribal societies where personalistic medical models attribute illness to supernatural causes or sorcery; people appreciate magic that reifies shamanic powers against malevolent forces (Foster and Anderson 1978, 116–17).

Lone Bear and Silver Horn described the typical scenario when medical emergencies arose in indigenous Kiowa society. First, a male relative of the afflicted person approached the chosen shaman with a lighted pipe, asking for help. A medicine man could not refuse such requests, though he had the right to question the man concerning the sufferer's symptoms before accepting the pipe, and he could then refuse treatment if he felt his powers were inadequate to treat the described illness. If the doctor felt his powers matched the symptoms, he took the pipe and smoked it, praying to the spirit that represented his power, evoking it to assist him in curing the patient.[44] Lone Bear, Mary Buffalo, Hunting Horse, Haumpy, Moth Woman, Jim Ahtone, and Sanko provided vivid details about what happened next. The medicine man purified his hands in sweetgrass smoke before proceeding any further. Black handkerchiefs obtained from Mexico, or perhaps buffalo calf skins, were used by many shamans to locate the source of illness, or "poison," in the patient's body. Placing the handkerchief over his eyes, he scanned the afflicted person's body, looking for the poison. After determining the location of the poison, the doctor took a sharp piece of flint, made a slight incision on the skin, and began sucking the wound. Most patients screamed in pain when the poison—stones, pieces of deerskin, skin, black handkerchief, fingernail pairings, or corpse hair—left their body. Variations of the sucking technique included the absence of incisions, placing hot coals in the mouth before sucking, applying different bird feathers smudged in cedar smoke to the afflicted area, or using a hollowed-out buffalo horn for sucking. Regardless of the method used, the shaman spit out the poison and showed it to everyone present to prove that his diagnosis had been accurate. Even though doctors did not charge fees, after treatments they were gifted with seven items, including horses, calico, blankets, and black handkerchiefs, unless the patient died. If so, nothing was said, but repeated failures led to the shaman's loss of popularity; if the patient lived, he or she was expected to follow his taboos until they were removed following a special feast provided for the healer.[45]

Kiowa shamans still used the sucking technique in the 1930s, usually in special doctoring meetings sponsored by members of the Native American Church. Biătonmá told Marriott that "real" doctors never joined the Christian church because they "hate[d] to give up the old power," and that those who joined the peyote religion lost their old power "but doctored by peyote." This represented a "transfer of power."[46] Sanko described a doctoring meeting north of Mountain View to LaBarre in which the patient was positioned south of the doorway of the east-facing peyote tipi. The peyote doctor treated him by brushing out the sickness like one would "sweep out dust" and by feeding him peyote during the meeting.[47] Sanko told Marriott that all Indian doctors used the sucking technique "at some time or other" to remove blood from the head causing headaches or blood clots in the lungs causing pneumonia.[48] Charley Apekaum said the same thing to LaBarre and identified Jim Ahtone as one of the remaining Kiowa doctors (1957, 13, 87). Gus Palmer Sr. told me about the nearly blind Yellow Wolf, another well-known shaman, who treated his father after he lost his vision.[49] Peyote doctors were paid like shamans in former times by the person requesting a meeting. Doctors were given seven articles, including a black handkerchief, Indian perfume, red earth paint, and other objects (LaBarre 1957, 13).

Peyote doctors were renowned for curing numerous afflictions, especially facial paralysis (Bell's palsy), rheumatism, and pneumonia. Apekaum identified Jim Ahtone as a well-known curer of the first two illnesses. During a doctoring meeting around 1930 in Shawnee country, Ahtone cured a Creek man suffering from rheumatism. The patient had tried Anglo doctors and had languished in Hot Springs, Arkansas, health spas before attending the meeting. Arriving in an ambulance in intense pain, the man was carried into the meeting on a blanket and situated south of the entryway. Ahtone fed him peyote and applied the sucking technique. By morning, the man felt better, sat up, and then exited the tipi without assistance. Happy with his recovery, he paid Ahtone handsomely, and Ahtone gained several Creek converts to the Native American Church (LaBarre 1957, 113–14).

Numerous accounts from the mid-twentieth century relate how peyote doctors treated pneumonia, a respiratory infection with symptoms including the buildup of pleural fluid in the space surrounding the lungs, causing severe chest pains. Charley Apekaum described how a jagged piece of glass was used to make incisions above each nipple so a cow horn could be placed over them to suck out the bad blood. After the poison was extracted, the sufferer regained full breathing. Charley claimed that he often treated pneumonia and that anyone could perform the technique (LaBarre 1957, 87). This procedure is analogous to thoracentesis, a surgery in which a pleural tap is inserted between the chest wall and lungs to drain the excess fluid.

Betty Tenadooah (Medicine Bird, b. 1932) wrote a story about Blue Jay, a peyote doctor who healed her when she was a small girl. According to Boyd (1983, 12), Blue Jay was a Ten Medicines keeper and an "Indian doctor." One morning during the summer of 1937, Betty slipped on her shoes that had been left out overnight in the brush arbor and was bitten by a black widow spider that had crawled into one of them. Shortly afterward, she became "sick with fever and convulsions," compelling her father to summon Blue Jay because he lived in the area. The nearest Anglo doctor was at least seven miles away, a lengthy journey by horse and buggy. Betty describes how Blue Jay doctored her:

> Old Man Blue Jay reached into his medicine pouch. Inside his pouch were different relics for other types of sicknesses. He sat at the foot of the bed where he found me in a coma. He began to cleanse the wound with warm water. Using a sharp flint, he made several small incisions around the wound and placed a cow horn with a hole at the end, over the cuts he had made. He then used the horn as a suction to transport the blood and poison to the upper part of the horn. This ritual continued until Blue Jay was satisfied that all the poison was out.
>
> He began to chew some herbs which only the medicine man can keep at all times. After chewing these herbs he began gently blowing the herb saliva from his mouth all over me. With a fan made of six eagle feathers to keep the fever down, he continued his ritual through the night.
>
> The next morning I awoke to a bright sunny day. I had recovered miraculously. The Kiowa Indian Medicine Man had saved my life.[50]

Other than the reports of the medicine performed by Jim Ahtone, Yellow Wolf, and Blue Jay, there is also Lone Bear's report to Collier that he doctored headaches and pneumonia. He also identified seven other shamans and the illnesses they treated: (1) Tsoodle, children's stomach ailments; (2) Yego, swelling, rheumatism, tuberculosis, and sorcery; (3) Frank Given, sorcery, eye trouble, and hemorrhages; (4) Conklin Hummingbird, sorcery, pneumonia, head ailments, and swollen limbs; (5) Polá, fever; (6) William "Cornbread" Tenadooah, hemorrhages; and (7) Harry Hall (Zotigh), pneumonia and head ailments. All used the sucking technique in their healing rites.[51] Tsoodle, Frank Given, and perhaps Blue Jay were Ten Medicines keepers, and Conklin Hummingbird was one of the last Buffalo doctors. Collier thought that Jim Ahtone and Polá also possessed Buffalo medicine, but Haumpy disputed this notion.[52]

Marriott's fieldnotes provide details about the powers of shamans displayed in curing episodes not found in the Santa Fe field party notes. Her information was mostly from Sanko and to a lesser extent from Frank Given and Tsoodle. According to Sanko, a man's power spoke to him, saying "I am so and so," told him what doctoring techniques to use, and then what fees, or gifts, were to be requested before and after doctoring. Vision recipients were given songs that "just came" to them; when a doctor sang a new song during a healing rite, others learned it and would always know "to whom it belonged." Before "going to work" on the patient, the shaman told everyone to be quiet and to concentrate on his success. Lighting a sprig of cedar, he held his feathered fan over the smoke, perfumed it, and then handed it to the person sitting next to him. Next, the shaman held a small trade bell over the fire, smoked it, rang it, and then sang four songs, accompanied by the men and women in attendance. Upon finishing the last song, he performed the sucking technique to remove the poison, which was thrown into the central hearth. He called for his pipe, which was lit, passed around, and smoked by everyone but the patient. Upon receiving the spent pipe, the doctor emptied the ashes in the fireplace and declared that the patient felt better and was recovering, which was confirmed by the patient. Afterwards, the patient was given instructions about adhering to the dietary and behavioral taboos of the shaman. All restrictions were lifted upon full recovery of the patient.[53] Important to the healing rite described by Sanko is the involvement of other participants, because healing is a community event in tribal societies. Also important is the positive, collective mindset urged by the shaman, referred to by William S. Lyon as the "observer effect," that enables the shaman's powers to work, especially through singing songs of power that connect to the supernatural; songs obtained from the spirit world allowed the shaman to utilize supernatural powers bestowed by the spirit world (Lyon 2012, 19–23, 86–87).

Sanko also described the medicine powers of Beaver doctors whose healing rites included dancing to the rhythm of a water-drum. Beaver doctors treated a variety of illnesses by sucking out decayed blood and matter from their patients. He recalled that Podaymgia, a powerful Beaver doctor, situated his patients at the place of honor—the west side of the tipi—with the head facing west. Singers sat around the perimeter of the tipi while Podaymgia danced from the center to the doorway, where he peered out, grunted, and then moved back to the patient. At this time, the singers and other guests told him he would not cure the patient "in order to put him on his mettle." Apparently disbelief challenged his medicine powers to work. Sanko then told a story about another Beaver medicine man who responded to such skepticism by swallowing his black handkerchief, pulling it out of his side, placing it over the patient, sucking the poison out, and then spitting it into the fire. This was his most powerful medicine.[54]

Marriott learned about spider bite medicine from Saoma, which concurs with the story written by Betty Tenadooah. A person bitten by a "deadly poisonous" spider was hurt "in his heart," regardless of where he was bitten. Employing the sucking technique on the wound, the doctor removed the spider's teeth, represented by a "long, needle-like thing," followed by yellow matter and the web, which were spat into a black handkerchief and shown to all present. Frank Given treated rattlesnake bites by drawing a line on the leg above the punctures, patting the area with an eagle wing feather, and then making incisions around the wound with glass in order to suck out the poison. He always spat out the two "teeth," a technique not performed by Comanche doctors. Sanko identified several women doctors who received power through dreams: one treated tics, another doctored general illnesses, and a third cured snake bites. Women could pass such doctoring powers to their daughters. Tsoodle, whom Marriott said had an "extremely practical and literal mind," discussed the treatment of trauma victims. Broken bones were "pulled into place and tied with stiff rawhide"; sprains were scratched with glass and "sucked like a head-ache, to reduce the swelling"; and boils were lanced with knives, drained, rubbed with buffalo fat, and bandaged. In former times toothaches only afflicted the older populations, but by the 1930s they were commonplace. In such cases, the gum was cut near the infected tooth to relieve the pain. Rheumatism was usually treated by bleeding. Sanko added that doctors treated kidney trouble, fever, chills, and overeating using the sucking technique. These treatments were being used in the 1930s.[55]

Employing the sucking technique was closely connected to the belief that many illnesses resulted from the sorcery of shamans, according to Haumpy and Lone Bear.[56] Although there were powerful medicine men blessed with beneficial healing powers, Hunting Horse and Moth Woman said that they were greatly feared because all powers are dichotomously good and evil; hence a curing power could be reversed to cause sickness and even death.[57] Haumpy said that angering a person of power potentially caused sorcery, so people were careful not to offend shamans, even though conflicts were unavoidable, a belief commonly found in tribal societies (Foster and Anderson 1978, 114–15), including some Plains groups (DeMallie and Lavenda 1977, 158; Bowers 1965, 157, 320, 351; DeMallie and Miller 2001, 578).[58] Lone Bear pointed out that medicine men practicing sorcery always seemed to know the restrictive taboos of their adversaries and used this knowledge to magically inject their victims with foreign objects.[59] Lone Bear and Haumpy described how the sorcerer typically drew an outline of the intended victim on the ground and then placed a needle, small feather, blade of grass, or other object into a pipestem and blew it at the body part to be afflicted.[60] Mary Buffalo and Hunting Horse said that sorcerers, besides employing sympathetic magic by "shooting" poison into victims, could harm enemies by merely pointing at them while casting a spell, or by aiming a painted bone toward the person and breathing on it, causing the bone to magically penetrate his body.[61]

More details about sorcery are found in Marriott's fieldnotes. Sanko, Saoma, and Frank Given expressed how people buried nail pairings, burned hair-combings, or wrapped loose teeth in meat and fed them to dogs to prevent them from falling into the hands of owls and witches that could "throw" these exuviae at them. Sometimes komt'o ada (ghost hair, or the fingernails or hair of a corpse) were "shot" into the body of victims, according to Sanko, who also identified a sickness manifested as sores caused by worms that were shot into the victim's neck. Margaret Hunt Tsoodle told how she was treated for an illness causing her face to "feel thick and heavy" and then "drawn and heavy" the next day. A white doctor failed to cure her, so she went to an Indian woman doctor and presented her a rolled cigarette and seven items. Burning sage, and then marking the ground and praying, the doctor examined Margaret by looking through a black handkerchief. She found a place around the eye toward the ear and began sucking, eventually removing a fingernail. Four days of treatment were required for full recovery. Sanko told the story of two rival shamans, Gudlkutoy (Much Paint) and Setandoa (Thunder Speaks), who "witched" one another. Much Paint, shot in the chest with a maggot, retaliated by shooting back at Thunder Speaks. Other doctors were unable to cure them, so shortly thereafter Much Paint died followed by Thunder Speaks. Everyone knew that medicine powers can be used for good or evil, but power was seldom used for evil because it was known that one of a sorcerer's relatives would die for every person he killed.[62]

George Hunt told Marriott that most illnesses were caused by shamans who *baita(p)be* (sun-shot) their victims. This form of shooting magic was "put in the victim's food [sic] drink or something he would touch. Water, weeds, frog tracks, air, or winds were also common media for it. *Baita(p)be* could be sent on a sunbeam." Ironically, the same shaman causing the illness was probably summoned to doctor the victim, which Hunt likened to a "death sentence, as the shaman would only pretend to cure, without making any real effort."[63] For instance, Gus Palmer Sr. related a story how his father, Choctaw Bill, a farmer in the Redstone community, was bewitched by Jim Ahtone sometime in the 1930s. Initial symptoms appeared as a film enveloping the eyelids, causing blindness. As his condition worsened, Palmer was approached by Ahtone, who offered to help in exchange for horses and other gifts. Despite treatment, Palmer's condition worsened, which compelled him to attend a peyote meeting, where he met Yellow Wolf, who took him aside and revealed that the man he was paying to cure him was the actual sorcerer causing his blindness. Taking over treatment, Yellow Wolf eventually restored Choctaw Bill's vision, and from that time on he was a welcome guest in the Palmer household.[64]

Oftentimes an ill person could identify the sorcerer by observing the behavior of suspected shamans in the vicinity. Either the sorcerer avoided speaking to the victim or treated that person with kindness to obfuscate the malign magic. According to Haumpy, victims could only achieve total recovery by identifying the sorcerer, approaching him with a drawn weapon, and forcing him to rescind the spell.[65] White Buffalo concurred with Haumpy that another method was to find a powerful shaman who could identify the sorcerer and send the poison back. In such instances, the medicine man was approached with gifts and implored to determine the aggressor's identity. Putting a black handkerchief over his eyes, the medicine man examined the patient to determine if indeed sorcery was responsible for the illness. If so, he could usually name the culpable sorcerer. Employing the sucking technique, he drew out the poison and by spitting it into a fire destroyed the spell. Recurrent symptoms implied that the sorcerer was still conjuring against the patient, which often precipitated power contests between the two medicine men.[66]

Haumpy and Tsoodle related to Bascom how shamans demonstrated their powers during curing episodes by employing the sucking technique and other magical feats, and that rival medicine men sometimes engaged in public power contests. In both instances they regurgitated the *gietso* from their stomachs to display their powers for public viewing. Osonte, or Okanti (No Voice, or Hoarse Voice), had Buffalo power and sometimes spat out a miniature bison that grew to a length of about ten inches. A woman named Tsodlte, or Tsodltoi (Spotted Wing), possessed Snake power and had the remarkable ability to eject up to four large rattlesnakes from her mouth. More incredible is the case of Pododlte, who could cough up a pistol and swallow it again. The pistol resided in his stomach with a spider, a centipede, a turtle, and a butcher knife.[67] Variations of these "swallowing powers" are found among the Klamaths, Hopis, Zunis, Poncas, Yanktons, Canadian Dakotas, Pawnees, and Tlingits (Lyon 2012, 303–10).

Frank Given, oldest son of Set'angya (Sitting Bear), the famed war leader called Satank by non-Indians, described his father's swallowing powers to Marriott. As a young man Set'angya knew an Eagle shield keeper who had been taken underwater, shown how to design a bird tipi and a fish tipi, and given a black-handled knife that he could swallow. Although the shield keeper offered to give Set'angya his power, the youth was afraid to take it because of the "rules" that accompanied it: he could not smoke with anyone wearing feathers, nor could he eat hearts or any food "cooked over a fire where a knife had been dropped in the ashes. If this happened, the ashes must be cleared away and the fire put out and a new one built." Nevertheless, Sitting Bear's father had a dream instructing that his son should take the power, which included an Eagle shield and the black-handled knife. During a sweat lodge ceremony the knife was given to Set'angya, who gifted the donor with horses. Given described his father's powers to Marriott:

> When this man had the knife it made him powerful in war and in everything he did. It gave him power. When Sĕtăi'giã [Set'angya] received it, he had the full power. I saw Sĕtăi'giã get up in a meeting and go round and around. Then he took coals from the fire and swallowed them and took that knife out of his mouth and it spun in the middle of the floor and stood up straight. Then he threw a black handkerchief over the knife and the knife turned into a crow feather. Then he swallowed that. That's what made him so powerful, and that's what he used to stab the guard when he was killed [by soldiers outside Fort Sill on June 8, 1871].[68] (see Mooney 1898, 328–33)

Undoubtedly the most famous power display was the performance of Tonakɔt, or Tonakai (Turtle, Water Turtle, or Wrinkle Tail), whose power came from Turtle and Underwater Monster. On an occasion still remembered by Kiowas, Tonakɔt survived after another man shot him in the face with a rifle; picking himself off the ground from the blast that had knocked him over, Tonakɔt spit the spent bullet into his hand.[69] Invulnerability to projectiles was also reported among the Comanches, Cheyennes, Pawnees, Lakotas, Chiricahua Apaches, Arikaras, Poncas, and Paiutes (Deloria 2006, 175–79; Lyon 2012, 287–91). Mary Buffalo, Moth Woman, and Jim Ahtone recalled that Wrinkle Tail was one of the most powerful and feared shamans in the 1880s. Tonakɔt received his medicine powers when he was a boy. One day while playing and fishing along the shallow part of a river, he became drowsy and fell asleep on the sandy riverbank and dreamt of underwater travel. In his watery dream, Turtle entered a strangely painted tipi through a door flap decorated like a softshell turtle and then encountered a multitude of fish and underwater animals lined up in rows to bestow him with their powers. Afterward, Tonakɔt painted his power symbol on a shield—a moss-green surface with a black circle in the middle, over a bullet with two zigzags coming out of it—and began doctoring. Turtle painted his tipi to resemble the underwater lodge where he obtained his power: a turtle-eagle, or a turtle shell with eagle wings, beak, and claws, with long-stemmed pipes protruding from the outstretched wings (fig. 2 in this volume; see also Ewers 1978, 27–28).[70]

Like most shamans, Tonakɔt used his dɔdɔ for good or evil purposes depending on the circumstances, according to Jim Ahtone, who narrated a well-remembered curing episode when Turtle took Tongyei (Clyde Coco) underwater for an extended period of time and then brought him up completely healed. Meanwhile, Water Turtle's physical unattractiveness perhaps contributed to his penchant for practicing malign magic. Even though he had several wives, Tonakɔt was reputed to make advances toward beautiful women who feared him because he had allegedly used sorcery to kill a young woman who had spurned his overtures. Since some of his dɔdɔ came from Gopher and Mole, Turtle could use their powers to create facial sores on his victims. Tonakɔt also used image magic to kill a Caddo shaman by fashioning a mud image of the man that he then carried underwater.[71] George Hunt told Nye (1962, 264–66) that sometime in the early 1890s, Turtle killed a Wichita man who had insulted him during a game of Monte. Ahtone claimed that Turtle died from drinking poisoned whiskey and that he had nine followers or apprentices in various stages of learning his powers through observing his power displays. However, Ahtone thought Turtle's rapid death prevented him from passing on his dɔdɔ, and he related to Bascom that because Tonakɔt was not very popular, "all the Kiowas were glad" after his passing. Moreover, Turtle's children preceded him in death, lending credence to the belief that shooting magic invariably reverses its course, causing harm to the practitioner and his family. Several years after his death Water Turtle's parents were visiting his grave site and found a small turtle on top of the grave. The turtle was given to a family friend and placed in a water dish, where it stayed for three days but vanished on the fourth morning, convincing everyone that indeed Tonakɔt possessed great powers.[72] Versions of this story collected by Marriott (1945, 173–87) and Nye (1962, 257–75) relate that Turtle died during a peyote meeting after his powers failed to kill his apprentice Sanko for converting to Christianity.

Controlling the weather was a feat sometimes achieved by medicine men in indigenous North America (Deloria 2006, 135–48). According to Botadli, his father, Gibai, had a hailstone as his gietso and "understood the rain." Gibai did not pass his dɔdɔ to Botadli, allegedly because it created "much mischief," though he gave it to T'aikɔbɔ, his grandson. Once the mischievous side of Gibai's power was manifested when he made it rain on a war party headed by Feathered Lance, who was Bert Geikauma's grandfather.[73] Geikauma acknowledged that he knew of someone who could still bring rain.[74] Conversely, Goomda maintained that Kiowas did not pray to make it rain, though he mentioned several individuals, including Gi·abai (Botadli's father) and Ayadltsohi (a woman), who could send rain clouds in another direction.[75] As noted earlier, Kiowa elders remember their grandparents standing outside tornado shelters with outstretched arms, singing and praying toward oncoming tornadic clouds to send them away.

Other powers of North American shamans included divinatory rites like the Lakota Yuwipi and Algonquian Spirit Lodge that were designed to find lost people, animals, objects, or to predict the future (Deloria 2006, 83–106). Similar rites practiced by the Kiowas involved the Owl doctors. Because Kiowa eschatological beliefs associated owls with spirits of the deceased, the spirits of shamans, or the transformed souls of evil sorcerers, Lone Bear noted that it was a major insult to call a man *sɔpodlk'i* (owl man) or a woman *sɔpodlma* (owl woman), the equivalent to saying they were already dead.[76] As representatives of the deceased, owls also caused "face twisting" or "face sticking" if encountered. Hunting Horse, Jim Ahtone, and Lone Bear emphasized that Kiowas feared and avoided owls and ghosts to prevent this illness.[77]

Unlike the Kiowa majority shunning owls, Owl doctors obtained their *dɔdɔ* directly from this dreaded bird. According to Moth Woman, Owl doctors understood Owl language and communicated with the dead using owls as mediums; each Owl doctor consulted his "all-knowing spirit" to discern future happenings, such as impending death, or to find lost objects and people. She referred to their special power as *a·tedɔ·dɔ* (spirit of dead power).[78] Haumpy stated that *ate* means "feather" and that *ate* and *sɔpodl* (Owl) were the same power.[79] Hunting Horse, whose father-in-law was an Owl doctor, said they could *atekyatl* (commune with the spirits). Perhaps the reference to *ate* derives from their medicine, white owl-feathered fans, "painted at the bottom with red clay."[80] Marriott learned from an unnamed collaborator that "*ate* is a ghost or an owl or a dead spirit."[81] Lone Bear referred to the owner of Owl power as an *a'tekiɔtɔ*.[82]

Owl doctors held séances in their tipis, analogous to the Algonquian Spirit Lodge rite, to locate missing persons or lost objects, or to prophesy the future; divination rituals attempted to divulge the whereabouts of men presumed dead or separated from war parties, or to pinpoint the location of missing horses, according to Lone Bear, Moth Woman, and Hunting Horse.[83] Moth Woman and Mary Buffalo vividly remembered how Owl doctors conducted divinatory ceremonies. When an Owl doctor was consulted, a special tipi was erected before sundown, then a smaller tipi, perhaps one and a half feet in height, was placed inside the larger tipi on the west side for the Owl spirit during the séance. Only the Owl doctor and his clients were permitted inside the tipi during the divinatory rite. Anyone else permitted in the area was required to prostrate himself on the ground outside the tipi, fearful of seeing the Owl spirit, incurring its wrath, and risking having dirt kicked in his eyes. Each ceremony began with drumming and low singing from inside the tipi, and then suddenly the Owl spirit was heard alighting on top of the tipi poles, causing the tipi to shake. Shortly afterward, the spirit spoke, identifying the soul of the deceased person it possessed, and then asked what information was sought. The Owl spirit departed, returning shortly afterward, but this time it entered the tipi through the smoke hole and descended into the miniature tipi, through which it spoke, imparting knowledge to the concerned family members of a missing relative, or the owner of a lost horse.[84]

Owl doctors were also consulted to heal sick people, especially those who had been bewitched by owls or ghosts. During healing episodes, Lone Bear, who claimed to understand Owl language, said they applied the usual sucking techniques to remove the foreign objects implanted by owls that caused facial paralysis.[85] Hunting Horse claimed that in earlier times Owl doctors sucked without horns but that cow horns were used by the extant practitioners. He also pointed out certain taboos, such as the avoidance of "balls and spices" (Bascom did not know the meaning of the former) or the spices of water plants like watercress. It was also forbidden to walk into a tipi during a doctoring ceremony. Hunting Horse recalled that a girl once walked behind Nesonte, "who saw her and grunted. The girl fell down on the ground twisted up in a fit." Nesonte then sucked out a burr from the girl and cured her.[86]

Since Owl doctors existed in his wives' family, Hunting Horse could identify two family lines of Owl power. Gɔgode, his father-in-law, who had one son and three daughters, obtained Owl power from fasting, and he eventually passed his power and Owl Shield to Tenézeptie, or Tene/epde, his son. Hunting Horse claimed that war power was also associated with the powers of Tenézeptie, who carried his shield into battle. Nesonte, his sister, obtained Owl power while mourning, and younger sisters Pitoma and Pitma also obtained Owl power, probably through inheritance. Hunting Horse claimed that Pitoma still used Owl power but that Pitma did not. Albert Horse, Bascom's interpreter, related that Pitma had dreamt about Owl power but did not have the knowledge to cure. According to Albert, in 1914 Pitma failed to cure Ramona, the oldest daughter of Pitoma. Ramona died and Pitma subsequently lost her power. Albert's story was not contradicted by his half-brother, Monroe Tsatoke.[87] Perhaps it was easy to accuse Pitoma of practicing Owl medicine because Hunting Horse had divorced her—a requirement for his conversion to Christianity—while staying married to her younger sister, Pitma. Dorothy Tsatoke Gray, Pitoma's granddaughter, noted that her family suffered hardships after the divorce, and that some divisions still exist between the two family lines descended through the two sisters.[88]

Another Owl doctor in the family line—though the kin connection is nebulous—was Gu/gu (Yellow Wolf), who obtained Owl power from his father, Tenehadlk'yaptɔ, who might have been another of son of Gɔgode. Bascom's fieldnotes do not provide any further information about the kinship ties. Nevertheless, Yellow Wolf—the healer of Choctaw Bill—passed his powers to his two sisters-in-law.[89]

The second family line of Owl power identified by Hunting Horse descended from K'ŏyiɛte, a woman who obtained her powers by mourning and passed them to a captive son, Kŭyóte, who gave them to his son Jim Ahtone (alias Tsódlte) before dying. Hunting Horse claimed that K'ŏyiɛte was the only member of the family who could *atekyatl* (commune with the spirits), that Kŭyóte "could understand what owl[s] were saying," but that Jim Ahtone was "just a straight doctor."[90]

Hunting Horse told Bascom how Gɔgode displayed his powers to groups of people by coughing up the head of an owl the size of a dime and passing it around so everyone could rub it on themselves for protection against witches. A disbeliever once laughed and refused to rub the owl head on his body, so Gɔgode swallowed the head, causing the man's face to twist. Begging for mercy in the names of Pitma and Pitoma, the man begged him to reverse the spell, so Gɔgode "sat him down and made motions over him and cured him."[91]

Moth Woman identified Pieguete, the father of Tepde and grandfather of Kiowa Six artist Spencer Asah, as an Owl doctor possessing a·tedɔdɔ (spirit of dead power). His medicine bundle contained the skin of "one of the smaller owls and was derived from dead people." Moth Woman described a séance in which the spirit of Kyahik'o (Male Buffalo) spoke through the owl to clarify the "obscure circumstances" of his death during a battle. Some thought his bridle had broken and that his horse had charged the enemy, whereas others believed that he had deliberately ridden to his death. Those inside the tipi heard the owl fluttering outside, and then it spoke: "I am come. I am come. I am the truth teller. I am the truth teller. I am Kyahik'o. I am Kyahik'o. I want a smoke. I want a smoke." His spirit came back to inform everyone that he had voluntarily charged the enemy. The spirit of Male Buffalo returned several times to provide information about lost warriors. On one occasion, the Kiowas were concerned about the whereabouts of Utes they had recently fought, so they consulted the Owl "oracle" through Pieguete. When the Owl entered the tipi Pieguete said, "There are seven pipes here for you. Tell us whether the Utes turned back after the battle or are they still trailing us." The owl replied, "No, they turned back" and then left and came back a half hour later and said, "You are all right. No danger." Pieguete then smoked the seven pipes to end the ceremony. During other séances, the Owl spirit specified the exact day a missing raiding party would return, identified the location of a missing woman, and located lost horses.[92]

Lone Bear and Moth Woman provided genealogical information about the Owl power of Pieguete, which was traced back to his grandmother Atesonhi (Old Owl Woman), who obtained it from her brother after his death. According to the story, Atesonhi had taken her infant son A·tekyaptɔ to mourn at her brother's grave when a whirlwind came along and threw them down a steep embankment, concomitantly bestowing Owl power on them. Upon his death, A·tekyaptɔ divided his power, giving the most important part, the "talking half," to Pieguete and the other half to

Ko'ɔkǫte. Half the power of Pieguete was given to Se'pa·goi, who passed it to his brother Qɔkiete, who eventually gave it to Lone Bear, his son. Apparently Tepde, Pieguete's son, got the other half.[93] Whether or not Lone Bear actually had Owl power is questionable, however. Lone Bear claimed that he and Yellow Wolf were the only two men at present who could still locate lost people, though Lone Bear claimed his information came from dreams whereas Yellow Wolf obtained his knowledge through the séance. Lone Bear related that once while fasting in the hills lying naked under a buffalo robe, an owl appeared to him and hooted; however, Collier noted that "the owl did not speak to him or give him power."[94]

Surprisingly, Kiowa collaborators said very little about Dɔhade (Medicine Man), also called Mamä'nte (Walking Above, or Sky Walker) (see Mooney 1898, 215), a very powerful Owl doctor who died on July 29, 1875, while serving prison time at Fort Marion, Florida. Lone Bear described Dɔhade as a "great medicine man who could understand the horned owl," which was very powerful.[95] Luther Sahmaunt related that Dɔhade fasted for Owl power, and he told the story about a war expedition he organized in 1872 after prophesying the killing of two people and a return time of seven days. After several days out from the Kiowa villages, Dɔhade spoke to an owl and asked several questions about the success of the war party. The owl responded, "Tomorrow noon you will meet what you're after. If it is foggy in the morning, I have told the truth." A second owl, interpreted as the ghost of the man to be killed, hooted in agreement. Indeed, it was foggy the next morning, and all predictions made by the Owl oracle came true. As they arrived at the chosen location, Dɔhade told everyone, a man on a wagon would pass by first and that they were to leave him unmolested. A second group, however, was to be attacked, according to the second owl. As prophesied, a man on a wagon passed by but was unharmed and was followed by a group of soldiers who stopped for water and dinner. Two of the soldiers were killed, and Dɔhade had correctly predicted the identity of the man who would count first coup. Moreover, the war party returned home exactly seven days after departing.[96]

Kiowa oral traditions imply that Sky Walker's powerful Owl sorcery was responsible for Kicking Bird's death in early May 1875. Kicking Bird, a "peace chief" recognized by U.S. Army personnel as Kiowa head chief at the conclusion of the Southern Plains wars, was assigned the ominous task of choosing twenty-six incorrigible Kiowa leaders and warriors to serve prison time, placing him in an uncomfortable situation since he was already at odds with most leaders of the "hostile" faction. Lone Wolf, Woman's Heart, White Horse, Bird Chief, Swan, Buffalo Bull's Entrails, and Sky Walker were the main chiefs selected by Kicking Bird, then thirteen lesser warriors and six Mexican captives were chosen (Mooney 1898, 215–16, 231; Nye 1937, 231; Levy 1959, 39; Hamilton 1988, 159). Unfortunately for Kicking Bird, being put in this position contributed to his death.

According to Charley Buffalo, one of the prisoners, as the shackled Kiowa prisoners were being loaded onto wagons on April 28 for transport to the nearest railhead, Kicking Bird reprimanded them for their behavior.[97] In return, he received a "hard look" from Lone Wolf and a curse from Sky Walker: "You will die for this deed. You see me in chains in this wagon. Look good at us all, for it is your last chance to see us before you die!" En route to the main railhead, the wagon train pulled over for the night near Rush Springs, where Sky Walker smoked and prayed to his Owl power. Sky Walker knew that he would perish following the death of Kicking Bird because sorcerers ultimately die from using malign magic against others. After supplicating his Owl power, Sky Walker informed the other Kiowa prisoners that they would return home but that he would die in Florida (Boyd 1983, 251–52). True to the prophecy, Kicking Bird died sometime between May 3 and May 5, although sources vary (Nye 1937, 233; Corwin 1958a, 104; Mooney 1898, 216; Battey 1968, 317; Mayhall 1984, 298; Hamilton 1988, 159; Methvin n.d., 84). Kiowa agent James Haworth's 1875 annual report indicates that Kicking Bird's death on May 5 occurred "so suddenly as to create the impression that he had been poisoned; but proof of it could not be had." Kicking Bird, interred in the Fort Sill cemetery, was the first Kiowa to receive a Christian burial, even though he had never converted to Christianity.[98] Also true to prophecy, Sky Walker died at Fort Marion on July 29 (Nye 1937, 234; Nye 1962, 223; Hamilton 1988, 213n).

Individual versus Collective Powers

In Plains societies, charismatic men with demonstrative powers typically assumed social and spiritual leadership roles because of their connections to cosmological power. Although many individuals possessed unique powers derived from inheritance and their visionary experiences, some men were empowered by the same dream spirit and typically belonged to the same warrior or medicine society (Wissler 1912a, 1913, 1916; Fletcher and La Flesche 1911, 133, 459; DeMallie 1987, 38–42; Walker 1980, 153–68; Densmore 1918, 285–305; Dempsey 2001, 615, 616; Dorsey 1884, 342; Howard 1965, 114–15; Wedel 2001, 439–40; Whitman 1937, 105–6, 111–13; Parks 2001, 532; Newcomb 2001, 558; DeMallie and Miller 2001, 579; Kavanagh 2001, 892; Grim 2005a, 764; Irwin 1994, 152). Among the Kiowas, charismatic men with war medicine were likely to become band leaders (*topadoga*), and gifted shamans were renowned for their healing powers. Men with curing power or war medicine belonged to medicine societies, shield societies, or warrior societies, whereas *ondedɔ* men who inherited the sacred tribal bundles composed a priesthood. At least one women's society existed during prereservation times, though it was extinct by 1935. Analogous to that of other Plains tribes, society membership typically crosscut kinship ties.

In a manuscript entitled "Shield Societies," Marriott identifies three men's societies in indigenous Kiowa society distinctly related to warfare, healing, and religious purposes. All three societies exhibited "distinct evidence of the shamanistic complex" and adhered to Mooney's "system of heraldry." Membership in the societies was mutually exclusive in that a man could only belong to one; he carried either an Eagle shield connected to war power, a Buffalo shield representing healing power, or a Taime shield associated with the Taime bundle and the Sun Dance. Frank Given revealed that the Taime shields were the oldest, followed by the Eagle shields and then the Buffalo shields. Other shields, including Owl shields, were more recent. Marriott distinguished the shield societies from dancing societies—identified as warrior societies by members of the Santa Fe field party—and a women's society, the Bear Society, which Given said was older than the others.[99]

Ideally, shamans belonging to societies were less likely to engage in power contests or sorcery because the cumulative powers within a society were stronger than individual powers. Moth Woman and Hunting Horse stated that since sorcery and the misuse of powers would ultimately come back against an evil medicine man and kill him or members of his immediate family, it was believed that the collective power of a society could "cause the evil to befall the sorcerer." Thus, ritual smoking in groups ensured peace and harmony within a village and potentially prevented hard feelings that could lead to sorcery.[100] Hence the importance of ceremonies and healing rites conducted by members of the Buffalo Society, or Buffalo Medicine Lodge, a name Bascom assigned to the consortium of Kiowa Buffalo doctors.

Buffalo Society or Buffalo Medicine Lodge

During the prereservation era, approximately twenty to thirty men possessing Buffalo doctoring power belonged to the Buffalo Society. Buffalo doctors were an elite group of medicine men who gained membership into the society through inheritance, purchase, or being cured by a Buffalo doctor. Mooney acknowledged that although Buffalo doctors were outnumbered by independent medicine men, the Buffalo doctors were more powerful.[101] Between 1891 and 1904, Mooney devoted much time to reconstructing Kiowa inheritance patterns of painted shields and tipis, and he commissioned several Kiowas to construct miniature replicas for the National Museum of Natural History, where they are still housed (Ewers 1978). The elders who helped Mooney were Gunavoi, or Gunaoi (Many Tipi Poles), born about 1814; Tenepidi, or Tenepaibi (Ridge Bird, or Hummingbird), whose birth date was circa 1850; Gaápiatañ (Feathered Lance), born around 1824; and T'ébodal (One Who Carries A Buffalo's Lower Leg), who was approximately the same age as Gunavoi. Information from these individuals contributed to descriptions of Buffalo doctors and Buffalo shields in Mooney's "Kiowa Heraldry Notebook."[102]

By 1935, the Buffalo Society and its associated rituals had ceased, but several Buffalo doctors were still living. Tsoodle told Marriott that Conklin Hummingbird still practiced Buffalo medicine and that Elk Creek Charley also had the healing powers of Buffalo.[103] Haumpy told Bascom that he had Buffalo power that would be passed to his son, whereas Hunting Horse had tried to obtain his brother's Buffalo medicine power but failed to secure the vision. Becaues they were familiar with the principal functions and rituals of the society, their stories augmented Mooney's data about the Buffalo Society, or Buffalo Medicine Lodge.[104] Bascom gathered extensive data about Buffalo doctors, mostly from Haumpy and to a lesser extent from Hunting Horse. Mary Buffalo added additional details, and Lone Bear provided some information to Collier. Marriott learned about Buffalo doctors through interviews with George Hunt, Biătonmá, Sanko, George Poolaw, and Atah, or Etadi (Ripe Fruit).

Versions of the origin myth of the Buffalo Society narrated to Mooney in 1897 by Gunavoi, Tenepidi, and T'ébodal describe how the Buffalo shields and doctoring society originated from a woman's vision. In 1935, Hunting Horse and Haumpy told variants of the origin myth to Bascom. Marriott's "Shield Societies" manuscript contains similar versions of the myth as told by George Hunt, Biătonmá, and George Poolaw.[105] The more recent stories, though consistent, vary slightly from Mooney's version recorded thirty-eight years earlier. Thus the origin myth recorded by Mooney is preferred because Many Tipi Poles, Hummingbird, and One Who Carries A Buffalo's Lower Leg could provide more precise information about the society's origins in the late eighteenth to early nineteenth centuries.

The story begins with two Kiowa women searching for their village after escaping from Pawnee captors. En route to their homeland, they were pursued by a bear, prompting one of them to scale a tree, although she was immediately devoured. Fortunately, the other woman procured a dead cedar tree, which she used to scale a large rock beyond the reach of the deadly claws. Later that night, the survivor, Etdá-i-tsoňhi (Old Woman Who Has Medicine On Her), slipped off the rock and escaped by stepping on dried buffalo chips to hide her tracks. Continuing her trek, Etdá-i-tsoňhi escaped an impending thunderstorm by seeking refuge under the rib cage and decomposing hide of a bison bull that had been partially consumed by coyotes. Exhausted from her ordeal, Etdá-i-tsoňhi immediately fell asleep under the protective buffalo bull robe. During her slumber, the spirit of the animal appeared, bestowing her with power and the design for a shield.[106] The existence of unsought, spontaneous visions occurring in the liminal space beyond the safety of an encampment happened in other Plains cultures; sometimes women and children were the recipients of these visions (Stewart 2001, 337; Bowers 1950, 335–36, 343; Fletcher and La Flesche 1911, 128–29; Whitman 1937, 81–88; DeMallie and Miller 2001, 578; Fowler 2001, 844; Kavanagh 2001, 892; Schweinfurth 2002, 132; Irwin 1994, 83–88).

Eventually finding her encampment, Etdá-i-tsoňhi informed her husband about her vision and then manufactured a shield from the thickest part of a buffalo hide, behind the neck. Because women were not allowed to own power shields, Etdá-i-tsoñhi presented the shield to her husband, who used it and eventually passed it on to their son, Mañka-i-gyäto (Flat Nose Old Man), who then received the name Pa-gyäto (Buffalo Old Man, or Bull Old Man). He married a woman who became Pa-tsoñhi (Buffalo Old Woman, or Old Lady Buffalo), and they had seven sons. Pa-gyäto fashioned seven Buffalo shields for his sons based on the original shield his mother had given him and then later made three more for his brother's sons. The ten shield keepers eventually passed the shield design and associated power down to their sons, creating the Buffalo Society. Notably, Hummingbird remembered the names of the ten original shield keepers who obtained their shields from Pa-gyäto, who died in 1824: (1) Pá-ïmhéte, the oldest son of Pa-gyäto, and the grandfather of Gunavoi, who was born between 1815 and 1817. Gunavoi remembered camp criers announcing the coming of the 1834 dragoon expedition; (2) Atä-gyäto (alias Atäti), who died around 1857 at a very old age; (3) Tsotaí-ádälton, who died in the summer of 1870 at a very old age; (4) Ósoñti; (5) Täbähóte; (6) Békáante; (7) Ódalpódalte (Hetkoñgya's father), who died in 1849, the cholera year; (8) Pá-gúak'ote (alias Doǵuatá-i), who died in 1866 at age sixty; (9) Gui·yanonte (Howling Wolf); and (10) Ka-ibä-te (alias Adlháñte [Silver]). Based on the lines of succession, Gunavoi estimated that the first shield was made sometime between 1750 and 1770.[107]

T'ébodal thought there were as many as twenty-seven Buffalo shields at one time, and years later Hunting Horse told Bascom that there had been forty Buffalo medicine shields. Sanko suggested to Marriott that once there had been between twenty and thirty Buffalo doctors "because the power was so freely divided."[108] According to T'ébodal, shield owners never refused apprentices and the number of shields was "always increasing," resulting in many different shield patterns; Buffalo shield designs varied in detail, but all were decorated with bunches of buffalo hair and eagle feathers. Gunavoi surmised that only twelve Buffalo shields remained in 1867, but by 1897 only one survived.[109] Hunting Horse said that most of the Buffalo shields "were taken away by the soldiers," along with the weapons and war paraphernalia confiscated after the Kiowas surrendered at Fort Sill in May 1875, marking the end of the Kiowa war complex and the subsequent breakdown of inheritance and purchase patterns.[110] By 1935 the shields were gone, according to Hunting Horse, Mary Buffalo, and Sanko, though Mary Buffalo noted that the medicines were still passed on without the shields.[111] Fashioned according to the original Etdá-i-tsoñhi design, the surviving Buffalo shield passed from Pa-gyäto (d. 1824) to his son Ódalpódalte (d. 1849), to Set-konkya (Black Bear) (d. 1896), and it was purchased in 1897 by Mooney for the National Museum (fig. 3, this volume). Though Etdá-i-tsoñhi constructed the original Buffalo shield, it was called the Pa-tsoñhi Shield. Like the others, Black Bear's shield was fitted with a decorated cover left unpainted except for two symmetrical circles on the upper portion painted Indian red, symbolizing blood. One circle was adorned with eleven antelope hoofs, the other with twelve, which represented an unspecified medicine. In between the red circles and farther up were eleven swift hawk tail feathers, and at the bottom were two pendant buffalo bull tails and a bell, which hung from the center. The actual shield was painted red with a large green circle in the center, surrounded by a thin yellow border, with two pendant fringes of red cloth covered with eagle wing feathers draping the sides. Attached at the top just above the green circle were two bunches of buffalo hair braided together with hawk and crow feathers all smeared with Indian red paint. The circles represented either a buffalo wallow or a buffalo eye, and the hair and feathers symbolized the shield's medicine power. Mooney bought the Pa-tsoñhi shield for forty dollars from Black Bear's nephew, who also sold the *kiätsó* (or *gietso*) that belonged to it—a hair ball from a buffalo bull's stomach. In former times, the shield and pendant *gietso* rested on a tripod outside the owner's tipi, facing west into the wind.[112]

The design of the shield purchased by Mooney was similar to the original Pa-tsoñhi shield carried into battle by Pa-gyäto's father. After learning its medicine power, he wore the shield across the chest affixed by a cord around the neck to render enemy arrows harmless. Importantly, the shield derived from the original vision was associated with the power to doctor battlefield wounds. When Etdá-i-tsoñhi presented her husband the shield, she blew her *gietso* into his mouth in the form of various colored paints derived from earth pigments, including red clay. Pa-gyäto's father—whose name has been forgotten—was instructed to blow the paint onto a wounded man to stanch the flow of blood and, as a consequence, became the first Buffalo doctor.[113] Haumpy noted that although the Buffalo shields were taken into battle for protection, their principal function was for curing. Buffalo doctors carried their medicine bundles, or pouches, under the shield covers, and when called upon to cure a patient they rocked their shields on the ground four times, removed the medicine pouches that were tied inside, donned their red-painted buffalo headdresses, and then leaned the shields against the patient's tipi, if they were in the base camp. The contents of the medicine bundle were used for curing purposes.[114]

In 1935, Haumpy permitted Bascom to examine the contents of his three Buffalo doctor medicine bundles. The bundle covers were fashioned from bison tails wrapped in buckskin adorned with buffalo hair, deer hooves, pieces of red, white, and blue paint (clay), bells, fragrant roots, and feathers—eagle plume, crow, and five types of hawk. Hair balls, the *gietso* of the buffalo, were also inside the bundles, in addition to sweetgrass, wild cherries, and buffalo root. Red and yellow clay covered most of the bundle contents. Bascom suggested that the buffalo symbolism represents Buffalo power in war and healing; the feathers connect bird and bison *dɔdɔ*; and the paint pigments are connected to Etdá-i-tsoňhi's curing vision: red symbolizes blood, and yellow represents the dust that falls off the hide of a wallowing buffalo. Haumpy stated that he used the roots and sweetgrass as purifying incense, the wild cherries were fed to patients for loss of appetite, and the bell was used to call back the soul to the body if the sufferer was close to death.[115] It is commonly believed in tribal societies that the soul partially detaches from the body during sickness and departs upon death. During states of ecstasy, shamans consult their other-than-human powers for assistance in reuniting the body and soul of the patient (Harvey 2006, 142; Foster and Anderson 1978, 65–66).

Besides shields and bundles, Buffalo doctors owned rattles described by Hunting Horse as the tips of deer or buffalo hooves tied to a bundle of falcon feathers.[116] George Poolaw told Marriott that the buffalo rattles represented the powers of the Buffalo doctors. During healing ceremonies, a Buffalo doctor activated his Buffalo power by shaking the rattle while singing Buffalo songs; there were at least twenty songs that the Buffalo doctors commonly knew. Poolaw possessed one of the original rattles and claimed that Danger Bear owned three and that Big Joe, who had recently died, also kept one. When not in use, the rattles were kept in cases and were never shown to anyone. Poolaw stated that the rattles and associated powers were typically passed from father to son. In the absence of a son, a nephew or other man might be chosen, but if an heir was not selected the rattle was buried with its owner.[117]

Mooney's collaborators, as well as Hunting Horse and Haumpy, concurred that Buffalo doctors accompanied raiding parties into Texas and Mexico in case they were needed to treat bullet and arrow wounds or injuries sustained from falling off horses but said that they did not attend broken bones; bone-setting was common knowledge, though some men were splint-making specialists. Stumbling Bear informed Mooney that Buffalo doctors once saved his life when he was shot by Pawnees.[118] George Hunt told Marriott that Buffalo doctors treated broken bones by singing and shaking their rattles but never by setting the bone.[119] Lone Bear and Hunting Horse noted that unless a war party was ambushed, all Buffalo doctors in attendance convened before an engagement with enemies to paint their bodies red and white while singing a Buffalo song. They were ready for combat when the protective rite concluded. Once the fighting began, Buffalo doctors rushed to assist their fallen comrades, spewing red paint on open wounds to coagulate the bleeding.[120] T'ébodal told Mooney that the war cry of the Buffalo doctors was the grunting of a buffalo bull, the same sound they made while healing.[121] According to Haumpy and Hunting Horse, wounded warriors were taken back to the home village whenever possible so the Buffalo doctors could better attend to their needs. A solitary tipi for the wounded was pitched at least one hundred yards away from camp, for the Buffalo doctors did not want their urgent work disrupted by barking dogs and noisy children.[122]

Buffalo doctors typically worked alone, though Haumpy observed that other Buffalo medicine men were summoned for severe cases. Initiating treatment involved offering a lit pipe to the most renowned Buffalo doctor in the village, along with gifts that included horses, buffalo robes, buckskin, and black handkerchiefs.[123] After examining the patient, other Buffalo doctors were solicited if their assistance was deemed necessary; four to five Buffalo medicine men could doctor a single patient, although Hunting Horse said that as many as fourteen were called for extreme cases.[124]

Haumpy and Hunting Horse described the protocol for Buffalo doctors summoned to treat a patient. Accepting their gifts upon arrival, the doctors entered the patient's tipi: the head Buffalo doctor sat on the west side, assistants and the remaining Buffalo doctors positioned themselves to the north, and the patient was placed on the south side. Next, the leader began the curative rite with a ceremonial smoke, after which he removed several hot coals from the center fireplace, placed them on the ground between himself and the fire, and sprinkled sweet-grass on them. Taking each doctor's medicine pouch, he held it over the incense and prayed and then gave it back. Standing by the patient holding their bundles, the doctors sang four Buffalo songs from the repertoire of approximately twenty-five songs that were common property of the Buffalo Society. When the songs were finished, the doctors were ready to treat the patient.[125] According to George Poolaw, sometimes a woman's voice was heard singing from the top of the tipi. Since women were not allowed to attend Buffalo doctoring meetings, the woman's voice was interpreted as the spirit of Pa-tsoňhi, which signified that the patient would recover. Sam Ahtone, Sanko, George Hunt, and Stephen Aitson all claimed to have heard her voice during a doctoring meeting; they said it sounded like it was coming from a radio.[126]

T'ébodal related that Buffalo doctors treated wounded men by spewing red paint (clay) on the patient's bodies and using the sucking technique to extract blood and pus from the wound. If a "candidate" or apprentice was present, he was given the blood to swallow, which would enable him to dream and learn more about the medicine.[127] Haumpy said that Buffalo doctors also sprinkled the patient with buffalo tails dipped in water. Once these rites were completed, the doctors rested in the tipi along with the patient's relatives. Keeping the patient under constant vigil, doctoring procedures occurred after breakfast, before a midday meal, and before an evening meal. Men with severe wounds were also doctored later in the night. On the evening of the fourth day of treatment, gifts were brought into the tipi and laid in piles. The doctors sang a closing song and made motions with their medicines over the patient, who was then painted by the leader. The gifts were distributed to the doctors, who shook hands with the family and left. If the patient's condition had not improved after four days, necessitating another four days of treatment, then another round of gifts was given to the doctors. However, the cycle would not be repeated a third time, as "the patient would either [be] cured or dead." In 1935, Haumpy still doctored patients. Besides healing those who were wounded, he treated hemorrhages, nosebleed, cuts, fever, swelling, pre-natal ailments, and urinary blockage.[128] Throughout the course of the curative rites, the patient assumed the taboos of the attending Buffalo doctors, restrictions that were lifted at the end of the four- or eight-day period by a ceremonial smoke and ritual meal with the doctors. Food prohibitions of the Buffalo doctors described by Gunavoi included not eating blood or raw meat, such as liver and kidney, and it was taboo to break bones in the vicinity where they were doctoring a wounded man. A Buffalo doctor could not break the limbs of animals—to extract the marrow—in the tipi where he lived, nor could he put buffalo horns, tails, hooves, or tipi pegs into the fire.[129] George Poolaw told Marriott that scraps of meat could not be thrown on the ground near Buffalo doctors, and that they could not eat the wounded part of an animal. However, they were allowed to eat cooked liver.[130] Haumpy agreed that the most common prohibition was avoiding "wounded meat," raw gizzards, kidneys, livers, and uncooked blood, and he also noted some peculiar qualms Buffalo doctors had while smoking with others in a circle. One doctor "was afraid to have someone else take hold of a pipe he was smoking below (closer to the bowl) than he held it. Thus when he passed it to another person he set the pipe down in front of them." Another feared having someone take the pipe above where he held it. Most feared red pipes "and would get skittish when they saw them." Breaching any of these taboos would result in power loss or possible bewitchment.[131]

Haumpy asserted that like other men possessing *dɔdɔ*, Buffalo doctors smoked and prayed to their medicine bundles on a daily basis, acknowledging the spiritual forces responsible for their doctoring abilities. Otherwise, Buffalo doctors differed from other shamans because they assembled at least once a year to conduct sweat lodges and society meetings. Collective gatherings occurred during the summers when the Sun Dance was performed, whereas sweat lodges and renewal meetings took place at least every few years to teach Buffalo songs to apprentices and to create new medicine bundles or repair old ones. Attendance of all society members was mandatory at the assemblies, which featured ceremonial smoking and praying.[132]

Whether acquired through purchase or inheritance, the recipient of a Buffalo shield and corresponding medicine bundle was required to sponsor a Buffalo Medicine Sweathouse after successfully completing his vision quest in the late spring or summer when the Kiowa bands coalesced. Haumpy's description of the sweat lodge ceremony differed little from T'ébodal's rendering to Mooney in 1897. Constructed by the initiate, the sweat lodge consisted of seventeen willow poles bound together at the top and covered with buffalo robes. A Buffalo shield and set of bison bull horns served as the door flap. The sweat lodge had to be large enough to accommodate men sitting cross legged on the sage-covered floor. In the center of the lodge a pit was excavated to hold the rocks, and excavated earth was mounded around the pit. Outside the lodge sat a stack of rocks next to the fire where they were heated. After completing the sweat lodge, the initiate went through the encampments to collect all available Buffalo shields from their tripods and carry them back. Bringing the shields to the sweat lodge, he was greeted by several older Buffalo medicine men previously notified about the ceremony. Feigning three entries, the candidate then circuited counterclockwise around the sweat lodge three times, then on the fourth circuit entered and stacked the shields face up on the west side. If the shields were too heavy, an assistant handed them in from the outside without entering. Finally, a long stem pipe was placed between the shields and the central mound.[133]

With everything in place, the initiate exited the sweat lodge. The shield donor, imitating the initiate's route, entered the sweat lodge on the fourth attempt and sat at the west side by the shields and pipes. Following the same counterclockwise circuit, the remaining Buffalo doctors entered and seated themselves at the north side of the lodge. When the north side was filled, those without seats entered the sweat lodge but then reversed their motion, moving to the south side. Having taken their places, the doctors stripped down to their breechcloths while the candidate waited outside, where his relatives had tethered several horses and stacked blankets for the shield donor. After the Buffalo doctors were seated, the initiate was summoned into the lodge. Bringing a live coal to light the donor's pipe, the candidate returned to the east and sat down south of the door entrance. Lifting the pipe upward, the shield donor first offered a prayer to Sun, lowered it to make an offering to Earth, and then motioned four times toward the winds of the four cardinal directions. Without being smoked, the pipe was passed across the south side until it reached the initiate, who drew from the pipe and handed it to the person on his left, who smoked and passed the pipe to the person on his left. The pipe circuited clockwise around the lodge in this fashion until the tobacco was spent. The initiate then went outside the sweat lodge, removed the stones from the fire with a forked stick, and passed them inside, where they were received with tongs and stacked in the central earthen pit. Returning inside, he closed the door and the sweat began when water was sprinkled over the hot stones, producing steam. A series of either four or seven Buffalo songs was sung, the last song of each set signifying the opening of the door flap to let in fresh air. After the ceremony the shield donor received the horses and blankets, though most of the blankets were left in place as an offering to the spirits, and perhaps a horse was sacrificed by staking it out to die.[134] Exactly when the initiate acquired his shield is unclear, but Haumpy said there was a special transfer meeting where the doctors blew clay on the candidate and then incensed his new medicine bundle by spewing clay on it.[135] T'ébodal told Mooney that the recent recipient of a shield could not doctor until he had carried the shield for several years, had made many sacrifices, and had learned to doctor from the older Buffalo shield owners.[136]

According to T'ébodal, the candidate to receive a Buffalo shield always went to where the Buffalo doctors were working, offering them a lit pipe, which they accepted and smoked. Taking pity on him, the doctors gave him feathers to wear in his hair as well as paint coughed up from their stomachs. Mooney described this procedure: "When teaching [the] recipient one would take earth in [his] mouth, preceded by several grunts, & then blow it on recipient or patient, when it appears as red or some other kind of paint. (Buffalo medicine is very fragrant & smells [a] long way off when making medicine-andres)."[137] Also, if Buffalo doctors employed the sucking technique to clean a wound, they gave some of it to the initiate to swallow, which "tastes as sweet as sugar," giving him more cause to learn about the medicine.[138] Tsoodle told Marriott that he once saw a Buffalo doctor suck the inflamed area of a wounded man and blow the pus into a young boy's mouth, saying, "It's sugar. It's sweet." This youth was the chosen successor of the doctor blowing the pus into his mouth.[139]

Haumpy stated that renewal meetings were conducted every five to seven years during the fall or spring to repair the medicine bundles housed in the Buffalo shields. Oftentimes casual conversations led to decisions about conducting repair meetings and selecting a sponsor. On the night before the ritual, the sponsor's female relatives pitched a tipi some distance from the encampment. Inside, the floor was scraped and swept clean, a four-inch-high earthen platform was constructed on the west side and covered with sage, and then a central fireplace was excavated. The finished renewal tipi was called *pɔpyatom* (the place where the buffalo rolls), which represented a buffalo wallow, a sacred place of power.[140]

Repair meetings described by Haumpy followed very closely the Buffalo Medicine Sweathouse ceremony except that the person sitting immediately south of the entryway was not a society member but someone suffering from sickness who received free treatment. Filing into the tipi, the Buffalo doctors placed their shields and bundles on the sage platform and then took their seats and passed around the pipe for a ceremonial smoke. After everyone had smoked, the runner brought in hot coals and set them in the fireplace, as requested by the leader, who sprinkled sweetgrass over them. Each bundle was passed through the smoke five times while praying to Pa-tsoñhi's spirit, informing her about the renewal ritual. Returning the bundles to the altar, the doctors lined up before the leader and each recited what repairs or objects his particular bundle needed, such as feathers or new rawhide covers. Assisted by the other Buffalo doctors, the leader tied and fastened the bundles that were replenished with all the necessary materials. For his services, the leader received seven gifts, in addition to a horse for every new strip of cut rawhide. Bundle renewal was time-consuming, so after every two or three repairs, the doctors assumed their sitting positions for another ceremonial smoke before continuing their work. The pattern of working and stopping was followed until all the bundles were repaired, which took at least a day and a half. After each bundle was finished, it was placed on the sage altar, and when they were all completed, the leader painted them with colored clay and passed them through incense again. Upon completion of the renewal rite, people with various illnesses congregating outside the tipi were invited inside to be incensed and treated by the Buffalo doctors, who blew clay on them and sang Buffalo songs. Patients were not expected to give the doctors gifts. Another ceremonial smoke and prayers to Pa-tsoñhi followed the treatment, and then the patients departed. Finally, the doctors left the tipi and were joined by their families for a feast that marked the end of the formal ceremony. Sometime after the meal, the old materials to be discarded were taken to a remote area and tied to a tree as offerings, completing the renewal procedure.[141]

Kiowa Vision Quests, Doctoring, and Sorcery after 1935

Although indigenous beliefs dating back to the horse and buffalo culture were still remembered by elders in the mid-1930s, many Kiowas now belonged to various Christian denominations or the Native American Church. Concepts of dɔdɔ were extant, and to some degree they had been amalgamated into the new religions as many former practices were fading into obscurity. For instance, vision-seeking in the Wichita Mountains occurred less frequently as this rite was not a central element of the introduced religions. The only current account of the vision quest collected by LaBarre was Geikauma's unsuccessful two-night attempt to find the source of gold, diamonds, or oil that would support his family, which he made because he was suffering from an inguinal hernia. When LaBarre returned to Southwestern Oklahoma in 1936, Charley Apekaum informed him that Bert wanted to "finish out the four days" fasting and praying in the mountains, but the vision quest never materialized because his daughter became ill, and he had to attend to her needs. She died shortly thereafter and Bert blamed his involvement in the peyote religion for her death. So he joined the Baptist Church and threw his peyote gear—including feathers and gourd rattle—into the river. Charley was not aware of anyone else seeking power at the time (LaBarre 1957, 101–2).

In 1987, Geikauma's granddaughter, Trina Stumblingbear, recounted the story of Bert's conversion to Christianity following the death of his daughter, who was Trina's mother. Trina stated that Geikauma, a celebrated peyotist who allegedly held the record for consuming 240 green peyote buttons during a three-day period, was so stricken with grief that he mourned at his daughter's grave. Kneeling at her gravesite with an open Bible on the ground in front of him, Geikauma cried out, "Lord, if you are really God, show me. Open my eyes that I can see. Give me a sign that I would know that my daughter is in Heaven with you. Is there a Heaven?" The answer came in the form of a whirlwind that kicked up and blew across the grave, turning the pages to the book of John, where Geikauma read the passage "I go to prepare a place for you. In my father's house are many mansions." Later Bert went home, built a fire, and destroyed his peyote regalia, "feathers and all." As in former times when visions became the visionary's autobiography, Geikauma's religious experience became his personal testimony: "I was an old fool living in the peyote and powwow way." Geikauma joined Redstone Baptist Church west of Anadarko and later became a Methodist.[142] Apekaum told LaBarre that Geikauma would "preach to you" (LaBarre 1957, 102).

Although it's unclear when this vision quest occurred, Frank Given told Marriott about the time he fasted on the west side of Mount Sheridan seeking assistance for an uncle whom others had failed to cure. On the fourth night a large mountain boomer appeared to him during a state in which "he seemed to fall asleep but he still saw it." The lizard did not speak but blew its breath on Given, who "felt words come into his heart." Through this heartfelt communication, Given learned that his uncle would have a brief recovery and live through the summer but would die the following autumn. Although Frank had always prayed to Sun and daylight, the mountain boomer told him to pray to *maindetak'oyk'i* (the white man above). As prophesied by the spirit of the mountain boomer, the uncle hemorrhaged and died that fall.[143] This story manifests syncretisms between indigenous beliefs and Christianity, indicative of changing times in the early twentieth century.

That fewer men sought visions led to the decline of power. Sanko related to Marriott that "Most of the men who had real power are gone now."[144] When Jerrold Levy interviewed Kiowa and Comanche peyotists in the late 1950s, he learned that the old-timers were not passing down their powers to the younger generation. Elders who had obtained *dɔdɔ* through vision quests were dying without passing them to heirs, resulting in the cessation of their powers when they died. Levy noted that the youth had options to utilize white doctors and hospitals, and he attributed the influence of Christianity to their ambivalence toward old-time powers (Levy 1958, 38–39).

Despite the decline of vision quests, Kiowas still maintain spiritual connections to the mountainous areas of their ancestral homelands in Montana and to the Wichita Mountains and the Slick Hills in southwestern Oklahoma; the Wichitas are granite formations, but the Slick Hills, just to the north, are limestone. Some Kiowas find inspiration through prayer pilgrimages to these locations. Patricia Ware treks to Elk Mountain on occasion because she believes it's a sacred mountain where buffalo go to die. According to Patricia, seeing buffalo on Elk Mountain "makes you feel good." Another elder told Justin Castro that she makes an annual trip to the Wichita Mountains looking "for a few certain buffalo and says prayers in their honor and of their ancestors."[145] Dorothy Tsatoke Gray (1924–2010), whose home was nestled beneath the Slick Hills near Dietrich's Lake, described how she often had revelations while praying in her garden and said that one of her sons received a vision from God after praying in the Wichitas.[146] Recent controversy surrounds gravel mining and the destruction of Longhorn Mountain, a lone sentinel of the Slick Hills. Ernest "Iron" Toppah related that Longhorn Mountain, south of Gotebo, is renowned for its cedar trees, which have an especially sweet smell. Even Crows are known to sojourn south from Montana to obtain this special cedar.[147] Pilgrimages to collect the sacred cedar used for smudging, or cedaring, ceremonies have occurred as long as Kiowas have lived in the area (see Meadows 2008, 92–93).

Today, five non-Indian families own Longhorn Mountain as the original Kiowa allottees sold the lands years ago; hence the mountain is not on trust or federal lands. In March 2013 staff members of the Kiowa Tribe Museum learned that two of the landowners had signed leases with Material Service Corporation for mining and water rights on the western side of the mountain. Mining permits were granted to MSC between 2005 and 2006 by the Oklahoma Department of Mines, and mining operations supervised by the Stewart Stone mining company of Cushing, Oklahoma, were set to begin at the end of the summer. Since learning of plans to quarry the west side of the mountain, the Kiowa Tribe Museum and NAGPRA Department have attempted to block the destruction of their sacred mountain.[148] In an interview with a reporter from Oklahoma City's KFOR TV4, Joe Fish explained his personal relationship with the mountain:

I tell that mountain I am a Kiowa. I am a Kiowa. I come here for something. This is the only place that I know of in the world where this evergreen, cedar, where it grows. And like I said, it has its own unique fragrance, and that's what God almighty gave us, the Kiowa. He gave us this sacred mountain, this sacred site, this sacred mountain, and this sacred cedar. That's what we hold dear to us.[149]

Kiowa Tribe Museum director Aime Tah-Bone added that "with the crusher up there, we're still losing that spirituality of the mountain." Tribal historian Phil Dupoint concurred that Longhorn Mountain is sacred because his ancestors put spiritual power there for future generations journeying to the mountain. He noted, "This is where we always come. This is where our elders used to come. Maybe they were searching for some kind of power."[150] The two landowners on the eastern side of Longhorn Mountain have refused to lease their lands and continue to allow tribal members to climb the mountain to pray and pick cedar.[151]

Modern-day visionary experiences often take place in people's homes during stressful times, what Lee Irwin (1994, 100) refers to as spontaneous visions that come "to the individual without any formal questing." Such experiences among the Kiowas occur in the context of the Native American Church and Christianity. In his lifetime, Gus Palmer Sr. (1919–2006) told many stories about his blessed life, and on several occasions he related the visionary experience of his daughter LaDonna, who at one time felt ambivalent about participating in peyote rites due to pressures from members of a Christian church she attended in Dallas. Significantly, Gus related this story to the U.S. House of Representatives Subcommittee on Native American Affairs of the Committee on Natural Resources, 103rd Congress, 1st session, on March 16, 1993:

My daughter, LaDonna Palmer, lived in Dallas. It spoke to her in spirit. She worked in the Environmental Health Building, 28th floor. She was driving home to Garland and had a weak feeling. [She] went home and went into the bathroom. It had a soft voice, but with authority. She was thinking, why did she go to Native American Church meetings? It spoke to her in spirit: "It's alright because I'm in it." He [God] made it, He created it. I am telling you this story my daughter told me. He's in it. It's not a god. He's in there. What can you eat that will tell you that? He's in there. He makes you humble; you sit in there [in tipi meetings] and He lets you know you can learn something. It's going to teach you something it's in your heart.[152]

Today's dreams and visions are recounted in such testimonials that are institutionalized in Native American Church as well as Christian practices. For instance, Lavena Pewo (1936–2009), a Baptist, described a life-saving encounter with Jesus that happened years ago following an argument while visiting her mother, Henrietta Tongkeamha. Following the quarrel, Lavena and her husband drove away from the old homestead south of Eagle Heart Springs and returned to their home. Later that night, Lavena was still angry when she went to bed. That night she dreamt that her parents were standing in the front door of their home, looking up into the sky at God (Jesus), who was instructing them about families in the Saddle Mountain community he wanted them to visit. Espying Lavena, he pointed his finger at her saying, "And for you, you have two weeks to get your act together!" Lavena awakened screaming and covered in sweat, vowing to turn her life around. From that time, she remained a staunch Christian until her death.[153] Her brother, Raymond Tongkeamha, acknowledges that this demonstrates that the older concept of *dɔdɔ* is inherent in God.[154]

Reading the accounts of early twentieth-century missionaries gives the impression that Christian converts readily gave up their indigenous beliefs and rituals, including Indian doctoring. However, because the Kiowas believed that variant forms of *dɔdɔ* were not mutually exclusive, many did not abandon their worldviews and traditions after converting to Christianity. Isabel Crawford, who established a Baptist mission at Saddle Mountain in 1896, described the conversion of Odlepaugh (Buffalo Bird) and his wife, Konanɔma (Buffalo Hoof Prints).[155] Odlepaugh — one of White Bear's four sons — and Konanɔma lived northwest of Saddle Mountain at the mouth of Odlepaugh Springs, which emanates from an underground source in the Slick Hills. On July 11, 1897, the couple sponsored a "Missionary Big Eat" to fulfill a pledge made by Konanɔma the previous winter to slaughter a beef if she recovered from an illness. After feeding Crawford and the other Saddle Mountain converts, Odlepaugh stated that he had "converted straight" to Christianity. Odlepaugh and Konanɔma were charter members of Saddle Mountain Kiowa Indian Baptist Church (Crawford 1915, 91–92, 222).

Henrietta Tongkeamah (1912–1993) told another version of the story. In 1916, Odlepaugh and Konanɔma adopted Henrietta and her sister Margaret after their parents died. The girls were raised in the Baptist Church by the grandparents, who rarely spoke about their indigenous beliefs. However, sometime in 1918 when Henrietta was six years old, Odlepaugh took her to a peyote meeting for doctoring. Though Odlepaugh died in 1923, she remembered the peyote satchel he took to peyote meetings, and that he specialized in fashioning cow horns used for treating pneumonia and removing blood clots. Like other early twentieth-century Kiowas, Henrietta's grandparents still believed in Indian doctoring.[156]

By the 1930s, the number of Indian doctors was declining due to the breakdown of inheritance patterns. In the autobiography *Remember We Are Kiowas* (Hall 2000), Tōʼákút (Pulled From The Water), also known as Harlan Hall (1932–2003), wrote that there were only two Kiowa doctors by the 1940s: his paternal grandfather Zótai (Zotigh), or Harry Hall (1882–1957), and William "Cornbread" Tenadooah (d. 1976). Hall described how his grandfather doctored an Indian soldier, Frank Blind Bull, at the Fitzsimons Army Medical Center in Denver after medical staff failed to determine the cause of his illness. Following two days of treatment "behind closed doors," the soldier was able to eat solid foods and drink lots of water. On another occasion, Zotigh was summoned to the Omaha Reservation in Nebraska to doctor a tribal council member who was suffering from chest pains. Employing the sucking technique, Zotigh sucked out "a dull yellow mass intermingled with some that was grey in color" through his cow horn. After four days of treatment the patient was fully recovered and the grateful family gave Zotigh four gifts: a bridle with hackamore bit and halter; a saddle blanket; a blue and red peyote blanket; and one thousand dollars. Zotigh once treated Harlan to stop a nosebleed. First, holding a cooled-off wood coal in his mouth, he scratched Harlan's temple, placed a cow horn over the scratch, and put a piece of well-chewed sinew in the small aperture at the opposite end and began sucking. After repeating the same procedure on the opposite temple, Zotigh placed a black silk handkerchief over Harlan's face and told him to rest. Within two days Harlan was fully recovered and learned from his father that Zotigh had sucked out small pieces of "something black" from his temples, possibly "slivers of very dirty finger nails that had been clipped." Afterward Zotigh was paid with a new black handkerchief, twelve silver dollars, a chamois drum cover, and groceries (Hall 2000, 47–53, 233–34). Apparently Indian doctors were now gifted with four instead of seven items.

In February 1987, Gus Palmer Sr. related how his father-in-law, Henry Oliver Tenadooah (1882–1966), treated him for pneumonia, probably in the 1950s or early 1960s. At the time, Gus, working as a painter at Fort Sill north of Lawton, came home on a Friday doubled-up in pain from the fluid that had collected in his pleural cavity. Tenadooah, also known as White Cloud, said to him, "I bet you've got pneumonia. I'll straighten that out, fix it up for you." Instructing Gus to take off his shirt and lie down, the old man began pressing on his chest to determine where it hurt the most. Cutting the bottom off a bottle to produce a sharp sliver of glass, Tenadooah lanced the skin at the base of Gus's lungs and then used his cow horn to suck out the fluid. Gus described the procedure:

> There's a hole on the top of the tip of the horn, see, and there's a hole. And he had this sinew he was chewin', so he placed that over here and he formed a suction, you know? Then he stuck that sinew there [at the sucking end of the horn], and there's a suction already. He waited a little while, and he had a piece of paper like that ... [, and] then he took that off there, where it don't drip. Boy, there's some of that, that blood. And there was, kind of that ... there was hardened, thick. Next time he said "You watch. I'll get it." Same way. Put a suction on that, and put that sinew. . . . Then after a while he took that off. Same way. And he poured it over here and said "There it is." Said, "But I'm not through yet." He said, "Now turn over." He said when you have that it ... it goes through you. So, the back through here. And that was the spot.[157]

As Gus explained further, placing the cow horn over the incision, creating suction, and then sealing the end of the horn with sinew to maintain pressure is the technique Tenadooah used to draw fluid from the pleural cavity. When asked what the fluid looked like, Gus described it as "dark" and "hardened." After the procedure was applied to his front and back sides, Gus could take a deep breath and the pain was gone! Snapping his fingers Gus said, "Pneumonia. They can cure it that quick. It's like taking a sticker out of you."[158] Using cow horns to suck out sickness undoubtedly ended with Tenadooah's generation.

Conversations with Kiowas today suggest that there is only one old-time Kiowa doctor left. Oftentimes he performs cedaring rites to purify homes marking the completion of mourning periods, or is summoned to offer blessings for the dedication of new construction projects. One fall afternoon in 1989 I visited with him to ask questions about treating type 2 diabetics because he allegedly prescribes peyote tea, which might act as a diuretic to lower blood sugar levels. Preferring to remain anonymous, he nonetheless described certain aspects of his practice. Since his youth he has suffered from epilepsy, which prevents him from working full-time jobs. Before dying his paternal grandfather passed his peyote doctoring medicine to him because his medical condition ostensibly allows him to "understand sickness"; hence his affliction enables him to have empathy and compassion for individuals coming to his home with tobacco offerings seeking help. The medicine he received is very powerful and to take it "you have to be the man of the house"—that is, one who is in control of everything. People come to him with many problems, but his specialty is treating strokes. If he feels he cannot handle a certain illness, then he refers the patient to other doctors, Indian and Western. Noting that some of his patients go to Western doctors first because "we're geared toward a white man's world," he added that they usually seek his help afterward. Whether he doctors inside or outside a tipi, it's important that all participants are in accordance because God is overlooking the procedure.[159] This gives credence to the observer effect—that the efficacy of belief is crucial to well-being (Lyon 2012, 40–41, 120–21, 241).

Toward the end of the interview the peyote doctor told a story about a Sioux who had recently visited asking what he could do to help his people. He answered his friend by advising him to be guided by religion, even if it meant reviving the Ghost Dance. "As long as it has something to do with God, that's the most important thing. Like Christians, if people believe in God, then they will find a cure." However, he also emphasized that he encourages his patients to follow the orders of their doctors, and to quit smoking and drinking, bad habits that exacerbate type 2 diabetes.[160]

As noted by William Lyon (2012, 279), the observer effect also applies to sorcery in that the victim of "witching" possesses something that has come into contact with bad medicine. This coincides with the Kiowa notion of good and bad medicine, that the powers to heal can be turned into the powers to harm others. Once while I was visiting Amos Aitson (1928–2003) he told me stories from the mid-1940s when he was a Golden Gloves and AAU (Amateur Athletic Union, now United States National Boxing Championships) boxer. In 1944–45 he was runner-up in the Oklahoma Golden Gloves bantamweight division as a representative of the Riverside Indian School boxing team, and on April 3, 1945, he won the 57th Annual National AAU Boxing Championship in Boston Garden. Sometime in 1945 he faced an opponent who apparently "witched" him, causing facial paralysis and dizzy spells that rendered him bedridden. An old Indian doctor came to his bedside, looked into his eyes, and proclaimed that he had been witched by his Seminole adversary. Touching a feather on Amos's forehead and then moving it downward between his eyes, he drew out the poison that had been placed there, claiming that he had sent it back against the perpetrator who had witched him. About a week later Amos faced the same guy in the ring and knocked him out after three or four punches. The unconscious man was then rushed to the hospital where he died four days later from head trauma. Amos maintained that the old adage "what comes around goes around" definitely applied to this situation.[161] Bad medicine has been used in other activities, including war dancing. John Tofpi once showed me a small red rock that he carried in his pocket and offered to take me to the source of this medicine, which helps individuals who dance in competitive powwows where prize money is awarded for different categories of dancing, including the Fancy Dance. He told me that rubbing the rock behind one's ear blocks the magic others send that causes feathers and other pieces of regalia to fall on the floor, which is a bad omen even in non-competitive dancing.[162]

Whether sorcery still occurs is a topic best left unexplored, though stories have been told about strange happenings linked to bad magic. For instance, an anonymous source disclosed some of the events linked to the violent takeover of the Kiowa Complex on the morning of January 7, 2004. At approximately 7:45 a.m., forty to fifty "political dissidents" stormed the tribal complex and seized control of the buildings. By 8:30 p.m., when the last tribal employees were evacuated, five of their co-workers had been taken to the city hospital to be treated for their injuries.[163] One witness to the events claimed she saw a snake "come out of" the body of one of the dissidents and leave the complex with him. She also saw the father's ghost of one of the dissidents as well as the spirits of people oppressed by the "takeover people."[164] Undoubtedly there are different opinions regarding the veracity of her observations, though most Kiowas are well aware that such events can still occur.

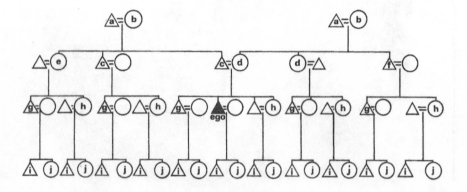

Fig. 1. Kiowa kinship terminology. Kin terms as used by a male ego for his consanguineal kin: (a) *k'o* (grandfather); (b) *t'a* (grandmother); (c) *toy* (father); (d) *ga* (mother); (e) *ʔam* (aunt); (f) *tsegi* (uncle); (g) *ba·bi* (brother); (h) *da* (sister); (i) *go·dl* (son); (j) *i·ta* (daughter). Drawing by Scott Kracht based on a table by Weston LaBarre in "Kiowa Fieldnotes, Summer 1935, Spiral Notebook #1." Courtesy of the Smithsonian Institution, National Anthropological Archives.

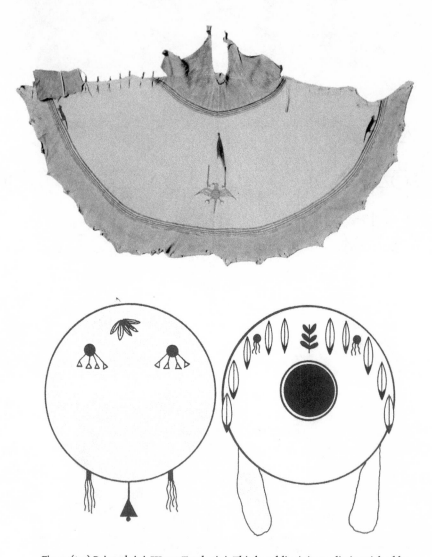

Fig. 2. (*top*) Painted tipi. Water Turtle tipi. This heraldic tipi was distinguished by the pictograph representing a turtle-eagle, a turtle shell with eagle wings, beak, and claws. Photograph of tipi model made for James Mooney, ca. 1897. Courtesy of the Smithsonian Institution, National Anthropological Archives (Smithsonian negative no. 1471 A8).

Fig. 3. (*bottom*) Pa-tsonhi Buffalo shield. *Left*: Outside shield cover; *right*: Pa-tsonhi Buffalo shield made for James Mooney in 1897. Drawing by Scott Kracht based on a sketch by Mooney, from "Kiowa Heraldry Notebook. Descriptions of Kiowa Tipis and Shields." Manuscript no. 2531, 1891–1905. Courtesy of the Smithsonian Institution, National Anthropological Archives.

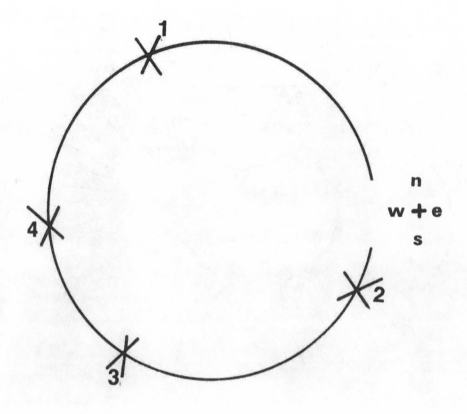

Fig. 4. Floor plan of a tipi, depicting the location of the three-pole tripod (1–3) and the fourth pole (4) used to push up the tipi cover. Medicine bundles were always attached to the fourth pole. Drawing by Scott Kracht based on a sketch by Donald Collier in "Notes on Kiowa Ethnography." Courtesy of the Smithsonian Institution, National Anthropological Archives.

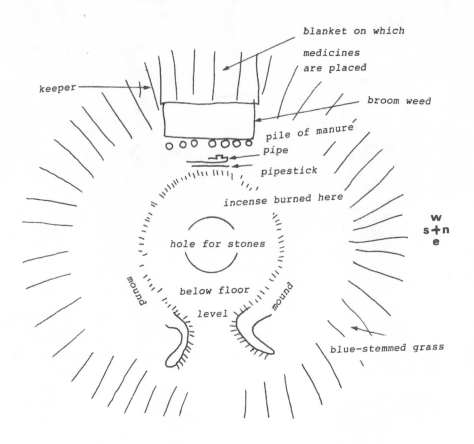

blanket on which
medicines
are placed

keeper

broom weed

pile of manure

pipe

pipestick

incense burned here

hole for stones

mound

below floor

level

mound

W
S ✛ N
E

blue-stemmed grass

Fig. 5. Floor plan of sweat lodge for the Ten Medicines. Note that the door opens to the east. Drawing by Scott Kracht based on a sketch by Donald Collier, "Notes on Kiowa Ethnography." Courtesy of the Smithsonian Institution, National Anthropological Archives.

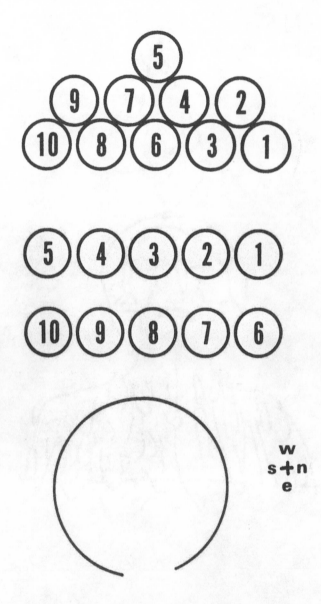

Fig. 6. (*top*) Stack of Ten Medicines in sweat lodge. Numbers refer to the order in which they were removed from the tipis. Drawing by Scott Kracht based on a sketch by Donald Collier in "Notes on Kiowa Ethnography." Courtesy of the Smithsonian Institution, National Anthropological Archives.

Fig. 7. (*bottom*) Arrangement of bundles outside sweat lodge. Drawing by Scott Kracht based on a sketch by Donald Collier in "Notes on Kiowa Ethnography." Courtesy of the Smithsonian Institution, National Anthropological Archives.

Fig. 8. Taime. Drawing by Scott Kracht based on a sketch by Weston
LaBarre from his fieldnotes, "Notes on Kiowa Ethnography." Courtesy
of the Smithsonian Institution, National Anthropological Archives.

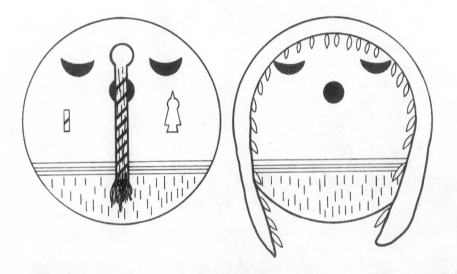

Fig. 9. Taime shield and cover. *Left*: Taime shield cover; *right*: Taime shield.
Note two black crescent moons and black sun on both. Also, the shield cover is
distinguished by a whistle on the left and crow skin on the right. "Rainbow colors"
constitute the stripes directly over the black "rain." A scalp wrapped in red cloth
is attached to the center of the shield cover. Drawing by Scott Kracht based on a
sketch by Weston LaBarre in "Kiowa Fieldnotes." Courtesy of the Smithsonian
Institution, National Anthropological Archives.

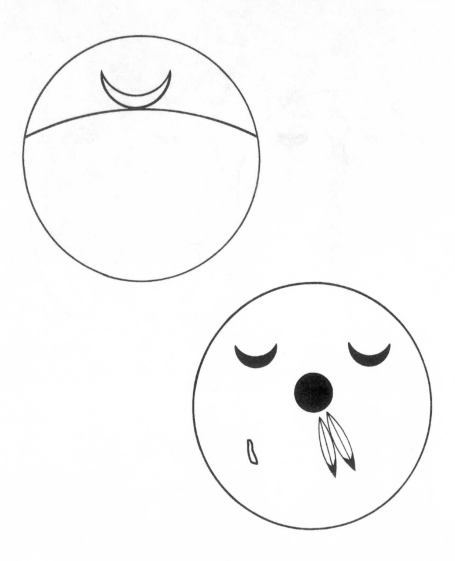

Fig. 10. (*top*) Koɔde shield. The lower part was painted dark red, the upper portion light red. A large white crescent moon adorned the top center— this lunar motif was also painted on the Koɔde dancer's sternum. Drawing by Scott Kracht based on a sketch by Weston LaBarre in "Kiowa Fieldnotes." Courtesy of the Smithsonian Institution, National Anthropological Archives.

Fig. 11. (*bottom*) Hotoyi shield. Note the solar and lunar motifs similar to those of the Taime shields. Also, the shield was adorned with a whistle on the left and two pendant eagle feathers. Drawing by Scott Kracht based on a sketch by Weston LaBarre in "Kiowa Fieldnotes." Courtesy of the Smithsonian Institution, National Anthropological Archives.

Fig. 12. Gudlgut dancer. Drawing by Scott Kracht based on a sketch by Andres Martinez for Rev. J. J. Methvin. From J. J. Methvin, *Andele: or, the Mexican-Kiowa Captive* (Louisville KY: Pentecostal Herald, 1899), facing p. 73.

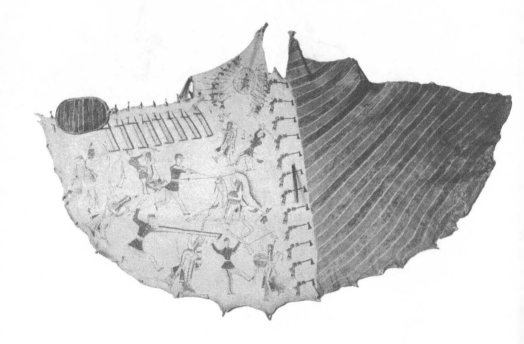

Fig. 13. Little Bluff's "battle tipi" designed for James Mooney by Ohettoint (Charley Buffalo), grandson of Little Bluff I. The darkest bars on the right represent successful war parties in which Little Bluff brought back enemy scalps without sustaining any losses. The twelve tomahawks in the center were painted by Heart Eater, who had the reputation of eating small pieces of slain enemies' hearts. The pictographs and eight horizontal lances near the entry flap allegedly were painted by the former Cheyenne owner. This tipi was always positioned so the half with the battle scenes faced north (Ewers 1978, 15). Photograph courtesy of the Smithsonian Institution, National Anthropological Archives (Smithsonian negative no. 1471 A1).

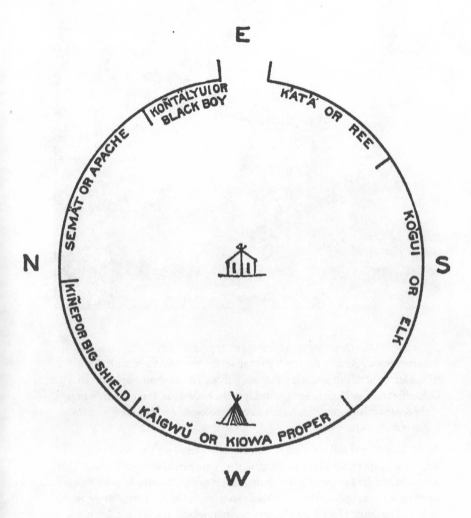

Fig. 14. James Mooney's reconstruction of the Kiowa Sun Dance circle, ca. 1867.
The five Kiowa Sun Dance "bands" were (1) K'at'a (Ree); (2) Ko'gúi (Elk); (3)
Gâ'igwû (Kiowa proper); (4) Kiñep (Big Shields); and (5) Koñtä'lyui (Black Boys, or
Sindi's [Saynday's] Children.) The Plains Apaches, called Semät (Thieves) by the
Kiowas, completed the circle. Drawing by Scott Kracht based on an illustration
by James Mooney. Image from James Mooney, "Calendar History of the Kiowa
Indians," in pt. 1 of *17th Annual Report of the Bureau of American Ethnology [for] 1895–
'96* (Washington DC: Smithsonian Institution Press, 1898), 229.

Fig. 15. (*above*) Sun Dance lodge, depicting center pole, circumference poles, and cross poles. Also note the brush piled about the base of the structure. The tribal identity of this structure is unknown, although it was photographed at an unspecified date by Hugh L. Scott, possibly in the early 1890s. Photograph courtesy of the Smithsonian Institution, National Anthropological Archives (Smithsonian negative no. 55,593).

Fig. 16. (*opposite top*) Make-buffalo ceremony. Men covered with buffalo robes supported by sticks. Wearing this costume, they were part of the "buffalo herd" that was lured into the Sun Dance lodge during the ceremony. Drawing by Scott Kracht based on sketches by Silver Horn for Hugh Scott. From Hugh L. Scott, "Notes on the Kado, or Sun Dance of the Kiowa," *American Anthropologist*, n.s. 13 (1911). *left*: p. 363; *right*, plate 24, facing p. 363.

Fig. 17. (*opposite bottom*) Sun Dance altar. Sacred objects placed in front of cedar-cottonwood screen at the western portion of the Sun Dance lodge: (a) sand censers; (b) dɔ, or chinaberry image; (c) buffalo skull; (d) Taime; (e) crow-feathered fan; (f) center pole of Sun Dance lodge; (g) stone at entryway of lodge, with a cloth underneath; (h) sand mound at base of center pole. Note that (a), (g), and (h) were constructed the morning following the processional and placement of the other sacred objects. Also, the light lines on the floor of the lodge represent the steps, or movement of the dancers. Drawing by Scott Kracht based on a sketch by Silver Horn for Hugh Scott. From Hugh L. Scott, "Notes on the Kado, or Sun Dance of the Kiowa," *American Anthropologist*, n.s. 13 (1911), plate 19, facing p. 351.

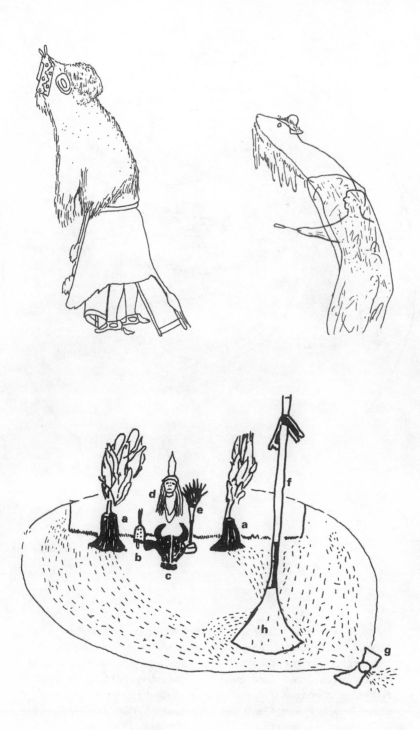

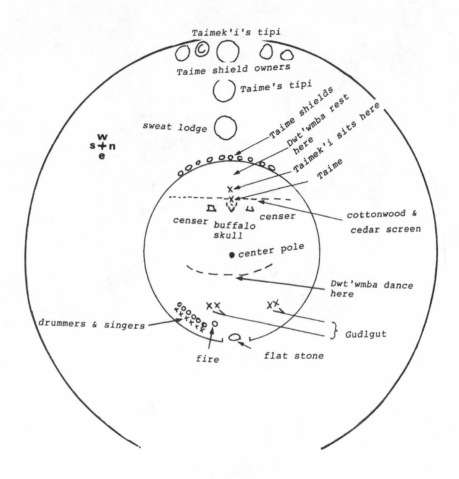

Fig. 18. Sun Dance lodge, floor plan. This diagram depicts the placement of the Taime shields, the altar, the fire, and the singers and drummers. Also note the location of the Demguk'os' (Taime keepers') tipis, located in the western portion of the sacred circle. Also shown is the rock at the entryway of the lodge as well as the dancing locations of the Dɔt'ɔmba and Gudlgut during the Sun Dance proper. Drawing by Scott Kracht based on a drawing by Donald Collier. Courtesy of the Smithsonian Institution, National Anthropological Archives.

4

Bundles, Shields, and Societies

During the zenith of the Plains horse and buffalo culture, men possessing *dɔdɔ* owned medicine bundles and shields representing powers that were activated by ritual and song. Since collective powers were more important than individual powers, the tribal medicine bundles were of utmost importance because they represented the spiritual well-being of the entire tribe. Properly caring for the bundles and performing the associated rituals was critical to maintaining spiritual integrity and harmony to ensure the perpetuation of Kiowa society. Both the Santa Fe fieldnotes and those of Marriott contain detailed information about the tribal bundles — the Ten Medicines and Taime.

All men carried war shields into combat, but men with war power kept dream shields emblazoned with symbols representing the *dɔdɔ* that gave them magical protection from enemy projectiles. As noted in the Santa Fe fieldnotes, most men owned distinctive war shields with individualized protective designs, though Marriott acknowledged the existence of a war shield society in which membership was based on owning Eagle shields. She also identified a religious shield society whose members owned Taime shields connected to Taime, the Sun Dance bundle. Whereas war shields and Eagle shields provided combat-related power and protection, the Taime shields were displayed with Taime during the Sun Dance, a ceremony of renewal.

Marriott noted that membership in the Buffalo, Eagle, and Taime shield societies was mutually exclusive, though men could also belong to one of the dancing — or warrior — societies. According to Marriott, the three shield societies "were always discussed in connection with one another and in connection with the dancing societies; the concept behind them was apparently considered as similar to, if not the same as, that behind the dancing societies."[1] All the societies played important roles during the Sun Dance. Marriott's fieldnotes and the Santa Fe fieldnotes provide extensive data on warrior societies, which compose the corpus of William C. Meadow's books (Meadows 1999, 2010), so coverage here will pertain only to society involvement in the Sun Dance.

The Tribal Medicines

Plains visionaries contacted by dream spirits inevitably learned divinatory rites that activated the powers connected to the medicine bundles they assembled. Whereas individually owned bundles were associated with success in hunting and warfare, healing, or overall well-being, owners of tribal bundles participated in sacred rituals beneficial to the entire community. Origin myths related how tribal bundles were alive with powers conferred by dream spirits, culture heroes, and other-than-human persons. Oral traditions also conveyed information regarding bundle taboos and proper performance of rituals, although changes caused by social or environmental circumstances often precipitated innovation, adaptation, and reinterpretation of bundles and rituals. Since tribal bundles represented group identity and history, releasing their powers through public rituals helped maintain group solidarity and provided hope for future fortune and well-being. Real power, however, resided within the visionaries, and the bundles, as the material representations of power, helped activate the dream powers of the bundle keepers (Harrod 1995, 23–24; Harrod 2000, 77–78; Harrod 2005, 95–97; Irwin 1994, 221–22, 213).

In indigenous Kiowa society, eleven *ondedɔ* men owned the principal tribal medicines: the Ten Medicines and Taime, the Sun Dance bundle. Assisted by their families, the keepers were responsible for the well-being of these sacred bundles. LaBarre called the owners "priests," but White Fox, a Ten Medicines keeper, said the keepers were medicine men different from curers because they did not employ "technology," or healing techniques, when called upon. Instead, they evoked spiritual assistance to help sick people and often assisted curers working on severe cases. The Ten Medicines or Split Boy bundle keepers often assembled to pray for the welfare of the entire tribe and, when solicited, assisted in conflict resolution. White Fox identified the Taime keeper as the "high priest" of the Sun Dance.[2] Through sacred rites, the eleven medicine men provided spiritual intercession to help maintain spiritual and social stability within Kiowa society.

The Ten Medicines: Bundles and Keepers
THE BUNDLES

Two different origin myths describe the Ten Medicines, often called the *talyi-da-i* (Boy Medicine) or *zaide-thali* (Split Boy) bundles. The earlier version, collected by Mooney, specifies that Sun-Boy, one of the Split Boys fathered by Sun, walked into a lake and transformed himself into the ten bundles (Mooney 1898, 239). The late Kiowa historian Linn Pauahty identified Spear Lake, Wyoming, as the location of the myth (Boyd 1981, 8, 134n). In 1935, Jimmy Quoetone and Moth Woman separately told the story about the giant bear chasing seven sisters up a huge boulder—Devil's Tower—that grew into the sky, transforming the siblings into the Pleiades constellation.[3] Moth Woman stated that shortly afterward, Kiowa hunters killed a huge bear and placed a claw inside each Ten Medicines bundle.[4] This story associates Bear power with the bundles, which partially explains why Kiowas respect bears despite their ambivalence toward them.

Mooney (1898, 239) made only a brief reference to the Ten Medicines, but the 1935 fieldnotes contain ample, albeit sometimes conflicting information about the bundles, perhaps due to confusion created by the breakdown of inheritance patterns. Collier and LaBarre collected the most information about the bundles. Collier worked primarily with Jimmy Quoetone and to a lesser extent with Red Dress, Mary Buffalo, Mrs. Hokeah, and Frizzlehead. Additional information was obtained from Mrs. Big Bow, Hunting Horse, Mausepe, and White Buffalo. Weston LaBarre learned about the bundles mostly from interviews with White Fox, using Ned Brace as interpreter, and Mary Buffalo, with Bert Geikauma translating. Some information was also provided by Jimmy Quoetone and Pitma. Jane Richardson obtained extensive information from Moth Woman, and Alexander Lesser even gathered data from conversations with Heap O' Bears. Marriott, though, had little luck learning about the Ten Medicines, probably because the two keepers she worked with, Tsoodle and Frank Given, refused to talk about the bundles. In her fieldnotes, Marriott describes her frustrations working with them in reference to her questions about the connections between the Bear Women Society and the Ten Medicines:

> (Tsoodle was probably evading, here. There is evidently some rela-
> tionship between the bear women and the gods, and he is a priest.
> He always avoids discussion of bears, and any mention of the gods
> is impossible. His extreme conservatism is making him even more
> rampant than F.G., who would I believe, discuss such matters freely,
> were he not afraid of T.)[5]

Although there are brief references to the Ten Medicines in Marriott's fieldnotes and publications, it is apparent that she did not obtain detailed information about them; that she called them "gods" and "grandmothers" reflects her lack of knowledge since the two Ten Medicines keepers she knew declined to discuss them with her. Likewise, Frank Given and Tsoodle did not provide any information about them to the Santa Fe field party students.

In the manuscript "Kiowa Indian Snapshots," LaBarre provides background information about three Ten Medicines keepers: Adalpaguit-ain (White Coyote, or White Fox), head keeper of the bundles, whom he allegorically referred to as the "Kiowa chief pontiff" of the "priestly Supreme Court" of Ten Medicine keepers; Tsoodle (Packing Stone), or Henry Tsoodle, also called Little Henry; and Charley Ohettoint (Buffalo).[6] As related by Mary Buffalo, her husband Charley died in 1934, but she could not pass the bundle to her only son, Homer, who was too young to care for it. Hence Jim Waldo (K'okoitadl, or Lean Elk) "bought" the bun-dle and gave it to his older brother Silver Horn to care for. Beforehand, the bundle had belonged to Poor Buffalo, who passed it to his son Doke Buffalo, who gave it to Ohettoint (see also Greene 2001, 31–33, 44, 136).[7] Although Tsoodle did not talk about the bundles, White Fox and Mary Buffalo shared firsthand knowledge about them with LaBarre.

Mary Buffalo told LaBarre that the word for the collective bundles was *tæ·dló'·kɔ*, and *tæ·dli* the word for a single bundle.[8] These words proba-bly derive from *zaide thali* (Half Boys) and correspond with Mooney's *tä' lyí-dá-i* (Boy Medicine) and the Split Boy myth (Mooney 1898, 239).

Red Dress called the ten keepers *tadl doga* (hole, or fire + to hold, or have possession), whereas Mrs. Big Bow called them the *doi doga* (medicine + to hold, or take care of). Mrs. Big Bow also said that the collective name for the bundles was ɔdlbeoi (lots of hair, or scalps), since enemy scalps were commonly offered to the bundles.[9] LaBarre found descriptions of the bundle contents somewhat ambiguous, especially since the keepers never exposed the bundles or looked at the contents, and they even averted their gaze when the bundles were opened during renewal meetings. Even though she never looked into the Poor Buffalo bundle, Mary Buffalo described its contents to LaBarre, who disbelieved the "official" ignorance about the bundles. According to Mary, older men probably knew "the contents of the outer bundle," but "perhaps only ten or twelve people know the other contents." Mary was not afraid of the bundles anymore due to being a Christian, though she said that talking about them gave her heart "shakes." Although Mary was "an unusually willing informant," she spoke about the Ten Medicines in "an almost inaudible whisper" because she was afraid that Homer would hear her talk about them. LaBarre noted that White Fox never discussed "the physical nature of the medicine [because] he shut up tight before that point was reached."[10]

Mary Buffalo identified the "central object" in the bundle as *gonk'o*, a small rock image shaped like a man's bust, swaddled "in a soft-tanned speckled fawnskin" wrapped in buckskin. This double-wrapped inner bundle measuring twelve to eighteen inches in length rested in a larger buffalo hide that allowed ample room for other individually wrapped medicines and offerings: "Indian perfume," red paint, cedar, buffalo chips, blends of old and new tobacco, a straight black pipe wrapped in a black handkerchief, human teeth, supposedly of the former keepers, "naval strings offered by women," and human scalps. Mary Buffalo believed that some bear part—a claw, ear, or piece of hide—was located in one of the little bags stuffed into the medicine bundle. Attached to this particular unpainted bundle were twelve Indian and four blonde scalps and a white gorget beaded with dark blue beads.[11] Jimmy Quoetone said each bundle was approximately one-half to two feet square and weighed between thirty and fifty pounds.[12] Since human-shaped figurines were the principal source of *dɔdɔ* for the Ten Medicines, Mary Buffalo and

White Fox said the bundles were treated like people and were spoken to because the image "understands when you talk to it," according to Mary. As living entities, if the images residing in the bundles perceived danger, they made it impossible for someone to lift them and carry them away.[13]

Housing and transporting the Ten Medicines required special protocol. White Fox pointed out that only the keepers' wives were authorized to touch or move the bundles and erect the tipis that protected them.[14] Red Dress told Collier that a typical Ten Medicines tipi frame consisted of twenty-two poles and two smoke flap poles, totaling twenty-four poles. Those erecting the typical Kiowa tipi began by lashing together three poles at one end, spreading out the untied ends to form a tripod base, and then resting the remaining poles against the frame. Ten Medicines tipis required a fourth pole at the west side called *dopagɔ* (tipi tied), referring to its use for pushing the tipi cover over the frame. Once the tipi was pitched, the medicine bundle was tied to the *dopagɔ* pole four feet from the ground (fig. 4, this volume). Beneath the bundle rested the keeper's smoking accessories: a straight pipe, tobacco pouch, and a flint.[15] Moth Woman and Red Dress both said that when women were moving camp, the bundle was carefully tied to the back of a saddle so that it hung over the left side.[16] Mary Buffalo added that when establishing a new village, the bundle owners' wives pitched their tipis some distance from the other lodges, preventing the disturbance of the medicines by the daily activities of camp life, especially crying infants or playing children. Importantly, the ten tipis, as sacred dwelling places of the bundles, were sanctuaries for refugees because any act of violence around a bundle would incur supernatural repercussions (see Richardson 1940, 11).[17]

Moth Woman explained that wives helped care for their husbands' bundles, and that in polygynous marriages, the senior wife was the primary assistant. A Ten Medicines keeper had *dɔdɔ* in his prayers, even if he was "away from his particular bag," and his wife, as handler, also had *dɔdɔ* "in her words." Noting that Ten Medicines keepers were ambivalent toward the powers of the bundles, and feared opening them to handle the contents, she said they circumvented harming themselves by summoning captives to open them in special cases when the contents needed inspection. Captives, however, did not inherit the bundles.[18] Besides wives and adopted captives, Moth Woman said, others were forbidden to touch a

Ten Medicines bundle unless the village was under attack; in such circumstances, anyone was eligible to enter the owner's tipi to rescue the bundle. Jimmy Quoetone stated that if a bundle keeper were compelled to leave camp for any reason, and if his wife and assistant were not available, then he was required to compensate a trusted individual to guard the bundle during his absence. Before his passing, Charley Buffalo told Mary that while he was in town, she was authorized to remove his bundle to a safe area if the house caught on fire.[19]

THE KEEPERS AND THEIR ROLE IN KIOWA SOCIETY

According to Mary Buffalo, Ten Medicines keepers were "supposed to be very peaceable, pleasant, non-truculent, obliging, [and] patient in their behavior" toward other Kiowas. No one could strike or hit them because "they like everybody." Bundle keepers were expected to have a peaceable demeanor, and Moth Woman noted that even great warriors like Sitting Bear were expected to be soft-spoken during war expeditions.[20] Moth Woman, Jimmy Quoetone, White Fox, Heap O' Bears, and Mary Buffalo described taboos followed by the keepers. Foremost was the avoidance of bear meat, hides, and any other bear part, justifiable on the grounds that the owners "received their power from the bear, and therefore [were] afraid of it," according to Heap O' Bears. Eating the source of one's power was strictly prohibited, especially one that protected the entire tribe. Bad fortune would beset a village if a keeper's bundle got wet, and for unknown reasons, the keepers were also ambivalent toward skunks. Those in the company of the keepers also had to follow certain rules of etiquette, such as not standing too close to them, and, even more important, not passing between a keeper and the fire when in the keeper's tipi. Throwing sticks at any tipis inhabited by the keepers was also taboo. Another restriction required that meat cooked for a keeper in a metal pot be stirred only with a buffalo rib. Other taboos or special rules unique to each bundle were connected to the personal power of each owner.[21]

Ideally, a Ten Medicines keeper possessed his bundle until naming a successor on his deathbed, according to Moth Woman, who said that in most cases the eldest son inherited the bundle, but if the keeper did not have a son, it was passed to a brother. In the absence of a close relative, or in the event of sudden death without naming a recipient, the remaining keepers convened to discuss an heir. Non-kin could be chosen based on their character and disposition toward the bundles; for instance, a man might be chosen if he periodically offered gifts of horses, blankets, and enemy scalps to the bundles contingent on successful war expeditions, or erected sweat lodges for one or more of the bundles. Upon the death of a keeper, his widow, sister, or daughter cared for the bundle until another relative assumed responsibility for it, circumventing the need for the other keepers to make a selection.[22] Moth Woman noted that the new keeper did not have to possess dɔdɔ, although it was possible he could obtain personal power through a vision quest, or that the collective dɔdɔ residing in the bundles could be transmitted to him through a transferal sweat bath. Praying to the collective dɔdɔ of the bundles during the ceremony put power in their prayers to empower the heir.[23]

Heap O' Bears related to Lesser how Ten Medicines keepers played two important roles in Kiowa society: as holy men, they prayed for the welfare and well-being of the Kiowas, and as civil servants, they settled disputes within the villages. Conflict resolution was necessary due to enmities arising from domestic problems, infidelity, and inheritance disputes. To thwart further trouble when such cases arose, relatives from the offending party dispatched a gift-bearing messenger to retrieve the nearest keeper. Leading several horses or bearing gifts, the suppliant approached the medicine tipi, pleading to the Ten Medicines keeper for assistance: "Help us. So and so has done thus and so and so is in trouble. We want you to help us. We want you to go with us and give the pipe to so-and-so."[24] According to Heap O' Bears, Jimmy Quoetone, Moth Woman, and Mary Buffalo, the plea signified the urgency of the matter, impelling the bundle owner to fill his pipe and depart with the conciliatory gifts or horses for the offended party. Keepers could not refuse the request, nor could the two factions once the keeper arrived and lit the pipe; both parties were obliged to accept the proffered pipe, smoke together, and agree on a peaceful solution to their dispute. Thus, the keepers of the Ten Medicines helped maintain social cohesion within Kiowa society by invoking the spirit world to witness agreements made by mortals. Violating agreements could evoke the wrath of the spirits.[25]

Mary Buffalo, Mrs. Hokeah, and Jimmy Quoetone described how the bundles functioned within Kiowa society. Every day the Ten Medicines keepers prayed for the protection and good health of the Kiowa peo-ple. Thunder in the fall and especially in the spring was the best time to pray to the medicines. After Thunder made its appearance, each keeper painted himself red, donned his gorget, filled his pipe, and prayed to the bundles. During the winter encampments, people brought offerings to the bundles to receive blessings or recover from illness. The gifts—scalps, dried pieces of meat, sticks representing horses, calico, tobacco, blankets, beads, buckskin, or black handkerchiefs—were brought into a bundle tipi and placed on top of the bundle while reciting a prayer. One of the most popular gifts was ten balls of dried meat in a rag bag. Gifts presented to one bundle symbolized a collective offering to all ten. For those seeking recovery from illness, the outer bundle was opened so the odor of the contents could be inhaled. Gifts remained on the bundles overnight and then were kept or given away, and the meat was offered to children to eat for health and good fortune.[26]

Besides transferal rites, White Fox related that sweat lodge ceremonies were also vowed to one or more Ten Medicines in cases of serious illness. For instance, a father seeking the healing powers of the bundles built a sweat lodge outside the community and then hobbled a horse near the newly constructed lodge. After proceeding to the tipi of a selected Ten Medicines keeper, he entered without saying a word, silently removed the medicine bag from its resting position, and carried it back to the sweat lodge. Then, after circling clockwise four times and entering, he placed the bundle on the west side of the sweat lodge. Next, heated rocks were brought inside and placed into the central pit. As this transpired, the Ten Medicines keeper understood what was happening and followed the man to the sweat lodge. When everything was prepared, the keeper took the sick child inside, opened the bundle, and "thrust the child's head into the mouth of the medicine bag," praying for her or his health and longevity. A sweat lodge ritual was also conducted shortly after the birth of a child or if a couple kept losing newborn children. When such ceremonies were held, anyone desiring a blessing could enter and pray.[27] Mary Buffalo told LaBarre that once when she was sick her parents took her into the sweat lodge with one of the medicines, which was hung on the west side and covered with a blanket. Rubbing oneself with the blan-ket utilized its curing power transferred from the bundle.[28] According to White Fox and White Buffalo, extreme medical emergencies or epidemics often necessitated bringing several of the Ten Medicines into the sweat lodge at the same time. Since prayers to one bundle represented all ten, all the keepers did not have to be present, although four keepers were considered a quorum when the well-being of the entire tribe was at stake. Sweat lodge ceremonies sometimes were held solely for the benefit of the bundles, which were revered as other-than-human persons. Sweating with the bundles was believed to confer power ensuring good fortune and overall well-being.[29]

Mrs. Hokeah, Jimmy Quoetone, Moth Woman, and Max Frizzlehead said that Ten Medicines keepers attempted to participate in a communal sweat lodge when all ten bundles were brought together every two to three years for a sweat lodge meeting second in importance only to the Sun Dance. During mid-June when the Sun Dance was held was the best time for these gatherings, since this was the only time when all the keepers were readily available. Pledges to sweat all ten bundles were made well in advance of a forthcoming Sun Dance and occurred when close relatives were critically ill or when war parties were on the brink of annihilation. Any man could pledge a sweat lodge when facing adversity with the expectation that he had to construct the sweat lodge without any help within a day's time, and that his relatives would help carry the bundles inside.[30]

Jimmy Quoetone provided detailed information about sweat lodge ceremonies for the Ten Medicines. One time during his youth—probably during the late 1870s or early 1880s before his conversion to Christianity—Quoetone went out to the open prairie with a needle and knife before sunrise, sliced four pieces of skin from his chest, held each one up to the rising sun, and offered a prayer: "Here is my flesh; I offer it to you that I may live to old age. I want to live the right life and be prosperous." After placing the skin on an altar of dried cow dung, he went home. Contemplating his sacrifice, Quoetone decided that a less painful method of obtaining a blessing was through the Ten Medicines, so he vowed to hold a sweat lodge ceremony for the *zaidethali* owned by Ahiädlso'hi, whose two grandsons were her apprentices. Following the sweat lodge ceremony Quoetone had "great faith" in the Ten Medicines and dedicated numerous sweat lodge ceremonies for them, especially the *kokɔigudl* (Red Elk) bundle. On one occasion he sponsored a sweat lodge for all ten bundles when they came together before the Sun Dance.[31]

Quoetone provided detailed descriptions of the sweat lodge ceremony for all the Ten Medicines. Additional information pertaining to other sweat lodges was provided by White Fox, Frizzlehead, Red Dress, and Moth Woman. The particular meeting recollected by Quoetone was officiated by Pɔtɔdlte and included bundle keepers Tomɔ·te, Tokɔigudl, and Pɔta·te and apprentices Aiseoi and Koikonhodlte. Willow-framed sweat lodges were built for the occasion. Smaller sweat lodges for single bundles were constructed from at least fifteen poles, whereas a lodge for all ten bundles required fifty poles, or even one hundred with two poles to a hole. Willow bark binding secured the frame, but Quoetone did not mention the materials used for the cover. It is assumed that buffalo robes were preferred, though bison scarcity and the availability of trade goods would necessitate the use of blankets and canvas by the 1860s. Inside the sweat lodge, the perimeter seating area for the keepers was lined with a blue-stemmed grass, and a blanket laid on the west side served as the resting place for the bundles. Earth scooped from the center of the lodge created a pit to accommodate hot rocks, and around its perimeter, the floor was leveled out so that it was lower than the sweat lodge floor. The excavated soil was formed into a low circular mound encompassing the central area, opening to the east with the edges of the mouth flanged out at ninety-degree angles. Immediately west of the circular mound, seven piles of buffalo chips were lined up in a north-south axis, then strips of broom weed, stems oriented east-west, were laid between the chips and the blanket where the medicines were placed (fig. 5, this volume). When the sweat lodge was finished, the ceremony was ready to begin.[32]

Quoetone noted that at this juncture, rocks were placed in a fire built outside the lodge, and then the pledger and three or four close relatives visited the tipis of the ten keepers to procure their bundles. Upon arriving at the first tipi, the pledger entered, made a clockwise circuit, carefully unfastened the bundle from its westerly resting place and brought it outside, and then hung it on the back of an assistant, a procedure performed until all of the Ten Medicines were secured and placed over the backs and under the arms of the pledger and his helpers. Although the keepers had not been informed of the pledger's intentions, people in the coalesced village fully understood what was happening as they gathered to watch the entourage. Upon leaving the tipi of the tenth keeper, the bundle-bearing party approached the sweat lodge located southeast of the village. Lining up at the door, each person feigned entering the lodge and then walked clockwise around it four times. Once the fourth circuit was completed, they lined up at the door again and waited outside while the pledger carried the first bundle into the lodge. In succession, the process was repeated for each bundle until they rested in a stack on the blanket with the mouths facing west (fig. 6, this volume). Frizzlehead added that upon completing the bundle stacking rite, the pledger took his own pipe, filled it with tobacco, and then placed it on the mound between the stacks of buffalo chips and the central pit, with the stem pointing south. While the final preparations transpired, the bundle keepers began assembling outside the sweat lodge. The first keeper to arrive took charge of the proceedings, unless he declined and someone else went into the lodge first.[33]

The sweat lodge ceremony described by Quoetone officially began when the leader feigned entering the lodge but circuited it clockwise before entering and moving along the south side and taking a seat south of the bundle pile. At the leader's request, a buffalo chip coal from the outside fire was brought in by the pledger with a forked stick and placed directly between the pipe and the central pit. The pledger left the tipi and the leader procured some cedar incense from his bundle, placing it on the coals after three feigns and a prayer. Passing his hands through the fragrant smoke and rubbing them through his hair and over his body, the leader prayed that he would receive blessings of prosperity and longevity. All ten bundles were manipulated by the leader's smoke-filled hands to receive the same blessing. Afterward, the pledger came back into the sweat lodge, blessed himself in the same manner, and then exited.[34]

Following the same ritual motions, the remaining keepers filed in and took their seats at the south and north sides of the sweat lodge. Those entering the sweat lodge and sitting at the south side followed the same ingress and clockwise circuit of the leader, already seated on the southwest side with the bundles. Protocol, however, would be breeched if someone passed between him and the central pit, compelling those seated on the north side to feign entering clockwise, but instead turning counterclockwise to approach their seats. Non-active participants and apprentices were required to sit on the north side. Once everyone was seated, the pledger reentered the sweat lodge brandishing a buffalo chip coal with a forked stick, and then sat down south of the sweat lodge entrance, where he waited for the leader to bring him the pipe. Holding the pipe so the pledger could light the tobacco/sumac mixture, the leader puffed and blew smoke into his hands and then blessed the fire pit, broom grass/chip altar, and the bundles by holding his hands over them. Next, he handed the pipe, stem first, to the pledger and returned to his position near the bundles. Accepting the pipe, the pledger puffed and blew smoke toward the bundles to bless them and everything in the sweat lodge, prayed for longevity and good fortune, and explained the reason for the ceremony. After finishing his prayer, the pipe was returned to the leader, who smoked again and passed the pipe around the sweat lodge in a clockwise circuit until the bowl was spent. Receiving the spent pipe, the leader emptied the ashes in the incense residue and then placed the pipe on the medicine bundles, with the stem propped up against the back pole of the lodge. Everything was ready for bringing in the heated rocks for the sweat.[35]

When the pledger exited the sweat lodge to obtain the hot rocks, the leader took his vacated space by the entrance. Balanced on a sturdy forked stick, the hot rocks were brought to the entryway, passed into the lodge after three feigns, and stacked in the central pit. A bucket of water and a "grass beating bundle" were passed in, and then the pledger secured the entryway with the leader's blanket and remained outside.[36] Striking a rhythm on the bucket, the leader prayed for everybody's good health and longevity and then poured water on the hot rocks four or seven times, filling the sweat lodge with steam. He then prayed to the powers of the universe, to the Ten Medicines, to Sun, to the "gods of the sky, wind, clouds, rocks, treetops, underwater" powers, and to practically every conceivable source of dɔdɔ. While praying, the leader whipped himself with the grass bundle to produce more sweat, and when finished, he requested the pledger to raise the door cover. In total, four cycles of sweating and praying were interspersed with short breaks when the door flap was lifted, higher at the end of each session. After the fourth and final sweat, it was lifted all the way back so the keepers could file out, followed by the leader, who walked around to the west side of the sweat lodge and sat down, facing west. Once the leader was situated, the pledger went back into the sweat lodge and in ten trips carried the sacred medicine bundles under his left arm and placed them in two parallel rows on a blanket situated between the leader and the sweat lodge (fig. 7, this volume). Each keeper then gathered his bundle and headed home, the leader once again going last. The sweat lodge ceremony was over.[37]

Repair meetings were periodically called, whenever one of the bundles needed mending, although not all the keepers needed to attend. Moth Woman and Pitma described repair meetings to Richardson and LaBarre. The individual whose Ten Medicines bundle needed repairs erected a special tipi and then requested a captive woman or her daughter to mend the bundle. Meetings began when the keeper entered the tipi and tied his bundle to the west pole, after which the other participants entered, sat down and covered their heads with buffalo robes so they would not inadvertently see the bundle's contents. Even the woman mending the bundle had her head covered. The leader of the ceremony then untied the lacing that fastened the bundle, and the woman, who possessed a special buffalo hide and deer sinew repair kit, patched the bundle. Upon finishing her task, the captive woman handed the bundle back to the leader, who uncovered his head to fasten it to the west pole. The woman was presented with gifts for her work, and the bundle keepers left.[38]

The Ten Medicines in the 1930s

Although Collier and LaBarre were primarily interested in collecting memory histories about the role of the Ten Medicines in the prereservation and reservation eras, they also garnered valuable information about their existence in the 1930s. White Fox told LaBarre that notable changes involved father-to-son inheritance patterns. Ideally, a bundle keeper appointed his oldest son heir before dying or passed the bundle to a younger brother, or alternatively the eldest daughter could keep a bundle until a younger brother was old enough to care for it.[39] However, as noted by Jimmy Quoetone and Moth Woman, some bundle keepers had died without sons since the 1920s, or their sons were too young, or perhaps they were single, which was problematical since it was the responsibility of each keeper's wife to help care for the bundle and to erect the tipi where it resided.[40] According to Moth Woman and Red Dress, if a keeper died suddenly without naming an heir, the remaining nine keepers were supposed to select the next heir after consulting with his family.[41] Despite rapid culture change and the breakdown of inheritance, LaBarre, Collier, and Richardson pieced together some information about the keepers in 1935, as related by White Fox, Lone Bear, Red Dress, and Moth Woman.

The ten keepers included (1) White Fox; (2) Pakosa (Buffalo-Cut-Up); (3) Tsoodle; (4) Frank Given; (5) Silver Horn; (6) Togyamot (Get Off In Front [of the enemy forces, in battle]); (7) P'asot'a'de (White Thunder); (8) Goɛtɛ (White); (9) Kohat'ægyɛ (Pretty Crow, also known as Big Joe); and (10) Old Lady Haumpo.[42] White Fox inherited his Ten Medicines bundle from his father, Afraid of Bears, leader of the Ghost Dance between 1894 and 1916. LaBarre identified White Fox as "the Kiowa chief pontiff, head of the Ten Medicines keepers," a new development since the horse and buffalo days. Pakosa, recognized as White Fox's assistant, was becoming too feeble to care for the bundle he had possessed for fifteen years. Tsoodle inherited the bundle of his father, Red Tipi, through his older brothers Koboho (Black Bonnet) and Sɛ'ki (Bear Shield). Frank Given (also spelled Givens or Gibbon), or Set'angya (Sitting Bear III), was the oldest son of the famed Sitting Bear killed in 1871. White Fox identified Given, who took his father's name later in life, as the only "medicine man proper in the whole society, that is, a medicine man who cures individual patients of diseases." K'okoitadl (Lean Elk), also known as Jim Waldo, owned a bundle that was cared for by his older brother Hongu (Silver Horn). Previously the bundle had been owned by their maternal uncle Patadlkyapta (Poor Buffalo), who passed it to his son Doke Buffalo, who then sold it to Ohettoint, or Charley Buffalo — Mary's husband — twin of White Buffalo and older brother of Lean Elk and Silver Horn (Greene 2001, 31–33). Wilbur Nye (1962, 51) claimed that Silver Horn, "a medicine man who did not go out of favor even in modern times," and Frank Given allowed him to see the bundles that they "guarded." That Given allowed Nye to see his bundle demonstrates the rapport that Lt. Nye developed with many Kiowas and Comanches during his tenure at Fort Sill.[43]

When T'ebodal died, his two sons were too young to care for his bundle, so it was cared for by his cousin Togyamot until the sons were old enough to care for it. Togyamot still had the bundle in 1935. The bundle kept by White Thunder had passed down from his maternal uncle Kyæɔgoma, who had obtained it from his brothers P'asot'a (White Thunder) and Zɛgæa (White Arrow). White inherited his bundle from his father, Mɔm'ɛ, the third son of Bayiîɛte, whose older sons Odltoɛdl and Butoɛdl had owned the bundle beforehand. Pretty Crow had recently died without any siblings or children. Richardson learned that the bundle, inherited from Big Joe's maternal uncle Guibɔde, was "in the care of Kɔsä [Pakosa] pending [a] decision" by the remaining bundle keepers. Hopode (Hook), also called Old Man Haumpo, died in 1922 (see Boyd 1983, 50). Since his daughter was very young, the other keepers allowed his widow, Old Lady Haumpo, to keep her husband's bundle, which was still in her possession in 1935. Old Man Haumpo had obtained the bundle from his maternal uncle Yiepa.[44]

Big Joe's recent death reflected the increased complexity of inheritance patterns during the postallotment era. Collier and Lesser attended a special meeting of the remaining nine keepers on June 27, which was held to decide the fate of Big Joe's bundle and discuss the transfer of the Pakosa bundle to White Horse, his nephew. Neither issue was resolved.[45] Adding to the confusion, Lone Bear and Moth Woman identified A·poma, a woman, as owner of two or three of the bundles; Nye (1962, 51) also identified her as a bundle keeper. In addition, they learned that T'enésɔhe' (Blue Bird, or Blue Jay) had received a Ten Medicines bundle from a woman named Aise'oi "because he was such a strong believer in it" according to Moth Woman.[46] Making matters more complicated, Gus Palmer Jr. (2003, 129n) revealed that one of the bundles "was destroyed in a fire in the 1930s," probably after completion of the Santa Fe field school. Though inheritance was becoming problematic, White Fox noted that bundle owners still met three to four times a year to conduct sweat lodge rituals and to pray for the well-being of the tribe, and that people continued to bring gifts to the bundles and offer prayers to them during austere times.[47]

The Taime and Taime Keeper
ORIGIN AND HISTORY OF THE TAIME

Taime, the sacred Sun Dance bundle, was the focal point of traditional Kiowa religious beliefs, for this sacred icon unified the Kiowa tribe during the Sun Dance. Mary Buffalo, a descendant of the Taime keeper lineage, told LaBarre that Taime symbolized Sun and was "etymologized" (LaBarre's term) as "lonesome" because it became lonely for the Kiowas when the bands dispersed at the conclusion of the Sun Dance.[48] Hugh L. Scott researched the Sun Dance shortly after its demise in 1890 and described "Taime [as] the mediator between the people and the Sun power" during the ceremony. Its presence at the western portion of the Sun Dance lodge provided "concreteness to their vague ideas of the Sun power" and was reputed to bestow them with good fortune (Scott 1911, 351). Of all the sacrosanct objects ever known to the Kiowas, the Taime Sun Dance image has the most unique history. Mary Buffalo, granddaughter of renowned Taime keeper Ansóte, or Onsokyapta (Long Foot), shared information about Taime with LaBarre, but Heap O' Bears III, the paternal nephew of Onsokyapta, provided LaBarre with the most data. Others who added their knowledge included White Buffalo, Mrs. Big Bow, Mrs. Hokeah, and George Hunt. Marriott's fieldnotes do not provide details about Taime other than its role in the Sun Dance. The origins of Taime date back to the late seventeenth century as the Kiowas migrated southeastward from the headwaters of the Yellowstone River, encountered the Crows, and formed an alliance (Mooney 1898, 153, 155). Robert Lowie suggested that the Siouan-speaking Crows probably introduced the Sun Dance to the Kiowas, noting that the Taime image is derived from the various Sun Dance dolls that the Crow priests attached to a cedar tree in the west side of their Sun Dance lodge (Lowie 1935, 298; Voget 1984, 107). According to the Taime origin story collected by Mooney, a poor Arapaho attending a Crow Sun Dance many years ago became awestruck by one of the Sun Dance dolls and danced long and hard in front of the effigy, never diverting his eyes from it with the aspiration that he would achieve personal power and wealth. A Crow priest associated with the image took pity upon the man, and after the completion of the Sun Dance, he presented the doll bundle to the Arapaho, who afterward participated in several successful raids through which he accumulated numerous horses. Thankful for his new status, the Arapaho sacrificed many horses to the image, being blessed in return by amassing the largest horse herd among the Crows. One day, determined to rejoin his people and share his recent wealth, the Arapaho departed for home. Meanwhile, several Crow warriors, jealous of his new fortune, discovered that he was leaving with the bundle, so they followed him and found an opportune time to steal the image from his tipi while he slept. Undaunted, the Arapaho fashioned some duplicates modeled after the lost doll and took them to his people. He eventually married a Kiowa woman and lived with her relatives, introducing the Taime image to the Kiowas (Mooney 1898, 240).

More recent renditions of the Taime origin myth are adaptations of Mooney's account (Boyd 1981, 31–32; Mikkanen 1987; Spier 1921a, 437–38), but a variant collected by Scott in the 1890s suggests that the Arapaho man had already been living with the Kiowas before traveling north with some Kiowas to visit the Crows (Scott 1911, 368). In 1935, George Hunt told LaBarre that the main character was Kiowa, not Arapaho, because the Kiowas did not make peace with the Cheyennes and Arapahos until 1840, although later in the same interview he contradicted himself and identified an Arapaho named Gienaha as the first Taime owner.[49] Regardless of the discrepancy, the Crows greatly influenced the creation of Taime and the Kiowa Sun Dance.

Little is known of the Taime image prior to the winter of 1832–33, the earliest recorded date in the Kiowa calendars, albeit 1830 is the approximate year that Onsokyapta became *taimek'i* (Taime man), or Taime keeper, a position held until his death in the winter of 1870–71, as remembered by Mary Buffalo, who was about twenty-three years old at the time of his passing.[50] His successor, Dó-héñte (No Moccasins), died in the fall of 1875 after the onset of the reservation period. He was succeeded by Set-dayá-iti (Many-Bears, or Heap O' Bears), the uncle of Heap O' Bears II killed by Utes in the summer of 1868, and the cousin (brother) of Taíméte, who inherited the bundle when Set-dayá-iti died in the summer of 1883. Émáa acquired the bundle when Taíméte died in 1894. Mooney claimed she was the ninth keeper of the bundle, which he estimated originated around 1770 (Mooney 1898, 241, 328, 340, 351). During his forty-year tenure as Taimek'i, Onsokyapta continuously innovated the Sun Dance and accepted several Taime images that replaced the original. According to Heap O' Bears, his first innovation was to discontinue the practice of leaving the Taime bundle on a mountaintop at the end of the Sun Dance. Before 1830, the bundle was placed facing the direction the Kiowas departed, "on guard" to ward off sickness or any enemies that might follow them, a custom referred to as "leav[ing] their prayer there."

In his first year as Taimek'i, Onsokyapta either retained the old Taime or constructed a new image; each year, a new cover was made for Taime at the next-to-last camp before the Sun Dance. LaBarre suggested that this probably was a survival of the earlier custom.[51] Such innovations reflect the adaptability of Plains religions to changing cultural and environment conditions; though certain motifs were borrowed from other tribes, they were transformed into specific tribal identities that were maintained through traditions and rituals (Harrod 1995, 28).

There is some confusion regarding the exact number of Taime images and their descriptions during the forty-year tenure of Onsokyapta, though Mooney reported that there were three images: one shaped like the bust of a woman, the other two smaller and resembling men (Mooney 1898, 241). In the early 1890s, a Taime replica was presented to Scott, who in turn gave it to Mooney to deposit in the National Museum of Natural History (Boyd 1981, 31). A photograph of this Taime image appears in *Calendar History of the Kiowa Indians* (Mooney 1898, plate 69). Mooney described the image:

> This is a small image, less than 2 feet in length, representing a human figure dressed in a robe of white feathers, with a headdress consisting of a single upright feather and pendants of ermine skin, with numerous strands of blue beads around its neck, and painted upon the face, breast and back, with designs symbolic of the sun and moon. The image itself is of dark-green stone, in form rudely resembling a human head and bust.... The ancient *taíme* image was of buckskin, with a stalk of Indian tobacco for a headdress. (Mooney 1898, 240)

LaBarre was given a similar description of the Taime by Heap O' Bears III, who was named after his father, Heap O' Bears II, killed by Utes in 1868. As the paternal nephew of Onsokyapta, Heap O' Bears II would have inherited the largest Taime image had he survived.

> The taime image itself was the bust of a man about down to the breasts, the head a little larger than a fist, made of sewed buckskin stuffed ("the brains were tobacco") with tobacco. The man's face has nose, eyes, and ears; there was an eagle-down feather on the forehead. A white stick

was attached to the "hollow" of the sternum. The head had a dark blue background with black lines to show features. The eagle feather was white [see fig. 8, this volume].[52]

The primary difference between the two descriptions is that LaBarre associated Taime with the male gender, whereas Mooney stated that the largest image was female.

In his role as Taimek'i, Onsokyapta was responsible for the well-being of the bundle, which was always suspended by a buffalo-hair rope from the cross poles of his tipi, facing west. On those occasions when Onsokyapta was absent from camp, his wife was entrusted to protect the sacrosanct image, a duty she faithfully performed in the fateful summer of 1833 during the massacre of numerous Kiowas by an Osage war party at K'ódaltä K'op (Beheading Mountain) (Mooney 1898, 257–60). Also known as Cutthroat Gap, this beautiful horseshoe-shaped valley in the Wichita Mountains is located on the west fork of Otter Creek, about twenty-five miles northwest of Fort Sill (Ellenbrook 1991, 2). As told by Heap O' Bears and Mary Buffalo, Long Foot's wife was killed in the massacre while attempting to cut down the Taime and carry it to safety. Recognizing the importance of the Taime bundle, the Osage warriors took it with them. Upon returning to the village after his absence, Onsokyapta found the mutilated remains of his wife, ascertained that Taime was missing, and then went out to the prairie to mourn.[53] Weakened by the ordeal of fasting and weeping, he fell asleep on the grass, where Crow took pity upon him and imbued him with a power vision. In his dream, described by Heap O' Bears and Mrs. Big Bow, Onsokyapta was instructed to construct a new Taime, a gorget to be worn by himself as *taimek'i*, and seven shields for Taime. In accordance with his power vision, he made them.[54]

After the tragedy at Cutthroat Gap, Heap O' Bears noted, the Kiowas did not conduct the Sun Dance during the summers of 1833 and 1834. Meanwhile, the recently chosen principal chief, Dohásän (Little Bluff), negotiated peace with the Osages. Fearing Kiowa retaliation, the Osages returned the bundle in the summer of 1834.[55] Following the peace, the Sun Dance was held in the summer of 1835 after the Kiowas were reunited with the sacred Taime image taken two years before (Mooney 1898, 262–63, 269). At this time, there were two Taime images.

During a running fight with Mexican soldiers in 1839 near Hueco Tanks, Texas, Kɔɔde, or Koñáte (Black Paunch; later known as Pá-tadal [Lean Bull] or Patadlkyäpta [Poor Buffalo]), was wounded and left for dead. Lying maimed on the ground, Kɔɔde was approached by a wolf that licked his wounds. Shortly afterward, the spirit of Taime spoke, telling him he would live, and then sent rain that cleaned his festering wounds. Kɔɔde was discovered later on by Comanches and returned to his people, where he fully recovered. Inspired by his vision, Kɔɔde carried a forked chinaberry stick called ä/poto as his medicine and danced with it inside the Sun Dance lodge (Mooney 1898, 301–2, 305). Heap O' Bears called the forked stick dɔ, describing it as an eighteen-inch-long chinaberry stick shaped like a man's bust colored red that tapered into the stick, complete with eyes and a nose.[56] According to Scott, dɔ was an ash-root digging stick with a head the size of a man's fist that was adorned with a golden eagle breath feather headdress. The breast was adorned with eagle body feathers. Though Scott did not understand the significance of dɔ, he claimed it lacked medicine power (Scott 1911, 350). Heap O' Bears said that Onsokyapta took pity on Kɔɔde, allowing him to place dɔ on the north side of Taime during the Sun Dance. He also acknowledged that Kɔɔde fashioned another Taime and seven red Kɔɔde shields that were incorporated into the Sun Dance. Heap O' Bears also said that Kɔɔde was crippled because of his wounds and stood sideways when he danced. Frank Given told Marriott a slightly different version of the story about dɔ, referring to it as konä and t'ä (digging stick), and said that Black Paunch's Taime image had been given to him by the Comanches, who had captured it from Blackfoot. Heap O' Bears and Frank Given both said that dɔ was given to T'ebodal, who gave it to Tanedooah, and that it was presently owned by Oliver Tanedooah. Mooney claimed that Kɔɔde gave the chinaberry stick to his nephew K'ayä'ñte (Falls-Over-A-Bank), who planted it in the ground inside the lodge as a sacrifice at the conclusion of the 1857 Sun Dance (see Mooney 1898, 301–2).[57]

The Taime effigies made by Onsokyapta and Kɔɔde probably were the two smaller Taime images kept with the original Taime in a kidney-shaped parfleche bag. Taime, the larger image, was kept at one end and the smaller two at the opposite end. Mooney referred to the small images as "man" and "bear kidney," whereas Taime was referred to as a "woman" not permitted to leave the village on war journeys (Mooney 1898, 241, 322–23). Scott (1911, 350) identified the miniature Taimes as "man" and "woman," the former taken on war expeditions but the latter never removed from the village. Boyd (1981, 34) later concurred that the two figures were male and female but emphasized that both were taken into combat. Perhaps these discrepancies about the Taime images reflect the fact that in the 1890s Mooney and Scott worked with people who were reticent to discuss or describe Taime due to its highly sacred nature because they were pressured by missionaries and Indian agents to discontinue the Sun Dance after its 1890 collapse. Nevertheless, that Scott obtained a Taime replica is undoubtedly attributed to the friendships he established as Indian scout commander at Fort Sill. Mooney was also well liked by the Kiowas (Scott 1911, 349). By 1935, however, those Kiowas who had converted to Christianity were perhaps less ambivalent about describing these venerated objects because forty-five years had passed since the last Sun Dance. Kiowa elders today maintain that once the Sun Dance ceased, the Kiowas put it away forever. Time and memory lapses, therefore, could account for some of the differences in the data gathered by the field party about Taime and the Sun Dance.

According to Heap O' Bears, Onsokyapta made the second, smaller Taime shortly after receiving his power vision while mourning the loss of the original image. Responsible for protecting Taime, he probably made the smaller replica to compensate for its loss but kept both images when the Osages returned the original over a year later. LaBarre identified the second image as the "female" Taime, which was positioned immediately below the Taime during the Sun Dance (Taime was exposed for public viewing toward the end of the Sun Dance, when it was simultaneously stuck in the ground and tied to a cedar screen in the western portion of the Sun Dance lodge). Integrating the female Taime into the Sun Dance with the larger "male" Taime was one of the innovations brought about by Onsokyapta. Heap O' Bears II, the paternal nephew of Onsokyapta, was chosen to inherit the Taime bundle. To prepare him for his forthcoming obligations, Onsokyapta gave him the small female image he had made as well as a Taime shield, because he was "training him for the job."[58] According to Scott (1911, 350), this was the female effigy that allegedly was never taken out of the village on a war expedition; the other small

Sun Dance Taime, the one Scott identified as the male image, was the one taken into battle as a talisman.

Despite assertions that the female image was never taken along on war expeditions, both of the miniature Taimes accompanied the ill-fated Kiowa-Comanche excursion against the Navajos in 1868. Along the way into Navajo territory, some of the Comanches killed and ate a bear, causing several Kiowa warriors to turn back toward home after witnessing the breaching of the bear-meat taboo. Mooney (1898, 322–23) stated that Heap O' Bears II believed that the power of his Taime effigy was stronger than the violated taboo, but he could not persuade many Kiowas to remain with the war party. Because Koɔde—now called Patadlkyäpta—had organized the expedition, he wanted to return home, but he was bound by his pledge to stay with the war party. According to Heap O' Bears, Patadlkyäpta entrusted his small male Taime image with his close friend Pagu·he, or Pagunhente (Hornless Bull). When the remaining members of the expedition encountered Ute warriors and were soundly defeated, Heap O' Bears II and Hornless Bull were killed, and the two small Taime images were captured, never to be seen again.[59]

Although the miniature Taimes were lost forever, Heap O' Bears said, during the summer of 1869 a new Taime effigy was introduced to the Sun Dance by Hotoyi, or Akopti (Timber Mountain), based on a power vision from his youth. In his dream, he was instructed to construct five shields and a Taime, all which were used during the 1869 "Bring in the War Bonnet Sun Dance," held at the confluence of Sweetwater Creek and the North Fork of the Red River near the present Texas-Oklahoma border (see Mooney 1898, 326).[60]

In total, there were four Taime images: (1) the original Taime, the largest, captured by the Osages in 1833 and returned the following year; (2) the miniature female image made by Onsokyapta after the original image was captured; (3) the other miniature Taime, the male effigy constructed by Koɔde; and (4) the Taime image fashioned by Hotoyi and introduced during the 1869 Sun Dance. Taime numbers 2 and 3 were captured by Utes in 1868 and never returned, and the surviving Taimes, numbers 1 and 4, undoubtedly resided in the same bundle under the care of the *taimek'i*, the principal Taime keeper and "high priest" of the Sun Dance. *Dɔ* was fashioned after the Taimes but was not one of the Taime images. Conflicting stories about Black Paunch's innovation incorporated into the Sun Dance by Onsokyapta are further complicated by Mooney's description of the Gadómbítsoñhi (Old-woman-under-the-ground), which he said was placed in front of Taime during the Sun Dance. According to Mooney, "by some unexplained jugglery the priest in charge of it caused it to rise out of the ground, dance in the sight of the people, and then again sink into the earth." The image was stolen, and for many years hunters in the Wichita Mountains encountered "a wailing dwarf with disheveled hair who vanished as soon as discovered." Many claimed this was the lost Gadómbítsoñhi (Mooney 1898, 239).

TAIMEK'I: THE TAIME KEEPER, OR "PRIEST"

Officiating the summer Sun Dance was the most important role of the Taimek'i. LaBarre described him as "one of the Ten Medicine Men Society ex officio, making eleven" total keepers of tribal medicine bundles. Heap O' Bears noted that ownership of the Taime bundle was hereditary, and that the Taimek'i smoked and prayed for the welfare of the Kiowas after the first appearance of Thunder in the early spring, as did the Ten Medicines keepers. People prayed to Taime and offered scalps and other gifts to the bundle. Sometimes pledgers requested that Taime accompany sweat lodge ceremonies for one of the Ten Medicines. During the Sun Dance, the Ten Medicines keepers left their bundles in their tipis and assisted the Taimek'i to "work for the Taime." During the four- to six-week period of the Sun Dance, the Taimek'i was the most important person in the tribe.[61]

When at home, the Taimek'i kept the Taime bundle suspended from the top of his tipi facing west, and when it rained, the bundle was swaddled in an additional cover to keep it dry. Heap O' Bears identified another bundle owned by the Taimek'i, which contained the accouterments that accompanied Taime: two large gourds rattles, a gorget, a crow-feathered fan, "many whistles," a rabbit-skin headdress, and a human scalp. A long-stemmed, black-bowled pipe — smoked at the Sun Dance ceremony — was carefully positioned inside the bundle, the mouthpiece facing south, and the bowl north. Perhaps this was the "great Straight Pipe" mentioned by Boyd (1981, 46). The paraphernalia bag was kept inside his tipi on the west side. According to Heap O' Bears, an assistant Taimek'i kept the miniature female Taime made by Onsokyapta. Heap O' Bears II held this position of "little Taime keeper" before he was killed in 1868. Part of the assistant's training as successor included "errand work" for the Taimek'i as well as performing four principal duties during the Sun Dance ceremony.[62]

In a manner analogous to the way the Ten Medicines keepers obeyed their own prohibitions, Mary Buffalo and Heap O' Bears pointed out, the Taimek'i adhered to several restrictions concerning food and material culture: mirrors, knife blades, and other image-reflecting metal objects were prohibited in his presence, for he would become blind if he saw his own reflection; it was permissible for the Taimek'i to pet dogs, but he could not eat their meat or the heart of any animal, nor could he wear wolf robes; and, critically, he could not don red blankets or any article of red clothing. Also important was abstaining from food and water during the Sun Dance proper, restrictions also followed by the Taime shield keepers.[63] Sharing the keeper's prohibitions, Taime would be offended if any of these forbidden objects were brought into the Sun Dance enclosure. Even though the Kiowas followed protocol, the prohibitions were violated on several occasions by outsiders who did not understand the rules. Frank Given told Marriott about a Comanche man who took a mirror inside the lodge. When asked to leave he refused and continued to dance until he was physically removed from the Sun Dance lodge and his mirror destroyed. Heap O' Bears and Mary Buffalo recalled incidents about red blankets brought to Sun Dances resulting in unfortunate circumstances for the offending guests. They told the story about a Comanche man wearing a red blanket during a Sun Dance. Overwhelmed and "hypnotized" by the powers of Taime, he ripped off his blanket, took it into the enclosure, offered it to Taime, and began dancing as if he were "crazy." Mary stated that on another occasion, a Kiowa dancer ripped the blanket off the shoulders of a Comanche spectator and offered it to Taime inside the Sun Dance lodge.[64]

Battey described an incident involving red blankets during the 1873 Sun Dance held along the banks of Sweetwater Creek west of the reservation just inside the Texas Panhandle. According to him it was so hot that the foliage of the Sun Dance lodge began to wilt, prompting No Moccasins to use his medicine powers to bring forth rain and clouds to cool off the dancers:

The rain came, with a tempest of wind and the most vivid lightning. Peal after peal of thunder shook the air. The ground was literally flooded. Two Cheyenne women were killed by the lightning. The next morning To-haint [No Moccasins] apologized for the storm. He was a young man, and had no idea of making such strong medicine. He hoped the tribe would pass by his indiscreetness. He trusted that, as he grew older, he would grow wiser. The Cheyenne women were dead, not because of his medicine, but because of their wearing red blankets. All Indians know they should not wear red during the great medicine dance of the Kiowas.

The apology was accepted, and it is to be hoped that all Indians who may in future incline to attend this, the great annual assembly of the Kiowas, will remember not to wear red blankets. (Battey 1968, 183–84)

Taime in the 1930s

By 1935, when members of the Santa Fe field party visited Anadarko, the Sun Dance religion was defunct, and the Taime bundles were still in the possession of Émáa, according to Lone Bear.[65] Émáa had inherited the bundles following the death of Taíméte in 1894 (Mooney 1898, 241). People continued bringing prayer requests and presents to Émáa until her death in 1939; shortly after her death, the Taime bundles were transferred to her son Botone (Boyd 1983, 48, 50; Nye 1962, 54–55). To complicate matters, Hugh Corwin identified Mo-keen, as a Taime keeper as well as "a helper with the ceremonies and the keeping of the Taime and other sacred articles used in the Sun Dance." Mo-keen, of Mexican descent, "joined" the Kiowa tribe in his youth and was adopted by Onsokyapta. According to Corwin, Mo-keen gave up the Taime image after his only son, Lucius Aitson, died in 1918 during the influenza pandemic. At the time, Aitson was pastor at the Saddle Mountain Baptist Mission Church, and Mo-keen converted to Christianity afterward (Corwin 1958a, 74, 77, 80–83). The fate of Mo-keen's bundle is not mentioned, but it was possibly the Hotoyi version of Taime. Because Mo-keen was the adopted son of Onsokyapta, and Émáa was his natural daughter, both of them probably possessed Taime images.

Warfare and Protective Powers

Besides its connections to the curative powers associated with independent shamans, Buffalo doctors, and the tribal bundles, *dɔdɔ* related to warfare, the most esteemed male occupation in prereservation times, was extremely important. War power existed among individuals, but also on a group level, as exemplified by the shield and warrior societies that played important roles during the Sun Dance.

The northward and eastward diffusion of horses from the New Mexican frontier in the late seventeenth century forever changed the physical and cultural landscape of the Southwestern Plains. Seeking this prized new mode of transportation, Comanches, Kiowas, and Plains Apaches adopted equestrian lifeways as they migrated south toward this region in the eighteenth century. By mid-century, high mobility increased contact among Plains tribes, though tenuous relations among tribal groups resulted after horse raids became the major method for acquiring this valued commodity. Intertribal warfare and conflicts with Euro-Americans were further exacerbated by increased raiding, retaliatory strikes, and competition over diminishing bison resources. Through the 1870s, Plains warfare centered on protecting territory and successfully accumulating horses and war honors (Mishkin 1940, 9; Foster 1992, ix; Ewers 1992, xi; Secoy 1953, 27–29; Osborn 1983, 565, 584; Kracht 1982).

Beyond economic and political dimensions, Plains warfare was also religiously motivated since war power was received from highly venerated dream spirits. Oftentimes younger men sought guidance from "war shamans," experienced combat veterans who had successfully obtained war power from the spirit world. Pending crises created by interloping enemies, confrontations during horse-stealing raids and revenge expeditions, and clashes in bison-hunting territories compelled ordinary men to seek war power through vision quests. Since power visions were highly personal mystical experiences not openly discussed, men possessing war medicine carried rawhide dream shields decorated with symbols of their defensive powers; war power protected combatants and enabled them to return home safely. Experientially, men of power who accumulated the most war honors and plunder usually became band leaders or commanded age-graded warrior societies, sodalities that crosscut kinship ties and band affiliation; membership in sodalities consolidated individual powers into a more powerful aggregate. Prior to engaging in combat, men participated in rites facilitating the transition into the realm of war-related violence, and upon their return, scalp dances were performed by women if the war party had not incurred any losses. Although men were killed and scalps were taken, the highest war honors derived from counting coup on enemies, a form of "spiritual warfare" (Irwin 1994, 81–82, 153, 228–32; Holm 2005, 1135–41; Grim 2005a, 764).

Kiowa Warfare

The prereservation Kiowas have been described as "the bravest and most courageous, yet the most warlike and defiant, of the tribes in the Southwest [Plains]" (Wright 1986, 169). According to Friend Thomas Battey, who lived with the Kiowas in 1873 during the outbreak of the Red River War, they were "the most fierce and desperately bloodthirsty tribe of Indian Territory" (Battey 1968, 59). Today, Kiowas, like most American Indians, strongly support the U.S. military, are proud of their soldiers, and adhere to the interpretation that Kiowas have always been fierce warriors. A Korean War veteran of the Eight Army, Clifton Tongkeamah often referred to the prereservation Kiowas as the "predators of the Plains."[66] Until their surrender at Fort Sill in May 1875, warfare played an important role in indigenous Kiowa society because it was founded in religious beliefs connected to war medicine obtained from dream spirits.

Bascom and Mishkin compiled the most materials about nineteenth-century Kiowa warfare; Mishkin used some of the data for his 1940 monograph *Rank and Warfare among the Plains Indians*. Guiguakoti (Yellow Wolf) recollected his experiences on war parties and provided the most information about warfare and war power, followed by Mary Buffalo, Luther Sahmaunt, Jimmy Quoetone, Max Frizzlehead, and Hunting Horse. Even Tsoodle, who was reluctant to discuss the Ten Medicines, openly discussed Kiowa warfare. Other contributors included Bagyanoi, Sankadota, Haumpy, Lone Bear, Heap O' Bears, and Sanko. As Nye (1962) learned around the same time, Kiowas willingly discuss their warrior valor. Jimmy Quoetone related a legend to LaBarre accounting for Kiowa prowess in warfare: The Kiowas and several tribes were encamped adjacent to a big lake. From the shoreline, it appeared that sharp objects, "rocks, spears, or knives," were floating on the surface, preventing anyone from jumping into the water without impaling himself. Lengthy boasting among the assembled men regarding the identity of the bravest warrior failed to compel anyone into action until a Kiowa warrior finally took the initiative to plunge into the water. Closing his eyes, he dove into the floating detritus, which turned out to be grass and water lilies instead of sharp objects. The man earned "warrior prowess" for his people, and from that time on, the Kiowas were "ahead of other tribes" in their fighting abilities.[67]

As related by Yellow Wolf, Jimmy Quoetone, Max Frizzlehead, and Hunting Horse, prereservation Kiowa warfare was waged against other tribes and Euro-Americans by two distinct types of war parties: (1) "general war expeditions," in which horses, scalps, other plunder, and war honors were sought; and (2) revenge war parties. On a micro-level, small raiding parties comprising two to ten warriors from the same band departed on year-round ventures to steal horses, capture wild horses, or trade at the Spanish settlements and with other Indians. Between 1770 and 1820, wild horses were abundant southwest of Kiowa country toward the "Big Mountains" (Rocky Mountains) but diminished afterward. Adjusting to the changing environment of the Southwestern Plains, Kiowas, Comanches, and others replenished their horse herds by raiding settlements and ranches. Small raiding parties also initiated sorties into present-day Texas, New Mexico, and Mexico in search of scalps from any enemy encountered (see Mishkin 1940, 28–43).[68] Similar patterns of raiding existed throughout the Plains, especially during the "buffalo culture" period (1850–1880). During this era, bison hunting accelerated as Plains societies became dependent on trade goods, especially firearms. Having an ample supply of horses enabled hunters to procure more buffalo hides for the trade, though a shortage of horses required warriors to conduct more raids to augment their herds. Accelerated hunting to produce bison robes brought about competition over bison hunting territories, which were rapidly shrinking because of overhunting (Klein 1993, 144, 147–50, 155–56; Moore 1996, 85–87).

Jimmy Quoetone, Yellow Wolf, Luther Sahmaunt, and Frizzlehead described larger-sized raiding parties numbering between twenty-five and ninety men that usually set out in the summertime following the completion of the Sun Dance; organization of the larger raiding parties crosscut band affiliation and military society membership. Large raiding expeditions were often accompanied by Plains Apache and Comanche allies, increasing the ranks to over two hundred warriors (see Mooney 1898, 282). Such war parties departed to the south or southwest searching for common enemies in present-day Texas, New Mexico, and northern Mexico. They sought foes that could be quickly encountered and overwhelmed, foraging for horses, booty, scalps, and captives. Contemporary Kiowas acknowledge the high degree of "captive blood" in the tribe because so many children were kidnaped on raids (see also Corwin 1959). Large war parties motivated primarily by revenge sought to avenge the death of comrades killed by specific enemies. For instance, if Mexican, Ute, or Navajo enemies defeated a Kiowa war party resulting in the death of one or several important warriors, a revenge expedition formed the following summer or winter, with the intent of killing the first Mexican, Ute, or Navajo encountered. Vengeance satisfied the aggrieved relatives of the deceased warrior, and trophies, including scalps, were brought back as evidence that retribution had been exacted.[69]

The Kiowa calendars chronicle revenge-motivated warfare between 1833 and 1875. Three successive winter counts from 1834 to 1837 identify Kiowa warriors killed in Mexico, as well as mortalities during the winters of 1844–45, 1850–51, 1853–54, and 1873–74. During the winter of 1840–41, a large expeditionary force traveled into Mexico seeking revenge. Warriors were killed by Texans in the winters of 1841–42, 1866–67, and 1868–69, and in the spring of 1870. In the winter of 1870–71, a Kiowa war party led by Walking Above killed five black soldiers in Texas, and on May 17, 1871, a war party of over one hundred men led by Sitting Bear and White Bear killed over seven teamsters near Fort Richardson in Northern Texas. Battles against the Cheyennes and Arapahos are recorded between 1837 and 1839 before the intertribal alliance of the Southwestern Plains tribes in 1840. Over the next two decades, encounters with Pawnee horse-raiding parties were recorded for the summer of 1841, the winters of 1846–47 and 1849–50, the summers of 1851 and 1852, and the winter of 1857–58. Revenge raids were launched against the Omahas in the winter of 1855–56, the Caddos in the winter of 1860–61, and the Navajos in the winter of 1867–68. In the first two occurrences, the calendars record the deaths of Kiowa warriors at the hands of the Omahas and Caddos the previous year, and in the last, the Navajos committed the offense of stealing Kiowa horses during the Sun Dance. Engagements with federal troops in Kansas are recorded for the summers of 1860 and 1864, and the winter of 1864–65 marks Kit Carson's pitched battle against the Kiowas,

Comanches, and Plains Apaches at Adobe Walls. In these battles, the army employed Caddo, Navajo, and Ute auxiliaries against the Southwestern Plains tribes, prompting revenge raids that culminated in the summer of 1868 debacle resulting in the loss of the miniature Taimes to the Utes (Mooney 1898, 257–333, 337–38).

War Power and the Rites of Warfare

Rumors about revenge war expeditions circulated quickly throughout the Kiowa encampments. Yellow Wolf, Bagyanoi, Jimmy Quoetone, and Hunting Horse described how war parties were organized. Young men, eager to improve their status and yearning to accompany war parties, eagerly awaited the announcement that a *toyopk'i* (war chief) had just pledged to assemble one. Ideally, a *toyopk'i* possessed protective war *dɔdɔ* connected to a dream spirit, carried a dream shield, and used his spirit-derived powers to prophesy the outcome of war ventures. Popular war chiefs almost always belonged to the *ondedɔ* class, were renowned warriors with distinguished combat records, and belonged to a shield or warrior society. War chiefs relied on strong war medicine and success-ful war records to attract recruits for war expeditions and were com-pletely responsible for the outcome of the sorties they commanded. They determined the logistics of the entire expedition, chose camping locations, delegated men to perform sundry camp activities, and, inev-itably, directed attacks on enemies. Every *toyopk'i* inevitably led a war party, though recent failures or disasters lessened his ability to recruit warriors. Consistent with the hierarchy of powers derived from dream spirits, Yellow Wolf noted that the most powerful war leaders invariably led the most successful raids.[70]

Bagyanoi told LaBarre that in Kiowa etymology, *toyopk'i* derives from *tonyop* (I carry the pipe), which probably refers to consecrating war pledges through ritual smoking, as pointed out by Luther Sahmaunt and Hunting Horse.[71] Due to their high status, Yellow Wolf said, war chiefs wielded the authority to pledge war expeditions by sponsoring ritual smokes with *ondedɔ* men. Pipe-smoking rites formalized large-scale tribal war parties but were unnecessary for smaller, band-centered raids.[72] Mooney (1898, 282) referred to the ritual activities during the Sun Dance of 1844 as "giving the pipe," in which a pipe was sent around to the different sodalities, summoning the members to war against Mexican foes. Mishkin (1940, 19) concurred with Mooney, adding that sending the pipe was motivated by revenge. Yellow Wolf provided details of the ritual. According to accounts, a *toyopk'i* summoned the higher-ranked leaders or chiefs of the warrior societies who also owned dream shields to his tipi that evening for a ritual smoke. After all had arrived and found seats, he lit a pipe and passed it around for all to smoke before revealing his plans. Those wishing to join the campaign volunteered their services, and then the subordinate chiefs and scouts were selected. Three to four highly ranked *toyopk'i* commanded the largest expeditions, which sometimes became intertribal enterprises, like the revenge expedition during the winter of 1844–45 (Mooney 1898, 282).[73]

Following the giving of the pipe ceremony, everyone was welcome to join a farewell dance described by Yellow Wolf, Luther Sahmaunt, and Bagyanoi. Anyone dancing to the *gudɔ·gie* (travel song) was entitled to leave with the expedition the following morning. Participating in the dance also allowed departing warriors to say goodbye to their wives and sweethearts. In the morning, the warriors congregated at the predetermined location before departing on the expedition.[74] Mooney (1898, 312) observed that smaller raiding parties were often initiated by a lone individual singing the *Gua-dayga* (travel song), compelling others to join the band-level raid. Concomitant to these nocturnal activities, some men appropriated the time to "make medicine," identified by Yellow Wolf and Luther Sahmaunt as a personal rite of seeking specific powers to subdue enemies or acquire property.[75] Young men desirous of improving their war records often trekked to nearby hills to supplicate the spirits for war power, a ritual still remembered by White Fox, Jimmy Quoetone, Sankadota, Haumpy, Tsoodle, and Mary Buffalo. Shortly before sunrise, some worshipers endured acts of self-mutilation by cutting off flesh strips—in combinations of two, four, five, or seven to represent cardinal directions—then placing them on bison chips as offerings to Sun for war power.[76] Such protective rites always have been important to American Indian warriors (Holm 2005, 1140).

Some men prayed to Taime and the Ten Medicines for spiritual guidance and protection while away, pledging scalps, horses, and other plunder to the sacrosanct objects if they returned unscathed. More scalps were offered to the Ten Medicines than to Taime, which seemingly contradicts the idea that Taime was more closely associated with warfare. Mary Buffalo explained that only large-scale, tribal revenge sorties involved pledges of scalps to Taime, whereas men involved in smaller, more common raids pledged scalps to the Ten Medicines. Her rationale was that fewer scalps were obtained from vengeance expeditions, so they were considered more valuable. Due to their rarity, presenting revenge scalps to Taime, connected to Sun — the principal source of war power — imbued them with them power and great importance. Pledging scalps to the Ten Medicines involved approaching a keeper with a lit pipe and offering it to him with the petition: "You and your medicine smoke this pipe and pray for me; if I kill some man, and you give me the courage to be brave, I'll give the scalp to this bag." Following the pledge and prayer, the Ten Medicines keeper blew medicine on the pledger to bless him with war power, enabling him to safely return from the war expedition.[77]

Once the war party was underway, Yellow Wolf noted that the *toyopk'i* consulted his personal power every evening to prophesy the outcome of the next day. After leaving camp, the *toyopk'i* sat on a hill, smoking and praying to the spirit representing his *dɔdɔ*. Following any communication with his spirit power, the war chief relayed the message to the rest of the group. Based on information conveyed by the oracle, the *toyopk'i* recommended the appropriate course of action. Sometimes he predicted the killing of enemies, or that a particular man would be wounded.[78] According to Mary Buffalo, the prophecies often proved to be true.[79] The ideal war expedition as described by Yellow Wolf and Hunting Horse closely followed the war chief's plans, giving the men enough time to prepare their protective medicines before any fighting happened. If chance encounters with enemies did occur, skirmishes were avoided if the warriors had not "made medicine." Unfavorable surprises were countered by dispatching scouts to reconnoiter the countryside in search of the best terrain for passing through undetected, and to scout for enemies. When enemies were sighted, the scouts rode back to the main group, circling it four times while howling like wolves. They also stacked up piles of buffalo chips to represent available horses and goods to plunder. When it was believed that all logistics were under control, it was time to make medicine.[80] Lone Bear, Luther Sahmaunt, Haumpy, and Heap O' Bears described the ritual, which began when the men stripped down to their breechcloths to prepare for battle; at this time, men of power began supplicating the dream spirits representing their *dɔdɔ*. Those without personal power petitioned the spirit force representing Sun, and sometimes left blankets and shield ornaments on the ground as offerings. Anyone was free to petition Taime or the Ten Medicines at this time, pledging horses, blankets, and scalps, or they could pledge a Sun Dance contingent on obtaining high war honors. All were considered to be extremely powerful prayers.[81] According to Lone Bear, men painted their faces black during war expeditions and then upon their triumphant return with scalps. Warriors also painted white, yellow, green, and blue power designs on their bodies to protect themselves from enemy projectiles.[82] Tsoodle said that the decorative dream-inspired symbols adorning their shields, bodies, and horses rendered enemy bullets and arrows ineffective, which coincides with Mooney's earlier findings.[83]

During revenge expeditions, the bodies of victims were mutilated when circumstances permitted. A fallen foe was decapitated, his skull smashed into a pulp, the chest cavity opened to remove ribs, fingers, arms, and legs were cut off, and severed genitals were placed into his mouth, if it was still intact. Sometimes the deceased was placed in a fire and reduced to ashes. According to Sanko, disfiguring the body made grieving relatives feel better, but when LaBarre asked whether or not mutilation had any effect on the victim's spirit, Charley Apekaum had difficulty interpreting Sanko's answer and said he was unsure.[84] Taking trophy scalps, however, was rewarding because scalps were honored more than plunder brought back from raids, including horses, according to Luther Sahmaunt and Yellow Wolf. Victorious war parties returning with scalps were elaborately welcomed, especially by the mourning relatives of warriors previously killed by the enemy.[85] Yellow Wolf, Tsoodle, and Mary Buffalo indicated that celebrations only occurred if a war party returned with scalps and no mortalities; if a single warrior had been killed, the war party silently entered the village, stopping only to speak to a camp crier who met them at the outskirts. Learning the dreadful details, the camp crier returned to announce the bad news at the encampment. Close female relatives of the deceased immediately began mourning by gashing their arms and breasts, cutting off fingertips, and cutting hair. There was no celebration, and the relatives remained in mourning up to eight months, the period of time it normally took to form a revenge party and gain retribution.[86]

Mary Buffalo, Max Frizzlehead, Yellow Wolf, and Tsoodle described the ritual that welcomed successful sorties. When victorious war parties approached Kiowa territory, two scouts were delegated to reconnoiter Kiowa encampments and report back so everyone could orchestrate the triumphant return. Before leaving the last resting place, the warriors painted their faces black to symbolize killing an enemy and donned their finest war regalia. Once prepared, they silently approached the village in single file, with the most accomplished warrior from the expedition riding in front, wielding the scalps draped over the ends of their lances. Reaching the camp, usually at midday, they fired bullets and arrows into the air to announce their arrival. Relieved that this was not an enemy attack, women greeted them at the edge of camp, each one leaping up and riding behind the warrior of her choice. Reaching the center of the village, the entourage was met by male singers drumming dried rawhide hand drums accompanied by women vocalizing tremolos. Following the triumphant arrival, the warriors ambled off to their respective warrior society tipis to eat and rest. In the interim, the Á'daldá-gúăn (hair-kill dance, or Scalp Dance) (Mooney 1898, 291) began when a widow danced into the circle with an enemy scalp affixed to a long stick or lance. The widow still in mourning, three or four horizontal black stripes were painted on her face, finger-width apart, and she wore a hairless buffalo robe. While dancing, she was joined by the mothers, sisters, and aunts of the returned warriors, who also wielded scalp-laden lances. In rhythm to the drumming, singing, and tremolos, the women pantomimed spear thrusts at imaginary enemies. Performance of the dance late into the night ended the mourning period, and the widow was supposed to feel better afterward.[87] The Kiowa calendars note performances of the Scalp Dance with Pawnee scalps in the winter of 1849–50, and in the winter of 1860–61 with a Caddo scalp (Mooney 1898, 290–93, 309).

Ancillary to the Scalp Dance, the same collaborators stated, public storytelling by the war chief recounted details of the expedition, particularly the prowess of the newly returned warriors, or even acts of cowardice. Each man's deeds were recited, accompanied by tremolos from his female relatives who danced with his weapons. Afterwards, gifts were given away in his honor.[88] All warriors strove to obtain the highest honors because war deeds were ranked in order of importance. Although Jimmy Quoetone and Yellow Wolf disagreed on the exact ranking of war honors, they agreed that counting first coup on a living or deceased enemy was the highest honor. Charging an enemy while one's allies were retreating was the second-highest honor. Equally important was rescuing a fallen comrade during a retreat or charging an enemy who had ridden ahead of his own ranks to fight. Collectively, these acts of bravery reflected high personal risk on the threshold of suicide. Counting second coup, killing an enemy, or suffering wounds earned the second-highest honors. The lowest honors were associated with counting third and fourth coup, and hand-to-hand combat on foot. Notably, scalping did not confer war honors but served to prove kills. Oral records of each man's accomplishments were kept, but war deeds did not count unless they were witnessed by other warriors. Lying or fabricating false stories of one's accomplishments was a serious offense that brought much ridicule.[89]

Dream Shields: Symbols of Power and Protection

War accouterments of the Plains warrior-shaman included a rawhide war shield about two feet in diameter, painted and decorated to represent the protective powers obtained through his vision. Only the visionary knew the true meaning of his shield, a "mystery object" that conveyed to enemies that the warrior was protected and given courage by powerful other-than-human persons. In contrast, unpainted shields possessed by men without war power offered little protection (Irwin 1994, 228–29). Very few Kiowa men owned what Tsoodle called *a/p'ǫki* (dream shield), since *a/p'o·dɔo/mgyɛ* (dreamed power) was difficult to obtain. Carrying such a "power shield" allowed a man to charge into enemy lines without being killed. Those wielding dream shields were identifiable by the way they painted themselves and their horses before engaging in combat.[90] Men lacking war power often fashioned "unconsecrated" shields decorated with solar motifs and other symbols of war power, as related by T'ebodal to Mooney. Young men entering their first fights unprotected experimented with shield designs that might bring them success. T'ebodal surmised there were twelve to fifteen of these ordinary shields lacking dream power and the associated power-sustaining rituals.[91] Although men without power lacked the sacred war paint used by shield owners, Tsoodle, Jimmy Quoetone, and Heap O' Bears said, they nevertheless painted their faces and bodies with their own designs; most warriors painted themselves anyway. A man would change his face paint several times during the course of a lifetime before finding a suitable design bringing war prowess and protection. Once a design was proven effective, it became his personal property.[92] Heap O' Bears noted that Sun designs represented the war power given by Sun, zigzag lines down from the eyes symbolized lightning and "tears," and black facial paint stood for victory.[93]

In a similar fashion, Mary Buffalo and Tsoodle explained that some men without war power also painted war symbols on their horses, and if a man achieved a high war honor riding a painted horse then his design became patented for life, entitling him to paint the design on his horse prior to battle or the parade before the Sun Dance. Popular designs included yellow Sun circles, zigzag lightning marks on the legs symbolizing Thunder, hand imprints, painting the right side of a horse red and the left side white, and other markings. Another popular practice was to paint bullet scars where the horse had been hit, for it was a high honor to recover from combat-inflicted wounds.[94] Symbolic painting, therefore, was important to all Kiowa warriors, even though dream shields magically provided the best protection.

Many who possessed dream shields actually inherited the shield designs originally inspired by power visions. Through inheritance and purchase, the shields were duplicated and given to sons or close male relatives. Origin visions usually specified the number of shields to be made, usually between four and eight; exceeding the limit attenuated the power of the shields. Jimmy Quoetone said that on one hand more *ondedɔ* shield owners acquired their power by purchase than through original visions but that on the other hand more lower-class men owned dream-inspired shields because they could not afford to purchase their power. Kiowas commonly believed that "vision support" for a shield gave the owner more confidence in himself, a factor favoring the rise of some men to *ondedɔ* status.[95] Quoetone's comments demonstrate that the *ondedɔ* class held onto its privileged status through inheritance (see Mishkin 1940).

Some of the individual shield designs and their owners were remembered by Tsoodle. Pɔdlta/n owned a *ona/dek'i* (Bear shield), Set'aide had a *tse/bak'i* (Cow-bull shield) representing the "wild bulls of Mexico," Aya/te had a *ki/sǫyeki* (blue shield), Kǫbo/ho possessed a solid-white shield with a red line circle in the center, Big Bow had a red shield with a white circle in the center, and Dohásän had a *k'oguk'oga* (yellow shield). Bascom made pencil sketches of these shields. Hunting Horse recalled that Dohásän's yellow shield had a blonde scalp attached to it, that Tsetainde (White Horse) and A·eoide (Yellow Smoke) owned black shields obtained in "private visions," that Be/dlk'ɔe (Teller) had a white shield adorned with two dragon flies, and that Tenézeptie had possessed an Owl shield. He also remembered that Maiten/de, Do·kyai, and Kɔto·nde shared the same shield design.[96]

Tsoodle also described a Sun shield owned by White Bear that was derived from a vision in which Sun blessed him with strong war power to defy death. White Bear hung the shield at the front of his tipi during the Sun Dance as opposed to at the back. Although this was improper placement, no one challenged White Bear, because of his great physique, strength, and defiant attitude.[97] Further information about White Bear's Sun shield comes from Scott's 1897 interview with T'ebodal, who described the shield as featuring a Sun design in the center with two concentric rings around it like "rings around the moon." Red strips of cloth adorned one side of the shield and yellow cloth strips the other, and a crane's head was attached to it. This was one of six shields made by Black Horse in 1792, who in old age presented the surviving shield to White Bear. T'ebodal related that White Bear's war regalia consisted of a war shirt painted red on one side and yellow on the other, like the cloth on his shield, and that he "wore the longest wing feather of a crane in his hair." According to accounts, the Sun shield had a "strong road" based on White Bear's exploits in combat. Witnesses saw him spear a man to death in Mexico and kill a Sac on the north side of the Arkansas River and a Pawnee near Fort Lyon, farther west along the Arkansas. The shield allegedly was carried into over one hundred fights.[98] Perhaps this is the Crane shield briefly mentioned by Scott (1911, 373) in his article on the Sun Dance. Clifton Tongkeamah also claimed that White Bear, his great-great-grandfather, owned a Crane shield.[99] Sanko told Marriott that White Bear's war shield was white with red around the edges.[100] Despite the different descriptions of his shield, all collaborators attributed the war power of Set'aide to Sun.

Besides these accounts, little is known about privately owned dream shields besides their connection to animal powers and Sun. Undoubtedly more information could be gleaned from Mooney's cryptic and almost impossible to read heraldry notebooks, and studies of the miniature shield replicas made for him that are housed in the National Museum of Natural History might provide further information.

EAGLE SHIELDS

As opposed to privately owned shields, "ceremonial" dream shields originated from a single vision and possessed magical powers to protect all who inherited the design and belonged to the same shield society. T'ebodal told Mooney that before battles shield society members would "make medicine" together, and that "every kind [of] shield had its own war cry."[101] Heap O' Bears said that men with the same war power painted their bodies and prayed together prior to combat and participated together in the Sun Dance.[102] Throughout the Plains, members of shield societies shared a common social identity sanctified by their connection to dream spirits (Irwin 1994, 229).

During an interview with Bascom, Tsoodle briefly mentioned Eagle shields that originated from the war power vision of Gɔ/biɛtɔ. Over a week later he identified Feathered Lance as the owner of one of the seven *guitok'i*, bird shields with fish-hawk designs. When not in use, each shield rested on a rack that represented an eagle's nest. On an earlier occasion he mentioned that Feathered Lance had carried a shield decorated with hawk tail feathers. Bascom seemed confused between these shields and the *to/ngudlk'i* (Red-Tailed Hawk shield) owned by a man who also owned a whistle "which he blew when he charged and made a noise like a hawk."[103] Fortunately, Marriott obtained ample data about the *gútōkī* (Eagle shields) from Frank Given, whose father, Set'angya, had inherited one of the shields and its powers. Additional information was provided by George Poolaw, Atah, Tsoodle, Saíoma, whose husband had owned a shield, and Sanko, whose father, an adopted son of Set'angya, had also possessed an Eagle shield.[104]

Perhaps Bascom's confusion derived from conflicting descriptions of the shields, which Tsoodle and Sanko claimed were no longer needed after the cessation of warfare in May 1875 when soldiers took away weapons and war accoutrements. Frank Given said that he knew of twenty-three Eagle shields that were decorated with "pictures of guns — two pictures on each side" and "an eagle's claw fastened on the shield." Conversely, George Poolaw described seven "bird shields" adorned with a "spread eagle in the center and a fringe of eagle-tail feathers"; and Saíoma noted that there were fourteen shields, each decorated by a pipe design in the center flanked on either side by an arrow and a gun, with "feathers all around the edge of the shield." Discrepancies in shield detail might be attributed to a sixty-year lapse since they had been confiscated, lost, or buried with the owners. Tsoodle pointed out that since Eagle shields were made by different men, the actual number of "visioned shields" constructed by each visionary depended on the instructions he received during his power quest. According to Sanko, the Eagle shields "were not just alike."[105] These statements account for the variation in shield designs that might have contributed to Bascom's confusion.

Frank Given related that the shields originated when a man sitting on a hilltop during a vision quest was taken underwater, given power, shown several Eagle shields, and instructed how to make them and also to fashion a tipi with bird designs and another with fish designs. When not in use, the shields were supposed to rest on a rack behind the bird tipi, lying flat like an eagle's nest. The man also received a small, black-handled knife, which he was told to swallow and keep inside his body. After creating the bird-design tipi he gave it to his daughter's son and then constructed a fish-design tipi that he gave to his son. George Poolaw told a different story about a man who dug a pit, covered it with brush, attached a dead rabbit on top of it as bait, and waited underneath for an eagle to alight. He caught four eagles in this fashion, but while sleeping on the fifth night, an eagle told him to stop catching eagles and taught him how to make the Eagle shields. Poolaw claimed that the *gútōkī* shields were "at least as old" as the Taime shields. Regardless of the origin of the shields, Marriott's collaborators all knew that the original owner gave Set'angya one of the shields and its associated powers.[106]

According to Frank Given, the man offered his power to a young Set'angya, who initially refused it, justifying to his father that "there is too much to it." In other words, he did not want to follow the taboos attached to the shield, including the avoidance of eating hearts, not smoking with anyone wearing feathers, nor eating food "cooked over a fire where a knife had been dropped in the ashes." Afterward, Sitting Bear's father dreamed that he should accept the shield, so he told the man they would build a sweat lodge for him if he could give Set'angya something else. When the man agreed to give away the black-handled knife, a sweat lodge was built for the transfer ceremony, and afterward Set'angya gave the donor several horses. Besides the shield and knife, Set'angya received the "full power," which included strong war power and the ability to swallow and regurgitate the knife.[107]

Given witnessed some of his father's feats with the black-handled knife. During a meeting when Eagle shield keepers repaired and repainted their shields, Set'angya took hot coals from the central hearth, swallowed them, and then extracted the knife from his mouth and spun it on the floor. The knife stood up straight, he covered it with a black handkerchief, and it turned into a crow feather, which he then swallowed. According to Given, this is how Eagle shield owners showed their power. Set'angya kept the shield on a four pole rack behind his tipi, where it rested "as if it were a bird resting on its nest."[108]

Frank Given described how Gähäbitä tested his Eagle shield during a battle with warriors from another tribe. Holding a bow and arrow and shield in one hand and a spear in the other, he motioned his hand up the bowstring and sang the war song:

I will run up the bowstring,
And let that arrow be carried away by the wind.

Because the song was supposed to render enemy arrows harmless, the first arrow shot at him went wide and missed, assuring Gähäbitä that his Eagle shield had strong war power. During an engagement with Utes, another Eagle shield owner gained power by singing the song, causing enemy projectiles to go wide despite the fact that the Kiowas were losing and enemy arrows were killing Kiowa horses. In another fight, a Cheyenne warrior was outfighting some Kiowas, so an Eagle shield owner sang the song and charged, causing the wind to blow away his adversary's arrows.[109] The last engagement must have occurred before 1840, when the Cheyennes and Kiowas finally quit fighting one another and made a lasting alliance.

Saíoma described a shield dance held inside a tipi in which seven shield keepers sat on the north side, and seven on the south side, with their shields "hanging on their backs between their shoulders." Set'angya sat at the west side flanked by two men, including Feathered Lance, who greeted the sunrise after this all-night meeting. In the vicinity where Set'angya sat was a beaver skin decorated with beadwork, ornaments, "and a big red disk of shell fastened to it." The beaver skin was treated as if it were a person: "they talked to it that way." A woman doctor who sat by the entryway had the power to bring up a black handkerchief from her mouth. After sundown the wives and relatives of the shield keepers entered the tipi to join the ceremony designed to make medicine and repaint the shields.[110]

Throughout the night the men sang and the woman by the door danced. Shortly before sunrise, "a big star came up" and everyone began singing and dancing. "One old man" rose from his seat "singing loud and fast" and then belched and blew on Frizzlehead's forehead and cheeks, leaving a "circle of greenish-yellow paint." While this was happening Sitting Bear danced and threw his magical knife, which she described as an eagle wing. Following this Set'angya passed a long-stemmed pipe to his left, and everyone on the north side smoked until the pipe reached the door, and then it was passed back to Set'angya, who passed it to the men on the south side to smoke. Sitting Bear prayed while smudging the beaver hide in cedar incense:

Earthmaker (*dämaiyamk'i*—he fixed the earth) you smoke. They are people who multiply and live happily on the earth. Let them grow up in peace. Let them go through life and through sickness and get well again. If they should have any trouble let them come out of it all right. Give them peace and plenty.

Next, Frizzlehead, the "man they had been making medicine over," wearing a beaver skin around his neck, rose with pipe in hand and danced to the door to greet the sunrise and ordered that the tipi flap be opened. The men stopped singing and Frizzlehead said, "Get ready. Sun is coming up." Each man then began to paint his wife or female relative; those sitting on the south side had a black cross design on their foreheads, and those on the north side had a red cross. As the sun rose the camp crier called the villagers to assemble to watch the participants emerge from the tipi. Before exiting, Frizzlehead took a black handkerchief that had been resting over the beaver skin, tore off strips, and handed them to each woman. Frizzlehead left the tipi first, followed by the men, who circuited counterclockwise before exiting. Any loose feathers that had fallen from their shields were placed in the central hearth.[111]

Exiting the ceremonial tipi, the shield owners walked to the east, and then south, where they stopped to dance. Afterward the women emerged and stood near the tipi to watch the men dance. Individuals among the assembled spectators often "came forward and prayed to the Earthmaker, even if they didn't know God." Then the men circled the tipi, went back inside to remove their paint, and smoked. Just before evening the men sent the women to cook an evening meal and then put their shields back in their protective bags and came outside. The shields that had been on the north side of the tipi were taken back to the owners' tipis and affixed at the top of the poles, whereas those from the south side were placed on the four pole racks behind their respective tipis.

In the account of the shield dance given by Saíoma, it appears that this ritual occurred for four consecutive nights. On the first three nights the ceremony began with a feast of "little puppy-dogs that were milk-fed and fat," and on the fourth morning everyone came out of the ceremonial tipi. Set'angya reportedly instructed the men to repaint their shields when they were removed from their protective bags for this ceremony, which was usually conducted when the coalesced Kiowa bands traveled to the Sun Dance. Because the ritual was so sacred, it was not performed every year but only when "somebody prayed to do this, like promising a Sun Dance." Saíoma said that Set'angya asked her husband to take the power, but he initially refused due to the responsibilities of shield ownership and the sacredness of the society. When he eventually acquiesced, Sitting Bear fashioned a shield for him.[112] Notably, the references to Earthmaker and God in Saíoma's description of the dance could reflect syncretisms with the Native American Church and Christianity, though her remembrances of a ritual that had not been performed in over sixty years might have been muddled by the passage of time.

Saíoma, Frank Given, and Sanko discussed the fate of the shields carried by their relatives. According to Saíoma, one time her husband and a friend narrowly escaped after being attacked by whites. Though he bled profusely from a wounded heel, her husband claimed that the powers of the shield saved his life. Based on his faith in the shield's power, he loaned it to his brother Hátä before traveling far to the south to obtain horses. While her husband was away, Hátä encountered enemies and received a fatal head shot that splattered blood and brains all over the Eagle shield. Learning that Hátä had been killed, the brother retrieved his body but not the shield, because it was spoiled. Someone else brought it back and it was buried with Hátä. Consequently, her husband was no longer a member of the Eagle shield society. Sitting Bear gave his shield to his youngest son, Set'angya II, who was killed in the summer of 1870 while leading a war expedition into Texas (see Mooney 1898, 327). The shield was thrown away, but Set'angya gave another shield to Sanko's father. Sanko claimed that when soldiers took weapons away from the Kiowas in 1875, his father hid the shield in the Wichita Mountains so it would not fall into their hands. By this time, most of the shields were destroyed or buried with their owners and the society became defunct.[113]

DEMGUK'O, OR TAIME SHIELDS

Like the Eagle shields, the Taime shields were associated with war power, but since they were also connected to Taime and the Sun Dance, Marriott claimed they were "religious in purpose." Frank Given told her that the Taime shields were older than the other shields but not as old as Taime. Marriott learned about the Taime shields mostly from interviews with George Poolaw, Sanko, Frank Given, and Tsoodle, and she obtained some information from Atah and Saíoma.[114] Among the Santa Fe field school students, LaBarre gathered the most data about the Taime, Koɔde, and Hotoyi shields, from Heap O' Bears and to a lesser extent from Mary Buffalo; comparatively, LaBarre's fieldnotes are more detailed than Marriott's. Mishkin obtained additional information from Jimmy Quoetone, and Collier from Max Frizzlehead and Mrs. Big Bow.

As related by Heap O' Bears, the Taime shields originated shortly after the 1833 Cutthroat Gap massacre. Having lost his wife and the Taime image, Onsokyapta lay on the prairie mourning his losses when a thunderstorm moved in and it began raining, prompting him to crawl under a buffalo robe to stay dry. Shortly afterwards, two large black-colored birds came under the robe to share his shelter. During the storm, something grabbed Onsokyapta by the wrist and flung him out of the robe three successive times. Each time he returned dry to the protective covering to guard the birds. Onsokyapta was yanked from the robe a fourth time, but a larger bird, Crow, the parent of the two, appeared to him and it stopped raining. Grateful that Onsokyapta had taken care of his "little ones," Crow bestowed on him the rain power that Crow and Thunder controlled. Inspired by his vision Onsokyapta fashioned the new Taime, the gorget, and the seven shields. The raindrops he painted on the shields represent the rain that did not fall on him and the two birds. Based on the labeled sketches in LaBarre's fieldnotes, each shield had a yellow background adorned with raindrop designs, signifying invulnerability from enemy bullets and arrows, and black crescent moons and a black sun, representing lunar and solar powers. Two buffalo tails hung from the bottom of the shield, and a crow skin was attached to the right side, honoring Crow and his ability to dodge enemy projectiles (fig. 9, this volume). On the fourth day of the Sun Dance proper, the shields were placed on a cedar screen located at the western portion of the Sun Dance lodge, right above Taime.[115]

Onsokyapta was also instructed by the dream spirits to control distribution of the seven Taime shields used exclusively in combat and during the Sun Dance proper, according to Jimmy Quoetone. The seven original Taime shield keepers chosen by Onsokyapta had to follow his prohibitions: against seeing their reflection in mirrors or other reflective surfaces, which would result in blindness; against being near skunks; and against eating rabbit meat or the heart of any animal. Violating any of these restrictions was believed to nullify the power of the shields.[116] In addition, they could not smoke while wearing their moccasins (Scott 1911, 373). Heap O' Bears noted that the Taime shield keepers, or *demguk'o* (yellow breasts), participated in the four dancing days of the Sun Dance proper. He also described their paint. Their bodies were painted white; a yellow line extended from the insides of their arms across the chest; a black sun on the sternum was flanked by two blue crescent moons; and their wrists and ankles, painted with dark blue or black vertical lines, were also adorned with sage wristlets and anklets. The legs above the ankles were painted yellow, the face was yellow with white around the eyes, and the lips and jaw were black. Each dancer tied a crow adorned with downy eagle feathers to his braided scalplock, symbolizing the power vision inspired by Crow. The *demguk'o* helped one another with their body paint as they prepared for their role in the Sun Dance.[117]

The Demguk'o held their positions as Taime shield keepers for life, and when one of them passed away, the remaining six chose his replacement. As with other shield owners, wives cared for the shields in their absence, but since the Taime shields played an important role in the Sun Dance, their wives were privileged to bring them into the Sun Dance lodge. Descended from one of the keepers, Heap O' Bears could identify the owners of the seven Taime shields: (1) Guepagoi, or GueBagoi (Lone Wolf), who gave the shield to his son Tɔagya, or Tɔagkya (Ambush The Enemy); (2) Dohedɔte, or Tainsaiti (Many Crosses); (3) Set'aBedoi (Dangerous Bear, or Afraid Of The Bear); (4) Ma·bodlt'aha, who gave it to his younger brother Zempadl, or Zempadalti (Gnawing On A Bone), also known as Basokyæ'ta (Thunder Old Man) because of his power vision; (5) Set'oyoide, or Set'dayati (Heap O' Bears) II, nephew of Onsokyapta, the leader of the seven; (6) Ɔdlpete, or Adalpepti (Frizzlehead); and (7) Mɔkin, or Mo-keen, the adopted son of Onsokyapta instructed in the Sun Dance religion.[118] Through his eagerness to learn about the Taime-inspired religion of the Kiowa, Mo-keen earned several important roles in the Sun Dance (Corwin 1959, 73–82). The Taime shields ended with these individuals, though Heap O' Bears remembered the design, as sketched by LaBarre (see fig. 9, this volume).

Frank Given provided Marriott a slightly different account of the Taime shields. He identified Mo-keen, Red Cloud, Lone Wolf, Dábo, Heap O' Bears II, and a Comanche man as shield keepers. Tsoodle added that only relatives of the Taimek'i owned the shields. According to Given, there were ten Taime shields kept in elkhide covers, and two were described as "special" shields that Heap O' Bears had constructed: one was white with a dark circle in the center, and the other was black with a white circle in the center. Attached to the circle was a horse-hair tuft. Heap O' Bears carried one and his son the other, though both shields were lost in the summer of 1868 when they were killed by the Utes. (Mooney [1898, 323] identified Heap O' Bears's son as an adopted Mexican captive.) George Poolaw added another twist by identifying Big Bow as a Taime shield keeper. Poolaw said the shields were made by taking the neck part of a buffalo bull hide, cutting it into a circle, burning holes in it, and then lacing a buckskin cover onto it that was painted green with yellow designs and bordered with black. Marriott also observed that "within comparatively recent years, two other shield societies were organized, but never reached the social power or numerical strength of the older ones."[119] These were the Kɔɔde and Hotoyi shields.

THE KƆƆDE SHIELDS

According to Heap O' Bears, the seven shields named after Kɔɔde (Patadlkyäpta) originated from his 1839 vision that also resulted in the creation of dɔ and the miniature Taime image. Sometime afterward, they were introduced into the Sun Dance and were placed in a north-south line about sixty feet east of the Sun Dance lodge. LaBarre's sketch (fig. 10, this volume) illustrates that the lower two-thirds of the Kɔɔde shields were painted Indian red and the upper third a light red with a white crescent moon in the middle. Heap O' Bears could not remember much about the shields, and LaBarre did not know the significance of the lunar motif but surmised it symbolized war protection.[120]

During the Sun Dance proper, Heap O' Bears said, the Kɔɔde shield owners danced along with the Taime shield keepers. Ceremonial adornment of the dancers included Indian red body paint with a dark blue moon on the sternum flanked by two dark-blue crescent moons and white faces with "blue strips or dots around [the] semicircle of [the] lower face." Their feet, ankles, and wrists were painted blue, and crow feathers were attached to the wrists and ankles. Heap O' Bears later contradicted himself and said that two eagle feathers were attached to their wrists but not to the ankles. He also stated that the shield keepers wore sage wreaths, contrary to an earlier claim that only Kɔɔde wore a headdress, because he was the leader. Kɔɔde wore a buffalo-hide bonnet with an eagle-down front similar to the rabbit bonnet worn by Onsokyapta, perhaps to signify their close friendship.[121] Contradictory data probably derive from the rapid collapse of the shield societies with the demise of the Sun Dance after 1887, as evidenced by interviews with Mrs. Big Bow and Max Frizzlehead, who had some difficulties trying to remember details from the mid-nineteenth century.[122] Heap O' Bears, whose childhood dated to the mid-1860s, could not remember the names of all seven Kɔɔde shield bearers except for Poor Buffalo, Sekoye, and Pagu·he, or Pagunhente (No Buffalo Horns, or Hornless Bull), who was killed in by the Utes in 1868 along with Heap O' Bears II.[123] Mary Buffalo—a young girl when Patadlkyäpta was living—and Bert Geikauma remembered that Big Bow, Two Hatchet, and Hollering Wolf possessed Kɔɔde shields, but they were unaware of their whereabouts. They did specify, however, that the "shields stop[ped]" because inheritance patterns had been disrupted by Anglos.[124]

THE TE·DLGU·DA, OR HOTOYI SHIELDS

As related by Heap O' Bears, the five Hotoyi shields, originating from the power vision of Hotoyi, or Akopti (Timber Mountain), were introduced along with a new Taime at the 1869 "Bring in the War Bonnet" Sun Dance. Incorporating the shields into the Sun Dance was probably one of Long Foot's last innovations before he died the following year. The shields were placed about sixty feet east of the Sun Dance lodge in a north-south line, either north or south of the Kɔɔde shields but not intermixed with them. In the morning, the Hotoyi shields were positioned east toward the rising sun, were rotated west to follow the setting sun, and then were covered at night. Moving the shields in sync with the sun strongly suggests their association with Sun and Taime, the two principal sources of war power invoked during the Sun Dance. The Hotoyi shields, also called *te·dlgu·da* (white-red) due to their light-red background, featured the same solar and lunar motifs found on the Taime shields (fig. 11, this volume). Two black crescent moons in the upper portion flanked a centrally located black sun, an eagle wing bone whistle was attached to the left side, and two eagle feathers hung at the bottom. The solar designs represented warfare and the Sun Dance, but the meaning of the lunar motifs remains unknown. The Hotoyi shields might be the Pokítekī shields that Frank Given mentioned to Marriott.[125]

Heap O' Bears said that Hotoyi shield owners painted their faces and bodies for the Sun Dance with the same white-red background. Dipping sage in white paint, they splotched their arms and chests with white spots and painted black lightning on their cheeks and their lips black. Their waist belts were adorned with black handkerchiefs and silver fox fur, and the leader was distinguished by buckskin moccasins. While dancing, they constantly blew eagle wing bone whistles. The five Hotoyi shield owners kept their shields for life and selected heirs to succeed deceased members. Nevertheless, since the Hotoyi shields were introduced in 1869, and probably were confiscated in 1875 with all other weapons and war accouterments, inheritance problems did not arise in this short-lived society. Nonetheless, Heap O' Bears identified the five Hotoyi shield owners: (1) OnGuæ, described as a later Taime keeper; (2) Adɔyete, or Adoetti (Big Tree), a young warrior later turned Christian; (3) Baitædlyi, or Paitayli (Son of the Sun, or Sun Boy), an older warrior who died in 1888; (4) Ɔndeinbin; and (5) Mak'i, or Mo-keen.[126]

On November 15, 1873, Friend Battey was visiting a "peaceful" Kiowa camp when Sun Boy offered the protection of his "medicine shield" based on his fear that "hostile" Comanches opposing Battey's presence in the camp might harm him. Sun Boy took Battey aside and presented his shield to Battey, who described it:

> Sun Boy rose up, and bade me follow him. I did so. He led the way, without the utterance of a word, some distance into the thick, brushy wood, to a large oak tree, where he had caused his medicine shield to be placed. This, as usual, was wrapped carefully in a blanket, and mounted upon poles, a little after the fashion of a painter's easel. Stopping at some distance from the shield, the chief bade me by signs to go forward and remove its covering. I did so, and found that it had still another covering of buckskin, with a painted representation of the sun in the centre, shedding rays of all colors, in straight lines, to the circumference. This he also bade me remove. . . . Upon this, the chief stepped forward, removed the covering, and desired me not only to pass before it and look at it, but to handle it.
>
> With all this I complied, feeling the thickness of the shield, and handling the raven feathers and bone whistle which hung upon its face. This latter article is made of the principal bone of an eagle's wing. . . .
>
> Kicking Bird explained the object of the adventure, which was to render me safe from the bullets or arrows of the Comanches and Cheyennes. I had looked the shield in the face, had handled the sacred ornaments, and the spirit residing in it had not been angry, and would now watch over and protect me. (Battey 1968, 208–9)

The shield Battey described was probably Sun Boy's Hotoyi shield, albeit the multicolored sunbeams radiating from Sun do not match LaBarre's sketch, nor did Battey mention lunar motifs. Nevertheless, the Sun motif, pendant feathers, and eagle bone whistle correspond to the Hotoyi shield sketched by LaBarre. Undoubtedly, memories wavered between 1873 and 1935 concerning shield details. Battey, however, observed ritual activity that few non-Indians of his era chronicled, so his rendition of the shield's spiritual protection provides an eyewitness account of Kiowa religious beliefs.

Heap O' Bears said that like the other shields, the Hotoyi shields were "disposed of," or "put aside," and the designs were not passed down, because of the cessation of warfare. After 1875 the shields were used only in the Sun Dance, which declined in the 1880s and became defunct after 1887. By then, shield keepers like Sun Boy knew that the old days of raiding were long over and that the Sun Dance was practically extinct, so he left his shield as an offering in the vicinity of Mt. Scott in 1888 shortly before his death (see Mooney 1898, 358).[127]

Kiowa Warrior and Women's Societies

Unlike shield societies and doctoring societies, prereservation Plains sodalities were not esoteric, secret societies with limited membership. Instead, membership in warrior societies was voluntary and crosscut kinship ties and band affiliation. Mandan, Hidatsa, Blackfoot, Arapaho, and Gros Ventre military societies were age-graded, but sodalities in other Plains tribes were non-age-graded, coordinate systems with ad hoc membership. Warrior societies usually did not fight together as military units, though members' feats of valor were announced at public gatherings in coalesced summertime encampments. Members also performed civic duties such as policing the summer bison hunts, participating and assisting in tribal rituals, and helping those in need. Most importantly, sodalities commemorated the ethos of the warrior through distinctive origin myths, regalia, songs, and dances. Women's societies often supported sodalities through rituals, and offered prayers to other-than-human persons to protect warriors departing on war expeditions. Military societies undoubtedly played critical roles in the mid-nineteenth century as Plains warfare escalated (Meadows 1999, 4–11).

Although *dɔdɔ* was restricted mostly to *ondedɔ* men, Kiowa warrior societies were important because practically every male belonged to one, even the lowest class *dapom* (bums), *go·bop* (captives), and Plains Apaches. Goomda, Sanko, Tsoodle, Silver Horn, and Jimmy Quoetone provided the Santa Fe field party with lots of information about the sodalities, though most were defunct by 1935. Extensive war records were not prerequisites for joining sodalities, as men were taken into the societies without any prior combat experience. More important was the institution of *kom* (blood-brothers), friendship pairs that were arranged when two youths were taken into a society together. Upon initiation, *kom* pairs were required to bump heads in front of the assembled society, followed by an exchange of horses ritually formalizing their lifelong friendship. Since a young man's relatives did not pressure him to join their societies, *kom* was a vital bonding mechanism for crosscutting kinship ties and band affiliation and socially integrating Kiowa society in the rites of war and war power (see Meadows 2010, 6).[128]

W. P. Clark (1885, 355) identified five Kiowa "soldier bands," whereas Mooney (1898, 229–30) named six ranked Yäpähe (warriors) organizations which were non-age-graded except for the first, or lowest order: (1) Polä'ñyup, or Tsäñyu'i (Rabbits); (2) Ädaltóyui, or Téñbeyu'i (Young [wild] Sheep); (3) Tseñtä'nmo (Horse Headdresses); (4) Toñkoñiko (Black Legs); (5) T'äñpéko (Skunkberry People), or Tséñ-â'dalka-i (Crazy Horses); and (6) Kâ-itséñiko (Real, or Principal, Dogs). Recent research by William Meadows (2010, 5) suggests that individual status increased with membership in the last three societies. According to Mooney (1898, 230), the warrior societies led tribal ceremonies, served as camp police, conducted hunts, and participated in raids. As noted by Red Dress and Silver Horn, warrior society meetings were only held during the Sun Dance period since the bands were dispersed most of the year. At the meetings, members privately discussed matters of importance to the society, such as the recruitment of new members. Private war dances were conducted inside large society tipis, and the public was invited when the tipi covers were rolled up to connect the participants with those sitting outside. Then everyone could join the singing and dancing (see Meadows 2010, 7).[129]

According to White Fox and Jimmy Quoetone, the best-known function of the military societies—except that of the Rabbits—was to take turns policing the communal bison hunts necessary to provision the coalesced Sun Dance encampment that lasted up to six weeks. Members of the society chosen to guard the camp prevented solitary hunters from sneaking ahead of the main hunting party. When unauthorized hunting occurred, those society members were entitled to confiscate or even destroy the offender's property, including horses and hunting accouterments. Hunting stampeded the herds, so the logic behind communal hunting was to maximize the amount of buffalo meat brought into the large encampment; thoughtless individuals risked driving off the herds, causing hunger and compelling the people to break camp in pursuit of the fleeing herds. No one was immune from the strict hunting bans, not even Ten Medicines keepers, the Taime keeper, or the band leaders. Sodalities also enforced decisions made by the Ten Medicines keepers concerning domestic disputes.[130] Law enforcement by warrior societies in other Plains tribes has been covered by McHugh (1972, 57–59), Llewellyn and Hoebel (1941), and Provinse (1955, 344–62). Thorough analysis of the origins and history of Kiowa societies, including the roles of the present-day Toñkoñko, T'äñpéko (also Daimpega), and Polä'ñyup can be found in Meadows (2010), who heavily relies on the 1935 Santa Fe fieldnotes, the Alice Marriott Papers from the Western History Collections (University of Oklahoma) to a lesser extent, and secondary sources.[131]

The Bear Society

Perhaps related to the connection between the Ten Medicines and Bear mythology, a women's society, the Bear Society, functioned as an auxiliary to the Ten Medicines keepers. The Septsónkyop, or Ɔnká·deyigo (Bear Society), had been defunct for quite some time before 1935, although several elders remembered details about this secret society and the meetings held during former times. As translated by her nephew, Monroe Tsatoke, Pitma cryptically referred to the meetings as an "ill omen," a statement that perplexed LaBarre.[132] Red Dress said that her mother had belonged to this organization,[133] but the most information about the Bear Society came from Moth Woman and Gontahap (Mrs. Blue Jay), former members, who described meetings and seating arrangements to Richardson.[134] According to Gontahap, the last meeting was held around 1905.[135] Such discrepancies are perhaps due to the women's different degrees of involvement in the Bear Society and to memory lapses since its collapse concomitant with the demise of the horse and buffalo culture during the reservation period. Kintadl suggested that the Bear Society was linked to the Ten Medicines keepers through the story of the giant bear chasing seven sisters who became the Pleiades.[136] Moth Woman and Gontahap identified nine former members, including themselves, and agreed that the women inherited their powers just like the Ten Medicines keepers. Pitma remembered that one woman, serving as the leader, wore a bear claw necklace as her insignia of office.[137] No other symbols of this organization were remembered, but Moth Woman recalled that husbands and children could never hit a member in the face, and that her food could never be transferred to another person.[138] As auxiliaries to the Ten Medicines keepers, the women composing the Bear Society were also responsible intermediaries between the Kiowa and the spirit world, particularly in relation to warfare. Analogous to the keepers, they prayed for the well-being and longevity of the Kiowas during the special sweat lodge meetings pledged by male nonmembers. Detailed coverage of the Bear women and their spiritual assistance for war parties can be found in Meadows (2010, 320–27).

The Tsædlyiesonhi

As the high priest responsible for officiating at the Sun Dance, the *taimek'i* was assisted by a women's auxiliary society dedicated to serving Taime, the Tsædlyiesonhi, also Tsädlyiesonhe and variant spellings (Old Women's Society).[139] Moth Woman's and Mary Buffalo's mothers had been members of this organization that, with exceptions, extended membership to women over age sixty, who were venerated for having lived beyond their child-bearing years. Due to their advanced age and high status, members of the Tsædlyiesonhi were "uninhibited" and had "no shame," as exemplified by their dances, which often included obscene gesticulations. Because post-menopausal women possessed extremely powerful *dɔdɔ*, members of the Old Women's Society were considered to be more powerful than Bear Society women.[140] Moth Woman observed that Bear, the Ten Medicines, and the Bear Society were affiliated with women, whereas "the taime, sun and old women's soc[iety] comprised a male complex so were more closely associated with men." Her comments suggest that the post-menopausal powers of the old women aligned them closer to the maleness of Taime and war power, making them slightly more powerful than the Ten Medicines and the Bear Society. Hence women of the Tsædl-yiesonhi were called upon more frequently than the Bear Society women because of their greater powers.[141] Notably, the Old Women participated in the Sun Dance festivities, particularly the sanding ceremony during the final stages of constructing the Sun Dance arbor. Other scholars assert that the Old Women's Society, largely affiliated with war power, was an auxiliary to the men's societies (Lowie 1916b, 849–50; Levy 2001, 912; Meadows 2010, 320), but these claims cannot be substantiated by the 1935 fieldnotes. Thorough coverage of the Old Women's Society can be found in Meadows (2010, 301–16).

Bundles, Shields, and Societies after 1935

By 1935, the shield societies were defunct and any extant shields were largely in museums and people's memories. The women's societies were extinct, as were the men's societies, with the exception of the T'añpéko, and the O-ho-mah Lodge, which had been founded in 1883 (Kracht 2012, 287). Many Kiowas had converted to Christianity and worshiped in Baptist, Methodist, and other denominational churches or belonged to the Native American Church and attended peyote meetings. There were some tensions between the two competing religions, and those brought up in strict Christian traditions were prohibited by their parents from attending Indian dances or participating in any religious activities outside church. Such stories were related to me by Agatha Paddlety Bates, whose father, David Paddlety, was one of the interpreters for the Santa Fe field party.[142] There was some degree of leniency, though. For instance, Evalu Ware Russell was raised in a Baptist home where her father, James Ware, disapproved of the peyote religion and kept his children away from it, though he allowed Evalu to attend O-ho-mah dances with her mother, "a wonderful dancer" who "danced very hard with feeling."[143] Amos Aitson, raised in the Holiness denomination, remembered being left with his paternal great-grandfather Mo-keen, who taught him about the Sun Dance.[144] In 1936, Charley Apekaum described how Kiowa beliefs had changed in the postallotment era:

We don't have our sundance anymore and the people aren't worshiping the Ten Medicines like they used to and about the only thing we got now is the peyote religion and it's new, still we're hanging on and the older people still hang on to the Ten Medicines. And the younger boys and girls are not taking advantage of those old ways of worship. (LaBarre 1957, 183)

Jerrold Levy (1959, 117) later wrote that the tribal bundles remained in the eleven *ondedɔ* families that traditionally kept the medicines, though he apparently was not aware that one of the Ten Medicines was lost in a blaze sometime in the 1930s (Palmer 2003, 129n). Since then, inheritance has become complicated in a rapidly changing world.

Notably, most Kiowas are hesitant to discuss the Ten Medicines, Taime, or personal medicine bundles. Elsie Clews Parsons (1929, xvii) discussed the secrecy of the bundles in the late 1920s, as did Jerrold Levy (1959, 122) thirty years later, followed by Maurice Boyd (1983, 52) in the early 1980s, around the time I began conducting fieldwork. Even Gus Palmer Jr., whose grandfather Henry Tanedooah possessed one of the Ten Medicines in the post–World War II era, has acknowledged Kiowa reticence to discuss the bundles: "Most Kiowa elders refuse to talk about them because the medicines are too sacred to discuss" (Palmer 2003, 129n). Betty Tanedooah Tongkeamah initially warned me that asking questions about the bundles would create hostility among elderly Kiowas, and that I should avoid the topic.[145] Since that time, I do not ask about the bundles but politely listen if someone brings up the topic. For instance, while visiting with the women attending a United Methodist Women's retreat in April 1987, I mentioned my interest in Kiowa religious beliefs since the days of the Sun Dance when asked about my research. Someone brought up the topic of the Ten Medicines, prompting another woman to perk up and proudly state that one of the bundles is cared for by her family.[146]

During the post–World War II era, inheritance patterns of the Ten Medicines broke down due to the strict prohibitions attached to the bundles. Gus Palmer Sr. related that the old-timers believed that the medicines were supposed to be kept in isolated tipis where they would not be disturbed. Rapidly changing lifestyles brought about by cars and houses, however, made it increasingly difficult to care for the bundles, so keepers had to make some changes to ensure their safety. "Some time ago" the keepers got together to clean out the bundles to prepare them for modern times. One old time "priest" conducted the purification ceremony; without looking into the bundles he reached into each one and pulled out things that were no longer necessary, such as "hair [scalps] and some beads," thereby removing all the "superstitions" from the sacred bundles.[147] When Gus Palmer Jr. was a boy, Henry Tanedooah took him into the room where he kept his bundle to pray for the boy's recovery from an illness. He told Gus, "All of those old things that these medicines contained were removed from them long ago" (Palmer 2003, 129–30n). Boyd (1983, 12) indicated that a blindfolded medicine woman conducted such a ceremony in 1934. Regardless of how the ceremony transpired, the bundles were purified so they could be transported in cars and safely stored in houses, according to Gus Palmer Sr. Hence older symbols, such as scalps connected to the nineteenth century, were removed to modernize the bundles and make them easier to care for, though they can never leave the Kiowa area.[148]

Gus Palmer Sr. said that sometime in the post–World War II era, individuals inheriting the bundles became less involved in the ceremonies associated with them, so certain practices subsequently disappeared. For example, Ten Medicines keepers used to take out their pipes and smoke over the bundles after hearing the first thunder in the spring, a practice that has been abandoned.[149] When she was very young, Betty's father Henry Tanedooah used to take his pipe to a lonely spot each full moon to pray for the Kiowas. In his later years, Henry and his wife lived in Carrollton, Texas, with Betty and her husband, Clifton Tongkeamah. Oftentimes Betty heard him praying before sunrise, and she claimed he was one of the last Ten Medicines keepers to perform the prayer rite in the old-time way. When Henry died in 1966 the family met to decide the fate of the bundle because there were no men kinfolk to properly care for it. One possibility was to bury the bundle with him since in former times men had been buried with their bundles and medicine shields, but the family feared grave robbers would exhume his grave if they found out about it. Thus Betty's sister was selected to keep the bundle and care for it, which she did for seventeen years, with her husband serving as an assistant.[150] During the Santa Fe field school, Moth Woman told Richardson that Kiowas were fearful of having their graves looted.[151]

Since the 1960s, finding eligible caretakers has become increasingly difficult, compelling some descendants of bundle keepers to care for multiple bundles. James Silverhorn, son of former keeper Silver Horn, reportedly owned five of the Ten Medicines in the 1970s (Boyd 1983, 12). Rev. Bob Pinezaddleby related to me that James collected bundles from some of the families unable to properly care for them.[152] Gus Palmer Sr. related that after James Silverhorn died in 1981, other people came to claim the bundles, but the status of their ownership has been somewhat confusing since a proposed meeting to determine their fate never transpired.[153] Before his death in 1997, Harding Big Bow, who lived west of Carnegie, presumably cared for four of the bundles, as stated by Libby Littlechief Ahtone during a history lesson at the Kiowa Complex.[154] In June 2004, Ira Kaulay and I visited the old homestead where he showed me a concrete slab behind the house that constituted the floor for the tipi where he ran peyote meetings, and where he periodically kept the bundles.[155]

Jerrold Levy (1959, 121–22) noted that the power of the Ten Medicines was not attenuated by culture change since the reservation period because respectful Christians even supplicated them with prayer offerings of calico, beadwork, and other goods, and that they also took groceries and gifts to the keepers. Gus Palmer Jr. (2003, 129n) identified some of the gifts taken to his grandfather's bundle: "shawls, blankets, quilts, fabric cuts, money, and even food." During the Vietnam War, Johnny Pinezaddleby was preparing to ship out to Southeast Asia but was troubled by the negativity of the anti-war movement. He told his father: "I would like . . . when I leave from here, I would like to have something that is part of my Indian culture, my Indian background." Since James Silverhorn was Bob's father's cousin—essentially his father too—Bob approached him to fill his son's "tall order." On the appointed afternoon, father and son drove a carload of meat and groceries to Silverhorn's home near Carnegie, where they espied him sitting under an arbor near a tipi. After visiting with his grandson, Silverhorn provided instructions on receiving the blessing, as narrated by Rev. Pinezaddleby:

"I'm your grandfather. And I was told that you were very concerned about how things would be for you. Especially as you are going to leave for a distant place." "So," he said, "I got ready for you. See that tipi? You go over there, and when you go in there, there will be the medicine.

They'll be in there." And he had that whole area fixed up, he's like, like having a regular Native American Church meeting. And he had it all, the fireplace was all fixed up and he had the peyote, the cacti that they use, it was all ready. And up there in the back there, where they usually sit, the head people, was hanging four of those, the bundles were hanging, the *zaide thali* [Split Boys]. Yeah. They were hanging there [on the tipi poles at the west end of the tipi]. So he told Johnny, he said, "When you go in there you, you touch yourself. Touch them, touch yourself, all over, each one of them."

So I went up there with him, and as we stepped inside the tipi, and I noticed all that was there. And I said, "First thing we want to do is have a prayer." So, I prayed, about what was what, was going to take place. Then after we got through, well I said, "Now you can go and touch them, all over your body." And he did, and he followed that procedure and he got through. Then I went up there and did the same. And I felt a lot better. Then after we got through, well we went out, and went back to the grandfather, he was sitting out there. And we told him that we did what he instructed us to do. And he said, "Alright grandson, when you move, when you go from here, when you leave from here, that's when my work will begin."[156]

Johnny Pinezaddleby served as point man for a scout dog unit in Vietnam, conducting over twenty-one missions clearing out booby traps before returning home unscathed. Whenever he was sent on a mission, Johnny thought of his grandfather and the medicines. As his father related, "Through the prayer and through the spiritual involvement there[,] that really made him feel good." Shortly after returning home, Pinezaddleby told his son, "Well, you said you wanted something Indian, and you got it."[157] Today, the bundles are ready when needed, as nicely illustrated by this story. Even among Christians, the medicine bundles remain a source of tribal identity and power. As in the old days, powers are not mutually exclusive, so it's not unusual for individuals to consult the medicine bundles.

The Taime bundle remained in the hands of Émáa from 1984 until her death in 1939 and then passed to her daughter, Nina Kodaseet (Boyd 1983, 50). According to Rev. Pinezaddleby, Nina served as a counselor helping different tribes with their problems and presumably visited the Wind River Shoshonis in Wyoming to help them, taking Taime with her. After her passing in 1989, the status of Taime became a mystery, though it was presumed that her daughter took the bundle.[158] Others, like Vanessa Paukeigope Jennings, maintain that the Botone descendants kept the bundle.[159] For the sake of protecting the sanctity of Taime, it's best to let the mystery remain intact.

Today, the tribal bundles still play an important role in Kiowa culture, though they exist in modified form, which is consistent with the earlier practices of Onsokyapta, the renowned Taime keeper who introduced so many innovations during his tenure as Taimek'i. The individuals who convened to modernize the Ten Medicines by removing the scalps were in concordance with his capacity for adaptability. Purifying the bundles ensured they would not be abandoned in modern times, especially in an era where women were becoming keepers and their husbands were their assistants, a vast departure from earlier customs. That the decision concerning Henry Tenadooah's bundle was made by family members in lieu of the other keepers illustrates how the old priesthood is now largely defunct. Had these changes not been made, it's unlikely that the bundles would still play roles in Kiowa lives today.

5

The Kiowa Sun Dance

The Plains Sun Dance

Scholars have emphasized for some time that "Sun Dance" is an improper translation of indigenous terms for the nineteenth-century ritual found in seventeen Plains tribes and among the Utes and Wind River Shoshonis, Great Basin tribes at the periphery of the western Plains. The term "Sun Dance" probably originated in the mid-nineteenth century from misconceptions of the Lakota *wiwanyag wacipi* (sun-gazing dance) (Scott 1911, 347; Spier 1921a, 490), though usage has become conventional. Contrary to popular belief, the Sun Dance did not involve sun worship but was a communal rite of personal sacrifice, power-seeking, and renewal, as suggested by the Gros Ventre and Arapaho "sacrifice lodge" and the Cheyenne "medicine teepee ceremony" or "new life lodge." According to JoAllyn Archambault, it was the "most public and dramatic" of all the Plains ceremonies (Archambault 2001, 983, 987–88; Liberty 1980, 166–67; Voget 1984, 77). Among most horse and buffalo cultures, Sun Dance celebrations occurred between late spring and midsummer, the time marked by the coalescence of bison herds and scattered hunting bands. Sun Dance festivities lasting several weeks featured gatherings of band leaders and members of shield, medicine, and warrior societies; raids and war expeditions were planned; bison hunts were coordinated and policed; personal and tribal bundles were renewed; friends and family reunited; courtship, marriages, and affairs transpired; and gifts were given and exchanged (Archambault 2001, 983).

Sun Dances occurred only when visionaries pledged to sponsor them according to the directives of dream-spirits, or to fulfill vows made while confronting imminent danger or a serious illness; hence the Sun Dance was not necessarily an annual affair. Dancers and other functionaries also participated to satisfy personal vows or to seek power. Sun Dance bundle keepers selected the location and timing of ceremonies; directed the construction of the circular, open-air arbor; and officiated the choreography. The principal feature of the Sun Dance lodge was a tree—a living entity, respectfully treated like an enemy—that was scouted, cut down, dragged back to the encampment, and installed as the center pole. Affixed to the center pole or placed at its base was a bison hide or skull, completing an altar on which dancers focused their attention and drew inspiration as they danced in this place of power. Incarnate in this sacred space was the powerful spirit of Buffalo, to which people prayed for strength, fertility, and plentitude of all living things. Even onlookers were allowed to attach their own offerings to the center pole in search of healing or personal power. Although the Sun Dance was a renewal rite of healing and well-being, martial symbols were abundant, signifying the importance of warfare in nineteenth-century Plains societies (Archambault 2001, 983–84; Grim 2005b, 1050–56).

Sources on the Kiowa Sun Dance

Held between mid-June and late July, the Sun Dance was the most important Kiowa ceremony, for it unified the tribe socially and spiritually. A rite of renewal, the Sun Dance was associated with the dɔdɔ of Sun, the life-giving power of the universe, and Buffalo, lord of lower-world animals that provided sustenance. Sun gave power directly to the buffalo on which the Kiowas depended, and Sun was regarded as the father of Buffalo and the Kiowas. Sun was also a source of war power transmitted through Taime, the Sun Dance bundle. Sun, Buffalo, and war power were intricately entwined and recurrent themes during performances of the Sun Dance, which empowered the people as they sought spiritual and physical renewal.

On a societal level, this near-annual ceremony marked the only time the Kiowa bands, as well as the Plains Apaches, coalesced in the summertime, primarily because the successful performance of this tribal ritual ideally required the participation of all Kiowas (Scott 1911, 347, 356). Max Frizzlehead told Collier that on a spiritual level the Sun Dance was a renewal ceremony, a time for people to pray for the spiritual and physical well-being of their families. Moreover, those enduring fasting and dancing during the four days of the Sun Dance proper hoped that their pitiful state would create strong prayers to ensure a prosperous future. Individuals blessed with good fortune since the last Sun Dance also gave thanks to the powers represented by Sun, Buffalo, and Taime.[1]

Several published accounts provide useful information about the Kiowa Sun Dance (Battey 1968; Mooney 1898; Methvin 1899; Spier 1921a; Scott 1911; Nye 1934; Boyd 1981; Mikkanen 1987). Each source has intrinsic value, but most have biases that should be taken into consideration. For instance, Friend Thomas Battey, the sole Euro-American to observe and write about a Kiowa Sun Dance, only witnessed part of the 1873 ceremony but did not have a Kiowa interpreter to explain details to him. Though his descriptions are helpful, Battey's Protestant bias is apparent in his negative views of the ceremony (Battey 1968, 166–84). The same bias is found in Rev. J. J. Methvin's (1899, 58–71) account, related to him by Andres Martinez, or Andele, a multilingual Mexican captive raised Kiowa. Despite his bias, Methvin's account is useful on a comparative basis since Andele also collaborated with Mooney and Spier. James Mooney (1898) did not write a comprehensive account of the ritual, though descriptions of the Sun Dance and related ceremonies are scattered throughout his calendar history. He depended on Battey's description of the Sun Dance lodge (1898, 243–44) and also received data from his friend Hugh L. Scott (Greene 2009, 21).

Hugh L. Scott's (1911) account of the Sun Dance is undoubtedly the best. Transferred to Fort Sill in 1889, the year before the aborted and final Sun Dance "when the forked poles were left standing," Lt. Scott became intrigued by the ritual he never witnessed. During his nine-year appointment, and as commander of Indian Cavalry Troop L, Scott made lasting friendships with prominent Kiowa elders, who provided him with valuable ethnographic data regarding the defunct ritual. His consultants, T'ebodal, Poor Buffalo, Frizzlehead (the elder), Feathered Lance, and Stumbling Bear, identified as the oldest living Kiowas, had witnessed and participated in the ceremony. Tahbonemah, or I-see-o (Plenty Fires), Scott's closest Kiowa friend, served as "spokesman" for the group. Silver Horn, noted artist and calendar keeper, provided Scott with illustrations. Because he was fluent in Plains sign language, Scott obtained information about the Sun Dance exclusively through this mode and wrote the original draft of his article in 1897 (Scott 1911, 355, 368; Greene 2001, 71; Greene 2009, 21). Scott's account offers insight into the ritual that other sources do not mention and, importantly, Silver Horn's drawings depict details of the Sun Dance lodge and altar. Scott accurately identified the Sun Dance as a drama that symbolized the "regeneration of life" but like many of his contemporaries wrongly surmised that it involved "worship of the Sun Father" (Scott 1911, 374).

Leslie Spier wrote the summary article for the Plains Sun Dance in volume 16 of the *Anthropological Papers of the American Museum of Natural History* (Spier 1921b) and also contributed an article on the Kiowa Sun Dance (Spier 1921a). Field data were collected in 1919, and like his predecessors, Spier engaged Andele's services as consultant. Using Scott's 1911 publication as a baseline, Spier elicited additional information on the Sun Dance and compared his data to Robert Lowie's (1916b) article on Kiowa sodalities (Spier 1921a, 437). In most instances, Spier's article concurs with Scott's. In the fall of 1933, Lt. Wilbur Nye was transferred to Fort Sill's artillery school and assigned the task of writing the history of the post (Nye 1937). Like Scott, Nye befriended many Indians and within a year published an account of the Kiowa Sun Dance (Nye 1934). George Hunt—who also served as an interpreter for Alice Marriott and the 1935 field party—rendered the account that corresponds closely with Scott's (1911) and Spier's (1921a).

In the 1970s, several Kiowa elders concerned with non-Indian accounts of Kiowa culture formed the Kiowa Historical and Research Society (KHRS), which led to the publication of *Kiowa Voices*, volume 1 (Boyd 1981). Chapter 3, "Skaw-tow," describes the Sun Dance and is partially based on the Susan Peters Collection. Susan Peters, a field matron among the Kiowas between 1918 and 1963, befriended many Kiowas and obtained death-bed interviews from individuals like Laura Pedrick, the Carlisle-educated daughter of Red Otter (and sister of Ä'piataň, or Ahpeatone [Wooden Lance], according to Ray C. Doyah) and T'ebodal, Mooney's principal collaborator (Boyd 1981, 35–53).[2] The bulk of materials used in "Skaw-tow" derive from interviews in the 1970s with knowledgeable Kiowa elders: Linn Pauahty, James Twohatchet, David Apekaum, Charley Redbird, Louis Toyebo, Parker McKenzie, and others. Because the last complete Kiowa Sun Dance was held in 1887, none of these individuals actually witnessed the ritual, albeit they maintained oral traditions passed down to them by their parents and grandparents. Collectively, these individuals possessed a rich storehouse of information on Kiowa culture, although their data on the Sun Dance should be differentiated from eyewitness testimonies. A major problem with *Kiowa Voices* is the absence of detailed citations in the text permitting the reader to identify the diverse Kiowa "voices" describing the Sun Dance, and because of this, it is often difficult to assess where some of the data were derived—from the 1970s interviews, or from the Susan Peters Collection. Moreover, it is impossible to determine whether some passages represent Boyd's viewpoint or interpretations from other published sources, though it is evident that he relied on secondary sources (Stahl 1983, 46–50). Another problem, as related to me by Gus Palmer Sr., is that the proper authorities for certain topics were not consulted.[3] Finally, Mikkanen's (1987) version of the Kiowa Sun Dance is largely based on *Kiowa Voices*, adding no new information concerning this extinct ceremony (Archambault 2001, 994).

Compared to published sources on the Kiowa Sun Dance and the larger body of Plains materials, the data collected in 1935 by the Santa Fe field party is invaluable. In the Sun Dance chapter written by LaBarre for the unpublished monograph, he acknowledged his collaboration with Collier, noting that they hashed out the ceremony until they practically knew it backwards. LaBarre identified the "chief informants" for this chapter as White Buffalo, Max Frizzlehead, Mary Buffalo, Heap O' Bears III, Red Dress, Hunting Horse, Mrs. Hokeah, and Mrs. Big Bow. Additional information was provided by White Fox, Jimmy Quoetone, and Pitma. The principal interpreters were Charley Apekaum, Conrad Mausape, and Bert Geikauma, and to a lesser extent Ned Brace, David Paddlety, and Monroe Tsatoke. From the fieldnotes gleaned for the present chapter, Heap O' Bears provided the most information to LaBarre—with Charley Apekaum interpreting—and also to Collier, who used David Paddlety as his interpreter. Richardson also gathered some information from Heap O' Bears. Mary Buffalo, granddaughter of Taime keeper Onsokyapta, also provided lots of data about the Sun Dance to LaBarre, who used Bert Geikauma and Charley Apekaum as his interpreters. Notably, Mary had witnessed and could name fifteen Sun Dances, dating back to 1867.[4] Old Man Apekaum also provided information to LaBarre through his son Charley's translations. Charley also translated for Collier's interviews with Max Frizzlehead and White Buffalo, whereas Guy Quoetone interpreted for interviews with Hunting Horse. Bascom also interviewed Hunting Horse with Monroe Tsatoke interpreting for his father. Other information used in this chapter was contributed by Lone Bear, White Buffalo, Sanko, Jimmy Quoetone, Andrew Stumbling Bear, White Fox, Goomda, Moth Woman, Red Dress, Mrs. Hokeah, Mrs. Big Bow, and White Horse. Occasional interpreters included George Hunt, Luther Brace, Ned Brace, and Conrad Mausape.[5] Had the Kiowa monograph been published, the Sun Dance chapter would have been the longest, for the cut and paste notes total 170 pages.

Through a handful of interviews during the summers of 1935 and 1936, Marriott also collected some information about the Sun Dance. On July 4, 1935, she conducted a lengthy interview with George Poolaw and interviewed Frank Given on four occasions in July and August. On August 19, 20, and 22, Sanko provided some insight about the Sun Dance. Ioleta Hunt MacElhaney served as Marriott's interpreter during these interviews. Marriott's typed fieldnotes on the Sun Dance total forty-five double-spaced pages, which pale in comparison to the Santa Fe fieldnotes, which are extensive and greatly detailed. Nevertheless, both sets of fieldnotes provide important information about the Kiowa Sun Dance, a ceremony that has not been performed in its entirety since 1887.

The Kiowa Sun Dance was divided into three periods of time: (1) the aggregation of the Kiowas and their guests at the "ride-around" camp, followed by up to two weeks of buffalo hunting; (2) the "getting-ready" period when the circular Sun Dance encampment was formed and the sacred Sun Dance lodge constructed, a period of approximately ten days; and (3) the Sun Dance proper, which involved the Sun Dance lodge dedication and three and a half days of dancing. After the Kiowas and Plains Apaches coalesced at the ride-around camp, they hunted until they had obtained enough meat to carry them through the getting-ready period and the Sun Dance proper, when hunting was prohibited. The getting-ready period began when the people ceremoniously arrived at the Sun Dance site and spent the first two days in camp staking out the camp circle and the Sun Dance lodge, in addition to procuring the center pole and the buffalo bull hide hoisted up the pole. Once this was accomplished, the walls and roof of the lodge were built, a process that consumed about four or five days. Day one of the Sun Dance proper consisted of several consecutive events officially dedicating the Sun Dance lodge: the kick fight, door-opening ceremony, bringing in Taime, building the altar and entryway, and the first series of dances. Day two commenced with the sanding of the Sun Dance lodge floor, placement of the entryway stone, and the painting of the dancers. The functionaries began dancing on day two, continuing intermittently until sundown of day four. Days two through four were also highlighted by the "fan chase." The dance officially ended when Taime and its accouterments were removed from the lodge. For the most part, upper-class men possessing dɔdɔ were the major participants in the ceremony, while everyone else watched.

Social Aspects of the Sun Dance: The Coalescence of Kiowa Bands and Socio-Religious Organizations

The Kiowa name for the Sun Dance, K'ado (river bank house, or bluff house, according to White Fox and Goomda, respectively), reflects that the ceremony was always conducted adjacent to a large stream or river, the sole ecosystem in the sun-parched Southwestern Plains that offered abundant enough shade, wood, and water necessary to sustain the coalesced Kiowa bands — together with the Plains Apaches and any other guests — longer than a week.[6] There is some controversy regarding the proper pronunciation of this word, for some Kiowa elders say it should be pronounced Skaw-tow, claiming that non-Indians mispronounce it K'ado because they cannot hear the muted word initial phoneme /s/ (Boyd 1981, 35; Mikkanen 1987). Mooney (1898, 408) and linguist John P. Harrington (1928, 97) transcribed it as K'ado, as did LaBarre and Collier. Regardless of the pronunciation or spelling, the word has the same meaning.

Except in instances calling for mutual protection, Kiowa and Plains Apache bands were dispersed most of the year but coalesced into a single encampment for several weeks in the late spring or early summer when Sun Dances were held. According to Heap O' Bears and Hunting Horse, interband and intertribal visiting, merrymaking, gossiping, warrior society meetings, and "love-making" were the social highlights of the Sun Dance encampment.[7] Social rules for courtship became relaxed, as noted by Hunting Horse, Mrs. Hokeah, and Bert Geikauma, because everyone knew that men and women were more prone to sexual liaisons at this time, much like bison aggregating into large herds prior to the rutting season. Before every Sun Dance, the Taimek'i announced that the time was ripe for lovemaking and affairs, and that any jealous reaction could endanger the entire tribe, because it was well understood that bloodshed would attenuate the efficacy of the Sun Dance. Since domestic quarrels were potentially dangerous, relatives of involved parties oftentimes intervened to mitigate tense situations, or sodality policemen ridiculed and shamed individuals to ensure that adultery did not lead to violence.[8] Thus social cohesion was prerequisite for the successful completion of the ceremony linked to the regeneration of the bison and the Kiowas.

Properly performing all the activities for the Sun Dance depended on the specialized ritual knowledge of the Taimek'i and his ability to solicit the cooperation and coordination of the Ten Medicines keepers, the shield societies, the men's and women's societies, and special groups of Sun Dancers, the "painted people."

Taimek'i: "High Priest" of the Sun Dance

The most important person during the Sun Dance was the Taime bundle keeper, who was responsible for directing the entire ceremony and praying to the powers of Taime for the benefit of the congregated people. During the Sun Dance festivities, he was referred to as K'ɔtok'i, or K'adok'i (Sun Dance man), by Mrs. Hokeah, Heap O' Bears, and Mary Buffalo, which implies his utmost authority during this sacred ritual.[9] Heap O' Bears said that the K'adok'i could be identified by the ceremonial regalia worn during the four dancing days of the Sun Dance proper:

> The k'adok'i is painted yellow all over, including his hair; and he wears yellow leggings. He has a jack-rabbit skin bonnet. He has a black circle on his breast and back representing the sun, but with no moons. Instead, he has another smaller sun circle at the hollow above the top end of the sternum. This throat circle is his life-breath; and the circle on the breast is the sun-creator. His lips are painted black also. He wears a long-haired scalp around his neck, with hair hanging down the back. . . . He may <u>carry</u> in his hand sage or cedar. He wears a single white down-feather in the front of his head-dress.[10]

The sun designs signified Sun and its life-giving force, as well as war power, also symbolized by the enemy scalp draped around his neck. The jack-rabbit bonnet was the insignia of his office, as was the yellow body paint. Besides the K'adok'i, only the Demguk'o, or Taime shield owners, wore yellow body paint, as related to Marriott by George Poolaw, Sanko, and Tsoodle.[11]

Heap O' Bears told LaBarre that Onsokyapta (Long Foot), the innovative Taimek'i from 1832 to 1871, often allowed his apprentices to assist in the rituals associated with the Sun Dance, especially his adopted son, Mo-keen, and Heap O' Bears II, his father, the "little Taime keeper" killed by Utes in 1868. Assistants frequently performed four tasks during the Sun Dance: (1) selecting the tree for the Sun Dance lodge center pole; (2) ritually smoking four times during the cutting; (3) running alongside the tree blowing a whistle as it was brought to the Sun Dance encampment; and (4) participating in the fan chase during the Sun Dance proper. These and other duties were performed whenever Onsokyapta needed their help. Following Long Foot's death in 1871, his successor, Dóhéñte, or Dɔhɛdɔtɛ, also spelled "Do-hente" or "Dohente" (No Moccasins), oversaw Sun Dance activities in 1873, 1874, and 1875 before his own death that fall, shortly after the Kiowas were confined to their reservation (Mooney 1898, 337, 340).[12] Undoubtedly Onsokyapta was still a renowned K'adok'i sixty-four years after his death since all the elderly collaborators described the Sun Dance as he had directed it.

The Ten Medicine Keepers: Assistants to Onsokyapta

Even though the Ten Medicines were not related to the Sun Dance, the keepers played significant roles during the Sun Dance activities; according to Heap O' Bears, they "work[ed] for the Taime."[13] They also assisted Onsokyapta by performing five important tasks identified by White Fox, Heap O' Bears, and Mary Buffalo: (1) during the "play buffalo" ceremony, a keeper lured the "buffalo herd" into the Sun Dance enclosure with a long-stemmed pipe; (2) several unloaded the buffalo bull carcass which was hoisted up the center pole; (3) they set up the "goal" in the middle of the Sun Dance camp circle; (4) one of them loaded the sacred pipe smoked to Taime during the Sun Dance proper; and (5) most important, they were the principal singers for the dance.[14] George Poolaw told Marriott that the Ten Medicines keepers waited inside the Taime keeper's tipi during the hunt for the buffalo bull hide, and that nine keepers sang inside the Sun Dance lodge while the tenth participated in luring in the buffalo herd into the Sun Dance enclosure. They also selected the four men called the "best warriors" after the herd entered the enclosure.[15]

Sodalities: Onsokyapta's Civil Servants

Heap O' Bears, Mary Buffalo, and Hunting Horse all agreed that once all the Kiowa bands aggregated in the first of several Sun Dance encampments, Onsokyapta assumed the role of K'adok'i and the warrior societies automatically became his assistants through the performance of civic duties: (1) policing the tribal buffalo hunts; (2) constructing the Sun Dance lodge; and (3) restraining society members prone to irrational behavior linked to jealousy. Hunting restrictions and social codes immediately went into effect as soon as the bands coalesced and were not lifted until the Sun Dance was completed.[16]

The Painted People: Principal Dancers at the Sun Dance

The painted people were the leading dancers during the four days of the Sun Dance proper. These special functionaries belonged to three groups identified by Mary Buffalo: (1) Gudlgut; (2) Dot'ɔmba; and (3) members of the three Sun Dance shield societies, also called Gudlgut.[17]

THE GUDLGUT

Gudlgut dancers were named for their elaborate body paint. In free translation, the morphemes *gudl* (colored, or red) and *gut*, or *kut* (to be painted) (Harrington 1928, 66), combine to mean "painted all over," as noted by Marion Kaulaity Hansson.[18] As specified by Heap O' Bears and White Buffalo, four Gudlgut were appointed to four-year terms that expired at the conclusion of a Sun Dance, at which time successors were chosen. Terms expired in different years, so the appointments overlapped. If a Gudlgut died in office, Onsokyapta selected a replacement, who assumed a four-year term. Gudlgut was a prestigious and honored position, so it was considered improper to refuse an invitation into this dance group. An incumbent was required to heavily gift a predecessor with horses and goods each time a Sun Dance was held during his term, so successors typically came from *ondedɔ* families, and from the Dot'ɔmba.[19]

Gudlgut dancers assumed the taboos of the Taimek'i. According to Old Man Apekaum and White Buffalo, they could not look in mirrors or eat tongue, heart, bear, skunk, or rabbit.[20] Andrew Stumbling Bear added that anyone stepping over them would become paralyzed.[21] Although these restrictions did not make this a desirable position, one could not refuse an appointment. White Buffalo said that some Dɔt'ɔmba avoided recruitment by sneaking away before the Sun Dance ended, forcing the Gudlgut to make an alternative selection, a permissible ploy because the Dɔt'ɔmba could leave the Sun Dance lodge at will, whereas the Gudlgut were required to remain in the lodge the entire four days, except to briefly step outside to relieve themselves. However, White Buffalo added that the Gudlgut only danced two of the four dancing days: one and two, two and three, or three and four.[22]

Former Gudlgut painted their appointed successors on the first morning of the Sun Dance proper. Mary Buffalo related a description of the paint and regalia to LaBarre:

The painter feints four times before finally painting the following designs: a blue circle over forehead, cheeks and chin, all around face, diagonal zigzags from the eyes outward on the cheeks; a circle representing the sun in the middle of the breast; two half-moons with the horns up, over each nipple; same on back (sun and moons); and bands of paint around each wrist and ankle—all in blue paint. They also have bunches of sage around each wrist and ankle; tied in two places, one inside one outside of wrist—the stalks inward at ankle and wrist, and the sage-brush plumes outward. Two of them have also a sage-brush crown, into which is stuck a single white eagle plume; two of them have beaver bonnets, which are kept at other times with the taime medicine bag. All have a whistle made of an eagle wingbone (humerus), at one end of which is a neck loop which suspends it on the breast when not in use; at the other end is a short 2–3 inch buckskin string to which is tied a loose big quill, which turns and flutters with the movements of the dancers.[23]

The dancer drawn by Andres Martinez for Methvin (fig. 12, this volume) matches this description. Heap O' Bears added that Gudlgut dancers also wore long, white-painted buckskin shirts, featuring the designs described by Mary Buffalo.[24] White Buffalo and Old Man Apekaum, however, specified that one Gudlgut wore a jackrabbit bonnet and the other a beaver bonnet.[25] Perhaps the Gudlgut wearing a jackrabbit bonnet was the leader since the K'adok'i also wore a jackrabbit bonnet.

THE DƆT'ƆMBA

Heap O' Bears and White Buffalo thought there were as many as fifty Dɔt'ɔmba,[26] which they referred to as the "other dancers" besides the Gudlgut.[27] Dɔt'ɔmba, men and boys, including some Comanches and Plains Apaches, began dancing the first evening of the Sun Dance proper, as remembered by Heap O' Bears, White Buffalo, and Old Man Apekaum. They continued to dance alongside the Gudlgut during the second and third days, constantly staring at Taime while dancing, petitioning its powers with prayers.[28] Since the Dɔt'ɔmba came from all social classes, they did not wear the elaborate regalia and paint characteristic of the Gudlgut. Heap O' Bears described their body paint:

> These are painted white all over, with one eagle down feather hanging <u>down</u> loose in the back and fluttering; whistles of eagle wing-bone hung around the neck, blown while dancing. They have white paint in the hair also; no sage anklets, wristlets, no head-dress, no designs on body or face. They might dance with sage or cedar in the hand.[29]

The Sun Dance Shield Societies

Following the incorporation of the Taime, Poor Buffalo, and Hotoyi shields into the Sun Dance, the shield keepers danced alongside the other dancers and were also referred to as Gudlgut. However, Heap O' Bears noted that they differed from their namesake because they inherited their positions and served life terms.[30]

THE DEMGUK'O GUDLGUT

Although seven Taime shields originating from the 1834 power vision of Onsokyapta were presented to seven Demguk'o (yellow breasts) who shared the collective powers of the shields (see fig. 8, this volume), Mrs. Big Bow and Mary Buffalo indicated that there were only four Demguk'o.[31]

Perhaps the breakdown of inheritance patterns after the cessation of warfare in 1875 contributed to the diminishing number of Taime shield keepers by the final performance of the Sun Dance in 1887, when there were four or five, as specified by Andrew Stumbling Bear and White Buffalo,[32] or fewer, according to Mrs. Hokeah.[33] Undoubtedly the rapid decline of the Sun Dance and the shield societies during the reservation period is reflected by fewer shield owners.

According to Heap O' Bears and Andrew Stumbling Bear, the Demguk'o Gudlgut danced without their shields, which were positioned west of the Sun Dance lodge. Demguk'o body paint was similar to the paint of the Gudlgut. Their chests and backs were adorned with solar and lunar motifs, and they wore sage anklets, wristlets, and headdresses. Likewise, the Demguk'o Gudlgut leader wore a beaver bonnet, and the Demguk'o danced barefooted, as did all the painted people.[34] Andrew Stumbling Bear, who witnessed the final years of the Sun Dance, denied that the Demguk'o wore painted sun and moon motifs, and specified that their wristlets were made of otter skin, not sage.[35] Mary Buffalo agreed that the Demguk'o did not wear sage but described paint designs consisting of yellow chests and white backs.[36] Information obtained from Mrs. Big Bow and Mrs. Hokeah suggest that some confusion might have derived from the fact that the Demguk'o Gudlgut danced with the Gudlgut.[37] Although whistles were attached to the Taime shields, none of the elders explicitly stated whether the Demguk'o blew eagle wing bone whistles while they danced, though they must have since the other Gudlgut danced while blowing whistles. Again, such discrepancies in detail reflect the rapid collapse of the Sun Dance in its final years between 1875 and 1890.

THE KOƆDE GUDLGUT

Originally there were seven Koɔde shields inspired by Poor Buffalo's Taime vision in 1839, but Mary Buffalo thought there were only four. As with the other shield societies, their numbers obviously dwindled during the reservation period. Nevertheless, owners of the dark-red shields painted themselves like their shields (see fig 9, this volume). Their bodies were a dark Indian red, with dark blue moon and sun designs like the other Gudlgut wore. Mary also stated that the leader of the Koɔde Gudlgut was painted yellow, wore buffalo moccasins, a "beaverskin over his left forehead," and a quill in his scalplock braid.[38] Heap O' Bears said that the leader wore a "buffalo-hide bonnet" adorned with an eagle down feather in the front, similar to the rabbit-skin bonnet of the K'adok'i.[39] This is possible because Max Frizzlehead acknowledged that Poor Buffalo was good friends with Onsokyapta, who permitted him to dance with his dɔ inside the Sun Dance lodge, and also allowed the Koɔde to become Gudlgut.[40]

THE TE·DLGU·DA OR HOTOYI GUDLGUT

Known as the "white-red" Gudlgut, the Te·dlgu·da became part of the Sun Dance Gudlgut in 1869, according to Heap O' Bears. The five shield keepers painted their bodies light red and wore sage anklets, wristlets, and chaplets like the Gudlgut and Demguk'o Gudlgut. However, they did not paint lunar and solar designs on their chests and backs, which is surprising since their shields were adorned with Sun and Moon motifs (see fig. 10, this volume).[41]

Lone Bear suggested that the Demguk'o Gudlgut were called the "yellow-paint band" and that the Koɔde and Hotoyi Gudlgut were the "red-clay paint band." LaBarre thought this suggested the presence of moieties, but Lone Bear said the "bands" were "religious faction[s]."[42]

The Sun Dance Ceremonies
Dedication of the Sun Dance and Preliminary Activities: From the Pledge to the Ride-Around Camp

Sun Dances were pledged by prominent Kiowa men during times of crisis, particularly before fighting enemies. As members of a war party prepared to engage a powerful foe, White Buffalo remarked that a man could say, "I'll put up a tipi for you, *kongi* (taime)," using the respectful kinship term *kongi* (grandfather) to address Taime.[43] His pledge implied that if he returned unscathed from the ensuing battle he was prepared to pitch Long Foot's tipi due west of the Sun Dance lodge, where Taime was kept prior to the Sun Dance. Such positioning of tipis for sacred tribal bundles and private rites also occurred in other Plains Sun Dances (Archambault 2001, 984). Sickness was another crisis resulting in Sun Dance vows. According to Heap O' Bears, White Buffalo, and Max Frizzlehead, pledges were made contingent on the full recovery of a family member from a serious illness.[44] Frank Given told Marriott that when a

Sun Dance was pledged for a person "at death's door," the person always recovered.[45] Although White Buffalo, Heap O' Bears, and Mrs. Big Bow indicated that "anyone" could vow a dance,[46] Mary Buffalo insisted that only painted people, the Taimek'i, the four Gudlgut societies, and the Dɔt'ɔmba, could make the vow.[47] LaBarre made the following statement about who could vow a Sun Dance after talking to Heap O' Bears:

> At first inf[orman]t says: "Anybody can vow a sundance," for recovery from sickness and success in war. Claims a poor man could do this even, since the "I'll put up a tipi for *kongi*" refers metaphorically to the enclosure, and the actual taime tipi is furnished by the owner of the taime. Claims owner never refuses to acknowledge a vow. But all information I have, with regard to cases points to vowing by prominent men exclusively. (Mary [Buffalo] gave groups of men who vowed.) "Anybody" business is of course untrue. . . .
>
> (In every case I have, the vower is an important person; and every one fits into the list that Mary gave of the people who could make the vow). Heap o Bears [*sic*] says that if the time for a sundance is drawing near, and no one has yet vowed, the taime-owner will make the vow; and that this happened frequently.[48]

Mary Buffalo agreed with Heap O' Bears about the Taime keeper's ability to vow a Sun Dance if no one else vowed one,[49] but White Buffalo said that if a Sun Dance was not vowed, one was not held.[50] His statement seems plausible, for there were years when the Sun Dance was not conducted, demonstrating that the ceremony was not an annual affair. Heap O' Bears observed that No Moccasins pledged the 1875 "Love-making spring Sun Dance" that occurred at "Flirtation Spring" in Greer County, Oklahoma (Mooney 1898, 339).[51] Perhaps this was one of the changes made following the death of Onsokyapta in the winter of 1870–71.

Sun Dance vows could be made any time of the year, though dream-inspired pledges were frequently made during the wintertime when some men had visions of dancing with the Dɔt'ɔmba, a circumstance that compelled them to vow a Sun Dance. During the winter of 1878–79, this happened to Max Frizzlehead's father, who reported the dream to his family and fulfilled his vow.[52] Also, if a man died after making a Sun Dance vow, the Sun Dance was still held, and the Taimek'i selected a replacement. For instance, Heap O' Bears related that Heap O' Bears II, killed by Utes in the summer of 1868, had pledged to sponsor a Sun Dance the following year but died before he could honor his pledge. Despite his death and the capture of the two miniature Taime replicas, the pledge was upheld when No Moccasins took his place during the 1873 "Rice Creek," or "Maggot Creek," Sun Dance.[53] Frank Given concurred that dances were still held if a sick person died after a vow had been made for his or her recovery.[54]

News about Sun Dance vows spread rapidly among the bands, as did most gossip, so when an important person pledged to put up the Taime keeper's tipi, everyone knew there would be a Sun Dance the following summer. White Buffalo mentioned that on two separate occasions two men independently pledged Sun Dances at the same time, and in both instances, the Sun Dance proper was extended one or two days and called a "twin" Sun Dance.[55] The Kiowa calendars specify that "repeated" Sun Dances occurred in 1842 and 1878 (Mooney 1898, 279, 343).

Heap O' Bears said that during the prereservation era, Sun Dance vows were announced during the recitation of coup stories by members of recently returned war expeditions, and the good news was transmitted by the camp crier to the remaining villagers, who gleefully listened to the proclamation. Within a short period of time, word of mouth carried the message to the other bands, and eventually to Onsokyapta, who often consulted the different band leaders concerning the most suitable location for the ceremony, based on the availability of pasturage, water, and wood (to support the immense horse herds of the coalesced bands) as well as on proximity to tall cottonwood trees for constructing the Sun Dance lodge. Once all the variables were sorted out, Onsokyapta dispatched criers to announce the time and location of the Sun Dance.[56] White Buffalo added that minor vows to participate in the Sun Dance one way or another followed the major announcement, usually by men who had safely returned from war parties or had sick family members. Men also volunteered to dance with the Dɔt'ɔmba dancers, or to don "bull" costumes and join the buffalo herd, which included women and children who pledged to spread sand on the floor of the Sun Dance lodge. Finally, anyone could vow to present gifts to Taime, which was exposed for public viewing during the Sun Dance proper.[57]

Sometime after the announcements, Heap O' Bears stated, Onsokyapta affirmed the performance of a *tɔdɔ* (gourd singing) ceremony in the special Taime tipi situated adjacent to his "living tipi." Older men normally attended the rite featuring ritual smoking and praying to Taime, followed by singing accompanied by the shaking of gourd rattles. As participants filed in to the Taime tipi, they beheld a buffalo skull altar at the west side, facing east. Leaning against the front of the skull, bowl down, was a black tubular pipe, and flanking the skull were two black elbow pipes, likewise bowl down, stems facing west. Halfway between the altar and the central fire pit was a small hole for burning cedar incense during the course of the ceremony, which began with a ritual smoke. The elbow pipe located immediately south of the bison skull was lighted and then, with a prayer, passed to Onsokyapta, who pointed the stem down at the buffalo skull and prayed, and then held it skyward and prayed. Next he smoked and exhaled two puffs of tobacco smoke above, below, to the left, and to the right of the pipe, which was then passed counterclockwise along the south side, where each man took his turn smoking and praying. The same procedure was repeated with the pipe to the north of the skull, passed clockwise along the north side of the lodge. Each pipe, spent by the time it reached the door, was passed back, reloaded, and replaced at the altar. Afterward, the men sang the opening Sun Dance song, followed by more Sun Dance songs interspersed with four ritual smokes and ending with the opening Sun Dance song. At the end of the song, someone vowed a feast for Taime, a *k'ɔtodɔp'ai Gɔ* (singing Sun Dance songs), to be held in the keeper's living tipi, with food provided by the sponsor's women kinfolk. Besides the consumption of food, and an additional hole for cedar incense, this ritual differed from the gourd sing because singing was accompanied by hand drums. Usually three or four of these feasts were held between the *tɔdɔ* ceremony and the Sun Dance.[58]

Lone Bear told Richardson that unless unmitigated circumstances arose, Onsokyapta chose to conduct the Sun Dance sometime between mid-June and late July, "between the time the cottonwood leaves are full, and when the melons are ripe," a period marked by the rising of Pleiades, the "seven sister" stars, in the east during the early morning hours.[59] By this time, White Buffalo and Heap O' Bears noted that the dispersed Kiowa bands and the Plains Apaches began camping closer together, maintaining communications regarding where Onsokyapta wanted them to meet so he could announce the establishment of the *k'ɔtodogiai* (gathering for the Sun Dance), a coalesced encampment also called the "ride-around" camp.[60]

THE RIDE-AROUND CAMP AND PROCEEDING ENCAMPMENTS UP TO THE SUN DANCE PROPER

In the evening following the aggregation of the bands into a single encampment, a crier proclaimed that Onsokyapta was going to lead the ride-around ceremony the next morning and that everyone was to remain in the village until the completion of the ride-around. As noted by Heap O' Bears, Mary Buffalo, and White Buffalo, from that moment until the end of the Sun Dance, Onsokyapta assumed the role of K'adok'i, the high priest of the Sun Dance whose supreme authority allowed him to prohibit the departure of war parties and hunting expeditions until the end of the Sun Dance.[61] Although the Ten Medicines were not part of the Sun Dance, Old Man Apekaum noted, at this time all the keepers inhabited the same encampment; every few years, they assembled the bundles in the renewal sweat lodge after the ride-around camp.[62]

As promised, Onsokyapta gathered Taime in his arms the next morning and mounted his horse, as recalled by Heap O' Bears. Starting from the east side of the encampment—scattered along a stream or river—he began his long clockwise circuit around the coalesced camp.[63] Mrs. Hokeah mentioned that sometimes the Sun Dance pledger, or *k'ɔtodɔsaik'i* (Sun Dance vow man), accompanied him.[64] Methvin learned from Andres Martinez how Heap O' Bears II bore Taime when he assisted in the ride-around:

> Heap O' Bears had made a circuit of the tepees of the whole Kiowa tribe, for it was to be a grand occasion. It was the custom for the chief "medicine man," when the time of this annual worship drew near, to hang his "medicine" or idol around his neck, tie a representation of it to his saddle, and circle every teepee. (Methvin 1899, 58–59).

Martinez specifies that Taime was attached to the assistant's neck and a "representation" was tied to the saddle, suggesting that at least one of the miniature replicas of Taime was affixed to the saddle. Scott's (1911, 356) account supports the notion that the K'adok'i wore Taime "in a sack tied on his back by a string around his neck," although he did not mention the replicas. Heap O' Bears II probably had a "representation" of Taime attached to his saddle since he was the assistant Taime keeper and Long Foot's nephew. Heap O' Bears, Sanko, and Max Frizzlehead all stated that Onsokyapta also allowed Frizzlehead and Mo-keen to conduct the ride-around.[65]

According to Martinez, if the ride-around failed to circle a tipi, its occupants would encounter misfortune the next year. Likewise, ill luck would befall anyone in the coalesced village refusing to attend the Sun Dance once the ride-around was completed (Methvin 1899, 59). Heap O' Bears agreed that no one quit the Sun Dance after the ride-around and reported that members of the warrior society policing the Sun Dance once prevented an individual from leaving.[66] Nevertheless, Old Man Apekaum and Heap O' Bears said, people were exempted from the Sun Dance for legitimate reasons: participation in a raiding party far from home; mourning the recent death of a relative; or serious illness in the family. In the latter instances, people avoided further misfortune by completely avoiding the Sun Dance encampment.[67] Frank Given, however, told Marriott that everybody was supposed to attend the Sun Dance and that there was "an unwritten law that if anyone left the sun dance or went anywhere else at that time, something would happen to him." He reported that one time during the Sun Dance a scouting party of six Kiowas and a Plains Apache headed south toward Texas but was attacked by Caddoes near present-day Apache, Oklahoma; only three Kiowas survived the ordeal.[68]

Camp was broken after the ride-around ended, and this was followed by the formation of several encampments as everyone moved toward the predetermined Sun Dance site. Elderly collaborators, however, could not agree on the actual number of encampments leading to the final Sun Dance site, perhaps because it had been forty-five years since the last Kiowa Sun Dance abruptly ended. Mary Buffalo stated that the fourth camp was the Sun Dance site,[69] White Buffalo and Hunting Horse said it was the fifth,[70] White Fox insisted there were not any predetermined number of stops,[71] and Max Frizzlehead noted that there were thirteen camps in 1866.[72] White Buffalo and Hunting Horse also emphasized that it was necessary for everyone to stay at the fourth encampment until enough dried buffalo meat was processed to last through the completion of the Sun Dance, which must have been difficult by the mid-1860s due to increasing bison scarcity throughout the Southern Plains.[73] Their assertions seem logical, because George Poolaw told Marriott that the "journey to the dance-place was slow" and that sometimes one encampment lasted ten days.[74] Mrs. Hokeah agreed that it was difficult to procure enough bison to feed everyone for several weeks, so the number of encampments between the ride-around and Sun Dance camps, and the duration of occupation in each encampment, must have been contingent on successful bison hunting, which became more and more challenging by the onset of the reservation period.[75] Nightly warrior society dances — with enforced attendance rules — began at the ride-around camp and the ensuing camp movements. Mary Buffalo said that following Long Foot's proclamation restricting unauthorized hunting and leaving the village, one of the warrior societies was selected to police the tribal encampment for the remainder of the Sun Dance.[76] She and Old Man Apekaum said that the Daimpega (or T'äñpéko) and Toñkoñko alternated every year,[77] but Heap O' Bears insisted that the Daimpega, composed of older warriors, was the most popular society for the task.[78] His statement lends credence to present-day references to the Daimpega — now the Kiowa Gourd Clan — as the "policemen" of the tribe, according to Clifton Tongkeamah (see Boyd 1981, 118).[79] While moving between camps, warriors of the policing society scouted for bison several miles ahead of the main group of Kiowas, Plains Apaches, and other guests that traveled strung out in a wide line. According to Heap O' Bears, White Fox, and Mary Buffalo, once a herd was spotted, the hunters worked cooperatively to maximize the amount of fresh meat to be butchered and divided among the people. Collective hunting was threatened by lone hunters scattering the herds before the departure of the main hunting party, so any selfish individual daring to go out alone risked having his horse shot out from under him, his weapons destroyed, and, if he were recalcitrant, a whipping with riding quirts. No one, not even Onsokyapta or the Ten Medicines keepers, dared violate these strict but necessary rules.[80]

Another rule announced by Long Foot during the ride-around camp was understood by everyone — the avoidance of domestic violence. Throughout the Plains, the Sun Dance, "a celebration of fertility," was marked by courtship (Archambault 2001, 983–84), lovemaking, and adultery. According to Hunting Horse and Mrs. Hokeah, in acknowledgement that sexual liaisons were inevitable Onsokyapta reminded the men to show restraint and not succumb to jealousies arising from wife-stealing, since it was believed that any bloodshed would attenuate the dance.[81] Hunting Horse emphasized that men were closely monitored by the policing society since retaliation for marital infidelity could lead to dire consequences. Nevertheless, Sun Dance festivities were marked by an air of joviality, evident in warrior society songs memorializing teasing and flirting regardless of marital status.[82] White Buffalo and Old Man Apekaum mentioned that society parades and nightly dances also contributed to the festivities.[83]

If repressed jealousies threatened to supersede gaiety, perhaps staging the *tseinkya'kya* (mud parade: *tsein* [mud] + *k'yadl* [to be wet]) [Harrington 1928, 194, 114]) helped ease the tension. Old Man Apekaum related that the mud parade often occurred whenever two bands camped together, but during the Sun Dance, one was conducted sometime between the ride-around camp and the Sun Dance proper.[84] Heap O' Bears said that the mud parade was announced in the evening and staged the following morning and began when several young men acquired the "poorest and funniest looking horses in camp," coating them with mud. Next, they stripped down to their breechcloths, knotted their hair, covered their bodies with mud, affixed mud noses to conceal their identities, and commenced entertaining. Some men clowned by dressing like women, carrying young boys in their arms and spanking them to make them cry. Others assumed the roles of threatening husbands, while some staged mock fights with one another as others rode on their horses sitting backwards. Society and non-society men participated, as did some women. All antics and gaiety ended when the celebrants rushed down to the river and dove in to wash off the mud.[85]

As the coalesced bands formed the third, or final, camp en route to the Sun Dance encampment, referred to by Old Man Apekaum as *k'ɔdoietɔ* (stop while near sundance), several important events transpired, as specified by Heap O' Bears, Red Dress, and Hunting Horse.[86] Assisted by the Demguk'o, or Taime shield keepers, Onsokyapta, who was fasting, rode out scouting for the Sun Dance lodge center pole, a tall, forked cottonwood tree situated east of the Sun Dance site. Affixing a red rag to a limb of the selected tree, Onsokyapta sat on the east side, held his pipe toward Sun—which Heap O' Bears called the "maker of earth"—supplicating it for the good health of the people. Sometime during the same day, the Demguk'o gathered sticks and arranged them into a tipi-shaped goal in the center of the predetermined Sun Dance circle.[87] Mary Buffalo, however, stated that the Ten Medicines keepers set up the goal.[88] Heap O' Bears and Old Man Apekaum pointed out that while these events transpired, the Taime keeper's wife painted a new parfleche bag for Taime, a practice dating back before 1832, when a new Taime was made prior to each Sun Dance and the old one left behind. After 1832, Onsokyapta discontinued leaving behind a Taime, although the old parfleche bag, painted like a Gudlgut dancer with a sun disk flanked by two crescent moons, was left in a tree outside the last camp as an offering.[89]

Hunting Horse said that breaking the last camp was contingent on completing these tasks and processing enough bison meat to last another ten plus days.[90] Once everyone was ready to move to the Sun Dance site, the ensuing ritual movement marked the beginning of the "getting ready" period, normally lasting ten days, when the Sun Dance circle was arranged and the Sun Dance lodge constructed.

SETTING UP THE SUN DANCE CAMP
AND BUILDING THE LODGE

On the morning of the final preliminary camp, Onsokyapta and the Taime shield keepers led the assembled people, dressed in their finery, toward the Sun Dance site to the east. Mary Buffalo, White Buffalo, and Hunting Horse recalled that everyone mounted up and left except for Daimpega (T'äñpéko) members, who waited until the last person departed before they started walking toward the Sun Dance site, where they would make their grand entrance later that evening.[91] According to Heap O' Bears, since "war is the meaning of the Sundance . . . somebody had to come up on foot, so the Dai-Bega [Daimpega] did this."[92] Walking symbolized the pre-horse period of Kiowa history, a time of pedestrian war parties (Meadows 2010, 126). Meanwhile, riders in the main procession, singing and playing hand drums, made four stops en route to the goal marking the center of the Sun Dance encampment, as recalled by Hunting Horse and Mary Buffalo.[93] Red Dress and Mrs. Hokeah noted that the Taime keeper's wife dismounted at each stop and placed Taime on a tripod facing east toward the Sun Dance camp, and then Onsokyapta smoked and prayed with the keepers of the Ten Medicines, while sodality members sang and danced.[94] Following the fourth smoke, members of the warrior societies sang society war songs as everyone mounted horses and formed lines in preparation for the race to the Sun Dance goal, approximately one-quarter to a half mile away. Mary Buffalo, Hunting Horse, Old Man Apekaum, and Heap O' Bears all had vivid memories of this event. Upon Long Foot's signal, the contestants urged on their mounts, but cheaters hid behind trees or blocked other riders, though such behaviors were tolerated. First coup honors were awarded to the first rider who knocked over the goal, which symbolized killing and counting coup on an enemy in battle, illustrating the connection between the Sun Dance and warfare. A society member making the first strike brought honor to his society.[95]

Completion of the race quickly gave way to arranging the Sun Dance circle, a major task consuming the remainder of the day. Heap O' Bears, Hunting Horse, and Red Dress described how the dance circle was laid out. Members of the Toñkoñko, Ädaltóyui, and Tseñtä'nmo staked out the site as two leaders representing each society marked the appropriate distances of the circle, approximately one-quarter mile in diameter, with an open end to the east about one hundred fifty to two hundred feet wide. Inner circle, or front-row, tipis were pitched first by arranging the three-pole tipi frames to form a perfect circle, with the doorways facing toward the Sun Dance lodge in the interior of the circle. Spacing between tipis ranged from three to twenty feet apart. *Ondedɔ* families inhabited the inner-circle tipis, which stood on reserved spots that could not be occupied by anyone else without their being asked to leave by the officiating warrior societies. Many lodges in the inner circle were the painted tipis (see fig. 2, this volume) decorated with the medicine designs of men possessing powerful *dɔdɔ*. The painted tipis were flanked by other tipis for cooking purposes, which implies the sacredness of these structures. Once the inner row of prominent and painted tipis was established, tipis were set up behind them until the entire Sun Dance circle was about four rows deep.[96]

Heap O' Bears identified two important places inside the Sun Dance circle: the west side, inhabited by the "Sundance people," including

Onsokyapta and the seven Demguk'o, and just south of the east entryway, a space reserved for the famous Dohásän "battle tipi" (fig. 13, this
volume). In his formative years as Taimek'i, Onsokyapta awarded this
honorary position to Dohásän shortly after he negotiated the return of
Taime from the Osages in 1834. Guarding the entrance to the Sun Dance
circle, the Dohásän tipi was directly opposite from Long Foot's tipi on
the west side.⁹⁷ Little Bluff's renowned tipi was given to him by the Cheyenne chief Sleeping Bear in 1845, five years after the alliance between the
two tribes. Before his death in 1866, Dohásän presented the tipi to his
nephew, who afterward assumed his uncle's name, becoming Dohásän
II (Ewers 1978, 15; Greene 1996, 230–31).

In his reconstruction of the 1867 Kiowa Sun Dance encampment—held
the summer preceding the Medicine Lodge Treaty—Mooney obtained
information regarding the location of the principal leaders' tipis in the
front, or inner row, in conjunction with the designated camping areas for
the five Sun Dance bands: (1) K'at'a (Biters, or Arikara); (2) Ko'gúi (Elk); (3)
Gâ'igwû (Kiowa proper); (4) Kiñep (Big Shields); and (5) Koñtá'lyui (Black
Boys, or Sindi's [Saynday's] Children) (fig. 14, this volume). Completing
the circle were the Plains Apaches, called Semät (Thieves) by the Kiowas.
In earlier times, the K'úato (Pulling Up) band had occupied the camp circle, but its members had been "exterminated by the Dakota about 1780"
(Mooney 1898, 228–29). Through an examination of Mooney's diagram
(Ewers 1978, 11, fig. 3), it is possible to identify prominent leaders whose
tipis were in the front row. Immediately north of the entryway, and opposite the battle tipi, stood the tipi of Dohade (Medicine Man), the renowned
yet greatly feared Owl doctor, whose camp site was with the Black Boys.
T'ebodal, Lone Wolf, Sun Boy, Big Bow, and Hotoyi camped with the K'at'a
band; White Bear, Kicking Bird, Stumbling Bear, and Heap O' Bears II
pitched their tipis with the Ko'gúi; Lone Bear camped with the Kiñep;
Feathered Lance, Little Bear, Frizzlehead, and Onsokyapta camped at the
west side of the circle with the Gâ'igwû. Behind the row of unpainted
and decorated heraldic tipis were the lodges of these prominent men's
brothers and their families, which were scattered throughout the vast
areas staked out for each band. Heap O' Bears and Hunting Horse noted
that although brothers usually belonged to the same band, residence in
the Sun Dance circle was based on the principles of bilocality. If a man

camped with his wife's family the previous winter, then his tipis were pitched in the area set aside for her band.[98] Perhaps this explains why Mooney (1898, 228) identified Big Bow as a prominent member of the Ko'gúi band, although Big Bow camped with the K'at'a, according to the diagram. Another problem interpreting Mooney's (1898, 229, fig. 55) configuration of the bands during the 1867 Sun Dance bands stems from confusing the Sun Dance bands with the *topadoga*, or kindred-based bands.

Heap O' Bears, Mary Buffalo, and Red Dress described how late in the evening on the first day in the Sun Dance circle, drumming, singing, and the blowing of White Bear's bugle from the west end of the encampment announced the arrival of the Daimpega society, accompanied by their "partners," the K'oitsegun (Kâ-itséñiko). Approaching the encampment from the west, the procession stopped to smoke four times, repeating the pattern performed earlier in the day. Upon reaching the camp circle, they marched to a member's tipi for a feast, attended by anyone in the village wishing to join in the all-night singing and dancing.[99]

Early the next morning on the second day in the Sun Dance circle, preparations were made to construct the Sun Dance lodge. By this time, the Taime tipi had been erected at the west side of the encampment. Immediately east of the Taime tipi was a sweat lodge opening to the east, with a fire outside the door. Four major events transpired on this day: (1) a sham battle between the warrior societies followed by the cutting of the forked cottonwood tree for the Sun Dance lodge center post; (2) the digging of seventeen post holes and the center post hole of the lodge; (3) the killing and skinning of a bison bull for the center pole offering; and (4) purification in the sweat lodge, followed by the tying of the bison bull hide and offerings to the center pole. These four tasks were performed almost simultaneously by specialized functionaries.

THE SHAM BATTLE AND OBTAINING THE CENTER POLE

Early in the morning, as Onsokyapta prepared for the ceremonial cutting of the forked cottonwood tree located east of the Sun Dance circle, he was joined by an entourage of society members painted and dressed in their finest attire, as related by Max Frizzlehead, Heap O' Bears, and White Buffalo. Two Toñkoñko scouts dispatched to find the cottonwood tree immediately returned, reporting that surrounding the sacred tree was a "flimsy fortification of sticks," which had been secretly made the night before by members of the Daimpega and K'oitsegun, who promptly rushed to its defense when members of the other three men's societies mounted their horses to charge the defenses. As the younger men swooped down upon the older warriors, discharging their weapons harmlessly in the air, they were greeted by a barrage of mud balls and sticks, but in return they struck back with brush switches as they charged the fort. Eventually the attackers managed to knock down the fortification, symbolically defeating the Daimpega and K'oitsegun.[100] Even though Heap O' Bears said the mock battle was a "hilarious time" enjoyed by everyone,[101] Max Frizzlehead claimed that many warriors sustained bruises or, more seriously, were "badly knocked up" by the end of the fight.[102]

Following the sham battle, the participants and spectators watched as Onsokyapta stood on the west side of the sacred tree, sang four songs, and feinted touching the south side of the trunk at the end of each song. Upon completion of the fourth song, he touched the tree with his pipe, signaling the start of the tree-cutting ceremony, performed by a young and chaste woman, according to Heap O' Bears and Max Frizzlehead.[103] Mary Buffalo said the preferred tree cutter was a Mexican captive, because the power of the forked tree, *do·gyäyädo* (medicine-center-pole) was so great it could harm the person cutting it. For many years, Hunting Horse's mother, Sɛidlbí·dl, or Sale-Beal (see Corwin 1958a, 32), a Mexican captive, performed this dangerous ritual, as confirmed by George Poolaw and Frank Given. Before cutting, she painted up to four red and black stripes around the base of the tree and then attached several eagle feathers to the middle to provide magical protection from the sacred tree. Feinting four cutting motions, the captive woman cut the tree so it fell west toward the Sun Dance camp, and as the tree crashed to the ground, Onsokyapta blew his eagle bone whistle four times, accompanied by men shouting and firing their guns in the air and women ululating. Silence ensued as the captive woman stripped off the bark and cut the forks down to size.[104]

Next, Onsokyapta stepped onto the trunk of fallen tree at the east end while the men sang four songs. Max Frizzlehead, White Buffalo, and Old Man Apekaum said that when the fourth song ended, Onsokyapta simultaneously blew his whistle and ran the length of the tree and then jumped off at the fork. A successful run implied good fortune for the

Kiowas, but if he fell, then misfortune would prevail. Volunteers from one of the men's societies then lifted the newly fashioned center pole and carried it to the Sun Dance circle, stopping three times en route where Onsokyapta sang four songs and ran the length of the pole.[105] Notably, Scott (1911, 361), Mary Buffalo, and Max Frizzlehead indicated that the pole was dragged back by horses, in what was perhaps a later variant of the ceremony.[106] Nevertheless, the third stop was at the opening of the Sun Dance circle, and the fourth was approximately three feet east of the center post hole, previously dug by members of the Tsædlyiesonhi, who were at this time clearing the ground within the sacred lodge. Following the fourth stop, a repetition of the first three, the pole was placed in the hole, the forks oriented on an east-west axis. White Buffalo contradicted Max Frizzlehead and Mary Buffalo by stating that the forked pole was oriented on a north-south axis.[107]

Before his death in 1868, Heap O' Bears II performed four tasks during the Sun Dance as assistant Taimek'i, three of which pertained to the cutting of the center pole: (1) selecting the forked tree; (2) smoking the Taime keeper's straight black pipe at the cutting; and (3) running along the tree as it was dragged back to the Sun Dance circle. Heap O' Bears said that sometime after his father was killed, Mo-keen, Long Foot's adopted son, became assistant Taime keeper and performed the same tasks (see Corwin 1959, 73–74).[108]

DIGGING THE POST HOLES FOR THE SUN DANCE LODGE

After the center pole was set, Mrs. Hokeah said, the t'amõnk'i (measuring man) marked off the distance for the seventeen circumference poles of the Sun Dance lodge. In the prereservation era, White Shield, Hunting Horse's half-brother (see Corwin 1958a, 35), performed this task, but after his death, Hunting Horse took over. Heap O' Bears agreed that the measuring man started at the center pole and stepped off seven paces toward the east, designating the location for the south entryway pole, and then, returning to the center pole, he walked seven paces to the south, marked the spot, came back to the center pole, and then repeated the same procedure to the west and then to the north. Having established markers representing the four cardinal directions, three markers were placed between each of them, bringing the total number of markers to sixteen. A seventeenth marker was placed at the northeast side of the lodge, marking the spot for the north entryway pole. After the center pole had been placed and the seventeen circumference markers established, members of the Old Woman's Society dug the seventeen holes for the main posts. Upon completion, the diameter of the Sun Dance lodge was between forty-five and sixty feet.[109] In comparison, according to what Frank Given told Marriott, the Sun Dance lodge consisted of the forked center pole, twelve uprights, and twelve beams. However, Hunting Horse, who measured the distance for the poles, as well as Max Frizzlehead, White Buffalo, and Mary Buffalo, concurred that there were seventeen uprights.[110]

PROCURING THE BUFFALO HIDE FOR THE CENTER POLE

According to Mooney, Dohásän III held the hereditary position of conducting the ritual of scouting and killing the bison bull (Mooney 1898, 349; Greene 1996, 233). Max Frizzlehead related that early in the morning, prior to the departure of Onsokyapta and his assistants to procure the center pole, Dohásän, his wife, and a distinguished "war chief" departed from the encampment seeking a buffalo bull whose hide would adorn the center pole later that day. T'ebodal, Gútokõgia (Blackbird), and Mayánte, or Mamä'nte (Coming From Above), were identified as some of the war chiefs. Starting east by the battle tipi, the threesome rode clockwise within the camp circle, stopped at the Taime tipi located at the west end, received a blessing from Onsokyapta, completed their clockwise movement, and then exited through the east opening of the Sun Dance circle. Obtaining the bull hide ideally involved encountering a lone bison bull on the prairie, drawing power from Sun. Such circumstances became progressively rare by the 1870s due to increasing bison scarcity, causing a half-day hunt to extend to several days.[111] Hunting Horse stated that sometimes it took up to thirty days to find the buffalo, undoubtedly by the 1870s.[112] Mary Buffalo, Jimmy Quoetone, Heap O' Bears, and Max Frizzlehead described the hunt. When a suitable young bull was found, it was stalked like an enemy. Praying to Taime, the war chief recited a coup, raised his arrow in the air three times, and then on the fourth motion launched the projectile toward the buffalo while saying "this is how I kill my enemies," according to Jimmy Quoetone. If the coup was truthful, the arrow flew straight and lodged in the animal analogously to how it had when an enemy had been killed. Moreover, good luck would follow if the mortally wounded bull faced east toward the morning sun—the life-giving force of bison herds and the Kiowas—and if it did not bleed profusely. After the bull expired, an eighteen-inch-wide strip was cut lengthwise along the backbone from the head to the tail. Since the slain bull represented an enemy killed on the battlefield, the carcass was left on the ground to rot. LaBarre wondered whether the strip was analogous to an enemy scalp, but his elderly collaborators disagreed. Mary Buffalo laughed when he asked why the meat was left on the ground to spoil, but Jimmy Quoetone said that the buffalo represented an enemy, so the Kiowas would not eat it because they were not cannibals.[113]

After the butchering of the bison bull, Mary Buffalo said the strip of fur was placed over the front of the horse ridden by Dohásän, the head hanging over the left side. Riding single file, Dohásän, his wife, and the war chief journeyed back to the Sun Dance encampment, where Onsokyapta and his assistants waited in the Taime tipi, praying for the successful return of the hunting party.[114] White Buffalo and Max Frizzlehead stated that the hunting party stopped four times, the third at the camp entryway, the fourth directly in front of the eight- to ten-foot-diameter sweat lodge located east of the Taime tipi. Dohásän then rode his horse in four clockwise circuits around the sweat lodge, stopping at the entryway and dismounting as Onsokyapta ventured out to greet the trio. Their account of the successful kill produced a loud cheer from the spectators rushing toward the sweat lodge bearing gifts for the hide that Dohásän presented to one of the Taime shield keepers, who placed it on the ground, head facing west. According to Max Frizzlehead, Long Foot's daughter tied eagle feathers and a shell gorget to the bull's nostrils prior to its placement on the ground.[115] Gifts that Mary Buffalo recalled included calico, feathers, and blankets that were affixed to the strip until it was "hidden under the mound of sacrifices,"[116] which Max Frizzlehead claimed was approximately two to three feet high and six feet long, to which prayers were made for good health and longevity.[117] Mary Buffalo said that meanwhile, Dohásän's contingent left, continuing their clockwise circuit until they retired to his tipi for food, breaking their fast for the first time since the beginning of the hunt.[118]

Mary Buffalo and Max Frizzlehead related that once everyone finished supplicating the powers represented by the buffalo strip, two men who had recently finishing construction of the sweat lodge sang three songs and feinted picking up the robe, and, after the fourth song, lifted up the strip, carried it clockwise around the sweat lodge to the opening, feinted entering, and then repeated the action three more times before entering and placing the strip at the west side with the head facing east. Both men took seats on either side of the entryway, and then Onsokyapta entered with Taime attached to a staff, which he planted in the ground to the west of the robe and then sat down due south of the altar. Filing in behind him were a number of elderly men who took seats around the perimeter of the sweat lodge. Immediately north of the altar was a long-stemmed pipe, bowl facing east, which Onsokyapta picked up, lighted, and then held over the buffalo strip while praying. Then, beginning with the elder sitting north of the altar, he pointed the pipe stem at each participant, moving around the sweat lodge in a clockwise motion. After everyone was blessed, Onsokyapta smoked the pipe, which circulated clockwise around the lodge.[119]

Max Frizzlehead related that when the smoking ritual was completed, seven large rocks heating in the outside fire pit were handed in with a forked stick and placed parallel to a line of seven holes starting in the center and radiating toward the eastern entryway. Reciting a prayer over the center stone, Long Foot pushed it into its hole after three feigns, unceremoniously pushed the remaining stones into their holes, then a container of water was passed in and the entryway flap closed. Onsokyapta prayed, sang four songs accompanied by the communicants, then sang four unaccompanied songs; at the conclusion of each song, he poured water over the hot rocks, and the entryway flap was opened seven times by the two men flanking the doorway. By the time the purification ceremony was completed, it was near sundown. According to Frizzlehead and White Buffalo, Taime was returned to its tipi while the two carriers transported the gift-adorned buffalo robe—making three prayer stops en route—to the Sun Dance lodge center post, where it was tied to a bed of green willows. Max Frizzlehead and Mrs. Big Bow said that every year, Kɔpitɔ (Bird Arrow), a youth, shinnied up the twenty-foot-tall center post and caught a rawhide rope attached to the buffalo strip, which he hoisted up and lashed to the south side of the east fork, head facing west. While this transpired, Onsokyapta blew his eagle-bone whistle and the people sang. Afterward, Long Foot and the elderly men retired to the front of the Taime tipi, where they rested and broke their fast. If there was any remaining daylight, the men's societies prepared to bring in the side wall posts for the Sun Dance lodge. Otherwise, the second day in the Sun Dance circle was over.[120]

COMPLETING THE SUN DANCE LODGE

Lodge construction activities continued unabated for the next two days, or for as many days as were necessary to complete the lodge, according to White Buffalo and Max Frizzlehead, although Hunting Horse and Pitma stated that sometimes two to six days were needed to build the entire lodge because this "was the time for love-making" and there was no hurry.[121] Procedures for constructing the Sun Dance lodge described by White Buffalo, Max Frizzlehead, and Mary Buffalo involved placing seventeen forked outer-wall posts twelve feet in length around the perimeter of the twenty-foot-tall center pole, forming a circle forty-five to sixty feet in diameter. Next, cottonwood branches and brush were placed around the outer wall until a foot thick, and then thirty- to thirty-five-foot-long cross beams were extended from the center pole to the forked circumference poles, leaving a slight overhang. Finishing touches were made by fashioning a cottonwood branch roof extending from the projecting cross beams about one-third up the lodge, providing shade for the spectators (fig. 15, this volume).[122]

As recalled by White Buffalo, Max Frizzlehead, Hunting Horse, and White Horse, members of the five military societies were delegated to bring in the seventeen wall posts, the thinner roof beams, and the wall and roof branches. Resplendently dressed in their finest clothes and paint, sodality members diligently dragged in the building materials on horseback in parade-like fashion, many accompanied by young women riding double behind them; most female riders wore cottonwood-leaf crowns to disguise their identities from jealous spouses. "Dragging the branch songs" were sung by all the participants as they brought in the cottonwood branches for the walls and roof. As each load was dragged in, four stops were made so society members could dance with their female companions in a circular dance featuring a "dragging" step.[123] Translated lyrics of the brush-dragging songs reveal tolerance of extramarital affairs during the Sun Dance period. For instance, a Daimpega love song sung by Mary Buffalo stated, "We're crazy [over women] having a good time."[124] A popular Toñkoñiko song remembered by Hunting Horse taunted the jealous husband: "When you hear of this [the affair] you can come and strike us both." Furthermore, he said that society members whose wives accompanied them on horseback during the brush-dragging rite were taunted in the nightly society meetings by songs of jealousy.[125]

During the building of the Sun Dance lodge, the Old Women's Society sponsored feasts for the warrior societies that had been pledged by members, according to Mary Buffalo. Although the elderly women refrained from obscene behavior during the Sun Dance, they occasionally performed dances, as witnessed by Battey (1968, 168) in 1873.[126]

The Sun Dance Proper
FIRST DAY

Typically, the final morning of lodge construction marked the first day of the Sun Dance proper. Mary Buffalo and Max Frizzlehead explained that finishing touches were applied when a Mexican captive painted four roof beams representing the four cardinal directions with alternating black and red bands running the length of each beam. Onsokyapta, his wife, and the Taime shield owners sang four songs at each painting session. A lintel over the doorway was also painted red. Members of the five societies hoisted up the beams beginning with the west beam — or the east beam according to White Buffalo — and then, moving clockwise, completed the Sun Dance lodge except for the altar.[127]

The Kick Fight

Finishing the sacred lodge by midday, members of three societies lined up on either the north or south side, in opposition to the other two, in preparation for the forthcoming *onmá·ta* (foot fight, or kick fight), as described by Hunting Horse, Max Frizzlehead, Mary Buffalo, and White Buffalo. Having constructed their side of the lodge, each team selected its strongest member to pair off against the others' in a wrestling contest, and when one of the contestants eventually hit the ground, the opposing sides squared off in a flurry of kick fights ending only when one side was routed. Like the sham battle, the violence associated with the kick fight often resulted in broken ribs and fractured bones. Wounds were exacerbated by bruises and abrasions sustained from blows from water-soaked moccasins that were dried to heighten the effect of the kicks. A badly beaten warrior or one who merely was tired fell to the ground when he no longer wished to participate, but most men fought as long as they could stand. Mary Buffalo indicated that the K'oitsegun were too old to participate and merely observed from outside the lodge. Given the possibility that the fight could escalate into bloodshed, the Ten Medicines keepers were always ready to step in with a lit pipe to force a peaceful settlement.[128]

Employing functionalist paradigms, Collier and LaBarre suggested that the kick fight was cathartic, since some men undoubtedly harbored suspicious jealousies against other tribesmen, and that ill-tempered men probably relished the opportunity to beat up their adversaries. That the event preceded the Sun Dance proper ensured that certain men could vent their frustrations toward one another prior to staging the sacred ceremony, which would be polluted and nullified by bloodshed. From a symbolic perspective, however, it appears that the kick fight connects warfare—as represented through a mock battle—to the war power symbols of the Sun Dance. Mock warfare, which could potentially turn violent, thereby attenuating the effectiveness of the Sun Dance, was kept in abeyance by the presence of the Ten Medicines keepers; ultimately, men in the warrior societies participating in the erection of the Sun Dance lodge were united.

The Door-Opening Ceremony

When the kick fight ceased, Max Frizzlehead said, the Sun Dance lodge dedication ceremony was performed by the most accomplished of the kiätaisɔpan (big chief[s]), men having achieved at least four top war honors; Heap O' Bears indicated that a Plains Apache was always one of the big chiefs. Accompanied by the Ten Medicines keepers and other singers wielding hand drums, the big chiefs entered the Sun Dance lodge, taking positions at the west side, where they sang four tsákɔtedldɔge (door-opening) songs while slowly moving eastward toward the entrance. Max

Frizzlehead said that the first three songs consisted of vocables whereas the fourth stated, "To place a rock at the entrance will bring us plenty and increase our population, our children will grow up without sickness." The lyrics refer to the entryway stone, or "rock," that members of the Old Women's Society were going to place by the entrance the next morning. After the chiefs finished singing the door-opening songs, they discharged their weapons into the air to ensure illness would not descend upon the people.[129]

Returning to the western end of the Sun Dance lodge after the dedication, each big chief, starting with the southernmost, recounted their four greatest war deeds to the assembled people watching through the sides of the lodge, as remembered by White Buffalo, Heap O' Bears, and Max Frizzlehead. A translator was provided if the Plains Apache chief did not speak fluent Kiowa. Once the coup tales were recited, family members threw goods in front of the chiefs, and then women came rushing in to gather the gifts from the ground, officially marking the beginning of the Sun Dance proper. Max Frizzlehead remembered four big chiefs conducting this ceremony in his boyhood: Stumbling Bear, Big Bow, Feathered Lance, and his father, Frizzlehead the elder.[130] Perhaps this is the ceremony observed in 1873 by Battey (1968, 170–71).

Calling the Buffalo

By the time the dedication ceremony was finished, it was late afternoon to early evening, time for what Mary Buffalo called the *ɛmgɔ·dlan* (make-buffalo) ceremony. Meanwhile, fifty or more children and adults of both sexes had donned buffalo robes supported by sticks (fig. 16, this volume), forming a "buffalo herd" that congregated about a quarter mile east of the Sun Dance encampment. Membership in the herd was open to everyone; in particular many were younger participants who had recuperated from illnesses after their parents had pledged their involvement as calves contingent on their recovery and well-being; in their youth, Bert Geikauma and Andrew Stumbling Bear had been buffalo calves. The herd also included an elderly woman dressed as a cow, leading the herd into the Sun Dance enclosure, and an elderly man disguised as an old bull, last to join the herd and last to enter the Sun Dance lodge. Mrs. Hokeah called the cow *kɔdlpɔtoma* (buffalo leader woman) and the old bull *bot'ɔ* (old hide). White Buffalo and Hunting Horse described the old bull as slow and lagging behind the rest of the herd. Young boys (bulls) in the herd constantly hooked him with their horns and touched him to ensure they would live into old age. Mary Buffalo said the old bull was chased by calves and fell down four times, adding a "clown performance" to an "otherwise serious ritual." Red Dress, Max Frizzlehead, Heap O' Bears, and Sanko also described the calling the buffalo ceremony.[131]

According to Mary Buffalo, once the herd had assembled east of the encampment, the *piáikuk'i* (man that runs with the fire), clad in a buckskin shirt and leggings, and with his shoulders and braid painted white, entered the Sun Dance circle. For many years this role was played by Daite (Star), who was accompanied by his son Bai/Gudl (Red Turkey). Sanko referred to the "buffalo driving man" as a wolf. After entering the circle, he turned left and made a clockwise circuit to the Taime tipi and then turned east and walked to the sweat lodge fire, where he was handed a burning torch by Gu'k'ohi (Yellow Son), identified by Mary Buffalo as a big chief. Carrying the brand to the south side of the enclosure, he peered at the distant herd, walked to the north side to gaze at the herd, and then repeated the same motions at both sides. Hunting Horse and Heap O' Bears noted that the *piáikuk'i* then exited the Sun Dance circle howling like a wolf (or coyote, according to Mary Buffalo) and approached clockwise from the north and circled the herd, which sprang up and stampeded toward the Sun Dance encampment behind the old cow.[132] While these activities transpired, Onsokyapta, adorned in his jackrabbit headdress and ceremonial regalia, along with the Ten Medicines keepers, had been waiting in the western portion of the Sun Dance lodge since the conclusion of the door-opening ceremony. From this position, White Horse said, they sang vocable *kɔdlkyadldogie* (buffalo-calling songs) accompanied by hand drums as the herd began its clockwise circuit around the lodge. Spectators positioned themselves halfway between the Sun Dance lodge and the circle of tipis.[133]

As the herd approached the Sun Dance lodge entryway, Onsokyapta removed the black-bowled, long-stemmed pipe from its resting place on the buffalo skull inside the Taime tipi, took it to the west side of the Sun Dance lodge, and then handed it unlit to one of the Ten Medicines keepers whose title was identified by White Buffalo and Red Dress as *kɔdlkiadlk'i* (caller of buffalo), who was positioned outside the lodge opening. Also referred to as the pipe-puller by Mary Buffalo, To·gudlte (Red Tipi), White Bear's father, had formerly played this role. Meanwhile, Daite ran alongside the old cow as the herd approached the entryway, but when they reached the doorway, the cow feinted entering and veered to the south, making a clockwise circuit around the lodge. After the fourth circuit, the *kɔdlkiadlk'i*, standing at the doorway holding the bowl end of the pipe toward the herd, began walking backward toward the center pole, drawing the cow into the lodge. She went in and sat down, facing the center pole, a sign for the remaining herd to replicate the same four circuits before entering the lodge and circling the center pole clockwise four times before sitting down, likewise facing east. Finally, after falling down, then resting four times, the old bull ambled into the lodge, followed by an onrush of spectators running to the lodge and sticking their heads through the walls to better view the festivities.[134]

After the old bull plopped down inside the lodge, the *kɔdlkiadlk'i*, often accompanied by other Ten Medicines keepers, went among the herd to examine the bulls. Mary Buffalo and White Buffalo indicated that the pipeman, or *kɔdlkiadlk'i*, performed this duty by himself. Conversely, White Horse said that two men usually performed this task, though Mary Buffalo contradicted herself and agreed with White Horse. Sanko told Marriott that two men performed this task. Max Frizzlehead, however, claimed that three men selected the "bulls."[135] Either one to three Ten Medicines keepers performed this task or else the passage of time had muddled memories. Nevertheless, the *kɔdlkiadlk'i* brandished the sacred Taime pipe in his left hand and four short sticks in his right, approached a particular young bull, and lifted the buffalo-hide costume, stating, "Listen people! I find a big fat buffalo. He will be a great chief; maybe when a battle comes you will need him," as recited by Mary Buffalo.[136] According to Max Frizzlehead, if the man were older, the *kɔdlkiadlk'i* might state, "Here is a fine old buffalo, the Kiowa have already depended on him and will continue to do so."[137] Then, motioning the pipestem four times toward the bull, he laid one of the sticks on his back while the men cheered and the women vocalized tremolos. This great war honor was bestowed on three other men, all of whom wore distinctive feathers or markings to facilitate their identification. After the four "chiefs" were honored for distinguished war records since the previous Sun Dance, the herd filed out of the Sun Dance lodge and the Ten Medicines keepers smoked the sacred Taime pipe and then placed it on the buffalo-skull altar inside the Taime tipi after they finished.[138]

Opening Ceremonies of the Sun Dance Proper: Bringing in Taime, Building the Altar, and Entrance of the Dɔt'ɔmba

Frizzlehead explained that during the buffalo-calling ceremony, the thirty to thirty-five Dɔt'ɔmba dancers prepared themselves in the Taime tipi for the final event of the day by painting their dancing designs on tanned buckskin shirts with white clay. Concomitantly, two men—at one time Dohásän III and Pododlte—gathered cedar branches and placed them in front of the Taime tipi, where several women ("any women") gathered and fashioned them into a cedar and cottonwood screen in the western end of the Sun Dance lodge, about three or four feet from the west wall and six or seven feet in height. Mary Buffalo said that during the Sun Dance, this private enclosure provided sanctuary where the Dɔt'ɔmba rested and painted.[139] Upon completion of these activities, Hunting Horse, Heap O' Bears, Max Frizzlehead, and Goomda described how all the participants queued outside the west end of the Sun Dance lodge for the grand finale of the day. Onsokyapta wielded Taime, unwrapped, on a stick, followed by the Dɔt'ɔmba, each carrying sacrosanct objects to be placed along with Taime in front of the screen. Singing a song at the west side of the lodge, the procession moved clockwise to sing songs at the north, east, and south sides, a process repeated three times, leaving the singers at the south side. Continuing their clockwise circuit, Onsokyapta and the Dɔt'ɔmba entered the lodge, walked due west, staying north of the center pole, and then placed the sacred objects about the screen, transforming it into a shrine for Taime (fig. 17, this volume).[140] According to White Buffalo and Heap O' Bears, the stick holding Taime was stuck into the ground directly at the center of the screen so that Taime was about six or seven feet off the ground, whereas the unpainted buffalo skull was set directly in front of and below Taime, which was flanked by dɔ—called konä by Frank Given—and tsai/kiädlä, a crow-feathered fan. Until 1868, at least one of the miniature Taime replicas was situated immediately north of Taime. After the placement of these objects, the Dɔt'ɔmba prepared for their all-night dance. Some of the details provided by Max Frizzlehead and Goomda slightly differ.[141]

While the Dɔt'ɔmba set up the altar for Taime, the wives of the seven Taime shield keepers—having carried their husband's shields in the processional—set the shields on poles, and after the fourth feinting motion hoisted them into position directly outside the west side of the lodge, as recalled by White Buffalo, Max Frizzlehead, Heap O' Bears, Sanko, and Mary Buffalo.[142] Likewise, Heap O' Bears said that the seven Kɔɔde shields derived from Poor Buffalo's vision were brought out and set on tripods in a north-south line about sixty feet east of the Sun Dance enclosure.[143] White Buffalo pointed out that the shields were important because of their Sun-derived war power.[144]

After the placement of the altar pieces and shields, a fire was kindled immediately south of the east door by a tender who maintained the flames throughout the remainder of the evening and for the next three dancing days. Mary Buffalo, Heap O' Bears, and Max Frizzlehead related that warriors wielding sticks were then summoned to fuel the rising flames. Each man, in turn, tossed his stick into the fire and recited a coup, accompanied by drumbeats and women's tremolos. Designed to illuminate the Sun Dance lodge during nighttime dancing, and for lighting pipes for ritual smokes, the fire was fueled in this fashion for the duration of the Sun Dance.[145]

Upon completion of the fire building ritual, the Ten Medicines keepers, positioned just south of the entryway to the Sun Dance lodge, sang the Starting Song of the Sun Dance proper, as remembered by White Horse: "Keep your eye on grandfather, Women! Shake those leaves!" The first verse signifies that the dancers stared at Taime—grandfather—throughout the course of the Sun Dance proper, and the second refers to spectators peering in through the side walls of the Sun Dance lodge, including sisters shaking the enclosure branches to encourage their dancing brothers.[146] Signaling the resumption of dancing after intermissions, the Starting Song also served as the Closing Song on the last day of the Sun Dance proper, according to Max Frizzlehead.[147] Mary Buffalo, Heap O' Bears, and Sanko specified that the Starting Song also signaled fasting restrictions and sexual continence for Onsokyapta, the Taime shield keepers, and the Gudlgut dancers entering the lodge that night. Onsokyapta remained in the lodge for the next three and a half days, overseeing the dance, stepping out only very briefly to relieve himself. Otherwise, any dancer wishing to quit before the end of the Sun Dance proper circled the center pole before leaving, which immediately lifted all restrictions.[148]

Beginning with the dancing of the Dɔt'ɔmba, Mary Buffalo, Heap O' Bears, and Max Frizzlehead said, the Ten Medicines keepers served as the principal musicians at the western end of the lodge during the Sun Dance proper, though they took brief breaks from drumming and singing whenever the dancers rested. Otherwise, men who knew Sun Dance songs filled in whenever a keeper fatigued. Unlike Onsokyapta and the dancers, however, the Ten Medicines keepers were not required to fast or exercise continence. Onsokyapta owned two other musical instruments played during the Sun Dance: a large yellow gourd rattle and a large blue gourd rattle. At the conclusion of each song, the rattles, filled with broken buffalo teeth, were lifted high in the air and shaken.[149]

SECOND DAY
The Sanding Ceremony

Heap O' Bears explained that sunrise marked the beginning of the second day of the Sun Dance proper, the first full dancing day. Having danced throughout the night and into the morning, the Dɔt'ɔmba retired behind the screen to rest and repaint, which signaled members of the Old Women's Society, brandishing hoes, to queue outside the Sun Dance lodge before entering and dancing clockwise inside the lodge, singing a song he remembered: "Little boys, bring in the sand and scatter it inside; we're preparing for a playground where we can play. I'm an old woman, but I still think about sweethearts."[150] Words to the song identify young boys of the Polanyi (Polä'ñyup) Society as their assistants during the ensuing sanding ceremony and insinuate them as potential sex partners, although it is more likely that the latter statement signifies the close bonding between alternate generations, particularly between grandmothers and grandsons. In such joking relationships, the grandmother could tease her grandson and tell him dirty jokes (Eggan 1955, 53–54; McAllister 1955, 120–21). Perhaps the teasing also symbolized fertility and regeneration of the Kiowas—as with the bison herds—inherent in the young Rabbits, who represented the next generation.

Following three more songs and clockwise circuits, Max Frizzlehead, Mrs. Hokeah, Mary Buffalo, and Heap O' Bears described how the elderly women feinted three motions with their hoes and on the fourth began clearing weeds, roots, stumps, and other obstructions inside the Sun Dance lodge. Once finished, they exited the lodge, walked to the river-bank, and located and excavated white sand, which was placed on blankets and buffalo robes and then carried on their backs to the lodge. Numerous granddaughters, recruited through pledges, helped their grandmothers excavate and carry back the sand. Returning to the lodge with the sand, they entered and repeated the four songs and clockwise circuits, and then after the fourth song they dumped the sand and spread it out, filling holes and irregularities in the ground. Three more trips were made, and between each one, Polanyi members filled in holes missed by the elderly women.[151]

Building the Censers and Painting the Buffalo Skull

Mary Buffalo and Max Frizzlehead related that following the sanding ceremony, two sand censers, approximately six inches in diameter and three inches high, were constructed in front of the altar, flanking both sides of the bison skull (see fig. 17, this volume). Each time before dancing, the dancers immersed themselves in cedar smoke emanating from the censers, coating their bodies with a pleasant scent for the spirit forces representing Taime, Sun, and war power. Sick people were also brought in for incensing during a designated period. According to Charley Apekaum, the Kiowas believe that evergreens, especially cedar and sage, represent "spring and new life," so bathing in the smoke was believed to promote longevity.[152] Scott (1911, 354–55) also learned from the Kiowas that Sun loved these evergreens because they were the only plants to stay green year-round, and that for one to bathe in their fragrant smoke was "pleasing" to Sun.

Once the censers were shaped, the eastward-facing bison skull was painted: north side black, south side red. Likewise, the north censer was painted black, the south censer red. According to Max Frizzlehead, Jimmy Quoetone, and Heap O' Bears, the north, or "winter," side of the skull, painted black, represented Kiowa country and "victory in war"; the south, or "summer," side, painted red, stood for enemy blood.[153] Perhaps this referred to Kiowa migrations from the north and encounters with Mexican and Texan enemies in the south.

Placing the Entryway Stone Ceremony

Following the floor sanding and the bison skull/censer painting, Old Women's Society members placed a bison robe in the Sun Dance lodge entryway and then—according to Mary Buffalo and Max Frizzlehead—after three feints Honɛp'igul, or Honbeigu (Not-afraid-of-it), laid *tsodóm* (rock sunk in ground), a flat stone about ten inches in diameter on top of it, while everyone sang, "Let this rock have no misfortunes." According to Heap O' Bears, "rock" really meant "us," because the rock represented the Kiowas; hence the song was sung for their well-being and good health. Therefore, everyone entering the Sun Dance lodge stepped on the stone and made a personal prayer to be strong like the stone, a practice that would ensure protection from illness the forthcoming year. According to George Poolaw, a man with "hereditary privilege" brought the rock in every year. For many years, Honɛp'igul performed this task, but prior to his death, responsibilities were passed to his son Botone (Beaver Lake) (see Meadows 2010, 141).[154]

Painting of the Dancers

As related by Mary Buffalo, Heap O' Bears, and Hunting Horse, placement of the entryway stone ended by mid-morning, allowing the four Gudlgut, the Demguk'o and the Koɔde Gudlgut to enter the Sun Dance lodge for their ceremonial painting. While the Dɔt'ɔmba rested and painted behind the cedar/cottonwood screen, wives of the Taime shield keepers went outside the west side of the lodge, where the shields were positioned on poles, and took them down. After circuiting the lodge clockwise four times, they entered and walked south, where their waiting husbands relieved them of the shields, which were placed up on the screen above Taime. Sometimes the Koɔde shields were also brought in and placed on the screen north of Taime.[155] Onsokyapta probably permitted the Koɔde shields inside the lodge since Koɔde danced with *dɔ*, the chinaberry image, inside the lodge.

Concomitant to these activities, the four Gudlgut without shields positioned themselves north and south of the entryway, while the Demguk'o maintained their positions on the south side of the lodge, as recalled by White Buffalo, Max Frizzlehead, Mrs. Big Bow, Mary Buffalo, and Heap O' Bears. Accompanying the four Gudlgut into the lodge were ex-Gudlgut dancers, who painted the former in exchange for payments, whereas the

Koɔde Gudlgut painted at the same time, likewise helping one another. After the four Gudlgut dancers were painted, they smoked by the fire south of the entryway and then lined up and walked to the south censer to bless themselves in the cedar smoke. While they purified themselves, the ex-Gudlgut tied on their sage wristlets and anklets and the leader donned his fur cap. When each Gudlgut finished, he circled the center pole four times and then proceeded to the north censer, again immersing himself in the smoke before circling the center pole four more times. Finishing the purification rite signified that the Gudlgut were ready to dance, prompting the Dɔt'ɔmba to emerge from behind the screen as the Ten Medicines keepers struck up the Starting Song. All the dancers assumed their dancing positions (fig. 18, this volume): the four non-shield-owning Gudlgut danced side by side on a bed of sage that had been brought in prior to the painting ceremony; the Dɔt'ɔmba danced in a semicircle immediately east of, and facing, the center pole; and the shield-owning Gudlgut danced with the Dɔt'ɔmba.[156]

Dancing

Max Frizzlehead and White Buffalo described the dance choreography. Raising their feet straight up and down in tune to the music, participants danced with outstretched arms, their unbraided hair flying about their shoulders as they blew their whistles while alternately staring at Taime and Sun. Individually and collectively, their prayers were directed to Buffalo, symbolized by the buffalo hide on the center pole, and they prayed to the collective spirit forces represented by Taime and Sun for good health and longevity. Dɔt'ɔmba dancers, including the pledger, had vowed to fast and dance as long as they could during the Sun Dance proper, and while they danced, they also prayed for their families, particularly their sons. Onsokyapta rarely danced with the Dɔt'ɔmba but normally stayed behind the screen, where he continuously prayed to Taime and Sun for the well-being of the entire Kiowa tribe.[157] Battey's description of the Dɔt'ɔmba dance during the 1873 Sun Dance provides some insights into the choreography of the dance:

> Presently the dancers came from behind the screen. . . . They faced the medicine . . . jumping up and down in true time with the beating

of the drums, while a bone whistle in their mouths, through which the breath escaped as they jumped about, and the singing of the women, completed the music. The dancers continued to face the medicine, with their arms stretched upwards and towards it, — their eyes as it were riveted to it. They were apparently oblivious to all surroundings, except the music and what was before them. (Battey 1968, 175)

During the course of the dancing, all the dancers "scattered around" and became "all mixed up," according to Mrs. Big Bow and Heap O' Bears.[158] Constantly staring at Taime and Sun, the dancers prayed the whole time. One of the more common prayers remembered by Moth Woman stated, "Grandfather, look at me, I'm poor; help me and assist me."[159] After dancing for a good part of the morning, it was time for the first "chase" as the sun moved toward its zenith.

The "Fan Chase"

By this time, it was close to noon, and if Onsokyapta had been dancing with the Dɔt'ɔmba, he retired behind the cedar-cottonwood screen. Otherwise, he was already resting within the seclusion of the small chamber preparing his paint and regalia, featuring the jackrabbit bonnet, yellow body paint, and a pendant scalp on his scalp lock. Once ready, he blew into a crane wing bone whistle while simultaneously peering at the dancing Dɔt'ɔmba, first through the screen due south of Taime, and then north, and then south and north again, according to Mary Buffalo, though Max Frizzlehead gave the directions as north-south-north-south.[160] Frizzlehead added that, while still blowing the whistle, Onsokyapta emerged from the screen opening north of Taime, ran clockwise around the inside perimeter of the lodge, stopped in front of Taime, and then reversing directions he ran counterclockwise around the lodge, once again coming to a brief stop before Taime. Repeating the clockwise-counterclockwise movements, Onsokyapta ended the final circuit in front of Taime.[161] Max Frizzlehead, Heap O' Bears, Mary Buffalo, Hunting Horse, White Buffalo, and Mrs. Big Bow vividly described how the fan chase proceeded.

From his position before Taime, Onsokyapta began chewing *dɔitodlɔ*, identified by Max Frizzlehead as a sweet yellow root, and then went about the Sun Dance lodge spewing the juice on the center pole, and on the dancers for success. Returning to Taime, Onsokyapta feinted three times and on the fourth movement removed the crow-feathered fan from its resting position next to Taime, blowing his whistle the entire time. Grasping the fan, Onsokyapta spewed root juice on both sides and then spit some of the yellow juice toward Taime. Then, turning around, he shook the fan at the dancers, a terror-instilling act compelling them to run around the pole in clockwise circles as Onsokyapta began chasing them with the crow-feathered fan in the part of the ceremony that Max Frizzlehead called *tsaikiadle* (frightened chasing), referring to the Kiowa belief that being struck by the fan caused paralysis. As the Dɔt'ɔmba and Gudlgut ran, Onsokyapta made sweeping motions at them with the fan, causing them to fall to the ground and roll over repeatedly. Fortunately for the dancers crashing to the ground, the soft, sand-lined floor prevented serious injuries. According Frizzlehead, as many as ten to twelve dancers fell simultaneously, although Mrs. Big Bow and White Buffalo stated that only a total of four were selected to be knocked over.[162] When Battey (1968, 177) observed the 1873 fan chase, he noted the "death-like terror" of the fleeing dancers.

Although the dancers apparently feared the crow-feathered fan, Max Frizzlehead stated, the act of being knocked down by the fan was "considered good luck," undoubtedly because the crow feathers were connected with Sun, war power, north, winter, and a multitude of other powers.[163] Since Onsokyapta received his power vision from Crow, the crow-feathered fan possessed his *dɔdɔ*. Heap O' Bears asserted that the noticeable fright of the dancers represented Kiowa ambivalence toward power sources, especially one as powerful as Crow.[164] Mary Buffalo said that those who fell under the influence of the fan received "good luck, life, old age, [and] war luck."[165] Sanko told Marriott that the crow-feathered fan gave the medicine power of Taime to the dancers (Marriott 1945, 84), and White Buffalo specified that the feathers had power.[166] According to Methvin (1899, 67), dancers lying on the ground "in apparent unconsciousness, hypnotized" often experienced visions. Hunting Horse stated that such power visions were quite unusual and related the story of a man going crazy after receiving a vision in the Sun Dance lodge.[167]

After four chasing circuits around the center pole, Max Frizzlehead said,

Onsokyapta returned to Taime, feinted three times with the crow-feathered fan, and on the fourth motion replaced it near Taime. Then a Dɔt'ɔmba dancer approached the custodians of the Ten Medicines brandishing a pipe, which was accepted, lit, and passed back. The pipe was passed among the seated dancers, who smoked and prayed while their relatives went to the river bank for wet sand that they would then spread across the floor so the dancers could lie down to cool themselves.[168] Since the singers and drummers performed practically nonstop, day and night, Heap O' Bears acknowledged, they also appreciated the well-deserved breaks.[169]

Continuation of Second-Day Activities

Following a short rest, the dancing resumed, interrupted by two more fan chases, one around midday or early afternoon and another in the evening. Max Frizzlehead and Mary Buffalo specified that dancing typically continued well past sundown, and sometimes past midnight. When the dancers finished for the day, they crawled into buffalo robes and curled up on the lodge floor to sleep, while the singers by the fire continued singing and drumming through the night. Mary Buffalo said the constantly burning fire symbolized "human life."[170] According to Heap O' Bears, the Dɔt'ɔmba continued dancing throughout the night,[171] which was possible since all the Dɔt'ɔmba did not necessarily dance together, for as many as half of them rested behind the cedar-cottonwood screen at one time, as noted by White Buffalo.[172]

THIRD DAY

Shortly after sunrise, Mary Buffalo, Frizzlehead, and White Buffalo related, the Dɔt'ɔmba emerged from behind the screen, the Gudlgut assumed their positions within the lodge, and dancing resumed that was similar to that of the previous day, with three fan chases and subsequent resting periods occurring in mid-morning, noon, and late afternoon.[173] By that time, Mary Buffalo said, many of the dancers were greatly fatigued after two and a half days of dancing, so any Dɔt'ɔmba wishing to quit the dance merely donned a buffalo robe, fur side in, circled the center pole clockwise, and then left the lodge. She recalled how Zempadltɛ (Coyote-Eat-Buffalo), a Demguk'o Gudlgut, used his special medicine powers to help dancers endure the ordeal of fasting and dancing. When dancers began dropping out due to exhaustion, Zempadlて went to the Taime shields suspended on the cedar-cottonwood screen, reaching behind them to extract a root, which he chewed, then spewed the juice over the bodies of the dancers to cool them. Possessing great medicine powers, Zempadlて was also renowned for the ability to continuously stare at Sun while dancing to achieve a trance like state. He was the only dancer not to flee the crow-feathered fan of Onsokyapta during the fan chase, and during the interludes, he brought gifts for Taime into the Sun Dance lodge. Sisters and female relatives, peering in through the Sun Dance lodge, shook the outer wall branches of the enclosure to encourage the dancers. Besides moral support, they brought in cool sand to spread on the floor during intermissions, and they provided sumac berries, the inner bark of cottonwood trees, and cattail roots for the dancers to chew to suppress their hunger and thirst.[174]

Throughout the third dancing day, fathers brought their sons into the Sun Dance lodge for blessings. Max Frizzlehead pointed out that young boys, clad in thongs, were led inside and tied to the center pole for several hours, while their fathers, usually Dɔt'ɔmba, danced beside them while praying for their well-being. Some of the boys occasionally cried, whereas others danced with their fathers to ensure growing up healthy and strong.[175] Onsokyapta or an assistant also blessed small children brought in by their fathers, according to White Horse. Each supplicant grasped his child in one arm and held a pole in his free hand with a pendant gift for Taime, usually a piece of calico; poles were used because it was taboo to touch any of the functionaries during the Sun Dance proper. Such gift-giving rites were accompanied by the *pa·k'ue dogie* (prayer-giving song). Onsokyapta accepted each gift after three feints and then placed it beneath Taime on the fourth motion, along with other gifts that often accumulated into a pile five to eight feet tall. Tally sticks representing horses were often presented to Taime in lieu of other gifts, and sometimes the horses were left tethered to the Sun Dance lodge entryway after camp was broken at the conclusion of the ceremony.[176] A horse sacrifice occurred after the 1861 "Sun dance when they left the spotted horse tied" as an offering to Sun and Taime (Mooney 1898, 310).

Battey noted the pile of goods brought in for Taime during the 1873 "Maggot Creek" Sun Dance:

Quite a quantity of goods, such as blankets, strouding [blue and scarlet list-cloth], calico, shawls, scarfs, and other Indian wares, had been carried into the medicine house previous to my entrance. (Battey 1968, 178)

Mary Buffalo told LaBarre that these goods, "given" to Taime, were mostly distributed to the Gudlgut dancers, who in turn redistributed them to other people the next day with the help of relatives, prompting LaBarre to posit that "the economic complex of constant exchange" was ritually expressed through these giveaways.[177] Weiser Tongkeamha told me that the purpose of the "old time" giveaway ritual was to give presents to unrelated people, particularly if they were visitors or total strangers, suggesting that giveaways strengthen non-kin relationships.[178] This may simultaneously have been one way upper-class families redistributed wealth to lower-class people, an act that undoubtedly reinforced their high status, creating bonds of obligation.

FOURTH DAY

On the fourth day, Mary Buffalo acknowledged, dancing proceeded as it had on the third day of the Sun Dance proper, featuring three more fan chases interspersed by two intermissions.[179] Few dancers remained— only those with greater powers of endurance. Mary Buffalo, White Buffalo, Max Frizzlehead, and Heap O' Bears explained that following the third and final fan chase late in the afternoon or early evening, the Starting Song was rendered, and the dancers retired to the west side of the Sun Dance lodge behind the cedar-cottonwood screen, signifying that the dance was over, prompting all the spectators to run into the lodge, where the gifts for Taime were redistributed. One of the spectators, a female relative of one of the dancers, brought in a container of water, into which Onsokyapta spewed masticated sweet root juice before the container was circulated around so the dancers could drink. According to Frank Given, the water contained wild celery root. Next, the wife of Onsokyapta, bearing the Taime bag, accompanied by the seven wives of the Taime shield owners bearing the Taime shield covers, entered the lodge and were met by Onsokyapta, who placed Taime into its bag, an act transforming Onsokyapta from K'adok'i back to his normal role as Taimek'i. Likewise, the Demguk'o placed the Taime shields into their covers. Once the sacrosanct icons were covered in their protective covers, Onsokyapta and his wife, followed by the Demguk'o and their wives, sang songs as they left the lodge, followed by the other dancers, making a total of four stops before exiting. Once everyone was outside the Sun Dance lodge, the Taime and Taime shields were returned to the tipis of the respective keepers. All restrictions now were lifted so people could resume their daily activities.[180]

Although the Kiowas prevented bloodshed by prohibiting violence and self-mutilation during the four dancing days of the Sun Dance, Hunting Horse related that after one particular Sun Dance, he and several individuals, including Ä'piatañ (Wooden Lance) and Gɔdltaite (White Buffalo Calf) offered skin sacrifices to Taime under the watchful eye of Onsokyapta. Characterizing this as a "special thing" that occurred "very seldom," Hunting Horse stated that this rite was as powerful as offering flesh strips to Sun. Accordingly, those making sacrifices stood in front of Taime, left in the Sun Dance lodge for this special occasion, while Onsokyapta wielded his *bak'a·œ* (sacrifice fan), fashioned from "crow, golden eagle, falcon, [and] hawk" feathers gifted to Taime over the last year. After four feints toward his chest with the fan, Onsokyapta placed it on the ground below Taime, sang a song, and then, turning to the dancers, announced that it was appropriate for them to sever flesh strips for Taime. LaBarre disbelieved Hunting Horse's account, stating that there were no other instances in which a skin offering was made to benefit anyone other than the "person making the sacrifice."[181] Despite LaBarre's skepticism, and the fact that this was the only instance where self-mutilation was associated with a Kiowa Sun Dance, the involvement of Onsokyapta lends credence to Hunting Horse's story.

Breaking Camp after the Sun Dance

Early the next morning, White Buffalo, Max Frizzlehead, Mary Buffalo, and Heap O' Bears stated, people brought old clothing and moccasins into the abandoned Sun Dance lodge and tied them to the center pole and the outer walls as substitutes for the Taime gifts that had been redistributed the previous evening. Notably, the censers, buffalo skull, entryway stone, and the buffalo bull hide draped in the forks of the center pole were left intact, because the Kiowas were not worried about their condition once the Sun Dance lodge was abandoned.[182] Following the 1857 Sun Dance, Mooney related that K'ayä'ñte (Falls-Over-A-Bank), who had recently been given dɔ, or chinaberry image, by his Uncle Koɔde, left it in its place as an offering. Later the next year, some Kiowa travelers returned to the location of the abandoned Sun Dance lodge at the confluence of Elm Creek and the Salt Fork of the Arkansas River in north-central Oklahoma, where they discovered that dɔ had "taken root and put fourth green leaves." Again, Kiowas passed this area in 1867 following the Medicine Lodge Treaty, and discovered that dɔ had grown into a tree, a feat attributed to its powers (Mooney 1898, 301–2).

As the women broke camp and packed their belongings, Lone Bear told Richardson, a camp crier went throughout the encampment announcing where each *topadok'i* planned to camp for the winter, decisions that had been made the night before. A meeting among the war chiefs had also resulted in decisions concerning the destinations of raiding parties. He concurred with Heap O' Bears that individuals and families were free to join their primary band at leisure, but until they aggregated with them at the predetermined winter village location, they hunted bison for several months along the way. Several bands frequently camped together after the Sun Dance, visiting and conducting policed hunts, and it was commonplace for them to camp with Cheyenne or Comanche bands.[183]

Thus ended the Kiowa Sun Dance, described by Mary Buffalo as a "lonesome" time because as the bands dispersed, visiting and extramarital affairs came to a conclusion, but most critically, Taime missed the people.[184] Until the next Sun Dance was vowed, there would be no tribal ceremonies, for all other Kiowa rituals were privately conducted by individuals and societies.

The Sun Dance in 1935

As evident by the above reconstruction of the Sun Dance, some of the information provided by elderly collaborators reflects fading memories about the ceremony that had been defunct for over forty-five years. Failed efforts in the late 1920s to revive the Sun Dance—last performed in its entirety in 1887—enhance the value of the Santa Fe fieldnotes. The first attempt to revive the ceremony began in November 1927, forty years after the Oak Creek Sun Dance near Rainy Mountain Creek, the last ever held.

While visiting in Anadarko, Major General Hugh L. Scott was approached by ex-serviceman Edgar Keahbone and presented a letter requesting him to manipulate political channels to create favorable circumstances for conducting the ceremony. In the letter, Keahbone specified that he wanted to preserve what "our older people have never forgotten . . . [and what] the younger generations had never known." Keahbone wrote that he wanted to ensure that the Sun Dance was recorded for future generations:

> I am asking only to imitate what was once the way of our people, asking [the] "Great Spirit" for our need's [sic] in time's [sic] of war and peace.
> This propose [sic] Sun Dance to be last and for ever gone the aim of this kind is as a bid of farewell and a memory by securing photographer to take every detail of ceremony for construction our one time customs.
> We older people do not wish to have our young generation to follow our customs, but this is one thing we want as a tribal history to be preserved and kept.[185]

General Scott passed the letter to Malcolm McDowell, fellow member of the Board of Indian Commissioners, and then McDowell forwarded it to Indian Commissioner Charles H. Burke, who in turn wrote a letter to Kiowa Agency superintendent John A. Buntin in mid-December.[186] Meanwhile, Keahbone sent Scott another letter toward the end of the year stating that certain matters had come up preventing him from holding the proposed Sun Dance the following summer.[187] About the same time, Scott learned from Buntin that Keahbone's attempt to revive the Sun Dance had created some controversy because "certain old Indians" favored a revival of the ceremony, whereas the Christian converts and educated Indians were against its restoration. Keahbone had abandoned his revitalization efforts in order to maintain harmony between the two factions.[188] Around the same time, the politically conservative Jasper Saunkeah wrote Buntin expressing his disapproval of even one last performance of the Sun Dance:

> You are aware how things frequently spread among the Indians. Dancing and other gatherings may be small at the beginning but they gradually increase until they seriously prevent Indians from staying at home

and looking after their crops, homes, etc., and keeping their children in school. The starting of a Sun Dance might result in the Indians of this reservation wanting another Sun Dance which would be a larger one. It might spread to the other tribes of western Oklahoma and become a great drawback. There is no law prohibiting dances among the Indians any more than among the whites. While the Sun Dance has been stopped for several years and practically forgotten by the Kiowa Indians, I cannot see why any excitement should be worked up among the Indians over the Sun Dance at this time.

Saunkeah believed that the missionaries and the "leading Christian Indians of western Oklahoma" shared his sentiments that reviving the Sun Dance would cause more harm than good.[189]

The second attempt to revive the Sun Dance occurred after Charles J. Rhoads became Indian Commissioner in April 1929. The following March, Lewis Ware and Edgar Keahbone sent him a letter seeking permission to conduct a dance sans "abusing and torturing."[190] Buntin and Rhoads both denied their request.[191] Hence the Sun Dance was a moribund ceremony that existed only in the minds of the elders interviewed by Marriott and the Santa Fe field party. Another sixty-seven years would pass before yet another unsuccessful attempt to revive the ritual.

The Sun Dance after 1935

The latest attempt to revive the Sun Dance began in the mid-1990s through the efforts of Vanessa Paukeigope Jennings and her husband, Carl, a non-Indian. In an unpublished manuscript, Jennings wrote that the "K'ado is dead" and that "there are no living Kiowa who have a first-hand knowledge of the K'ado." She planned to sponsor the Sun Dance near their home on the old Mopope allotment three and a half miles southeast of Fort Cobb from June 1 through June 8, 1997. Two summers earlier, Jennings had obtained copies of Sun Dance songs recorded by Richardson that were in a museum curator's research collection and then attended the O-ho-mah Society dance held in Anadarko that July and "spoke with Mrs. Tom Bitseedy, the Taime Keeper, about the possibility of reviving the Sundance." That August, a meeting was held at the Jennings home attended by twenty-five men and five women to discuss the pending Sun

Dance revival. Seven months later, in March 1996, Crow-Shoshoni Sun Dance priest T. Larson Medicine Horse Sr. attended another meeting at the Jennings home in Fort Cobb. In June, several Kiowa families accompanied the Jennings to Crow Agency, Montana, where they attended the Big Lodge Ceremony presided over by Medicine Horse. During the dance their son, Gabriel Po-Kei-Tay Morgan, who participated in the dance, "fell and had a powerful vision which involved the Sundance, its medicine and return to the native grass of southwest Oklahoma." Their logic was that the original Taime and Sun Dance had been a gift from the Crows to the Kiowas "before the beginning of tribal memory."[192]

As rumors spread throughout Kiowa country in the spring of 1997 about the pending Sun Dance, several Kiowa elders led by Nelson Big Bow sent faxes and letters to Crow Agency leaders petitioning them to block Medicine Horse's forthcoming journey to Oklahoma to reintroduce the Sun Dance to the Kiowas. Big Bow's resolution referred to the performance of the Crow Sun Dance on Kiowa lands as "a giant leap backwards for traditional Kiowa societies as a whole." Moreover, it alleged that the planned dance was causing "emotional and psychological abuse among some of our Kiowa elders." Big Bow rationalized that late nineteenth-century Kiowas had "put away" the Sun Dance and that out of respect for them it should not be revived. Vanessa Jennings countered that their protest "isn't a case of being elders, or tradition, or respect—it's male domination."[193] On Friday, May 30, the Big Bow faction prevailed as Court of Indian Offenses judge Phil Lujan issued a temporary injunction prohibiting the dance "from being performed on Kiowa tribal land."[194] After the decision was rendered, Jennings stated that she was being denied the right to pray: "How many people do you know that have ever been stopped from prayer? This is America. You have that right to pray. You have that right to assemble."[195] Kiowas opposed to the revival of the Sun Dance acknowledged that women had traditionally played important roles in the Sun Dance but also that if the dance were to be revived, the decision would have to be made by the Taime keeper's family. Moreover, they stated, groups, not individuals, plan ceremonies (see also Palmer 2003, 98–99).[196] Sadly, Harding Big Bow, Nelson's brother, died on June 24, shortly after the Sun Dance revival was defeated.[197]

Despite the failed attempt to revive the Sun Dance in 1997, a handful of Kiowas participate in Sun Dance ceremonies conducted by other Plains tribes. In 1987 I met Dennis Cannon—brother of deceased artist T. C. Cannon—of Kiowa/Anglo heritage, who was raised by his Kiowa grandmother who had remarried a Northern Cheyenne. Through affiliation with his Cheyenne grandfather, Dennis was instructed in the Sun Dance ritual. Over the years, he participated in the ceremony as an assistant to other dancers, or as a dancer within the Sun Dance lodge. In the mid-1980s, he danced for the first time in the Northern Cheyenne Sun Dance through the encouragement of his grandfather, who approved of his participation because he had assisted the pledger in a previous dance. Cannon said that other Kiowas with Cheyenne or Arapaho spouses often participate in their Sun Dance ceremonies.[198] Another Kiowa, Ray Doyah, described his involvement in the Cheyenne Sun Dance near Concho, Oklahoma: "It is sacred to me and when I enter the gate, I leave certain negative things outside and concentrate on the positive aspects of the ceremony." Every year his prayer cloth is tied to the center fork of the Sun Dance lodge, and for several years before the passing of his mother, it was meant for her. Doyah finds participating in the Sun Dance to be spiritually fulfilling.[199]

The Kiowa Sun Dance has been defunct for over one hundred twenty-five years and will never be revived. It abruptly ended along with the horse and buffalo culture during the reservation period, as described in the next chapter. Perhaps its demise is the reason why Kiowa elders provided so much detailed information about it in 1935.

Conclusion

The Collapse of the Horse and Buffalo Culture and the Sun Dance

The Last Days of Freedom

Mooney (1898) and Nye (1937) are the best secondary sources describing Kiowa history between 1868 and 1875, though a handful of articles appearing in *The Chronicles of Oklahoma* also describe events during this period.[1] Eyewitness accounts by Friend Battey (1968) relate details about events related to the Red River War. Jerrold E. Levy's doctoral dissertation (1959) and entry in the Plains volume of the *Handbook of North American Indians* (2001) also include important historical data. Information pertaining to Cheyenne-Kiowa relations can be found in Stan Hoig's (1979) *The Battle of the Washita*, Donald Berthrong's *The Southern Cheyennes* (1979), John H. Moore's *The Cheyenne Nation* (1987), and *The Cheyenne* (1996), and the descriptions of their interactions with the Comanches in Thomas W. Kavanagh's *The Comanches: A History, 1706–1875*. Indian office correspondence appears in the Annual Reports of the Commissioner of Indian Affairs published in the Congressional Serial Set.

Prior to the Medicine Lodge Treaty sessions of October 1867, the Southern Plains tribes had occasionally been issued rations and presents to demonstrate the good will of the federal government, although the gifts were nonessential luxury items to the horse-rich KCA tribes, wealthy interlopers in the intertribal Plains trade network (Ewers 1980, 22–23; Osborn 1983, 566). In the last days of freedom, the horse herds of the KCA tribes were estimated at 14,090 head, more than those of any other Plains tribe (Osborn 1983, 572–74).[2] Ratification of the Medicine Lodge Treaty by the U.S. Senate in August 1868, however, established the distribution of annuity goods to the Southern Plains tribes—Cheyennes, Arapahos, Comanches, Plains Apaches, and Kiowas—for a thirty-year period ending in 1898, based on the premise that the migratory tribes would eventually settle down to a farming existence after the abandonment of bison hunting and raiding.[3] Shortly afterward, interim agent Gen. W. B. Hazen requested his charges report to Fort Cobb that fall for ration distribution; those failing to register would be considered hostile and subject to military action. By November, more than seventeen hundred Indians had reported to Fort Cobb, including Kiowa bands led by Lone Wolf, White Bear, and Sitting Bear, whereas bands under Kicking Bird, Woman's Heart, and Big Bow camped about two miles east of Cheyenne and Arapaho camps along the Washita River, approximately one hundred fifty miles west of Fort Cobb. Among the fifteen-mile-long string of band encampments along the Washita was Black Kettle's doomed Cheyenne village that was attacked by Lt. Col. George A. Custer on November 27, 1868. Turmoil following the battle compelled many to flee west to the Staked Plains, though the majority of the Kiowas and Comanches congregated near Fort Cobb. By early December, at least one-fourth of the Kiowas led by Woman's Heart were still unaccounted for. Rations eventually were distributed in late December when the Kiowas, minus Woman's Heart's band, came to Fort Cobb, and again in mid-February, 1869.

Meanwhile, on January 8, 1869, sites for the future KCA agency and Fort Sill were staked out near the confluence of Medicine Bluff and Cache creeks at the eastern edge of the Wichita Mountains. On March 12, the agency was moved from Fort Cobb and Col. Albert Boone was named agent for the KCA Indians and the Wichita and affiliated tribes. Friend Lawrie Tatum replaced Boone as Indian agent on July 1 at the new agency, located a mile and three-quarters south of the newly constructed Fort Sill, commanded by Col. B. H. Grierson. Assisted by Tatum, the KCA Indians were expected to learn "the arts of civilization and self-support"[4] by learning how to subsist on "crops raised by themselves," though they were preoccupied by the summer bison hunt.[5] Biweekly rations, consisting of "beef, bacon, flour, coffee, sugar, soap, tobacco, and soda," were issued to band leaders and then redistributed to women in each family. Scanty food supplies were typically exhausted well before the next issue day (Steele 1939, 371n). Since bison were not yet extinct in the late 1860s, the expectation was that fresh meat would supplement rations, but in order to procure buffalo, the KCA tribes had to hunt well beyond the reservation boundaries. Tatum maintained that of all the Indians in his charge, he did not expect the Kiowas to remain on the reservation given the shortage of biweekly rations and their inclination "to continue in their old habits of roaming and stealing horses and cattle from Texas citizens."[6]

Unhappy with their meager rations and fretful over the war between the Cheyennes and Arapahos and the army, the Kiowas spent the winter of 1869–70 off the reservation in northwestern Indian Territory near present-day Fort Supply, Oklahoma. In his annual report, Tatum remarked that following the 1870 Sun Dance, "the Kiowas, Apaches, Cheyennes, and about half the Comanches concluded to remain on the Plains for a time and commit some depredations." By the end of the summer, raids into Texas were so frequent that "the frontier settlements . . . [were] withdrawn near[ly] 150 miles." Tatum blamed the Kiowas and the "Quaha-da, a roving band of Comanches," for the raids.[7] Several Comanche bands and "all hostile bands of Indians in the southwest" (Steele 1939, 373) composed the Kwahada band, considered most troublesome and a bad influence on KCA Reservation inhabitants. Armed with weapons supplied by New Mexico traders, the Kiowas and Kwahada Comanches plundered north Texas settlements for horses, mules, and captives. Numbering anywhere between five hundred and two thousand members in 1870, the Kwahadas represented a sizeable number of the so-called "hostiles," given census counts for the Kiowas at 1,896, the Comanches 2,742, and the Plains Apaches 300, a total of 4,938.[8] Openly defiant, the Kwahadas roamed the Staked Plains in the Texas Panhandle and invited other Indians into their camps, where they planned large raids. Referred to as "out" Indians because they ignored pleas by Hazen and Tatum to report to the agency, the term Kwahada became synonymous with all "out" Indians, regardless of whether they were Kiowas or Comanches. The coalesced Kwahada band fought many skirmishes against the Utes, Navajos, Texans, and U.S. Army between 1867 and 1875.

During this era, multiethnic, militant bands led by "soldier chiefs" instead of council, or "peace," chiefs, developed in other Plains societies. For instance, in 1837, Porcupine Bear, leader of the Dog Soldier Society, and his relatives were banished following the murder of Little Creek, another Cheyenne (Powell 1969, 45–46; Grinnell 1915, 49). Disgraced and outlawed by the Cheyenne nation, the Porcupine Bear faction, numbering ten to twenty lodges, camped along the Smoky Hill and Republican Rivers in northwestern Kansas, an area also inhabited by Oglalas and Brules. Combined Cheyenne-Lakota war parties soon drove the Pawnees from this region. Within a short period of time, the Dog Soldier society-turned-band rapidly grew through defections from the main body of Cheyennes and through intermarriage with Lakotas. Between 1838 and 1856, raiding replaced trading as a subsistence strategy, and in the 1860s, the Dog Soldiers grew more militant in response to the encroachment of Euro-Americans, dwindling natural resources, Anglo dominance of the hide trade, and increased dependency on manufactured goods. Shortly before their defeat at the battle of Summit Springs in 1869, the Dog Soldiers numbered several hundred lodges. By this time, "Dog Soldiers" was synonymous with "hostiles" in the Central Plains, as was "Kwahada" in the Southwestern Plains. The presence of "peace" and "war" factions among the Comanches, Cheyennes, and Kiowas parallels the "red" and "white" structure found among the Creeks, Seminoles, and Cherokees (Moore 1987, 196–202; Klein 1993, 150–55).

The Guhale Band

Hunting Horse (b. 1847), Jimmy Quoetone (b. 1861), Mary Buffalo (b. 1847), Luther Sahmaunt (b. 1860), Bagyanoi, Moth Woman, and Red Dress recollected the Kiowa faction that camped with the Kwahada Comanches between 1867 and 1875. According to Hunting Horse, Bagyanoi, and Max Frizzlehead, this offshoot was called the Guhale (White Deer) band, a word derived from the Comanche language.[9] Formerly a member of the Guhale band, Red Dress said the Guhale ranged near the town of Goodnight in the Texas Panhandle. Max Frizzlehead stated that the Guhale band formed sometime after the Medicine Lodge Treaty council when several families from the various Kiowa bands camped with the Kwahadas near Goodnight; Guhale refers to the abundant white-tailed deer in the Staked Plains where the Kwahadas ranged.[10] Charley Apekaum suggested to Collier that the formation of the Guhale band created a third tribal division. Since Guhale migrations made them the southernmost group, they became known as the southern division, causing the old southern division to be called the middle division.[11] Establishing the reservation ultimately resulted in the northern division abandoning its hunting territories adjacent to the Arkansas River Valley in Kansas and the reformation of the Kiowa band divisions, since there undoubtedly was a high degree of interband movement between 1867 and 1875 as families moved back and forth due to Kiowa-Anglo hostilities. Moth Woman indicated that if a portion of a band moved south, it was identified with the Guhales.[12]

All collaborators stated that the Guhale band was ill-disposed toward whites, and Bagyanoi said the more peaceful northern division was ridiculed by them in songs.[13] Red Dress added that young men seeking war honors were attracted to the Guhale band camp, which served as a base for raids south and west to the Brazos Mountains and the Rio Grande River.[14] According to Hunting Horse, Big Bow was conspicuously absent from the Medicine Lodge treaty council.[15] Luther Sahmaunt and Jimmy Quoetone said he joined the Kwahadas and became the *dopadok'i* of the Guhales, initially composed of five families related to him and five non-kin families.[16] Hunting Horse and Red Dress identified several noted Kiowa warriors who rose to prominence through their affiliation with the Guhales, including White Horse, Bird Chief, Swan, Buffalo Bull's Entrails, and Coming Up Above; their involvement with the Guhale band, however, later resulted in their incarceration at Fort Marion, Florida. Other leaders included Dohásän's nephew, Little Bluff II (Greene 1996, 230–31), Gutokyo, or Gútokõgia (Blackbird), Soondeton (Tail Of An Industrious Bird), Tsoodle, Two Hatchet, and Poor Buffalo.[17] Moth Woman told Richardson that membership in the Guhale band crosscut band and sodality affiliation.[18]

Since all "out" Indians between 1869 and 1875 were classified as "hostiles," the Guhale and Kwahada camps swelled with young warriors during the last years of the Southern Plains wars. Moreover, large intertribal war parties consisting primarily of Kiowas, Cheyennes, and Comanches were common during this period. Whenever the Kiowas and Comanches felt threatened by the army while on the reservation, they fled to the Staked Plains, which happened during the "outbreak" of 1874–75. Hunting Horse stated that the Guhale band numbered 100 tipis and the Kwahadas 150, suggesting that the high incidence of warfare caused the formation of these large camps.[19] By the summer of 1870, White Horse, Big Tree, Big Bow, Poor Buffalo, and Woman's Heart, frequent visitors in Kwahada camps, were involved in raids into Texas while avoiding the agency. The formation of the Guhale band occurred when the Bureau of Indian Affairs and the U.S. Army identified "peacefuls" as those who stayed on the KCA Reservation, asked permission to leave during the summer hunt and Sun Dance, and did not participate in raids into Texas and Mexico. Even though "hostile" and "peaceful" factions were identified, the Kiowas as a whole were not interested in adopting farming or sending their children to school at the agency, as stipulated by the Medicine Lodge Treaty.[20]

"Peacefuls," "Hostiles," and the Last Days of Raiding: 1870–74

By 1870, Kicking Bird emerged as the Kiowa chief favored by Grierson and Tatum, much to the consternation of Lone Wolf and his supporters who believed he had succeeded Dohásän as head chief. Kicking Bird emerged as the leader of the "peacefuls," along with his cousins Stumbling Bear and Cat and brother Feathered Lance.[21] Lone Wolf, White Bear, Big Bow, Sitting Bear, White Horse, and Big Tree were among the leading *dopadok'i* affiliated with the "hostiles," or "out" Kiowas. Intermittent raids into north Texas continued through the spring of 1871. Undoubtedly the most remembered raid in Kiowa history occurred on May 18, 1871, near Jacksboro, Texas, and was subsequently dubbed the Warren Wagon-Train Massacre. Leaders of the expedition included Sitting Bear, White Bear, Eagle Heart, Big Tree, and Dɔhade, the Owl doctor. Seven teamsters were killed, resulting in the eventual arrests of Sitting Bear, Big Tree, and White Bear. Sitting Bear was killed outside Fort Sill on June 8 following a failed escape attempt using his black-stone "medicine knife," whereas Big Tree and White Bear were tried and sent to the state prison in Huntsville, Texas.

Meanwhile, White Horse and the Guhale band, still out on the Staked Plains, were joined by twenty Cheyenne lodges between the summers of 1871 and 1872 as a result of Cheyenne-Kiowa intermarriage. In addition, numerous Comanche and Plains Apache warriors were willing to join Kiowa raiding expeditions that resumed in the spring and summer of 1872.[22] That fall, a Kiowa-Comanche delegation led by Lone Wolf, Sun

Boy, and Wolf Lying Down traveled to the nation's capital, where Indian Commissioner Francis J. Walker informed them that White Bear and Big Tree would be released from prison if raiding into Texas and around the agency ceased and if the tribes camped within ten miles of Fort Sill.[23]

Despite some military actions against the Kwahadas and Guhales in September, the winter of 1872–73 found the majority of the Kiowas and Comanches camped near the agency, a first for many who had lived in the Kwahada camps. Kicking Bird's band of forty tipis camped near old Fort Cobb, whereas Lone Wolf's band of "hostiles" occupied a larger village north of Mount Scott.[24] As winter turned into spring, the majority of the Kiowas stuck to the agreement not to send out raiding parties, although some Kwahada war parties still slipped off the reservation to raid. Otherwise, Kicking Bird and Lone Wolf restrained Kiowa warriors from joining any forays leaving the reservation. Dismayed that White Bear and Big Tree would probably be released from prison, Agent Tatum resigned on March 31, 1873, and was replaced the next day by Friend James P. Haworth, who promptly dismissed the agency military guards; naively, he did not realize that the majority of the Kiowas and Comanches refrained from raiding because their chiefs were being used as bargaining leverage.

Through the spring and summer of 1873, raiding largely ceased, so White Bear and Big Tree were finally paroled on October 8 with the caveat they would be rearrested if Kiowa raids into Texas resumed. While visiting the encampments of Kicking Bird and Lone Wolf in early December, Battey learned that staying close to the agency prevented the Kiowas from procuring an ample supply of buffalo meat and robes to make it through the winter. Hunting prohibitions and inadequate ration issues had created hardships, causing many to eat their horses and mules through the winter.[25] On December 5, Battey encountered seven triumphant, scalp-laden warriors returning to Kicking Bird's camp, where they were greeted by a Scalp Dance. Moreover, he learned of a recent intertribal council initiated by a visiting Osage delegation complaining to the assembled Southern Plains tribes that government surveyors were destroying the bison herds. Hence the ensuing Kiowa-Comanche "outbreak," or Red River War, was caused by continuous raiding into Texas and was also fueled by vengeance based on the belief that Anglos were purposely killing off the bison herds.

The Red River War, 1874–75

Following the release of White Bear and Big Tree, most young Kiowa warriors refrained from joining Comanche war parties, although some, including Lone Wolf, managed to accompany expeditions into Texas and Mexico during the winter of 1873–74. Besides raiding for plunder and revenge, another catalyst leading to the final Southern Plains wars was the disappearance of the Southern Plains bison herds brought about by forts, railroads, and settlements engulfing the KCA Reservation from all sides by the early 1870s, resulting in the dispersal of the herds, making hunting more difficult.[26] Hunger caused by diminishing bison herds was exacerbated by white marauders plaguing Indian encampments at the Cheyenne-Arapaho and Kiowa agencies. The Cheyennes struck back in early February 1874 when a revenge war party entered the KCA Reservation and killed a surveyor, an act for which the Kiowas were blamed. In March and April, unidentified war parties fired upon troops within the boundaries of the KCA Reservation. That spring, Battey learned that Woman's Heart had accepted the war pipe circulated from the Kwahada Comanches to the Cheyennes and Kiowas.

Extinction of the herds accelerated after March 1873, when white buffalo hunters reoccupied the Adobe Walls trading post, formerly built by the Bent brothers, as their base of operation on the South Canadian in the Texas Panhandle. In May 1874, a Kwahada shaman and prophet, Isatai (Wolf's Vulva), announced that he was invulnerable to soldiers' bullets and organized a war party to punish the buffalo hunters operating at Adobe Walls. Estimated between three hundred and seven hundred strong, the revenge party was chiefly composed of Kwahadas, Cheyennes, and a handful of Kiowas and was led by Woman's Heart.[27] Hunting Horse later told Nye that other Kiowa attackers included White Bear, White Shield, Lone Wolf, White Horse, Big Bow, and Howling Wolf, contra Mooney, who stated that most of the Kiowas remained near the agency and that the Plains Apaches and Arapahos did not participate in the battle of Adobe Walls or in the ensuing Red River War. Nevertheless, the attack on Adobe Walls beginning on June 27 failed to dislodge the white buffalo hunters.

Subsequent raids in southwestern Kansas were blamed on the Kiowas, who completed their Sun Dance in early July. Afterward, a raiding party composed of Coming Up Above, Lone Wolf, Swan, and many prominent Kiowa warriors skirmished with Texas Rangers in the Lost Valley Fight near the Loving Ranch. That summer, young warriors raided about Fort Sill and the agency. On August 19, young Cheyenne and Kiowa warriors killed a white man near Signal Mountain, west of Fort Sill, and the next day four more Anglos were killed by warriors from White Bear's band after receiving their rations, causing all Kiowa bands except Kicking Bird's to flee the agency. Among the refugees were Poor Buffalo, White Bear, and Woman's Heart. Fleeing north toward Anadarko, they met up with Lone Wolf's band and several Comanche bands, including Nokoni Comanches led by Red Food on August 21 at the Wichita Agency, where they joined the encampment of registered Penateka Comanches. Warriors from the coalesced bands demanded food from the agency employees and their Caddo, Wichita, and Delaware charges and then raided the gardens. The next day, four companies of the Tenth Cavalry arrived at the Wichita Agency, resulting in a firefight with the Indians. By the time the "Anadarko affair" ended, the agency trading store was pilfered and Red Food's village was burned, resulting in the destruction of supplies and several tons of dried buffalo meat. Most of the Kiowa and Comanche participants fled to the Staked Plains. In his annual report, Commissioner Smith wrote that one-third of the 1,050 Kiowas escaped to the Staked Plains following the Wichita Agency skirmish.[28]

According to Hunting Horse and others interviewed by Nye, members of the Kiowa bands led by Woman's Heart and Poor Buffalo participated in the Anadarko affair, as did Big Tree and White Bear. Mooney, however, stated that the four men were in Anadarko when the fight broke out but fled to the Darlington Agency to surrender on October 4. According to Haworth, Poor Buffalo was still at large when the other three chiefs were taken into custody.[29] Despite this discrepancy, the leaders and warriors who surrendered were imprisoned at Fort Sill, except for White Bear, who was promptly returned to Huntsville Prison, where he remained imprisoned until his suicide on October 11, 1878.

The primary reason for the capitulation of the Kiowa leaders at the Darlington Agency on October 4 and the subsequent surrender of the remaining "out" Indians was the pressure exerted by the four-directional attack employing five columns, led by Major William R. Price, Cols. Nelson A. Miles and Ranald S. Mackenzie, and Lt. Cols. John W. Davidson and George Buell, comprising forty-six companies of cavalry and infantry and totaling three thousand men. The purpose of the campaign was to drive the "out" Indians back to their respective agencies, constantly keeping them moving to prevent them from hunting to procure the necessary winter provisions. Keeping the Indians tired and hungry through relentless pursuit was the primary goal of the five columns, which hoped to converge somewhere in the Texas Panhandle. On September 27 Mackenzie delivered a devastating blow in a surprise attack on a large village in Palo Duro Canyon, inhabited by Kiowa bands led by White Horse, Lone Wolf, Poor Buffalo, and Coming Up Above coalesced with several Cheyenne and Comanche bands. Caught completely off guard, the Indians were able to scurry up the canyon walls with few losses, although they abandoned their tipis, winter food supply, and a horse herd estimated at fourteen hundred head, which Mackenzie ordered destroyed to ensure that they were not recaptured. Rousted from their base camp, the bands scattered in different directions.

After the defeat at Palo Duro Canyon, the Indians were driven by the converging military columns to the Staked Plains, which were swept by a blizzard in mid-November, causing great suffering. Destitute and on the verge of starvation, the majority of the "out" Indians headed back to the Darlington and Fort Sill agencies, yet some remained in the Texas Panhandle during the winter of 1874–75. Skirmishes and troop movements that kept the Indians constantly on the run eventually forced even the toughest warriors to capitulate. In February 1875, Haworth sent Big Bow, who had not been arrested, out to the Staked Plains to round up the hostile chiefs "Lone Wolf, Red Otter, Swan, Qua-ha-da, Tehausen [Dohásän II], and Poor Buffalo."[30] On February 26, Big Bow returned to Fort Sill accompanied by Lone Wolf, Red Otter, Swan, Dohásän II, Poor Buffalo, and about 250 Kiowas, although Red Dress remembered that a number of warriors remained in the Guhale and Kwahada camps.[31] By June 2 the remaining Kiowa, Cheyenne, Comanche, and Plains Apache warriors surrendered.

Upon surrendering at Fort Sill, the Kiowa and Comanche warriors forfeited their horses as well as their firearms, bows, arrows, lances, war shields, and other accouterments of war, which were either burned or placed in storage. Noncombatant women and children were housed in a detention camp on Cache Creek; the most feared leaders, particularly White Horse, Big Tree, and Woman's Heart, were shackled and kept in the basement of the guardhouse; and the remaining warriors were imprisoned in an unfinished icehouse, where they lived in tents and were fed once a day when raw meat was tossed over the walls. Once all the warriors were confined, army-appointed leaders were instructed to select the most notorious men to serve prison time at Fort Marion, near St. Augustine, Florida: at the Darlington Agency, thirty-three Cheyennes and two Arapahos were shackled and chained, and at Fort Sill, nine Comanches and twenty-six Kiowas received the same treatment. Altogether, a total of seventy prisoners of war awaited their boxcar journey to Florida.[32] Kicking Bird, recognized as Kiowa head chief by the army following the "outbreak," received the ominous task of choosing twenty-six incorrigible Kiowa leaders and warriors to serve prison time, placing him in an uncomfortable situation since he was already at odds with most leaders of the so-called "hostile" faction. Lone Wolf, Woman's Heart, White Horse, Bird Chief, Swan, Buffalo Bull's Entrails, and Dɔhade were the main chiefs selected by Kicking Bird, then thirteen lesser warriors and six Mexican captives were chosen. Unfortunately for Kicking Bird, being put in this position contributed to his death between May 3 and May 5 through the Owl sorcery of Dɔhade, who also died at Fort Marion on July 29. As prophesied by Dɔhade, his own death was inevitable for using his Owl powers to kill another Kiowa. The deaths of Kicking Bird and Dɔhade marked the demise of the horse and buffalo culture and the final days of the Sun Dance.

The Collapse of the Sun Dance

Undoubtedly, discussing the death of the Sun Dance was a painful memory for those who had lived during the passing of the horse and buffalo culture. In *The Way to Rainy Mountain*, Pulitzer Prize–winning author N. Scott Momaday describes that his grandmother, Aho, or Florence Mammedaty (1880–1965), was a young girl when the 1890 Sun Dance at the great bend of the Washita River was aborted. He noted that "for as long as she lived, she bore a vision of deicide" (Momaday 1969, 10). Kiowa elders discussing the end of the Sun Dance in 1935 who had lived during this transitional period included Heap O' Bears III, Goomda (b. 1867),

Mrs. Hokeah, Mary Buffalo (b. 1847), White Buffalo (b. 1855), White Fox (b. 1869), and Hunting Horse (b. 1847). The most information about the collapse of the Sun Dance was related by Heap O' Bears to LaBarre, with Charley Apekaum interpreting.

The cessation of warfare, the extinction of the bison herds, the confinement of the Kiowas near Fort Sill following the Red River War, and ultimately the anti–Sun Dance policy of Indian Commissioner Thomas J. Morgan (1889–93) all contributed to the collapse of the Sun Dance, which also became impractical to perform due to drought conditions on the Southern Plains. By 1890, the Sun Dance rite had disappeared with the horse and buffalo culture.

Change had begun in 1871 with the death of Onsokyapta, who had served as Taimek'i and Kadok'i for forty years. The 1869 "Sun Dance when they brought the war-bonnet," performed near the juncture of Sweetwater Creek and the North Fork of the Red River, and the 1870 "Plant-growing Sun Dance," held on the North Fork of the Red River in present-day Greer County, Oklahoma, were the last Sun Dances he directed (see appendix). Notably, the 1869 ceremony had been conducted to fulfill a Sun Dance pledge made by Heap O' Bears II prior to his death in 1868 and was also marked by the inclusion of the Hotoyi shields and the Hotoyi Taime image in the Sun Dance lodge, as remembered by Heap O' Bears. He also pointed out that dances were not held in 1871 and 1872 following the death of Onsokyapta but that his successor, Dó-héñte, vowed and directed the 1873 Rice Creek, or "Maggot Creek Sun Dance," on Sweetwater Creek, a tributary of the North Fork of the Red River, near the western edge of the reservation.[33] Friend Battey attended the dance, also remembered by Heap O' Bears as the "Black Buffalo's horses killed" Sun Dance because Gui-badai (Appearing Wolf), killed seven horses belonging to Pa-konkya (Black Buffalo) after the latter ran off with Appearing Wolf's wife. Intercession by the Toñkoñko Society policing the Sun Dance prevented Appearing Wolf from killing Black Buffalo. Dó-héñte oversaw the 1874 "Sun Dance at the end of the bluff," near Last Mountain (Mount Walsh)—the last Kiowa Sun Dance prior to the surrender—and then vowed and conducted the 1875 "Flirtation Spring," or "Love-making spring Sun Dance," also held near Last Mountain but this time monitored by troops.[34]

Further changes in leadership transpired with the death of Dó-héñte in the fall of 1875 and his replacement by Heap O' Bears, the uncle of Heap O' Bears II. Heap O' Bears officiated five Sun Dances: the 1876 "Sun Dance when Sun-boy's horses were stolen" by Mexicans, held at the confluence of Sweetwater Creek and the North Fork of the Red River; the 1877 "Measles Sun Dance," staged at the Salt Fork of the Red River in Greer County, again monitored by soldiers; the 1878 "Repeated Sun Dance" conducted somewhere along the North Fork of the Red River; the 1879 "Horse-eating Sun Dance" on the Elm Fork of the Red River, named because the Kiowas were compelled to eat some of their horses that summer due to a low meat supply resulting from the failure to find any bison the previous winter, compounded by a poor summer hunt; and the 1881 "Hot-Sun Dance" on the North Fork of the Red River near the "end of the mountains," which was not held until late August due to the inordinate amount of time it took to find a bison for the ceremony— the last Heap O' Bears presided over.[35] There was no Sun Dance during the summer of 1880 due to the paucity of bison, and also no Sun Dance in the summer of 1882 because Dohásän III—Dohásän's son—who for many years had procured the bison bull hide for the Sun Dance lodge center pole, failed to find buffalo (Greene 1996, 233).

Named after a visiting delegation, the 1883 "Nez Perce Sun Dance" occurred on the north side of the Washita River inside a fence-enclosed cattle pasture, about ten miles from Rainy Mountain Creek, near modern Cloud Chief, Oklahoma, and was led by a new Taime keeper, Taíméte, who replaced Heap O' Bears following his death that spring. No Sun Dance occurred during the summer of 1884, again due to the inability to find bison, but Taíméte presided over his second ceremony, the 1885 "Little Peninsula Sun Dance" at the bend of the Washita River twenty miles west of the agency, at the location of the 1839 Sun Dance. According to Mooney, Dohásän III had to travel west to the Staked Plains to obtain the bison bull in order to stage the ceremony. The Sun Dance was not performed during the summer of 1886, once again due to the failure to find buffalo. Held in a grove of black-jack oaks near the confluence of Oak Creek and the Washita River above Rainy Mountain Creek, the 1887 or "Oak Creek Sun Dance," called the "Oak-Leaf" Sun Dance by Charley Apekaum, occurred only after the approval of Agent J. Lee Hall and because Charles Goodnight supplied a buffalo from his small domestic herd in northern Texas.[36] A Sun Dance was not held in 1888, nor was one conducted in 1889, due to opposition from Agent W. D. Myers, who threatened to summon the military to arrest any Kiowas attempting to stage a dance.[37] The Sun Dances in the 1880s were obviously plagued by the extinction of the Southern Plains herds, hot weather and drought conditions, and, finally, staunch opposition from Agent Myers.

Several Kiowa leaders, including Dohásän III, solicited special permission from Agent Charles E. Adams—Myer's replacement—to sponsor one last Sun Dance during the summer of 1890. Adams initially consented to their wishes but then received commands from Commissioner Morgan to prohibit the dance, although the Kiowa celebrants had already built a Sun Dance lodge at the bend in the Washita, near the site of the 1885 Little Peninsula Sun Dance. By the time Adams received his instructions, many tipis had already been pitched in the great camp circle, and Dohásän III had even improvised by procuring an old buffalo robe to hoist up the center pole. According to Mooney, on July 19, Adams informed the commander at Fort Sill that the Kiowas intended to conduct a Sun Dance despite his warnings, and so on the next day, three cavalry troops were dispatched toward Anadarko to thwart any attempt to hold the ceremony. Learning that soldiers had been deployed, Quanah Parker informed Stumbling Bear—who had stayed away from the Sun Dance because his son had recently died—that troops were coming from Fort Sill to stop the dance. Wishing to avoid unnecessary bloodshed, Stumbling Bear directed two young men to the Sun Dance encampment to warn the participants to break camp and go home unless they wanted to stay and risk getting killed by soldiers. After some discussion, the Sun Dance camp was abandoned, leaving behind an unfinished Sun Dance lodge, recorded in the Kiowa calendars as the "Sun dance when the forked poles were left standing."

Rev. Methvin remembered a slightly different version of events:

The Indians declared they would disregard orders and hold it [the Sun Dance] anyhow. The agent wired the situation to Washington, asking for advice, and received back instructions to stop it if it took all the soldiers at Fort Sill.

Big Tree[,] . . . who was the war chief at the time, declared they would fight, repaired with his band up the [Washita] river, apparently to get ready for the conflict. During the night three or four hundred soldiers reached Anadarko from Fort Sill and camped in the agency. Messengers were sent to Big Tree to come in and surrender, which he did after a few days, and peace again reigned in our midst. This was the last effort the Indians [Kiowas] ever made to hold the sun dance. (Methvin n.d., 73)

Although Methvin's account differs, the Kiowa Sun Dance ended in 1890 and has not been performed to this day. During the reservation era, thirteen Sun Dances were performed by four different Taime keepers, and the last ceremony was aborted (Mooney 1898, 241, 340, 351).

Mooney stated that Emáa, a woman, inherited the Taime bundles when Taíméte died in 1894, as noted by Goomda, who identified Emáa as Long Foot's daughter, who still possessed the Taime bundle in 1935.[38] Conversely, former missionary Rev. Harry Treat later told Corwin that Mo-keen, Long Foot's adopted son, became the Taime keeper after the passing of Taíméte,[39] which is supported by a statement Max Frizzlehead made to Collier that Mo-keen "later had [the] Taime."[40] Presumably, only Mo-keen knew how to conduct the Sun Dance ceremony after Taíméte died (Corwin 1959, 73–77). Both interpretations are plausible because Mo-keen was raised by the ever innovative Onsokyapta, who also fathered Emáa, the unnamed daughter in Corwin's accounts. Given the different incarnations and replicas of Taime, perhaps Mo-keen inherited the Hotoyi version of Taime, or even the principal image.

Extant records and oral histories reveal little about Kiowa feelings during the final years of the Sun Dance, albeit the death of Heap O' Bears II and the loss of the two miniature Taime images following the 1868 Sun Dance surely must have been ominous signs, because even sixty-seven years later, Heap O' Bears III referred to the "misfortune" and "bad luck" connected to his father's lost female image that was never re-created.[41] That the Kiowas did not conduct a Sun Dance in 1871 following the passing of Onsokyapta the previous winter is not surprising, nor is its absence in 1872 in the wake of the White Bear and Big Tree incarcerations and the death of Sitting Bear. Further bad omens must have accompanied the tragic event witnessed by Battey during the 1873 dance when two Cheyenne women were killed by lightning (see chapter 4). That they were wearing red blankets undoubtedly contributed to their deaths. The prohibition against the Taimek'i and the Taime shield keepers wearing red blankets or articles of clothing during the Sun Dance undoubtedly applied to everyone in attendance. Elders interviewed in 1935 did not mention this particular event, though Heap O' Bears III and Mary Buffalo did recollect a similar occurrence during an unspecified Sun Dance when a Comanche visitor wearing a red blanket initially refused to offer it to Taime and then "went crazy," ripped off his clothing, ran into the lodge, placed the blanket under Taime, and then danced with the Dɔt'ɔmba. Neither elder, however, attributed misfortune to the event.[42]

The cessation of warfare and raiding after May 1875 undoubtedly contributed to the demise of the Sun Dance, since most pledges were made by prominent men during war expeditions and announced back home during the recitation of coup stories. Otherwise, recovery from illness was the only other way to pledge a Sun Dance, unless the Taimek'i, or one of the Dɔt'ɔmba, Gudlgut, or Demguk'o, vowed to sponsor one. Pledgers of specific dances during the reservation period included Heap O' Bears II, who pledged the Sun Dance of 1869 prior to his untimely demise; Dóhéñte, who pledged the 1873 and 1875 dances; Big Bow, Lone Wolf/Bird Chief, or both pledged the twin Sun Dance of 1878; and Frizzlehead vowed the 1879 Sun Dance when he was twenty-eight or twenty-nine years old, according to his son, Max.[43] Heap O' Bears identified Teme'to (Bird Tail), a non-shield-owning Gudlgut, as another pledger,[44] and Max Frizzlehead claimed that Mo-keen had pledged a dance.[45]

Shield societies connected to the Sun Dance—Demguk'o, Hotoyi, and Kɔɔde—rapidly declined during the reservation period, especially at the end of the Red River War, when the U.S. Army confiscated shields and weapons. Moreover, following the cessation of warfare, many shield designs were not passed down. During the prereservation era, there had been as many as ten Demguk'o, or Taime Shields, but by the last complete Sun Dance performed in 1887, there were only five left, mostly because the shields were buried with the owners, who did not pass on the dɔdɔ connected with them, as noted by Max Frizzlehead.[46] In 1935, Heap O' Bears remembered the fate of the last seven Taime shields:

(1) Lone Wolf obtained his shield from Onsokyapta and then passed it to his son, Ambush The Enemy, who was killed around 1870, and the shield "stopped" because it was captured by whites; (2) Many Crosses also received his shield from Onsokyapta, and it "stopped" when it was buried with him; (3) Dangerous Bear likewise acquired his shield from Onsokyapta, but its fate was undetermined, although he "disposed of it in some way"; (4) Gnawing On A Bone inherited a Taime shield from his older brother Ma·bodlt'aha after his death and then sometime after 1875, because there were "no more war parties," left it as a sacrifice on Mount Scott with a prayer; (5) Heap O' Bears II obtained his shield from his uncle, Onsokyapta, but lost it along with the miniature Taimes when killed by Ute warriors in 1868; Heap O' Bears III had a replica of his father's shield but claimed that "Boak" had it; (6) Frizzlehead procured his shield from Onsokyapta and eventually left it in the Wichita Mountains with prayers to Sun; and (7) Mo-keen had a shield, but whatever happened to it was not recorded by LaBarre.[47] Perhaps Mo-keen disposed of his shield and Taime image upon converting to Christianity following the death of his son, Lucius Ben Aitson (Kills Him On The Sly) during the 1918 influenza pandemic; Mo-keen undoubtedly was motivated by guilt because his son had become the first Indian pastor at Saddle Mountain Mission Church (Baptist) in 1913 while Mo-keen tenaciously adhered to the old Sun Dance beliefs (Corwin 1959, 80–81).

Increased bison scarcity also contributed to the collapse of the Sun Dance, particularly by the mid-1870s when Kiowa hunters, monitored by army patrols, encountered difficulties providing fresh meat and enacting the ritual hunt for the bull. In 1935 Mrs. Hokeah told Collier that the absence of bison caused the number of encampments between the ride-around camp and the Sun Dance circle to increase proportionally each year; she recalled that in earlier years strict hunting prohibitions went into effect once the ride-around camp dispersed but that in later years—after 1875—there were fewer opportunities to hunt, so the Kiowas pursued any game encountered while traveling to the Sun Dance encampment.[48] According to Mary Buffalo, Heap O' Bears, and White Buffalo, ideally four encampments were made en route to the Sun Dance site.[49] However, White Fox, Max Frizzlehead, and Hunting Horse insisted that there were often more than four camps.[50] Max Frizzlehead related that thirteen camps were made during the 1866 Sun Dance, though this was before his time.[51] Since the purpose of the movements between the ride-around camp and the Sun Dance circle was to provide enough fresh and dried meat for at least the next month, Mrs. Hokeah noted that bison shortages beginning in the mid-1860s lengthened the number of encampments.[52]

Before the demise of the Southern Plains herds, the hunt for the bison bull only took a half day because there were plenty of buffalo, but, Max Frizzlehead said, in "later days it took sometimes two or three days" to find any buffalo.[53] Hunting Horse even stated that it often took over thirty days to find bison, and he recollected that the 1879 "Horse-eating Sun Dance" was not affected by the buffalo shortage because the hunters fortunately found the needed bull. Even though the ritual proceeded without hesitation after the ride-around camp, there were few feasts due to the lack of fresh meat and inadequate government rations, so it was not necessary for a warrior society to police the hunt that summer.[54] During the 1880s, the final Sun Dances were difficult to perform due to the fact that the only surviving bison in the Southern Plains lived in captivity.

Religious Transformations during the Reservation Period

The final surrender in May and June 1875 marked a new beginning for the Kiowas confined within the boundaries of the KCA Reservation. Gone were the days of communal bison hunts, the great war chiefs, raids, and the importance of war power, as the former bison hunters and raiders were now beef- and-commodity-dependent peoples living in kin-based communities north of the Wichita Mountains. A short twenty-six years later, reservation lands were opened for homesteading, and the Kiowas were forced to select individual allotments and settle into homes. Reservation life accelerated the end of the horse and buffalo culture, beginning with military defeat, confinement, the demise of the Southern Plains bison herds, the collapse of the Sun Dance, the passing of the shield societies, the death of some sodalities, and dormancy in those that survived. Disrupted inheritance patterns also caused the medicine shields to "stop" because many Kiowa shield and bundle owners died without passing on their dɔdɔ. Although inheritance patterns for the Taime bundle and the Ten Medicines bundles were disrupted, an elite few managed to care for them and whenever necessary renewed the bundles they possessed. This period of rapid change was also characterized by the emergence of new religions, including prophet movements, the peyote rite, the Ghost Dance, and, inevitably, Christianity. By 1935, some indigenous beliefs and practices were discontinued and some were absorbed into the new religions or taken underground due to external pressures. Indeed, like other Plains cultures, the Kiowas adapted their religious beliefs and practices to the changing social and physical environments of the Plains (Harrod 1995, 28).

Two prophet movements occurred in the 1880s, the first developing from Kiowa dissatisfaction with government commodities. In 1882, Dátekâñ (Keeps His Name Always) changed his name to Pá-tépte (Buffalo Bull Coming Out) based on a vision in which he was instructed to bring the buffalo back from the underworld, from where they had originally emerged to populate the surface of the earth. For the next year Pá-tépte conducted sweat lodges and rituals in a medicine tipi to conjure the bison back into existence. After failing to revive the bison for the 1883 Nez Perce Sun Dance, Pá-tépte "just got sick, [and it] didn't take him very long till he died" early in the winter of 1883–84, according to Tsoodle, who said the Kiowas believed that Pá-tépte died because he had lied about his medicine powers.[55] Early in 1887, Pá-iñgya (In The Middle) claimed his dɔdɔ, partially derived from Whirlwind and Fire, was more powerful than that of his predecessor and prophesied that his powers would destroy all whites and any Indians living like them. Setting up camp on Elk Creek at the western edge of the reservation, Pá-iñgya announced sanctuary to those who joined his encampment. His followers were called Baiyop (Sun People, or Sons of the Sun), based on their adherence to the religion of the Ten Medicines and the power of Sun. These events were remembered by Tsoodle, Andrew Stumbling Bear (b. 1874), Jimmy Quoetone, and Max Frizzlehead.[56] As with Pá-tépte, Pá-iñgya became unpopular after his powers failed to produce an apocalypse in the summer of 1888 (Mooney 1898, 350, 356–57).

Despite his decline in popularity, Pá-iñgya maintained a small following. Members of the Sun People, including Lone Bear, Wooden Lance, and Big Bow, opposed the peyote religion, which was becoming very popular among the Mount Scott Kiowas. According to Tsoodle and Jimmy Quoetone, Pá-iñgya and his disciples disliked the peyote rite because they perceived it was a foreign religion that went against the Ten Medicines, the oldest form of religion among the Kiowas. Ironically, many of In The Middle's followers turned to peyote after 1890 when he became involved in the Ghost Dance movement. The death of several members was largely responsible for the disbandment of the Sons of the Sun (LaBarre 1938, 112).[57]

Peyote (*Lophophora williamsii*), a small green, spineless cactus occurring in single or small clusters of "buttons" attached to a taproot, grows naturally on both sides of the Rio Grande River (Stewart 1987, 3). Kiowa war parties traversing into Mexico in the mid-nineteenth century were exposed to the hallucinogenic cactus and its rituals. Bagyanoi said that around 1850, Big Horse consumed peyote to prophesy the well-being of war parties feared lost, and by 1870, members of Kiowa and Comanche raiding parties into the Southwest and Mexico learned the nascent form of the peyote rite from the Mescalero or Lipan Apaches (see also LaBarre 1938, 111; Stewart 1987, 47–51).[58] According to Lone Bear, Sankadota, and Apekaum, Zempadlte obtained the ceremony by the mid-1880s from Comanche warriors recently returned from the Southwest, and the earliest remembered peyote meeting occurred in the summer of 1885. On that occasion, some of the Sun People placed a rotten bear head inside the tipi to protest the ceremony.[59] Despite opposition from conservative groups like the Sun People, the crescent moon peyote rite that became popular in the 1880s outlived the other religious movements of the late nineteenth century, except for Christianity.

In the summer of 1890, finally convinced that the bison would not return, most Kiowas invested their energies in the Ghost Dance, a syncretic amalgam of Christianity, tribal beliefs, and prophecy. As related by Jimmy Quoetone and Andrew Stumbling Bear, Pá-tadal (Poor Buffalo) visited the Darlington Agency in June and learned about the Ghost Dance from Sitting Bull, the Arapaho proselytizer whose version of the ritual resulted from his pilgrimage to see the "messiah" Wovoka near Mason Valley, Nevada. Pá-tadal returned to the Anadarko Agency and introduced the dance while the Kiowas and Plains Apaches were assembled for a grazing lease payment. Shortly after the gathering in Anadarko, another Ghost Dance occurred at a large encampment near Saddle Mountain, about thirty-five miles southwest of the agency, where numerous Kiowas became instant converts. On such occasions, new followers received the dance through the "giving the feather" rite in which seven men (and often seven women) were presented an eagle feather or two crow feathers, indigenous symbols of power incorporated into the Ghost Dance. Early in the fall, Sitting Bull came to the KCA Reservation and set up a camp near the confluence of Rainy Mountain Creek and the Washita River, just west of present-day Carnegie.[60] The ensuing Ghost Dance in October was the largest ever among the Kiowas; even old chief Stumbling Bear came to give his support (Mooney 1898, 359–60; Mooney 1896, 919).

As taught by Sitting Bull, the "typical" Southern Plains Ghost Dance began in the midafternoon, or after sundown, and often continued until sunrise. Participants painted their faces with sacred red paint given by Wovoka to Sitting Bull and wore upright crow and eagle feathers in their braids. Many dances were preceded by a rite in which the dance leader sprinkled a special powder on the dance ground while praying. Once the arena was "consecrated," men, women, and children formed an inward facing circle while holding hands with fingers interlocked, then shuffled clockwise in rhythm to chanted Ghost Dance songs with no instrumental accompaniment. Entering the dance circle, holding a handkerchief or feather in one hand, the Ghost Dance leader moved about and hypnotized some of the dancers, who fell to the ground in trances. Whenever this happened, the dancing stopped and everyone sat down to smoke and visit while those in trances were making the transcendent journey to the spirit world, where they witnessed old-time activities or communicated with deceased relatives. Upon regaining consciousness from trances that lasted from ten minutes to several hours, the visionaries related their experiences while everyone listened attentively. Mooney, who witnessed dances at the Darlington Agency in January 1891, noted that trances were the central element of the Ghost Dance and suggested that hypnotism was the secret of the trance, though the Ghost Dance leaders claimed that they were merely conduits for a higher power that caused the trances (Mooney 1896, 918–24).

Having recently lost a favorite son, Ä'piatañ (Wooden Lance) took interest in the Ghost Dance doctrine that promised reunification with deceased relatives and consulted a council of Kiowa chiefs, who agreed to finance his trip to Mason Valley to meet the messiah, Wovoka.[61] Ä'piatañ departed in September as the Ghost Dance was gaining momentum among the Kiowas. Traveling north, he visited Lakota friends at Pine Ridge Agency and then continued west and finally met Wovoka in early January, 1891. Undoubtedly affected by the tragic Wounded Knee massacre of December 29, 1890, Wovoka told Ä'piatañ to return home and tell everyone to discontinue the dance. Convinced that Wovoka was not omnipotent as many claimed, a discouraged Ä'piatañ returned home and spoke to a large intertribal gathering at the Anadarko Agency on February 19. During the ensuing council—which was lengthy because all communications had to be translated into Kiowa, Caddo, Wichita, Comanche, Arapaho, and English—Ä'piatañ denounced the Ghost Dance and proclaimed that Sitting Bull was a fraud. Most left the council crestfallen believing that the Ghost Dance doctrine was powerless (Mooney 1896, 908–9, 911–14).

Not everyone was convinced, however; many Caddo, Wichita, Plains Apache, and Kiowa devotees still adhered to the Ghost Dance doctrine. Pá-tadal, Setæpetoi (Afraid-Of-Bears), and other Kiowa leaders kept the religion alive, and in September 1894, a large four-day Ghost Dance in the Washita River encampment west of Carnegie attracted several thousand Indian participants (Mooney 1896, 914; Methvin n.d., 77). Afraid-Of-Bears, White Fox's father, emerged as a popular leader for his ability to induce trances enabling visionaries to visit the spirits of deceased kinfolk. Participation in the revived dance also represented stability in the face of rapid culture change through forced allotment, which was inevitable by 1901. Indian agents often referred to the Ghost Dance faction as the "dance crowd" because they maintained traditions of song and dance, shamanism, games—especially the hand game—clothing, hairstyles, and other vestiges of the horse and buffalo culture. Ghost Dancers opposed progress associated with allotment, especially the construction of houses and fences, which to them signified "cutting up" the land. Moreover, Ghost Dancers opposed a rival group that followed a new religion—Christianity.

Christianity was introduced to the Kiowas by Quaker agents and Friend Battey in the early 1870s through the auspices of U.S. president Grant's "peace policy" stipulating that Quaker Indian agents were to hire teachers and other personnel to administer provisions of the Medicine Lodge Treaty—chiefly, to "civilize" Indians through education and religious instruction. By 1877, when the Quaker agents were replaced, they had established a school at Fort Sill for Indian children and had provided religious services at the agency. In the wake of the Quakers, there were no missions among the KCA Indians for the next ten years. Between 1877 and 1887, several religious organizations unsuccessfully attempted to bring Christianity to the KCA Indians, perceived as "wild blanket Indians" in "darkness" without Christians in their midst. Following the passage of the 1887 Dawes, or General Allotment, Act, several Christian denominations petitioned the Department of the Interior to build missions on the KCA Reservation. For the next fourteen years, a number of churches and mission boarding schools operated in Kiowa country (Kracht 1989, 626–27).

Rev. John J. Methvin (Methodist) was the first missionary to arrive in the fall of 1887, followed by Baptists, Catholics, Reformed Presbyterians, and Presbyterians. By 1901, nineteen mission churches with 448 members and four mission-operated boarding schools operated on the former KCA Reservation (Kracht 1989, 627–28). Although missionaries encountered initial resistance, their persistence and charitable works, particularly their efforts to facilitate the difficult transition from tipis to houses, helped them gain converts. Isabel Crawford, who lived with the Saddle Mountain Kiowas from 1896 to 1906, conducted prayer services, gospel meetings, and funerals and tended to the sick and dying. One of the best-remembered missionaries, Crawford assured her converts that the *dɔdɔ* of Dɔk'i (God) and Jesus could heal the sick and that deceased Christians went "to live with Jesus" in heaven. Jesus was perceived as a guardian spirit, a positive force available to everyone, as opposed to a personal dream spirit for a select few possessing *dɔdɔ* (Crawford 1915, 16, 239–40; Corwin 1958a, 113–42; Kracht 1989, 660–72; Kracht 2000, 241–42).

Opposition to Christianity subsided after 1916 when the Ghost Dance movement died out; many former Ghost Dance followers converted to Christianity, and Ghost Dance songs were reworked into Christian hymns. By the early 1920s, at least one-third of the Kiowa population had converted to Christianity. Others adhering to the peyote religion officially had organized into the Native American Church in 1918. Christianity and peyotism were the two major religions among the Kiowas in 1935.

Santa Fe Field Party: Aftermath

After nine weeks in southwestern Oklahoma, the five graduate students composing the Santa Fe field party ended their field stint among the Kiowas on the night of August 28. Professor Lesser, satisfied that each student had completed at least forty-five days of work with over thirty-five collaborators and twelve interpreters, anticipated publishing the collaborative monograph the following summer, which never happened.[62] Weston LaBarre returned the next year to collect data on the peyote religion for his dissertation and introduced ethnobotanist Richard Evans Schultes to many of his Indian friends in Oklahoma. A side project of his fieldwork was an autobiography of Charley Apekaum, which remains unpublished, though it was later duplicated by Microcard Publications (LaBarre 1957). In 1937, LaBarre and Collier both testified on behalf of the Native American Church and helped defeat Senate bill 1399, the same year that Schultes (1937) published an article identifying the alkaloids, or active ingredients, of peyote. As a Stanley Fellow at Yale University greatly influenced by Edward Sapir, LaBarre defended his dissertation documenting the peyote religion in 1937, which was published the following year (LaBarre 1938).

In 1946 he became a faculty member at Duke University, where he received the endowed James B. Duke Professorship of Anthropology in 1970. Throughout most of his career, LaBarre studied the psychoanalytical dimensions of religion and collaborated with Schultes and R. Gordon Wasson in the study of shamanism and altered states of consciousness. Although his classic *The Peyote Cult* was reissued several times during his lifetime, LaBarre never returned to Oklahoma for extensive fieldwork. In March 1996, he passed away at home in Chapel Hill, North Carolina.

Donald Collier served as a curator of South and Central American archaeology and ethnology at the Field Museum in Chicago, and from 1950 to 1970 he taught classes at the University of Chicago, where his PhD was conferred in 1954. Besides his brief article on Kiowa sorcery (Collier 1944), Collier never produced another publication on indigenous Kiowa belief systems. He passed away in January 1995.

Following the conclusion of the field school, Jane Richardson returned to Berkeley for two more years of graduate studies and in 1938 completed her doctoral dissertation on Kiowa law at Columbia University under the guidance of Ruth Benedict. Richardson also collaborated with psychologist Abraham Maslow in a study of the Blackfeet in Canada. In 1940, Richardson's dissertation was published in the *Monographs of the American Ethnological Society*, though her PhD was not conferred until 1943 due to technicalities. In 1950, Richardson and her husband, Lucien Hanks, published their Blackfeet research in *Tribe under Trust: A Study of the Blackfoot Reserve*. Her *Law and Status among the Kiowa Indians* (Richardson 1940) remains a classic in Plains anthropological studies. Richardson Hanks survived all members of the 1935 field party and was 105 years old when she passed away on July 27, 2014, in Bennington, Vermont.

William Bascom enrolled as a doctoral student at Northwestern University. In 1938 Bascom traveled to Nigeria, where he conducted ethnographic fieldwork with the Yorubas and completed his dissertation in 1939 as Melville Herskovits's first PhD student. In September 1981, he passed away due to complications that ensued following open-heart surgery. His Kiowa fieldnotes remain unpublished.

Of all the Santa Fe field school students, Bernard Mishkin had the shortest career, which was cut short by a heart attack when he was only forty-one years old. In 1937, Mishkin completed his dissertation on Kiowa warfare at Columbia University; three years later it was published by the American Ethnological Society as *Rank and Warfare among the Plains Indians* (Mishkin 1940). Though he never worked with the Kiowas again, his monograph on Kiowa warfare demonstrated the economic significance of Plains warfare.

Prior to directing the 1935 field school, Alexander Lesser and his wife, Gene Weltfish, conducted ethnographic fieldwork with the Pawnees in Oklahoma beginning in 1928, resulting in publications on the practice of the levirate and fraternal polyandry (1930), the cultural significance of the Ghost Dance (1933), the incorporation of the hand game into the Ghost Dance (1933a), and Caddoan kinship (1979). Lesser had completed his dissertation on Siouan kinship at Columbia University in 1929, though his PhD was not conferred until the publication of *Siouan Kinship* in 1958. In August 1982, Lesser died of a heart attack in Levittown, New York.

Alice Marriott worked independently of the Santa Fe field party but nonetheless collected relevant information through her interviews primarily with George Hunt, Margaret Hunt Tsoodle, Ioleta Hunt MacElhaney, Sanko, Frank Given, and Tsoodle. After finishing her bachelor's degree at the University of Oklahoma in 1935, Marriott stayed connected with the university and continued interviewing her Kiowa friends. From 1936 to 1942 she was employed as a field agent for the Indian Arts and Crafts Board (IACB) created by passage of the Indian Arts and Crafts Act in August 1935. Although the Texas-Kansas-Oklahoma region to which she was assigned required her to maintain contact with fifty-seven federally recognized tribes, Marriott managed to maintain relationships with Kiowa collaborators. One of the highlights of her career with the IACB was coordinating an exhibition of American Indian art at the 1939 San Francisco World's Fair, during which she met famed San Illdefonso potters Julian and Mariá Martinez. Funding for the IACB waned during World War II, but Marriott remained employed through the American Red Cross and worked in the Southwest from 1942 through 1945. For the next three years Marriott remained in the Santa Fe area supported by a fellowship that allowed her to focus on writing: *The Ten Grandmothers* (1945), *Winter-Telling Stories* (1947), and *Maria: The Potter of San Illdefonso* (1948) were published during this period. Marriott spent the rest of her career living in Oklahoma City and collaborating with archaeologist Carol R. Rachlin. Individually and collaboratively, Marriott authored over twenty books on American Indians. In 1958 she was nominated into the Oklahoma Hall of Fame, in 1963 became a consultant to the Oklahoma Indian Council, and in 2004 was posthumously installed into the Oklahoma Historians Hall of Fame. In the mid-1960s Marriott taught anthropology classes at the University of Oklahoma. She passed away in March 1992.

Aside from Marriott (1945, 1963), Nye (1934, 1937, 1962), and later on Levy (1959) and Corwin (1958a, 1959, 1962), other scholars did not work with the survivors of the horse and buffalo culture, which abruptly ended in 1875. Though these works are meritorious, they are not as ethnographically comprehensive as the 1935 Santa Fe Laboratory of Anthropology fieldnotes. Marriott's statement that fieldnotes "are an anthropologist's investment in the future" holds many truths, especially due to the liberties she took in presenting Kiowa culture to the public through her publications, as noted by Kiowa linguist and anthropologist Gus Palmer Jr. (2003, 115–16). That Marriott wrote for a non-Indian audience as opposed to scholarly, anthropological publications increases the value of her field-notes, which nicely complement the more detailed Santa Fe fieldnotes.

Perhaps the greatest value of the interviews conducted in 1935 by Marriott, Lesser, LaBarre, Bascom, Collier, Richardson, and Mishkin lies in the fact that many of their Kiowa collaborators died shortly afterward. Although vital records are oftentimes muddled—especially birth dates—at least eight of the collaborators and interpreters died within seven years after working with Marriott and the Santa Fe field party students. Max Frizzlehead died on August 15, while all the students were in the field, followed by Monroe Tsatoke (d. 1937), Mary Buffalo (d. 1939), Frank Given (d. 1939), Silver Horn (d. 1940), Tsoodle (d. 1941), Sankadota (d. 1941), and George Hunt (d. 1942). Another seven born before the reservation period passed away in the 1950s, including Belo Cozad (d. 1950), Haumpy (d. 1951), Hunting Horse (d. 1953), Jimmy Quoetone (d. 1956), Luther Sahmaunt (d. 1958), White Fox (d. 1959), and Goomda (d. 1959). The passing of these individuals (and others not mentioned) marks the end of firsthand knowledge about the horse and buffalo culture. Among the interpreters playing key roles, Charley Apekaum died in 1965 and Bert Geikauma (d. 1971) survived him by a few years. The contributions made by these individuals provide some insight into this bygone era.

Impact and Significance of the Fieldnotes

It's been over eighty years since Alexander Lesser and the five anthropology students concluded their summer residence in Kiowa country and returned to their respective universities and careers. In early December 1935, Lesser drafted a tentative outline for a Kiowa ethnography, though the project was never finished. Within a few years, LaBarre published his research on the peyote religion (1938), which was then followed by Mishkin's work on Kiowa rank and warfare (1940), Richardson's examination of law and status (1940), and Collier's article on Kiowa sorcery (1944). Today, the Typescript of Student's Notes is located in the Papers of Weston LaBarre housed in the National Anthropological Archives at the Smithsonian Institution. The compilation includes 1,320 cut-and-paste, typed and handwritten pages of the daily notes of the field party members (Merrill et al. 1997, 170). Digital copies of the individual fieldnotes of LaBarre, Collier, Mishkin, Bascom, and Lesser are located in the

Alexander Lesser Collection, American Indian Studies Research Institute, Indiana University, Bloomington.

After years of languishing in archival repositories, the Santa Fe field-notes have been accessed in recent years by scholars studying Kiowa ethnohistory. For instance, Smithsonian Institution ethnologist Candace S. Greene consulted them—as well as Mooney's fieldnotes—for a biography of Ten Medicines bundle keeper Silver Horn (2001), an analysis of the recently discovered Silver Horn pictographic calendar (2009), and identification of the three men named Dohásän (1996). Sometime in August 1990, William C. Meadows photocopied my copy of the fieldnotes (Meadows 2008, 4). Meadows utilized portions of the fieldnotes for his monographs on Kiowa, Comanche, and Plains Apache military societies (1999), Kiowa ethnogeography (2008), and Kiowa military societies (2010). Notably, his citations follow my pagination used to index my copy, which differs slightly from the actual pagination used in the typescript. More recently, Michael P. Jordan's dissertation discussing Kiowa family reunions and descendants' organizations cites the fieldnotes (2011), as does a book chapter coauthored with Daniel C. Swan about tipis and warrior traditions (Swan and Jordan 2011).

Other recent publications on Kiowa history and culture have not consulted the fieldnotes, for instance Gus Palmer Jr.'s short treatise on Kiowa storytelling (2003), Jacki Thompson Rand's overview of Kiowa-federal relations during the reservation period (2008), and Clyde Ellis's history of Rainy Mountain Boarding School (1996). Likewise, in their collaborative research on the Kiowa Gourd Dance and Southern Plains pow-wows, historian Clyde Ellis and anthropologist Luke Eric Lassiter have not cited the Santa Fe fieldnotes (Lassiter 1993, 1997, 1998; Ellis 1990, 1993, 1999, 2003). Additionally, their collaborative monograph on Kiowa Christian hymns omits the fieldnotes (Lassiter, Ellis, and Kotay 2002). Understandably, not referencing the Santa Fe fieldnotes does not lessen the significance of these publications, though useful information could have been gleaned from them.

During the summer of 1987, I obtained a copy of the Santa Fe fieldnotes through a graduate student fellowship at the Smithsonian Institution; the fieldnotes served as the major corpus of my doctoral dissertation (Kracht 1989). Since then, I have mentioned the fieldnotes to some Kiowa friends, but nobody seems to be aware of their existence other than a handful of Kiowas engaged in scholarly research, including Gus Palmer Jr. at the University of Oklahoma and Marian Kaulaity Hansson, a Native American fellow in the Department of Anthropology at the Smithsonian Institution. In June 2004, I visited with Fred Tsoodle and gave him a copy of his grandfather's interview with LaBarre, but Fred was vaguely aware of the anthropologist who visited with Tsoodle. Likewise, Gus Palmer Sr. remembered that anthropologists participated in Native American Church ceremonies in the 1930s and helped defeat anti-peyote legislation, but he did not specifically identify LaBarre. All the elderly consultants I worked with, though, are familiar with Mooney, and some even have a copy of *Calendar History of the Kiowa Indians*. Once I asked Gus Palmer Sr. a question and he went into the back room and returned with his copy! Many Kiowas are also familiar with Alice Marriott and *The Ten Grandmothers*, and some point out that the Ten Medicines are not called Grandmothers.

Mooney conducted fieldwork in southwestern Oklahoma from 1891 to 1918, whereas Marriott stayed in close touch with Kiowa friends after her 1934–36 field stints and spent her final years in Oklahoma City, just a short distance away. Both are well known for their publications on Kiowa culture. The Santa Fe Laboratory of Anthropology field expedition of 1935, however, was of short duration compared to the amount of time Mooney and Marriott spent among the Kiowas. That most contemporary Kiowas are unaware of the 1935 Santa Fe field party is not surprising, especially since the planned ethnography never materialized. Had it been published, perhaps LaBarre, Collier, Mishkin, Richardson, Bascom, and Lesser would be household names like Mooney and Marriott. Nevertheless, the fieldnotes remain a largely untapped wealth of information regarding nineteenth-century Kiowa culture. As noted by Lesser, future scholars utilizing the fieldnotes will find "ample, perhaps exceptional, material on Kiowa economics, political organization, authority, law, rank, kinship, family life, warfare, societies (men's and women's), religious conceptions, the vision complex, medicine men and sorcery, the Sun Dance, the Ten Medicine complex, cult movements, etc."[63]

Appendix

Kiowa Sun Dance Chronology, 1833–1890

1833 No Sun Dance. "Summer that they cut off their heads." There was no Sun Dance because Taime was lost to the Osages (Mooney 1898, 257; Frederickson n.d., 5).

1834 No Sun Dance. Taime still missing (Mooney 1898, 261; Frederickson n.d., 5).

1835 "Cat-tail rush Sun Dance." Held "on the south bank of the North Canadian River, at the red hills, about 30 miles above the present Fort Reno, Oklahoma" (Mooney 1898, 269–70; Frederickson n.d., 5).

1836 "Wolf-river Sun Dance." Held on Wolf Creek Fork of the North Canadian River (Mooney 1898, 271; Frederickson n.d., 5).

1837 No Sun Dance. "Summer that the Cheyenne were massacred." While preparing for the Sun Dance, the Kiowas, Comanches, and Plains Apaches were attacked by Cheyennes carrying the Medicine Arrows at Scott Creek, a tributary of the North Fork of the Red River in the Texas Panhandle. There was no dance, because some Kiowas were killed (Mooney 1898, 217–72). The Kiowa calendar housed in the museum at Berkeley, however, indicated that a Sun Dance occurred that summer (Frederickson n.d., 5).

1838 No Sun Dance. "Summer that the Cheyenne attacked the camp on Wolf River," a tributary of the North Canadian River (Mooney 1898, 273; Frederickson n.d., 5).

1839 "Peninsula Sun Dance." Held on south side of the Washita River below Walnut Creek (Mooney 1898, 273; Frederickson n.d., 5).

1840 "Red-bluff Sun Dance." Held at the confluence of the South Canadian River and Mustang Creek in the Texas Panhandle (Mooney 1898, 275; Frederickson n.d., 5–6).

1841 No Sun Dance. Kiowas on the move all summer (Mooney 1898, 276; Frederickson n.d., 6).

1842 "Repeated Sun Dance." Held on Kiowa Medicine Lodge Creek, a tributary of the North Canadian River (Mooney 1898, 279; Frederickson n.d., 6).

1843 "Nest-building Sun Dance." Held on same creek as in the previous Sun Dance in 1842 (Mooney 1898, 281; Frederickson n.d., 6).

1844 "Dakota Sun Dance." Held on the same creek for the third consecutive year (Mooney 1898, 281; Frederickson n.d., 6).

1845 "Stone-necklace Sun Dance." Again, the dance was held at the same location (Mooney 1898, 283; Frederickson n.d., 6).

1846 "Sun Dance when Hornless-bull was made a Kaitsenk'ia." Held on a tributary of the North Canadian River, slightly above Kiowa Medicine Lodge Creek (Mooney 1898, 283–84; Frederickson n.d., 6).

1847 No Sun Dance (Mooney 1898, 286–87; Frederickson n.d., 6–7).

1848 "Kaitsenko initiation Sun Dance." Held on Arkansas River near Bent's Fort in present-day Colorado (Mooney 1898, 387; Frederickson n.d., 7).

1849 "Cramp (cholera) Sun Dance." Held on Mule Creek, between Medicine Lodge Creek and the Salt Fork of the Arkansas River (Mooney 1898, 289–90; Frederickson n.d., 7).

1850 "Chinaberry Sun Dance." Held near the junction of Wolf Creek and the North Canadian River near Fort Supply, Oklahoma (Mooney 1898, 292; Frederickson n.d., 7).

1851 "Dusty Sun Dance." Held close to the spot of the previous Sun Dance in 1850 (Mooney 1898, 293; Frederickson n.d., 7).

1852 No Sun Dance (Mooney 1898, 294–95; Frederickson n.d., 7).

1853 "Showery Sun Dance." Third Sun Dance in a row at the same location. Mirror taboo broken during dance (Mooney 1898, 295–96; Frederickson n.d., 7).

1854 "Timber-mountain Creek Sun Dance." Held near Medicine Lodge Creek, Kansas (Mooney 1898, 297).

1855 No Sun Dance. Hot weather, grass dried up, horses weak (Mooney 1898, 300).

1856 "Prickly-pear Sun Dance." Held late in the fall ten miles south of Bent's Fort (Mooney 1898, 301; Frederickson n.d., 8).

1857 "Sun Dance when the forked stick sprouted." Held at the confluence of Elm Creek and the Salt Fork of the Arkansas River in Oklahoma. When dɔ was planted (Mooney 1898, 301–2; Frederickson n.d., 8).

1858 "Timber circle Sun Dance." Held on Mule Creek, which joins the Salt Fork of the Arkansas River near Medicine Lodge Creek (Mooney 1898, 305–6; Frederickson n.d., 8).

1859 "Cedar-bluff Sun Dance." Held at the confluence of Timber Creek and the Smoky Hill River near present-day Fort Hays, Kansas. Buffalo were more abundant there (Mooney 1898, 306; Frederickson n.d., 8).

1860 No Sun Dance (Mooney 1898, 308; Frederickson n.d., 8).

1861 "Sun Dance when they left the spotted horse tied." Held at the confluence of Walnut Creek and the Arkansas River, near Great Bend, Kansas (Mooney 1898, 310; Frederickson n.d., 8).

1862 "Sun Dance after the smallpox." Held on Mule Creek, where 1858 Sun Dance took place (Mooney 1898, 311; Frederickson n.d., 8).

1863 "No-arm's River Sun Dance." Held on the south side of the Arkansas River below the mouth of Walnut Creek (near Great Bend) close to a trader's store (Mooney 1898, 313; Frederickson n.d., 9).

1864 "Ragweed Sun Dance." Near sites of the 1858 and 1862 Sun Dances, at the confluence of Medicine Lodge Creek and the Salt Fork of the Arkansas River (Mooney 1898, 313; Frederickson n.d., 9).

1865 "Peninsula Sun Dance." Held near the bend of the Washita, near the mouth of Walnut Creek (Mooney 1898, 317; Frederickson n.d., 9).

1866 "Flat metal (German silver) Sun Dance." Held near the mouth of Medicine Lodge Creek in Oklahoma (Mooney 1898, 318; Frederickson n.d., 9).

1867 "Sun Dance when Black-ear was stolen." Held on north bank of the Washita River, near the western edge of Oklahoma. Last K'oitsenko initiation (Mooney 1898, 319–20; Frederickson n.d., 9).

1868 "Sun Dance when the Ute killed us," or "Timber-hill River Sun Dance." Held on Medicine Lodge Creek, a favorite Sun Dance site (Mooney 1898, 322; Frederickson n.d., 9).

1869 "Sun Dance when they brought the war-bonnet." Held near the confluence of Sweetwater Creek and the North Fork of the Red River, near western Oklahoma line (Mooney 1898, 326; Frederickson n.d., 10).

1870 "Plant-growing dance," or "Dusty Sun Dance." Held where previous Sun Dance was held in 1868 in present-day Greer County, Oklahoma (Mooney 1898, 327; Frederickson n.d., 10).

1871 No Sun Dance (Mooney 1898, 328). The Taime keeper Onsokyapta died that year (Frederickson n.d., 10).

1872 No Sun Dance (Mooney 1898, 335; Frederickson n.d., 10).

1873 "Maggot Creek Sun Dance," or "Black Buffalo's horses killed." Held where 1862 and 1870 Sun Dances were conducted (Mooney 1898, 336). Dó-héñte was the new Taimek'i (Frederickson n.d., 10).

1874 "Sun Dance at the end to the bluff." Held at the confluence of Elm Fork and North Fork of the Red River, near Last Mountain, Greer County, Oklahoma (Mooney 1898, 338). White Bear gave away his Zebɔt. Last Mountain is also known as Mount Walsh (Mooney 1898, 338; Frederickson n.d., 10).

1875 "Love-making Spring Sun Dance." Held on the north bank of the North Fork of the Red River near Last Mountain. The Kiowas were escorted by troops; the "outbreak" was not quite over (Mooney 1898, 339; Frederickson n.d., 10).

1876 "Sun Dance where Sun Boy's horses were stolen." Held at the fork of Sweetwater Creek. Many Bears, uncle of the late Heap O' Bears, was the new Taimek'i (Dó-héñte died the preceding fall). Mexicans stole the horses (Mooney 1898, 340; Frederickson n.d., 11).

1877 "Star-girl-tree River," or "Measles Sun Dance." Held at the Salt Fork of the Red River in Greer County, Oklahoma. Troops accompanied them (Mooney 1898, 341–42; Frederickson n.d., 11).

1878 "Repeated Sun Dance." Held somewhere along the North Fork of the Red River. Two parties vowed the dance: (1) buffalo hunters and (2) those who stayed home. Troops accompanied them (Mooney 1898, 343; Frederickson n.d., 11).

1879 "Horse-eating Sun Dance." Held at the Elm Fork of the Red River. The failure to find any buffalo the previous winter coupled with a poor summer hunt compelled the Kiowas to eat their horses that summer (Mooney 1898, 344–45).

1880 No Sun Dance. Failure to find bison (Mooney 1898, 346; Frederickson n.d., 11).

1881 "Hot Sun Dance." Held in late August because it took a long time to find a bison for the ceremony. The dance was performed at the North Fork of the Red River near the "end of the mountains" (Mooney 1898, 347; Frederickson n.d., 11).

1882 No Sun Dance. Dohásän II could not find a bison (Mooney 1898, 349; Frederickson n.d., 11).

1883 "Nez Perce Sun Dance." Held on Upper Cache Creek, near Washita River bottoms (present-day Cloud Chief, Oklahoma). Led by Taíméte, because Many Bears had died that spring (Mooney 1898, 351; Frederickson n.d., 12).

1884 No Sun Dance. Failure to find a bison (Mooney 1898, 352; Frederickson n.d., 12).

1885 "Little peninsula Sun Dance." Held at the bend of the Washita River twenty miles above the agency. (A previous dance was held at the same location in 1839.) Dohásän II procured the bull from a Texan rancher (Mooney 1898, 353–54; Frederickson n.d., 12).

1886 No Sun Dance. Failure to find buffalo compelled them to return home. First Kiowa grass payment (Mooney 1898, 254; Frederickson n.d., 12).

1887 "Oak Creek Sun Dance." Held above Rainy Mountain Creek. Charles Goodnight supplied a buffalo from his small domestic herd in Texas (Mooney 1898, 355; Frederickson n.d., 12).

1888 No Sun Dance. New agent prohibited dance (Mooney 1898, 356; Frederickson n.d., 12).

1889 No Sun Dance. Everyone stayed home (Mooney 1898, 358; Frederickson n.d., 12).

1890 "Sun Dance when the forked poles were left standing." The aborted dance was held at the bend of the Washita where two other Sun Dances had been conducted. Stumbling Bear sent word to discontinue the dance (Mooney 1898, 358–59; Frederickson n.d., 12).

Notes

KIOWA PRONUNCIATIONS

1. J. P. Harrington (1928, 9) described the ejective Kiowa consonants: "[*k', t', ts',*
   p'] are simultaneously glottalized. . . . The buccal release precedes the laryn-
   geal, thus producing a click like that of suddenly opening a chamber of partial
   vacuum, like the sound of pulling a cork from a bottle, the buccal consonant
   retaining of course its characteristic resonance. In glottalized [*ts'*] the laryn-
   geal opening comes after the *s*, not between the *t* and the *s*."
2. Harrington (1928b, 9) likewise described the aspirated consonants: "Like the
   sounds of the glottalized series . . . those of the aspirated series [*kh, th, ph*]
   are also immersed, not in a glottal clusive but in an aspiration. . . . The corresponding aspirated form of *ts* was not found."
3. In syllable-final position, /l/ becomes [d¹], a slightly affricated form. Sometimes long vowels are replaced by affricated d¹ in syllable-final position.
4. All six Kiowa vowels are long [designated by /·/ following the vowel] or short,
   oral or nasal.

PREFACE

1. Handwritten page, chapters written by W. LaBarre for a proposed general ethnography, "The Kiowa Indians," Papers of R. Weston LaBarre, series 1: Kiowa
   Studies, box 2, Smithsonian Institution, National Anthropological Archives
   (hereafter KFN). Henceforth, all archival materials will be referenced in end-
   notes. All secondary sources are cited in the text.
2. "Laboratory Offers Field Method Training Scholarships," undated newspaper
   clipping from unknown newspaper, box 1, folder 10, Arthur & Shifra Silberman Native Art Collection, Dickinson Research Center, National Cowboy &
   Western Heritage Museum, Oklahoma City, Oklahoma [Hereafter NCWHM].
3. LaBarre et al., KFN.
4. Alexander Lesser, field leader, to Director Jesse L. Nusbaum, September 19,
   1935, Kiowa–Alexander Lesser Anthropology Field Program, 1935 notes and
   letters, Arthur & Shifra Silberman Native Art Collection, NCWHM.

5. Alexander Lesser, field leader, to Director Jesse L. Nusbaum, September 19, 1935, Kiowa–Alexander Lesser Anthropology Field Program, 1935 notes and letters, box 1, folder 10, Arthur & Shifra Silberman Native Art Collection, NCWHM.

6. Alexander Lesser to Director Jesse L. Nusbaum, September 19, 1935, Kiowa–Alexander Lesser Anthropology Field Program, 1935 notes and letters, box 1, folder 10, Arthur & Shifra Silberman Native Art Collection, NCWHM.

7. Other copies of the 1935 field party fieldnotes and related correspondence are found elsewhere, including the Jane Richardson Hanks Kiowa Papers, 1935–1968, Roger and Julie Baskes Department of Special Collections, Newberry Library; R. Weston LaBarre Papers, Duke University; and Kiowa–Alexander Lesser Anthropology Field Program, 1935 notes and letters, box 1, folder 10, Arthur & Shifra Silberman Native Art Collection, NCWHM.

8. LaBarre, spiral notebook no. 3, box 1 of 14, KFN.

INTRODUCTION

1. Anonymous to Forrest E. Clements, April 11, 1935, Kiowa–Alexander Lesser Anthropology Field Program, 1935 notes and letters, box 1, folder 10, Arthur & Shifra Silberman Native Art Collection, Dickinson Research Center (hereafter DRC), NCWHM.

2. Alexander Lesser to Jesse L. Nusbaum, director, Santa Fe Laboratory of Anthropology, September 19, 1935, Kiowa–Alexander Lesser Anthropology Field Program, 1935 notes and letters, box 1, folder 10, Arthur & Shifra Silberman Native Art Collection, DRC NCWHM.

3. Donald Collier to Jesse L. Nusbaum, director, Santa Fe Laboratory of Anthropology, September 19, 1935, Kiowa–Alexander Lesser Anthropology Field Program, 1935 notes and letters, box 1, folder 10, Arthur & Shifra Silberman Native Art Collection, DRC NCWHM.

4. Field and Office Disbursements form and receipt, June 27, 28, 1935, Kiowa–Alexander Lesser Anthropology Field Program, notes and letters, box 1, folder 10, Arthur & Shifra Silberman Native Art Collection, DRC NCWHM.

5. Alexander Lesser to Jesse L. Nusbaum, director, Santa Fe Laboratory of Anthropology, September 19, 1935, Kiowa–Alexander Lesser Anthropology Field Program, 1935 notes and letters, box 1, folder 10, Arthur & Shifra Silberman Native Art Collection, DRC NCWHM.

6. John Collier to Donald Collier, March 30, 1937; Donald Collier to John Collier, March 31, 1937; Weston LaBarre to John Collier, March 31, 1937; John Collier to Weston LaBarre, April 2, 1937; Weston LaBarre to John Collier, April 5, 1937, Papers of R. Weston LaBarre, series 2: Peyote Studies, box 5, National Anthropological Archives, Smithsonian Institution.

7. Hugh D. Corwin, "50 Years with the Kiowa Indians, 1850–1900" (unpublished manuscript, 1962), 64, D'Arcy McNickle Center for the Study of the American Indian, Newberry Library, Chicago, Illinois; Special Agent E. E. White to

Indian Commissioner John H. Oberly, August 18, 1888, Annual Report of the Commissioner of Indian Affairs 1888. [Congressional Serial Set 2637] (hereafter cited as ARCIA with the serial number in brackets).

8. Hugh D. Corwin, "50 Years with the Kiowa Indians, 1850–1900," 64.

9. Kiowa orthography is somewhat problematic due to various spellings of names. Names appearing in this study are spelled according to the source. In the case of the 1935 fieldnotes, spellings remain the same with one exception: the typewritten fieldnotes used /w/ to represent low-back vowel /ɔ/. In this study, the latter is used. When possible, modern spellings will be used, e.g., Gueton or Quito appear as Jimmy Quoetone.

10. "Kiowa Indian Snapshots, 1935 Santa Fe Laboratory Field Trip to the Kiowa," Papers of R. Weston LaBarre, series 4: Photographs and LaBarre Term papers, box 13, National Anthropological Archives, Smithsonian Institution (hereafter cited as "Kiowa Indian Snapshots").

11. "Kiowa Indian Snapshots."

12. "Kiowa Indian Snapshots."

13. "Kiowa Indian Snapshots."

14. Alice Marriott fieldnotes, August 22, 1935, Ioleta Hunt MacElhaney, interpreter, Alice L. Marriott Collection, box 9, folder 27, Western History Collections, University of Oklahoma Libraries (hereafter cited as Marriott fieldnotes).

1. KIOWA HISTORY

1. Richardson fieldnotes, n.d.; Mishkin fieldnotes, August 1, 1935, KFN.

2. LaBarre fieldnotes, June 25, 1935, KFN.

3. LaBarre fieldnotes, June 25, 1935, KFN.

4. Letter from Ray C. Doyah to author, August 5, 2004.

5. Bascom fieldnotes, July 10, 1935; Collier fieldnotes, August 16, 23, 1935, KFN.

6. LaBarre fieldnotes, June 25, 1935, KFN.

7. Bascom fieldnotes, July 10, 1935; Collier fieldnotes, August 6, 1935; Mishkin fieldnotes, July 27, 1935, KFN.

8. Bascom fieldnotes, July 10, 1935, KFN.

9. LaBarre fieldnotes, July 25, 1935, KFN.

10. Richardson fieldnotes, late July, 1935, KFN.

11. Collier fieldnotes, July 18, 1935; Bascom fieldnotes, July 6, 11, 1935; Mishkin fieldnotes, July 8, 9, 1935, KFN.

12. Richardson fieldnotes, n.d.; Lesser fieldnotes, n.d., KFN.

13. Bascom fieldnotes, July 11, 1935; Richardson fieldnotes, late July, 1935, KFN.

14. Collier fieldnotes, July 11, 1935, KFN.

15. Collier fieldnotes, July 11, 1935, KFN.

16. Mishkin fieldnotes, July 9, 11, 12, 1935; Collier fieldnotes, July 8, 1935, KFN.

17. Collier fieldnotes, August 6, 1935; Bascom fieldnotes, July 31, 1935, KFN.

18. Collier fieldnotes, July 11, 1935, KFN.

19. Thomas W. Kavanagh's (1996) spelling of "Kwahada" is used here.

20. Richardson fieldnotes, July 3, 5, 1935, KFN.

21. Mishkin fieldnotes, July 8, 9, 11, August 6, 1935; 1935; Bascom fieldnotes, July 6, 8, 1935; Collier fieldnotes, June 28, 1935, KFN.

22. Kracht fieldnotes, July 1985.

2. KIOWA BELIEFS AND CONCEPTS

1. LaBarre fieldnotes, July 24, 1935, KFN.

2. Mishkin fieldnotes, June 27, 1935, KFN. Belo Cozad, or Bedalatena (They Caught Him By The Bridle), was also referred to as Kozad.

3. Mishkin fieldnotes, June 27, 1935, KFN.

4. LaBarre fieldnotes, July 20, 1935, KFN.

5. LaBarre fieldnotes, July 16, 1935, KFN.

6. LaBarre fieldnotes, n.d., June 28, 1935, KFN.

7. LaBarre fieldnotes, n.d., June 28, 1935, KFN.

8. Kracht fieldnotes, February 18, 1987. Bryan "Jake" Chanate was the veteran's advisor at Northeastern State University when he passed away in May 2005.

9. Collier fieldnotes, July 29, 1935, KFN.

10. Collier fieldnotes, July 29, 1935, KFN.

11. Collier fieldnotes, July 29, 1935; LaBarre fieldnotes, August 2, 1935, KFN.

12. Collier fieldnotes, July 29, 1935, KFN.

13. Richardson fieldnotes, n.d.; Collier fieldnotes, July 6, 1935; Bascom fieldnotes, July 18, 1935, KFN. Spellings, tonal markers, and capitalization for the term *dɔdɔ* vary slightly in the typewritten and handwritten fieldnotes.

14. LaBarre fieldnotes, July 6, 9, 1935, KFN.

15. Bascom fieldnotes, July 18, 1935; Collier fieldnotes, July 11, 1935, KFN.

16. Bascom fieldnotes, August 9, 1935, KFN.

17. Richardson fieldnotes, n.d., KFN.

18. Parker McKenzie, quoted in William C. Meadows, "On Kiowa Concepts of Power, God, Song, and Spirit: The Ongoing Need to Integrate Language in Native American Cultural Studies," typewritten manuscript in author's possession. McKenzie and Meadows assert that both morphemes in *dɔdɔ* have rising tones.

19. LaBarre fieldnotes, July 29, 1935; Bascom fieldnotes, July 18, 1935, KFN.

20. LaBarre fieldnotes, July 9, 1935, KFN.

21. Collier fieldnotes, July 11, 1935, KFN.

22. LaBarre fieldnotes, July 23, 1935, KFN.

23. Jane Richardson, fieldnotes, n.d., KFN.

24. Collier fieldnotes, July 24, 1935, KFN.

25. LaBarre fieldnotes, July 24, 1935, KFN.

26. Mishkin fieldnotes, July 5, 1935, KFN.

27. Bascom fieldnotes, August 9, 1935; Richardson fieldnotes, n.d.; LaBarre fieldnotes, July 23, 29, 1935, KFN.

28. LaBarre fieldnotes, July 10, 1935, KFN.

29. Bascom fieldnotes, August 16, 1935, KFN.

30. Collier fieldnotes, July 24, 1935, KFN.

31. LaBarre fieldnotes, August 1, 1935, KFN.

32. LaBarre fieldnotes, June 28, 1935, KFN.

33. LaBarre fieldnotes, July 8, August 7, 1935, KFN.

34. LaBarre fieldnotes, June 24, 1935, KFN.

35. LaBarre fieldnotes, August 22, 1935, KFN.

36. LaBarre fieldnotes, July 8, 29, 1935, KFN.

37. Bascom fieldnotes, August 26, 1935, KFN.

38. LaBarre fieldnotes, August 22, 1935, KFN.

39. LaBarre fieldnotes, August 22, 1935, KFN.

40. LaBarre fieldnotes, July 12, 1935, KFN.

41. Bascom fieldnotes, August 23, 1935, KFN.

42. LaBarre fieldnotes, July 12, 1935, KFN.

43. LaBarre fieldnotes, August 22, 1935, KFN.

44. LaBarre fieldnotes, July 16, 1935, KFN.

45. LaBarre fieldnotes, July 12, 1935, KFN.

46. LaBarre fieldnotes, July 12, 23, 1935; Richardson fieldnotes, n.d., KFN.

47. Bascom fieldnotes, August 23, 1935, KFN.

48. LaBarre fieldnotes, July 22, 29, 1935, KFN.

49. LaBarre fieldnotes, July 9, 1935, KFN.

50. Collier fieldnotes, July 24, 1935, KFN.

51. LaBarre fieldnotes, August 1, 1935, KFN.

52. LaBarre fieldnotes, August 1, 1935; Collier fieldnotes, July 24, 1935, KFN.

53. LaBarre fieldnotes, July 23, 1935, KFN.

54. LaBarre fieldnotes, July 12, 1935, KFN.

55. Marriott fieldnotes, July 19, 1935.

56. LaBarre fieldnotes, July 12, 1935, KFN.

57. Marriott fieldnotes, July 19, 1935.

58. Kracht fieldnotes, 1984, May 18, 1994, July 8, 17, 2003. Note that there are two different spellings: "Tongkeamah" and "Tongkeamha."

59. Letter from Doyah to author, August 5, 2004. He learned this in a Kiowa language class taught by David L. Paddlety.

60. Richardson fieldnotes, July 14, 1935, KFN.

61. Collier fieldnotes, July 11, 1935; LaBarre fieldnotes, July 23, 1935, KFN.

62. Collier, July 11, 1935, KFN.

63. Bascom fieldnotes, July 18, 1935, KFN.

64. LaBarre fieldnotes, August 6, 1935, KFN.

65. Collier fieldnotes, July 11, 1935; LaBarre fieldnotes, July 23, 1935, KFN.

66. LaBarre fieldnotes, July 1, 1935, KFN.

67. LaBarre fieldnotes, August 2, 1935; Bascom fieldnotes, July 18, August 9, 1935, KFN.

68. Collier fieldnotes, July 24, 1935, KFN.

69. LaBarre fieldnotes, August 1, 1935, KFN.

70. Collier fieldnotes, July 24, 1935; LaBarre fieldnotes, August 1, 1935, KFN. Coincidentally, as I wrote this section, thunder-sleet and thunder-snow occurred during the Tulsa blizzard of January 31 and February 1, 2011.

71. LaBarre fieldnotes, July 29, 1935, KFN.

72. Collier fieldnotes, July 24, 1935, KFN.

73. LaBarre fieldnotes, August 6, 1935, KFN.

74. Collier fieldnotes, July 6, 1935; Richardson fieldnotes, n.d.; LaBarre fieldnotes, July 20, 1935, KFN.

75. Collier fieldnotes, July 11, 1935, KFN.

76. LaBarre fieldnotes, July 3, 9, 1935, KFN.

77. Collier fieldnotes, July 29, 1935; Bascom fieldnotes, n.d.; LaBarre fieldnotes, July 29, 1935, KFN.

78. Collier fieldnotes, July 29, 1935, KFN.

79. LaBarre fieldnotes, July 20, 1935, KFN.

80. Bascom fieldnotes, August 9, 1935, KFN.

81. Bascom fieldnotes, July 18, 1935, KFN.

82. Richardson fieldnotes, July 14, 1935, KFN.

83. Bascom fieldnotes, July 13, 1935, KFN.

84. Collier fieldnotes, July 6, 11, 1935; Bascom fieldnotes, July 13, 18, 1935; Richardson fieldnotes, July 14, 1935, KFN.

85. Bascom fieldnotes, July 18, 1935, KFN.

86. Richardson fieldnotes, n.d., KFN.

87. Collier fieldnotes, July 6, 1935; Bascom fieldnotes, July 18, 1935, KFN.

88. Bascom fieldnotes, n.d., KFN.

89. "City teen killed in one-car accident," *Anadarko Daily News*, June 21, 2004, 1. In recent years, this deadly curve has been straightened out by the highway department.

90. Kracht fieldnotes, June 24, 2004.

91. LaBarre fieldnotes, August 1, 1935, KFN.

92. Bascom fieldnotes, July 18, 1935, KFN.

93. LaBarre fieldnotes, July 18, 23, August 6, 1935, KFN.

94. LaBarre fieldnotes, August 2, 1935, KFN.

95. Collier fieldnotes, July 29, 1935, KFN.

96. LaBarre fieldnotes, July 23, 1935, KFN.

97. Richardson fieldnotes, n.d.; Collier fieldnotes, July 6, 1935, KFN.

98. Bascom fieldnotes, August 26, 1935, KFN.

99. LaBarre fieldnotes, July 29, 1935, KFN.

100. LaBarre fieldnotes, July 9, 1935, KFN.

101. Kracht fieldnotes, June 2004.

102. LaBarre fieldnotes, July 9, 1935, KFN.

103. Bascom fieldnotes, August 9, 1935, KFN.

104. LaBarre fieldnotes, July 6, 9, 1935, KFN.

105. LaBarre fieldnotes, July 23, 1934, KFN.

106. Meadows fails to mention that the Kiowas maintain a spiritual connection to mountains, especially the Wichitas.

107. Bascom fieldnotes, July 18, 1935, KFN.

108. Mishkin fieldnotes, July 3, 1935, KFN.

109. Mishkin fieldnotes, July 25, 1935, KFN.

110. LaBarre fieldnotes, June 27, July 3, 1935, KFN.

111. Mishkin fieldnotes, July 25, 1935, KFN.

112. Richardson fieldnotes, July 14, 1935; LaBarre fieldnotes, June 27, July 3, 23, August 2, 1935, KFN.

113. Collier fieldnotes, July 29, 1935; LaBarre fieldnotes, July 2, 1935, KFN.

114. LaBarre fieldnotes, June 28, July 2, 3, 11, 23, 24, 1935; Richardson fieldnotes, July 5, n.d., 1935, KFN.

115. LaBarre fieldnotes, August 6, 1935, KFN.

116. Bascom fieldnotes, August 23, 1935, KFN.

117. Bascom fieldnotes, July 18, 1935, KFN.

118. Bascom fieldnotes, August 23, 1935, KFN.

119. LaBarre fieldnotes, July 23, 1935, KFN.

120. LaBarre fieldnotes, July 24, 1935, KFN.

121. Letter from Doyah to author, August 5, 2004.

122. LaBarre fieldnotes, July 22, 24, 26, 1935, KFN.

123. LaBarre fieldnotes, July 23, 1935, KFN.

124. LaBarre fieldnotes, July 6, 1935, KFN.

125. LaBarre fieldnotes, July 6, 9, 12, 15, 23, 1935, KFN.

126. Richardson fieldnotes, n.d., July 1, 1935; LaBarre fieldnotes, August 12, 1935; Collier fieldnotes, July 2, 1935; Bascom fieldnotes, August 27, 1935, KFN.

127. LaBarre fieldnotes, July 24, 1935, KFN.

128. LaBarre fieldnotes, July 12, 25, 1935, KFN.

129. Richardson fieldnotes, August 12, 1935, KFN.

130. LaBarre fieldnotes, August 1, 1935; Bascom fieldnotes, August 9, 1935, KFN.

131. LaBarre fieldnotes, July 17, 18, 20, August 20, 1935, KFN.

132. Bascom fieldnotes, July 18, 1935, KFN.

133. Bascom fieldnotes, July 9, 1935, KFN.

134. Bascom fieldnotes, July 9, 18, 1935; LaBarre fieldnotes, July 9, 1935, KFN.

135. LaBarre fieldnotes, July 9, 1935, KFN.

136. Bascom fieldnotes, July 18, 1935, KFN.

137. LaBarre fieldnotes, June 27, 1935, KFN.

138. LaBarre fieldnotes, July 29, 1935; Bascom fieldnotes, July 18, 1935, KFN.

139. Bascom fieldnotes, August 9, 1935; Collier fieldnotes, July 11, 1935; LaBarre fieldnotes, July 9, 1935; Richardson fieldnotes, n.d., KFN.

140. Bascom fieldnotes, August 9, 1935, KFN.

141. Bascom fieldnotes, July 24, 1935, KFN.

142. LaBarre fieldnotes, August 15, 1935; Bascom fieldnotes, August 27, 1935, KFN.

143. Richardson fieldnotes, July 5, 1935, KFN.

144. Richardson fieldnotes, July 5, 1935; LaBarre fieldnotes, July 18, 23, 1935, KFN.

145. LaBarre fieldnotes, July 6, 24, 1935; Bascom fieldnotes, July 18, 1935, KFN.

146. LaBarre fieldnotes, June 28, July 18, 1935; Richardson fieldnotes, n.d., KFN.

147. Bascom fieldnotes, July 18, August 9, 1935, KFN.

148. Richardson fieldnotes, n.d., KFN.

149. LaBarre fieldnotes, July 29, 1935, KFN.

150. Bascom fieldnotes, August 9, 1935; LaBarre fieldnotes, August 5, 1935, KFN.

151. Kracht fieldnotes, July 2003, June 2004.

152. LaBarre fieldnotes, August 5, 1935, KFN; Kracht fieldnotes, July 2003, June 2004.

153. Bascom fieldnotes, July 15, 1935; LaBarre fieldnotes, July 9, 17, 1935, KFN.

154. LaBarre fieldnotes, August 6, 1935, KFN.

155. Bascom fieldnotes, August 9, 1935; LaBarre fieldnotes, July 17, 1935, KFN.

156. LaBarre fieldnotes, July 9, 1935, KFN.

157. Bascom fieldnotes, July 18, 25, August 9, 1935; Collier fieldnotes, July 11, 1935; LaBarre fieldnotes, August 5, 6, 1935, KFN.

158. LaBarre fieldnotes, July 17, 1935, KFN.

159. Bascom fieldnotes, August 9, 24, 1935, KFN.

160. Mishkin fieldnotes, July 5, 1935, KFN.

161. Big Tree to Interior Secretary Franklin K. Lane, February 7, 1916, National Archives Records Administration: Records of the Bureau of Indian Affairs, 1907–39, Record Group 75, 063, Dances (hereafter cited as RG 75).

162. Kracht fieldnotes, February 20, 1987.

163. Kracht fieldnotes, February 20, 1987.

3. ACQUIRING POWER

1. Collier fieldnotes, July 6, 1935; Bascom fieldnotes, August 6, 1935, KFN.

2. Mishkin fieldnotes, July 26, 1935, KFN.

3. LaBarre fieldnotes, July 22, 25, 1935; Mishkin fieldnotes, July 25, 1935, KFN.

4. Mishkin fieldnotes, July 5, 1935, KFN.

5. James Mooney, "Kiowa Heraldry Notebook: Descriptions of Kiowa Tipis and Shields," Ms. 2531, 1891–1904, National Anthropological Archives, Smithsonian Institution. (hereafter cited as Kiowa Heraldry Notebook).

6. Collier fieldnotes, July 5, 1935, KFN.

7. Mishkin fieldnotes, July 26, 1935, KFN.

8. Marriott fieldnotes, January 29, July 11, 14, August 12, 1936, folders 27, 28; Collier fieldnotes, July 5, 1935, KFN.

9. LaBarre fieldnotes, July 23, 1935, KFN.

10. Mishkin fieldnotes, July 3, 1935, KFN.

11. Marriott fieldnotes, August 9, 1935, folder 28.

12. LaBarre fieldnotes, July 23, 1935, KFN.

13. Richardson fieldnotes, July 5, 1935; LaBarre fieldnotes, July 23, 1935; Bascom fieldnotes, July 18, 1935, KFN.

14. LaBarre fieldnotes, July 6, 1935, KFN.

15. Mishkin fieldnotes, July 3, 1935, KFN.

16. Mishkin fieldnotes, July 3, 1935, KFN.

17. Mishkin fieldnotes, July 3, 1935; Bascom fieldnotes, July 18, 1935; Collier fieldnotes, July 6, 1935, KFN.

18. Kiowa Heraldry Notebook.

19. Bascom fieldnotes, August 6, 1935, KFN.

20. Mishkin fieldnotes, July 3, 1935, KFN.

21. LaBarre fieldnotes, July 23, 1935; Mishkin fieldnotes, July 3, 1935, KFN.

22. LaBarre fieldnotes, n.d., KFN.

23. Bascom fieldnotes, August 25, 1936, KFN.

24. Kracht fieldnotes, June 4, 1993. Cutthroat Gap, part of the Jack Haley Ranch, is located east of Cooperton and northwest of the Wichita Mountains National Wildlife Reserve.

25. Bascom fieldnotes, August 25, 1936, KFN.

26. Bascom fieldnotes, August 25, 1936, KFN.

27. Bascom fieldnotes, August 25, 26, 1935, KFN.

28. Bascom fieldnotes, August 20, 1935, KFN.

29. Bascom fieldnotes, August 20, 1935, KFN.

30. Bascom fieldnotes, July 18, August 16, 1935; Mishkin fieldnotes, July 3, 1935, KFN.

31. Marriott fieldnotes, January 28, July 14, 1936, folders 27, 28.

32. Collier fieldnotes, July 6, 1935, KFN.

33. Bascom fieldnotes, July 25, 1935, KFN.

34. Collier fieldnotes, July 6, 1935, KFN.

35. Bascom fieldnotes, August 23, 1935, KFN.

36. Richardson fieldnotes, July 22, 1935, KFN.

37. Collier fieldnotes, July 11, 1935, KFN.

38. Bascom fieldnotes, July 15, 1935; Collier fieldnotes, July 6, 1935, KFN.

39. LaBarre fieldnotes, July 23, 1935; Bascom fieldnotes, August 2, 9, 1935, KFN.

40. Richardson fieldnotes, n.d., KFN.

41. Mishkin fieldnotes, July 5, 1935, KFN.

42. Collier fieldnotes, July 6, 1935; Mishkin fieldnotes, July 5, 11, 1935, KFN; Kiowa Heraldry Notebook.

43. Bascom fieldnotes, August 20, 24, 25, 1935, KFN.

44. Mishkin fieldnotes, July 3, 1935; Collier fieldnotes, July 6, 1935, KFN.

45. LaBarre fieldnotes, July 6, 1935; Bascom fieldnotes, July 18, August 9, 24, 1935; Collier fieldnotes, July 6, 11, 1935; Richardson fieldnotes, n.d., KFN; Marriott fieldnotes, August 21, 1935, folder 27.

46. Marriott fieldnotes, July 31, 1935, folder 27.

47. LaBarre fieldnotes, August 26, 1935, KFN.

48. Marriott fieldnotes, August 21, 1935, folder 27.

49. Kracht fieldnotes, February 11, 20, March 12, April 30, 1987.

50. Betty Tenadooah, "Kiowa Indian Medicine Man" (handwritten manuscript, ca. 1984, in author's possession).

51. Collier fieldnotes, July 11, 1935, KFN.

52. Collier fieldnotes, July 11, 1935; Bascom fieldnotes, July 27, 1935, KFN.

53. Marriott fieldnotes, August 21, 22, 1935, folder 27.

54. Marriott fieldnotes, August 22, 1935, folder 27.

55. Marriott fieldnotes, August 21, 1935, July 13, 1936, August 12, 1935, July 10, 1936, January 28, 1936, folder 27.

56. Bascom fieldnotes, August 6, 1935; Collier fieldnotes, July 6, KFN.

57. Bascom fieldnotes, July 15, 1935; Richardson fieldnotes, July 2, 1935, KFN.

58. Bascom fieldnotes, August 9, 1935, KFN.

59. Collier fieldnotes, July 6, 1935, KFN.

60. Collier fieldnotes, July 6, 1935; Bascom fieldnotes, KFN.

61. LaBarre fieldnotes, July 6, 1935; Bascom fieldnotes, July 18, 1935, KFN.

62. Marriott fieldnotes, January 28, July 7, 1936, August 21, 1935, folder 27. I utilize E. E. Evans-Pritchard's (1937) classification that witchcraft is an unconscious, perhaps inborn propensity for causing harm, whereas sorcery is intentional and malicious. Most Kiowas use the word witchcraft or witching when referencing acts of sorcery.

63. Marriott fieldnotes, 1934, folder 28.

64. Kracht fieldnotes, February 20, 1987.

65. Bascom fieldnotes, August 9, 1935, KFN.

66. Collier fieldnotes, July 9, 1935; Bascom fieldnotes, August 9, 1935, KFN.

67. Bascom fieldnotes, August 9, 28, 1935, KFN.

68. Marriott fieldnotes, n.d., folder 1.

69. Bascom fieldnotes, August 9, 28, 1935, KFN.

70. LaBarre fieldnotes, August 6, 1935; Richardson fieldnotes, n.d.; Bascom fieldnotes, August 24, 1935, KFN.

71. Bascom fieldnotes, August 24, 1935, KFN.

72. Bascom fieldnotes, August 24, 1935, KFN.

73. Bascom fieldnotes, August 25, 1935, KFN.

74. LaBarre fieldnotes, July 9, 1935, KFN.

75. Bascom fieldnotes, August 23, 1935, KFN.

76. Collier fieldnotes, July 6, 1935, KFN.

77. LaBarre fieldnotes, July 29, 1935; Bascom fieldnotes, August 29, 1935; Collier fieldnotes, July 11, 1935, KFN.

78. Richardson fieldnotes, July 14, 1935, KFN.

79. Bascom fieldnotes, August 9, 1935, KFN.

80. Bascom fieldnotes, July 18, 1935, KFN.

81. Marriott fieldnotes, January 21, 1936, folder 27.

82. Collier fieldnotes, July 6, 1935, KFN.

83. Collier fieldnotes, July 6, 1935; Richardson fieldnotes, July 14, 1935; Bascom fieldnotes, July 18, 1935, KFN.

84. Richardson fieldnotes, July 13, 1935; LaBarre fieldnotes, July 9, 1935, KFN.

85. Collier fieldnotes, July 11, 1935, KFN.

86. Bascom fieldnotes, July 13, 18, 1935, KFN.

87. Bascom fieldnotes, July 18, 1935, KFN.

88. Kracht fieldnotes, May 1993.

89. Bascom fieldnotes, July 18, 1935, KFN.

90. Bascom fieldnotes, July 18, 1935, KFN.

91. Bascom fieldnotes, July 18, 1935, KFN.

92. Richardson fieldnotes, July 14, 1935, KFN.

93. Richardson fieldnotes, July 15, 1935, KFN.

94. Richardson fieldnotes, July 15, 1935; Collier fieldnotes, July 11, 1935, KFN.

95. Collier fieldnotes, July 6, 1935, KFN.

96. Bascom fieldnotes, July 31, 1935, KFN.

97. Mooney (1898, 215–16) did not list Ohettoint (Charley Buffalo) as one of the Fort Marion prisoners, although other sources indicate that he was (Ewers 1978, 12; Boyd 1983, 249–52). An article in the May 15, 1934, *Anadarko Daily News* (reprinted in *The Anadarko Daily News Visitors Guide* 1986–87, 20) states that Charley Buffalo was chosen to go in Dohasan II's place due to the latter's old age.

98. Agent James M. Haworth to Indian Commissioner Edward P. Smith, September 20, 1875, ARCIA 1875:776 [1680].

99. Marriott fieldnotes, n.d., box 9, folder 1.

100. Richardson fieldnotes, n.d., July 2, 1935; Bascom fieldnotes, July 15, 1935, KFN.

101. Kiowa Heraldry Notebook.

102. Kiowa Heraldry Notebook.

103. Marriott fieldnotes, n.d., box 9, folder 1.

104. Kiowa Heraldry Notebook; Bascom fieldnotes, July 8, 9, 18, 25, 27, August 6, 1935, KFN.

105. Bascom fieldnotes, July 8, 26, 1935, KFN; Marriott fieldnotes, n.d., box 9, folder 1.

106. Kiowa Heraldry Notebook.

107. Kiowa Heraldry Notebook.

108. Kiowa Heraldry Notebook; Bascom fieldnotes, July 24, 1935, KFN; Marriott fieldnotes, n.d., box 9, folder 1.

109. Kiowa Heraldry Notebook.

110. Bascom fieldnotes, July 18, 1935, KFN.

111. Kiowa Heraldry Notebook; Bascom fieldnotes, July 18, 23, 1935, KFN; Marriott fieldnotes, n.d., box 9, folder 1.

112. Kiowa Heraldry Notebook.

113. Kiowa Heraldry Notebook.

114. Bascom fieldnotes, July 27, August 6, 1935, KFN.

115. Bascom fieldnotes, July 27, August 6, 1935, KFN.

116. Bascom fieldnotes, July 9, 1935, KFN.

117. Marriott fieldnotes, n.d., box 9, folder 1.

118. Kiowa Heraldry Notebook; Bascom fieldnotes, July 8, 27, 1935, KFN.

119. Marriott fieldnotes, n.d., box 9, folder 1.

120. Collier fieldnotes, July 11, 1935; Bascom fieldnotes, July 27, 1935, KFN.

121. Kiowa Heraldry Notebook.

122. Bascom fieldnotes, July 27, 1935, KFN.

123. Bascom fieldnotes, July 27, 1935, KFN.

124. Bascom fieldnotes, July 18, 1935, KFN.

125. Bascom fieldnotes, July 8, 9, 27, 1935, KFN.

126. Marriott fieldnotes, n.d., box 9, folder 1.

127. Kiowa Heraldry Notebook.

128. Bascom fieldnotes, July 27, 1935, KFN.

129. Kiowa Heraldry Notebook.

130. Marriott fieldnotes, n.d., box 9, folder 1.

131. Bascom fieldnotes, July 25, August 6, 1935, KFN.

132. Bascom fieldnotes, August 6, 1935, KFN.

133. Kiowa Heraldry Notebook; Bascom fieldnotes, August 6, 1935, KFN.

134. Kiowa Heraldry Notebook; Bascom fieldnotes, August 6, 1935, KFN.

135. Bascom fieldnotes, August 6, 1935, KFN.

136. Kiowa Heraldry Notebook.

137. Kiowa Heraldry Notebook. Andres Martinez, or Andele, was a Mexican captive raised in the Kiowa tribe. He often interpreted for missionaries and anthropologists.

138. Kiowa Heraldry Notebook.

139. Marriott fieldnotes, n.d., box 9, folder 1.

140. Bascom fieldnotes, August 6, 1935, KFN.

141. Bascom fieldnotes, August 6, 1935, KFN.

142. Kracht fieldnotes, April 9, 1987, June 1, 1993. The Bible verse (KJV) in reference is John 14:2, which reads, "In my Father's house are many mansions: if it were not so, I would have told you. I go to prepare a place for you."

143. Marriott fieldnotes, August 9, 1935, box 9, folder 28.

144. Marriott fieldnotes, August 21, 1935, box 9, folder 27.

145. Kracht fieldnotes, June 8, 2004; Castro fieldnotes, June 8, 23, 2004. Justin was one of the students who worked with me in the field in 2003 and 2004.

146. Kracht fieldnotes, June 10, 2004.

147. Kracht fieldnotes, June 22, 2004.

148. Amie Tah-Bone [museum director/NAGPRA representative], "Status Report to the Kiowa Indian Council on Longhorn Mountain," Kiowatribe.org, June 24, 2013.

149. Courtney Francisco, "Kiowa Tribe Fights for Sacred Longhorn Mountain," July 1, 2013, http://kfor.com/2013/07/01/kiowa-tribe-fights-for-sacred-long horn-mountain/.

150. Brian Daffron, "Gravel Mining Puts Kiowa Sacred Place in Peril," July 12, 2013, http://indiancountrytodaymedianetwork.com/2013/07/12/gravel-mining -puts-kiowa-sacred-place-peril-150378.

151. Tah-Bone, "Status Report to the Kiowa Indian Council on Longhorn Mountain."

152. Kracht fieldnotes, July 14, 2003. This is a longer, elaborated version of the story he told the Subcommittee on Native American Affairs.

153. Kracht fieldnotes, July 8, 2003.

154. Kracht fieldnotes, June 26, 2004.

155. Crawford identified Odlepaugh's wife by the name "Ananthy," possibly derived from *ananti* (cross, or ill-tempered). This might have been a nickname, as Ananthy referred to herself as "mean and cranky" (Crawford 1915, 123).

156. Kracht fieldnotes, May 24, June 2, 6, 1993.

157. Kracht fieldnotes, February 20, 1987.

158. Kracht fieldnotes, February 20, 1987.

159. Kracht fieldnotes, October 11, 1989.

160. Kracht fieldnotes, October 11, 1989.

161. Kracht fieldnotes, May 17, 1993.

162. Kracht fieldnotes, May 1994.

163. Sam Lewin, "Violent Takeover at Kiowa Headquarters Alleged," *Native American Times*, January 15, 2004, 1, 9; *Kiowa Dispatch*, January 2004; Kracht fieldnotes, June 10, 17, 22, 2004.

164. Kracht fieldnotes, June 14, 2004.

4. BUNDLES, SHIELDS, AND SOCIETIES

1. Marriott fieldnotes, n.d., box 9, folder 1.

2. LaBarre fieldnotes, July 19, 1935, KFN.

3. LaBarre fieldnotes, July 24, 1935; Richardson fieldnotes, n.d., KFN.

4. Richardson fieldnotes, n.d., KFN.

5. Marriott fieldnotes, July 10, 1936, box 9, folder 24.

6. LaBarre, Kiowa Indian Snapshots, KFN.

7. LaBarre fieldnotes, July 19, 1935, KFN. Charley Buffalo was also known as Padai (Twin) because of his twin brother, White Buffalo (Greene 2001, 31–33).

8. LaBarre fieldnotes, July 6, 1935, KFN.

9. Collier fieldnotes, July 17, August 5, 1935, KFN.

10. LaBarre fieldnotes, August 5, 6, 1935, KFN.

11. LaBarre fieldnotes, July 6, August 6, 1935, KFN.

12. Collier fieldnotes, July 30, 1935, KFN.

13. LaBarre fieldnotes, August 5, 1935, KFN.

14. LaBarre fieldnotes, July 23, 1935, KFN.

15. Collier fieldnotes, August 5, 1935, KFN.

16. Richardson fieldnotes, n.d.; Collier fieldnotes, August 5, 1935, KFN.

17. LaBarre fieldnotes, August 5, 1935, KFN.

18. Richardson fieldnotes, n.d., KFN.

19. Richardson fieldnotes, n.d.; Collier fieldnotes, July 30, 1935; LaBarre fieldnotes, August 5, 1935, KFN.

20. LaBarre fieldnotes, August 5, 1935; Richardson fieldnotes, n.d., KFN.

21. Richardson fieldnotes, n.d.; Collier fieldnotes, July 30, 1935; LaBarre fieldnotes, July 6, 19, August 6, 1935, KFN.

22. Richardson fieldnotes, n.d., KFN.

23. Richardson fieldnotes, n.d., KFN.

24. Lesser fieldnotes, August 9, 1935, KFN.

25. Lesser fieldnotes, August 9, 1935; Collier fieldnotes, July 30, 1935; Richardson fieldnotes, n.d.; LaBarre fieldnotes, July 6, August 5, 1935, KFN.

26. LaBarre fieldnotes, August 5, 1935; Collier fieldnotes, July 19, 20, 30, 1935, KFN.

27. LaBarre fieldnotes, July 19, 1935, KFN.

28. LaBarre fieldnotes, July 6, 1935, KFN.

29. LaBarre fieldnotes, July 19, 1935; Collier fieldnotes, n.d., KFN.

30. Collier fieldnotes, July 19, 25, 30, 1935; Richardson fieldnotes, n.d., KFN.

31. Collier fieldnotes, July 30, 1935, KFN.

32. Collier fieldnotes, July 30, 1935, KFN.

33. Collier fieldnotes, July 25, 30, 1935, KFN.

34. Collier fieldnotes, July 30, 1935, KFN.

35. Collier fieldnotes, July 25, 30, 1935, KFN.

36. Collier fieldnotes, July 39, 1935, KFN.

37. Collier fieldnotes, July 30, August 5, 1935; Richardson fieldnotes, n.d., KFN.

38. Richardson fieldnotes, n.d.; LaBarre fieldnotes, August 12, 1935, KFN.

39. LaBarre fieldnotes, July 19, 1935, KFN.

40. Collier fieldnotes, July 23, 1935; Richardson fieldnotes, n.d., KFN.

41. Richardson fieldnotes, n.d.; Collier fieldnotes, n.d., KFN.

42. LaBarre fieldnotes, July 19, 1935; Collier fieldnotes, n.d., July 6, 1935; Richardson fieldnotes, July 8, 1935, KFN.

43. Richardson fieldnotes, n.d.; LaBarre, "Kiowa Indian Snapshots"; LaBarre fieldnotes, July 19, 1935; Collier fieldnotes, July 6, August 5, 1935, KFN.

44. LaBarre fieldnotes, July 19, 1925; Richardson fieldnotes, n.d., July 8, 1935; Collier fieldnotes, n.d., July 6, 1935, KFN.

45. Collier fieldnotes, August 5, 1935, KFN.

46. Collier fieldnotes, August 6, 1935; Richardson fieldnotes, July 8, 1935, KFN.

47. LaBarre fieldnotes, July 19, 1935, KFN.

48. LaBarre fieldnotes, July 11, 1935, KFN.

49. LaBarre fieldnotes, August 26, 1935, KFN.

50. LaBarre fieldnotes, n.d., KFN.

51. LaBarre fieldnotes, August 1, 1935, KFN.

52. LaBarre fieldnotes, August 1, 1935, KFN.

53. LaBarre fieldnotes, n.d., July 30, August 1, 1935, KFN.

54. LaBarre fieldnotes, July 30, 1935; Collier fieldnotes, n.d., KFN.

55. LaBarre fieldnotes, August 1, 1935, KFN.

56. LaBarre fieldnotes, August 15, 1935, KFN.

57. LaBarre fieldnotes, August 10, 1935, KFN; Marriott fieldnotes, July 1, 29, 1936, box 9, folder 1.

58. LaBarre fieldnotes, August 1, 15, 1935, KFN.

59. LaBarre fieldnotes, August 1, 15, 1935, KFN.

60. LaBarre fieldnotes, August 1, 1935, KFN.

61. LaBarre fieldnotes, August 1, 1935, KFN.

62. LaBarre fieldnotes, August 1, 1935, KFN.

63. LaBarre fieldnotes, n.d., KFN.

64. Marriott fieldnotes, July 17, 20, 1936, box 9, folder 1; LaBarre fieldnotes, n.d., KFN.

65. Collier fieldnotes, July 6, 1935, KFN.

66. Kracht fieldnotes, n.d. I knew Clifton from May 1983 until his death ten years later. After he took me as his son in 1984, I often drove us from Dallas to Oklahoma for dances and ceremonials. During our visits, he talked about his two years of military service and other Kiowa war exploits.

67. LaBarre fieldnotes, July 24, 1935, KFN.

68. Mishkin fieldnotes, July 15, 24, 30, 1935; Bascom fieldnotes, June 28, July 2, 1935, KFN.

69. Mishkin fieldnotes, July 24, 26, 30, 1935; Bascom fieldnotes, June 28, 1935, KFN.

70. Bascom fieldnotes, June 28, July 2, 13, 1935; LaBarre fieldnotes, July 17, 1935; Mishkin fieldnotes, July 8, 1935, KFN.

71. LaBarre fieldnotes, July 16, 1935; Mishkin fieldnotes, July 16, 1935; Bascom fieldnotes, July 15, 1935, KFN.

72. Bascom fieldnotes, June 28, 1935, KFN.

73. Bascom fieldnotes, June 28, 1935, KFN.

74. Bascom fieldnotes, June 28, 1935; Mishkin fieldnotes, July 26, 1935; LaBarre fieldnotes, July 17, 1935, KFN.

75. Bascom fieldnotes, June 28, 1935; Mishkin fieldnotes, July 26, 1935, KFN.

76. LaBarre fieldnotes, n.d., July 23, August 5, 1935; Richardson fieldnotes, n.d.; Mishkin fieldnotes, July 5, 1935; Bascom fieldnotes, August 9, 16, 1935, KFN.

77. LaBarre fieldnotes, August 5, 1935, KFN.

78. Bascom fieldnotes, June 28, 1935, KFN.

79. LaBarre fieldnotes, August 6, 1935, KFN.

80. Bascom fieldnotes, June 28, July 8, 1935, KFN.

81. Collier fieldnotes, July 6, 1935; Mishkin fieldnotes, July 26, 1935; Bascom fieldnotes, August 9, 1935; Richardson fieldnotes, August 5, 1935, KFN.

82. LaBarre fieldnotes, June 27, 1935, KFN.

83. Bascom fieldnotes, July 16, 17, 1935, KFN; "Kiowa Heraldry Notebook."

84. LaBarre fieldnotes, n.d., KFN.

85. Mishkin fieldnotes, July 26, 1935; Bascom fieldnotes, June 28, July 1, 2, 1935, KFN.

86. Bascom fieldnotes, June 28, 1935; Bascom fieldnotes, August 28, 1935; LaBarre fieldnotes, July 6, 1935, KFN.

87. LaBarre fieldnotes, July 6, August 6, 1935; Mishkin fieldnotes, July 29, 1935; Bascom fieldnotes, June 28, August 28, 1935, KFN.

88. LaBarre fieldnotes, July 6, August 6, 1935; Mishkin fieldnotes, July 29, 1935; Bascom fieldnotes, June 28, August 28, 1935, KFN.

89. Mishkin fieldnotes, July 22, 24, 1935, KFN.

90. Bascom fieldnotes, August 16, 27, 1935, KFN.

91. "Kiowa Heraldry Notebook."

92. Bascom fieldnotes, August 27, 1935; Mishkin fieldnotes, July 22, 1935; LaBarre fieldnotes, August 1, 1935, KFN.

93. LaBarre fieldnotes, August 1, 1935, KFN.

94. LaBarre fieldnotes, August 27, 1935; Bascom fieldnotes, August 27, 1935, KFN.

95. Mishkin fieldnotes, July 11, 22, 1935, KFN.

96. "Kiowa Heraldry Notebook"; Bascom fieldnotes, July 13, August 27, 1935, KFN.

97. Bascom fieldnotes, August 27, 1935, KFN.

98. Gillett Griswold, director, Library of Congress, to James Auchiah, June 30, 1960, enclosure of Hugh L. Scott's account of "Tsait-ante's Shield," General Scott Papers, Kiowa–Tipis, Shields, 1960–1979, box 1, folder 14, Arthur & Shifra Silberman Native Art Collection, DRC, National Cowboy & Western Heritage Museum, Oklahoma City, Oklahoma.

99. Kracht fieldnotes, n.d.

100. Marriott fieldnotes, "Shield Societies," box 9, folder 1.

101. "Kiowa Heraldry Notebook."

102. LaBarre fieldnotes, August 1, 1935, KFN.

103. Bascom fieldnotes, July 13, August 16, 27, 1935, KFN.

104. Marriott fieldnotes, "Shield Societies," box 9, folder 1.

105. Marriott fieldnotes, "Shield Societies," box 9, folder 1.

106. Marriott fieldnotes, "Shield Societies," box 9, folder 1.

107. Marriott fieldnotes, "Shield Societies," box 9, folder 1.

108. Marriott fieldnotes, "Shield Societies," box 9, folder 1.

109. Marriott fieldnotes, "Shield Societies," box 9, folder 1.

110. Marriott fieldnotes, "Shield Societies," box 9, folder 1.

111. Marriott fieldnotes, "Shield Societies," box 9, folder 1.

112. Marriott fieldnotes, "Shield Societies," box 9, folder 1.

113. Marriott fieldnotes, "Shield Societies," box 9, folder 1.

114. Marriott fieldnotes, "Shield Societies," box 9, folder 1.

115. LaBarre fieldnotes, July 30, 31, August 1, 1935, KFN.

116. Mishkin fieldnotes, July 22, 1935, KFN.

117. LaBarre fieldnotes, July 30, 1935, KFN.

118. LaBarre fieldnotes, July 30, 1935, KFN.

119. Marriott fieldnotes, "Shield Societies," box 9, folder 1.

120. LaBarre fieldnotes, August 1, 18, 1935, KFN.

121. LaBarre fieldnotes, August 1, 18, 1935, KFN.

122. Collier fieldnotes, July 17, 25, 1935, KFN.

123. LaBarre fieldnotes, August 1, 18, 1935, KFN.

124. LaBarre fieldnotes, July 10, 1935, KFN.

125. LaBarre fieldnotes, July 30, August 1, 18, 1935, KFN; Marriott fieldnotes, "Shield Societies," box 9, folder 1.

126. LaBarre fieldnotes, July 31, 1935, KFN.

127. LaBarre fieldnotes, July 31, 1935, KFN.

128. Richardson fieldnotes, August 16, 1935; LaBarre fieldnotes, August 13, 1935; Mishkin fieldnotes, July 1, 1935, KFN.

129. Collier fieldnotes, July 2, 1935; Mishkin fieldnotes, July 2, 1935, KFN.

130. LaBarre fieldnotes, July 25, 1935; Mishkin fieldnotes, July 23, 1935, KFN.

131. Copies that he obtained from me in August 1990. Meadows also adopted the handwritten pagination I used for indexing data. Linguistically, Meadows has altered original spellings to what he identifies as the standardized Parker McKenzie orthography, though he takes great liberties and does not explain that most of the fieldnotes were typewritten, though some handwritten transcriptions appear in International Phonetic Alphabet. Not only do these modifications take original spellings out of context, but his translations are based on modern-day speech and do not take dialect differences into consideration (Meadows 2010, 385, xix–xx).

132. LaBarre fieldnotes, August 12, 1935, KFN. In his coverage of the Bear Society, William C. Meadows (2010) imposes the modern-day Parker McKenzie orthography on the 1935 spellings and translates differently, calling it the Bear Old Women Society.

133. Collier fieldnotes, August 2, 1935, KFN.

134. Richardson fieldnotes, n.d., July 1, 1935, KFN.

135. Richardson fieldnotes, July 1, 1935, KFN.

136. Richardson fieldnotes, n.d., KFN.

137. LaBarre fieldnotes, August 12, 1935, KFN.

138. Richardson fieldnotes, n.d., KFN.

139. Again, Meadows (2010, 309) changes orthography from the 1935 fieldnotes into the Parker McKenzie notation but also adds a new gloss, "Calf Old Women," a translation not found in LaBarre's spiral notebooks or the typed fieldnotes.

140. Richardson fieldnotes, n.d.; LaBarre fieldnotes, July 2, 1935, KFN.

141. Richardson fieldnotes, n.d., KFN.

142. Kracht fieldnotes, May 1, 1987.

143. Kracht fieldnotes, May 28, 1993.

144. Kracht fieldnotes, May 17, 1993.

145. Kracht fieldnotes, January 13, 1987.

146. Kracht fieldnotes, April 11, 1987.

147. Kracht fieldnotes, March 12, 1987.

148. Kracht fieldnotes, March 12, 1987.

149. Kracht fieldnotes, March 11, 1987.

150. Kracht fieldnotes, March 26, 1987.

151. Richardson fieldnotes, July 22, 1935, KFN.

152. Kracht fieldnotes, May 21, 1993.

153. Kracht fieldnotes, March 11, 1987.

154. Kracht fieldnotes, June 4, 1993.

155. Kracht fieldnotes, June 21, 2004.

156. Kracht fieldnotes, May 21, 1993.

157. Kracht fieldnotes, May 21, 1993.

158. Kracht fieldnotes, May 24, 1993.

159. Carl Jennings and Vanessa Paukeigope Jennings, "SUNDANCE '97" (unpublished manuscript), 4, in the author's possession.

5. THE KIOWA SUN DANCE

1. Collier fieldnotes, n.d., KFN.

2. Kracht fieldnotes, August 5, 2004; letter from Doyah to author, August 31, 2005.

3. Kracht fieldnotes, February 19, 1987.

4. LaBarre fieldnotes, July 11, 1935, KFN.

5. "Chapters written by Weston LaBarre for a general ethnography of the Kiowas," n.d., KFN.

6. LaBarre fieldnotes, July 18, August 26, 1935, KFN.

7. Richardson fieldnotes, August 5, 1935; Collier fieldnotes, August 13, 1935; LaBarre fieldnotes, July 29, 1935, KFN.

8. Collier fieldnotes, n.d., July 13, 1935; LaBarre fieldnotes, July 11, 29, 1935, KFN.

9. Collier fieldnotes, n.d.; LaBarre fieldnotes, July 30, August 7, 1935, KFN.

10. LaBarre fieldnotes, July 30, 1935, KFN.

11. Marriott fieldnotes, n.d., box 9, folder 1.

12. LaBarre fieldnotes, July 30, August 1, 1935, KFN.

13. LaBarre fieldnotes, August 1, 1935, KFN.

14. LaBarre fieldnotes, July 9, 19, 20, August 1, 1935, KFN.

15. Marriott fieldnotes, July 4, 1935, box 9, folder 1.

16. Collier fieldnotes, n.d., August 13, 1935; LaBarre fieldnotes, July 10, 11, 1935; Bascom fieldnotes, n.d., KFN.

17. LaBarre fieldnotes, n.d., KFN.

18. Kracht fieldnotes, July 1987. I met Ms. Hansson at the National Anthropological Archives in the Smithsonian Institution in the summer of 1987, and she provided invaluable insights into the Santa Fe fieldnotes, including this interpretation.

19. LaBarre fieldnotes, July 30, 1925; Collier fieldnotes, July 8, 9, 1935, KFN.

20. LaBarre fieldnotes, August 21, 1935; Collier fieldnotes, July 8, 9, 1935, KFN.

21. LaBarre fieldnotes, August 21, 1935, KFN.

22. Collier fieldnotes, July 8, 9, 1935, KFN.

23. LaBarre fieldnotes, n.d., KFN.

24. LaBarre fieldnotes, July 30, 1935, KFN.

25. Collier fieldnotes, July 8, 9, 1935; LaBarre fieldnotes, August 21, 1935, KFN.

26. LaBarre fieldnotes, July 30, 1935; Collier fieldnotes, n.d., KFN.

27. LaBarre fieldnotes, July 30, 1935, KFN.

28. LaBarre fieldnotes, July 30, August 21, 1935; Collier fieldnotes, n.d., KFN.

29. LaBarre fieldnotes, July 30, 1935, KFN.

30. LaBarre fieldnotes, July 30, 1935, KFN.

31. Collier fieldnotes, n.d.; LaBarre fieldnotes, n.d., KFN.

32. LaBarre fieldnotes, August 21, 1935; Collier fieldnotes, n.d., KFN.

33. Collier fieldnotes, July 19, 1935, KFN.

34. LaBarre fieldnotes, July 30, August 21, 1935, KFN.

35. LaBarre fieldnotes, August 21, 1935, KFN.

36. LaBarre fieldnotes, n.d., KFN.

37. Collier fieldnotes, n.d., July 19, 1935, KFN.

38. LaBarre fieldnotes, n.d., KFN.

39. LaBarre fieldnotes, July 30, 1935, KFN.

40. Collier fieldnotes, July 25, 1935, KFN.

41. LaBarre fieldnotes, July 30, 1935, KFN.

42. LaBarre fieldnotes, n.d., KFN.

43. Collier fieldnotes, n.d., KFN.

44. LaBarre fieldnotes, July 30, 1935; Collier fieldnotes, n.d., KFN.

45. Marriott fieldnotes, August 1, 1935, box 9, folder 1.

46. LaBarre fieldnotes, n.d., July 30, 1935; Collier fieldnotes, n.d., KFN.

47. LaBarre fieldnotes, July 11, 1935, KFN.

48. LaBarre fieldnotes, July 30, 1935, KFN.

49. LaBarre fieldnotes, July 11, 1935, KFN.

50. Collier fieldnotes, n.d., KFN.

51. LaBarre fieldnotes, July 30, 1935, KFN.

52. Collier fieldnotes, n.d., KFN.

53. LaBarre fieldnotes, July 30, 1935, KFN.

54. Marriott fieldnotes, August 1, 1935, box 9, folder 1.

55. Collier fieldnotes, n.d., KFN.

56. LaBarre fieldnotes, July 30, 1935; Collier fieldnotes, n.d., KFN.

57. Collier fieldnotes, n.d., KFN.

58. Collier fieldnotes, n.d., KFN.

59. Richardson fieldnotes, n.d., KFN.

60. Collier fieldnotes, n.d., KFN.

61. Collier fieldnotes, n.d.; LaBarre fieldnotes, n.d., July 30, 1935, KFN.

62. LaBarre fieldnotes, August 21, 1935, KFN.

63. LaBarre fieldnotes, July 30, 1935, KFN.

64. Collier fieldnotes, n.d., KFN.

65. Collier fieldnotes, n.d.; LaBarre fieldnotes, n.d., July 30, 1935, KFN.

66. LaBarre fieldnotes, July 30, 1935, KFN.

67. LaBarre fieldnotes, n.d., July 30, 1935, KFN.

68. Marriott fieldnotes, August 1, 1935, box 9, folder 1.

69. LaBarre fieldnotes, n.d., KFN.

70. Collier fieldnotes, July 9, August 6, 1935, KFN.

71. LaBarre fieldnotes, n.d., KFN.

72. Collier fieldnotes, n.d., KFN.

73. Collier fieldnotes, July 9, August 6, 1935, KFN.

74. Marriott fieldnotes, July 4, 1935, box 9, folder 1.

75. Collier fieldnotes, n.d., KFN.

76. LaBarre fieldnotes, n.d., KFN.

77. LaBarre fieldnotes, August 7, 21, 1935, KFN.

78. Collier fieldnotes, n.d., KFN.

79. Kracht fieldnotes, n.d.

80. Collier fieldnotes, n.d.; LaBarre fieldnotes, July 25, August 7, 1935, KFN.

81. Collier fieldnotes, n.d., August 13, 1935, KFN.

82. Collier fieldnotes, August 6, 13, 1935, KFN.

83. Collier fieldnotes, August 8, 9, 1935; LaBarre fieldnotes, August 21, 1935, KFN.

84. LaBarre fieldnotes, August 21, 1935, KFN.

85. LaBarre fieldnotes, August 15, 1935, KFN. Some confusion arises from Maurice Boyd's reference to a "Mud Head" ceremony on the sixth, or final, "getting-ready" day preceding the Sun Dance proper. Mud Heads are indigenous to Southwest Pueblo tribes like the Zunis and Hopis. Perhaps this is a borrowed term that could possibly be linked to the addition of mud heads to the annual parade at the Anadarko American Indian Exposition, which began in 1932 (Mikkanen, n.d.; *Anadarko Daily News Visitors Guide* 1985, 6) and features dances from the Plains, Southwest, and Mexico.

86. LaBarre fieldnotes, August 21, 1935, KFN.

87. LaBarre fieldnotes, July 30, 1935; Collier, n.d., August 6, 1935, KFN.

88. LaBarre fieldnotes, July 9, 1935, KFN.

89. LaBarre fieldnotes, August 1, 21, 1935, KFN.

90. Collier fieldnotes, August 6, 1935, KFN.

91. LaBarre fieldnotes, July 8, 1935; Collier fieldnotes, July 9, August 6, 1935, KFN.

92. LaBarre fieldnotes, July 30, 1935, KFN.

93. Collier fieldnotes, August 6, 1935; LaBarre fieldnotes, July 8, 1935, KFN.

94. Collier fieldnotes, n.d., KFN.

95. LaBarre fieldnotes, July 8, 31, August 21, 1935; Bascom fieldnotes, July 8, 1935, KFN.

96. Richardson fieldnotes, August 5, 1935; Bascom fieldnotes, n.d.; Collier field-notes, n.d., KFN.

97. LaBarre fieldnotes, August 1, 1935, KFN.

98. Richardson fieldnotes, August 5, 1935; Collier fieldnotes, August 6, 1935, KFN.

99. Richardson fieldnotes, August 5, 1935; LaBarre fieldnotes, July 8, 11, 1935; Collier fieldnotes, n.d., KFN.

100. Collier fieldnotes, n.d.; LaBarre fieldnotes, July 30, 1935, KFN.

101. LaBarre fieldnotes, July 31, 1935, KFN.

102. Collier fieldnotes, n.d., KFN.

103. LaBarre fieldnotes, n.d.; Collier fieldnotes, n.d., KFN.

104. LaBarre fieldnotes, July 9, 1935, KFN; Marriott fieldnotes, July 1, August 1, 1935, box 9, folder 1.

105. Collier fieldnotes, n.d.; LaBarre fieldnotes, n.d., August 21, 1935, KFN.

106. LaBarre fieldnotes, n.d.; Collier fieldnotes, n.d., KFN.

107. Collier fieldnotes, n.d.; LaBarre fieldnotes, n.d., KFN.

108. LaBarre fieldnotes, August 1, 1935, KFN.

109. LaBarre fieldnotes, n.d.; Collier fieldnotes, n.d., KFN.

110. Marriott fieldnotes, July 4, 1935, box 9, folder 1; Bascom fieldnotes, n.d.; LaBarre fieldnotes, n.d.; Collier fieldnotes, n.d., July 20–25, 1935, KFN.

111. Collier fieldnotes, July 20–25, KFN.

112. Bascom fieldnotes, n.d., KFN.

113. LaBarre fieldnotes, July 9, 24, 31, 1935; Collier fieldnotes, July 20–25, 1935, KFN.

114. LaBarre fieldnotes, July 9, 1935, KFN.

115. Collier fieldnotes, n.d., July 20–25, 1935, KFN.

116. LaBarre fieldnotes, July 8, 1935, KFN.

117. Collier fieldnotes, July 20–25, 1935, KFN.

118. LaBarre fieldnotes, July 8, 9, 1935, KFN.

119. LaBarre fieldnotes, July 9, 1935; Collier fieldnotes, July 20–25, 1935, KFN.

120. Collier fieldnotes, n.d., July 20–25, 1935; LaBarre fieldnotes, n.d., KFN.

121. Collier fieldnotes, n.d., July 20–25, 1935; Bascom fieldnotes, n.d., KFN.

122. Collier fieldnotes, n.d., July 20–25, 1935; LaBarre fieldnotes, July 8, 9, 1935, KFN.

123. Collier fieldnotes, n.d., July 20–25, August 13, 1935; Bascom fieldnotes, n.d.; Richardson fieldnotes, July 31, August 2, 1935, KFN.

124. LaBarre fieldnotes, July 9, 1935, KFN.

125. Collier fieldnotes, August 13, 1935; Bascom fieldnotes, n.d., KFN.

126. LaBarre fieldnotes, July 9, 1935, KFN.

127. LaBarre fieldnotes, July 9, 1935; Collier fieldnotes, July 20–25, 1935, n.d., KFN.

128. Bascom fieldnotes, July 6, 1935; Collier fieldnotes, July 20–25, 1935; LaBarre fieldnotes, July 9, 11, 31, 1935, KFN.

129. Collier fieldnotes, July 20–25, 1935; LaBarre fieldnotes, July 31, 1935, KFN.

130. Collier fieldnotes, n.d., July 20–25, 1935; LaBarre fieldnotes, July 31, 1935, KFN.

131. LaBarre fieldnotes, July 9, 31, 1935; Collier fieldnotes, n.d., July 2, 17, 20–25,

1935; Bascom fieldnotes, n.d., KFN; Marriott fieldnotes, August 19–20, 1935, box 9, folder 1.

132. LaBarre fieldnotes, n.d., July 9, 31, 1935; Bascom fieldnotes, n.d.; Collier fieldnotes, July 2, 20–25, 1935, KFN; Marriott fieldnotes, August 22, 1935, box 9, folder 1.

133. Richardson fieldnotes, July 31, August 2, 1935, KFN.

134. LaBarre fieldnotes, July 9, 31, 1935; Bascom fieldnotes, n.d.; Collier fieldnotes, July 2, 20–25, 1935, KFN.

135. LaBarre fieldnotes, n.d., July 9, 1935; Bascom fieldnotes, n.d., KFN; Marriott fieldnotes, August 19–20, 1935, box 9, folder 1; Collier fieldnotes, July 20–25, 1935, KFN.

136. LaBarre fieldnotes, n.d., KFN.

137. Collier fieldnotes, July 20–25, 1935, KFN.

138. LaBarre fieldnotes, n.d., July 9, 31, 1935; Collier fieldnotes, July 20–25, 1935; Bascom fieldnotes, n.d., KFN.

139. Collier fieldnotes, July 20–25, 1935; LaBarre fieldnotes, July 9, 1935, KFN.

140. Bascom fieldnotes, n.d.; LaBarre fieldnotes, July 31, August 22, 1935; Collier fieldnotes, July 20–25, 1935, KFN.

141. Collier fieldnotes, n.d., July 20–25, 1935; LaBarre fieldnotes, July 31, August 22, 1935, KFN; Marriott fieldnotes, July 17, 20, 1936, box 9, folder 1.

142. Collier fieldnotes, July 8, 9, 25, 1935; LaBarre fieldnotes, July 9, 31, August 26, 1935, KFN.

143. LaBarre fieldnotes, August 1, 1935, KFN.

144. Collier fieldnotes, July 8, 9, 1935, KFN.

145. LaBarre fieldnotes, July 9, August 1, 1935; Collier fieldnotes, n.d., KFN.

146. Richardson fieldnotes, July 31, August 2, 1935, KFN.

147. Collier fieldnotes, n.d., KFN.

148. LaBarre fieldnotes, n.d., July 7, August 7, 10, 1935, KFN.

149. LaBarre fieldnotes, July 9, 30, 1935; Collier fieldnotes, n.d., KFN.

150. LaBarre fieldnotes, August 10, 1935, KFN.

151. Collier fieldnotes, n.d., July 18, 19; LaBarre fieldnotes, July 9, August 1, 1935, KFN.

152. LaBarre fieldnotes, June 25, July 9, 1935; Collier fieldnotes, n.d., KFN.

153. Collier fieldnotes, July 25, 1935; LaBarre fieldnotes, n.d., July 31, 1935, KFN.

154. Collier fieldnotes, n.d.; LaBarre fieldnotes, July 9, 31, 1935, KFN; Marriott fieldnotes, July 4, 1935, box 9, folder 1.

155. LaBarre fieldnotes, July 9, 31, August 1, 1935; Collier fieldnotes, August 20, 1935, KFN.

156. Collier fieldnotes, n.d., July 8, 9, 20–25, 1935; LaBarre fieldnotes, July 9, August 1, 1935, KFN.

157. Collier fieldnotes, n.d., July 8, 9, 1935, KFN.

158. Collier fieldnotes, n.d., KFN.

159. Bascom fieldnotes, August 26, 1935, KFN.

160. LaBarre fieldnotes, July 9, 1935; Collier fieldnotes, n.d., KFN.

161. Collier fieldnotes, n.d., KFN.

162. Collier fieldnotes, n.d.; LaBarre fieldnotes, July 9, 31; Bascom fieldnotes, n.d., KFN.

163. Collier fieldnotes, n.d., KFN.

164. LaBarre fieldnotes, August 1, 1935, KFN.

165. LaBarre fieldnotes, July 10, 1935, KFN.

166. Marriott fieldnotes, August 19–20, 1935, box 9, folder 1; Collier fieldnotes, n.d., KFN.

167. Bascom fieldnotes, July 18, 1935, KFN.

168. Collier fieldnotes, n.d., KFN.

169. LaBarre fieldnotes, August 1, 1935, KFN.

170. Collier fieldnotes, n.d.; LaBarre fieldnotes, July 10, 1935, KFN.

171. LaBarre fieldnotes, July 31, 1935, KFN.

172. Collier fieldnotes, n.d., KFN.

173. LaBarre fieldnotes, July 10, 1935; Collier fieldnotes, n.d., KFN.

174. LaBarre fieldnotes, July 10, 1935, KFN.

175. Collier fieldnotes, n.d., KFN.

176. Richardson fieldnotes, July 31, August 2, 1935, KFN.

177. LaBarre fieldnotes, n.d., July 10, 1935, KFN.

178. Kracht fieldnotes, August 30, 1986.

179. LaBarre fieldnotes, July 10, 1935, KFN.

180. LaBarre fieldnotes, July 10, August 1, 1935; Collier fieldnotes, n.d., July 20–25, 1935, KFN; Marriott fieldnotes, July 17, 20, 1936, box 9, folder 1.

181. LaBarre fieldnotes, July 29, 1935, KFN. Underline is LaBarre's.

182. Collier fieldnotes, n.d., July 20–25, 1935; LaBarre fieldnotes, July 10, 31, 1935, KFN.

183. Richardson fieldnotes, n.d.; Collier fieldnotes, August 2, 1935, KFN.

184. LaBarre fieldnotes, July 11, 1935, KFN.

185. Keahbone to Scott, copy of original letter, n.d. (probably sometime in November 1927), RG 75.

186. McDowell to Burke, December 5, 1927; Burke to Buntin, December 14, 1927, RG 75.

187. Keahbone to Scott, December 27, 1927, RG 75.

188. Buntin to Scott, December 31, 1927, RG 75.

189. Saunkeah to Buntin, December 29, 1927, RG 75.

190. Ware and Keahbone to Rhoads, March 14, 1930, RG 75.

191. Buntin to Rhoads, March 25, 1930; Rhoads to Ware, June 5, 1930, RG 75.

192. Carl Jennings and Vanessa Paukeigope Jennings, "SUNDANCE '97" (unpublished manuscript), 4–6, in possession of C. Blue Clark, executive vice president, Oklahoma City University.

193. Charles T. Jones, "Kiowa Tribal Elders Condemn Revival of Banned Sun Dance," *Daily Oklahoman*, May 27, 1997, 1–2.

194. Lillie-Beth Brinkman, Lawton Bureau, "Tribal Judge Delays Ritual of Sun Dance," *Daily Oklahoman*, June 6, 1997.

195. Associated Press, "Judge Grants Bid to Halt Sun Dance," *Daily Oklahoman*, Saturday, May 31, 1997.

196. Dewey D. Tsonetokoy Sr., "Exploitation of Traditions Weakens Tribal Identity," *Daily Oklahoman*, June 3, 1997.

197. Kracht fieldnotes, June 21, 2004.

198. Kracht fieldnotes, April 30, 1987.

199. Kracht fieldnotes, June 9, 2004; Letter from Doyah to author, August 15, 2005.

CONCLUSION

1. The articles include those written by Muriel H. Wright (1956), Gillett Griswold (1958), Martha Buntin (1932), T. Ashley Zwink (1978–79), Grant Foreman (1941), Aubrey L. Steele (1939), and Forrest D. Monahan (1971–72)

2. Agent J. M. Haworth to Indian Commissioner E. P. Smith, September 1, 1874, ARCIA 1874:410–11 [1639].

3. Indian Commissioner Nathaniel G. Taylor to Interior Secretary O. H. Browning, January 25, 1868, House Executive Document 124, 40-2, V. 11 [1337].

4. Interior Secretary Jacob D. Cox to Speaker of the House of Representatives J. D. Blaine, May 21, 1870, House Executive Document (hereafter HED) 284, 41-2, V. 12 [1426]; see HED 65, 41-3, V. 8 [1454].

5. Executive Committee of Friends to Indian Commissioner Ely S. Parker, January 27, 1870, HED 125, 41-2, V. 3 [1417].

6. Agent Lawrie Tatum to Superintendent Enoch Hoag, August 12, 1869, ARCIA 1869:827, 478 [1414].

7. Tatum to Hoag, August 12, 1870, ARCIA 1870:727 [1449].

8. Tatum to Hoag, August 12, 1870, ARCIA 1870:727–29 [1449].

9. Bascom fieldnotes, July 5, 1935; LaBarre fieldnotes, July 17, 1935; Mishkin fieldnotes, July 8, 1935, KFN.

10. Collier fieldnotes, July 1, 10, 1935, KFN.

11. Collier fieldnotes, July 10, 1935, KFN.

12. Richardson fieldnotes, July 5, 1935, KFN.

13. Richardson fieldnotes, July 3, 1935; Collier fieldnotes, July 1, 10, 1935; Bascom fieldnotes, July 5, 1935; Mishkin fieldnotes, July 8, 1935; LaBarre fieldnotes, n.d., July 17, 1935, KFN.

14. Collier fieldnotes, July 1, 1935, KFN.

15. Mishkin fieldnotes, August 21, 1935, KFN.

16. Bascom fieldnotes, July 31, 1935; Mishkin fieldnotes, August 6, 1935, KFN.

17. Bascom fieldnotes, July 8, 1935; Collier fieldnotes, July 2, 1935, KFN.

18. Richardson fieldnotes, July 5, 1935, KFN.

19. Bascom fieldnotes, July 5, 8, 1935; Richardson fieldnotes, July 5, 1935; Mishkin fieldnotes, July 8, 1935; Collier fieldnotes, July 2, 1935, KFN.

20. HED 125, 41-2, V. 6 [1417]; HED 284, 41-2, V. 12 [1426].

21. Levy (2001, 917; 1959, 37) identified Stumbling Bear and Cat as Kicking Bird's

cousins and said that Feathered Lance was his brother. Conversely, Nye (1937, 137, 92, 141) identified Stumbling Bear as Kicking Bird's older cousin and said that Cat was Stumbling Bear's cousin and Kicking Bird's brother-in-law, though Feathered Lance's relationship to the others was not mentioned.

22. Tatum to Hoag, September 1, 1872, ARCIA 1872:632 [1560]; Captain Alvord to Indian Commissioner Francis A. Walker, October 10, 1872, ARCIA 1872:521 [1560].

23. Alvord to Walker, October 10, 1872, ARCIA 1872:517–18 [1560].

24. ARCIA 1872:482 [1560].

25. Hoag to Smith, October 29, 1873, HED 23, 43-1, V. 8 [1606].

26. Hoag to Smith, October 1, 1873, ARCIA 1873:569 [1601].

27. Hoag to Smith, November 20, 1874, ARCIA 1874:522 [1639].

28. ARCIA 1875:567 [1680].

29. Haworth to Smith, September 20, 1875, ARCIA 1875:774 [1680].

30. Haworth to Smith, September 20, 1875, ARCIA 1875:774 [1680].

31. Collier fieldnotes, July 1, 1935, KFN.

32. In her study of Fort Marion art, Joyce M. Szabo (2007, 25) identifies seventy-one prisoners and one Cheyenne woman who accompanied her husband. Her count consists of thirty-three Cheyennes, two Arapahos, one Caddo, nine Comanches, and twenty-seven Kiowas, for a total of seventy-two prisoners. Her math seems to be slightly off, though it should be said that several prisoners did die during the journey from the Southwestern Plains to Fort Marion (Szabo 2007, 176n).

33. LaBarre fieldnotes, August 10, 1935, KFN.

34. LaBarre fieldnotes, n.d., KFN.

35. Agent P. B Hunt to Indian Commissioner Ezra Hayt, August 30, 1879, ARCIA 1879:171 [1910].

36. LaBarre fieldnotes, June 25, 1935, KFN.

37. Agent W. D. Myers to Indian Commissioner Thomas J. Morgan, August 27, 1889, ARCIA 1889:190–91 [2725].

38. LaBarre fieldnotes, n.d., KFN.

39. "50 Years with the Kiowa Indians, 1850–1900," 53, 167.

40. Collier fieldnotes, n.d., KFN.

41. LaBarre fieldnotes, n.d., August 1, 1935, KFN.

42. LaBarre fieldnotes, n.d., KFN.

43. Collier fieldnotes, n.d., KFN.

44. LaBarre fieldnotes, July 30, 1935, KFN.

45. Collier fieldnotes, n.d., KFN.

46. Collier fieldnotes, n.d., KFN.

47. LaBarre fieldnotes, July 30, 31, 1935, KFN.

48. Collier fieldnotes, n.d., KFN.

49. LaBarre fieldnotes, n.d., July 39, 1935; Collier fieldnotes, n.d., KFN.

50. LaBarre fieldnotes, n.d.; Collier fieldnotes, n.d.; Bascom fieldnotes, n.d., KFN.

51. Collier fieldnotes, n.d., KFN.

52. Collier fieldnotes, n.d., KFN.

53. Collier fieldnotes, July 25, 1935, KFN.

54. Bascom fieldnotes, n.d.; Mishkin fieldnotes, August 20, 1935, KFN.

55. LaBarre fieldnotes, August 17, 1935, KFN.

56. LaBarre fieldnotes, August 17, 21, 1935; Collier fieldnotes, July 29, 1935, KFN.

57. LaBarre fieldnotes, July 29, 1935; Collier fieldnotes, July 29, 1935, KFN.

58. LaBarre fieldnotes, July 17, 1935, KFN.

59. LaBarre fieldnotes, n.d., KFN.

60. Collier fieldnotes, July 30, 1935; LaBarre fieldnotes, August 21, 1935, KFN.

61. There are variant spellings for Ä'piatañ, including Ahpiatan and Ahpeahtone. I will stick with Ä'piatañ (Letter from Doyah to author, August 31, 2005).

62. Alexander Lesser, field leader, to Director Jesse L. Nusbaum, September 19, 1935 notes and letters, box 1, folder 10, Arthur & Shifra Silberman Native Art Collection, NCWHM.

63. Alexander Lesser to Director Jesse L. Nusbaum, September 19, 1935, Kiowa–Alexander Lesser Anthropology Field Program, 1935 notes and letters, box 1, folder 10, Arthur & Shifra Silberman Native Art Collection, NCWHM.

Bibliography

Amos, Pamela T. 1997. "The Power of Secrecy among the Coast Salish." In *The Anthropology of Power: Ethnographic Studies from Asia, Oceania, and the New World*, edited by Raymond D. Fogelson and Richard N. Adams, 131–40. New York: Academic Press.

Archambault, JoAllyn. 2001. "Sun Dance." In *Handbook of North American Indians*. Vol. 13, *Plains*. Edited by Raymond J. DeMallie, 983–95. Washington DC: Smithsonian Institution Press.

Baird, W. David. 1980. *The Quapaw Indians: History of the Downstream People*. Norman: University of Oklahoma Press.

Bates, Russell. 1987. "Legends of the Kiowas." *National Fortean Organization Info Journal* 11:4–10.

Battey, Thomas C. 1968. *The Life and Adventures of a Quaker among the Indians*. Norman: University of Oklahoma Press.

Beals, Ralph L. 1935. *Ethnology of Rocky Mountain Park: The Ute and Arapaho*. Berkeley: U.S. Department of the Interior, National Park Service.

Bean, Lowell John. 1997. "Power and Its Application in Native California." In *The Anthropology of Power: Ethnographic Studies from Asia, Oceania, and the New World*, edited by Raymond D. Fogelson and Richard N. Adams, 117–29. New York: Academic Press.

Benedict, Ruth F. 1922. "The Vision in Plains Culture." *American Anthropologist*, n.s., 24:1–23.

———. 1938. "Religion." In *General Anthropology*, edited by Franz Boas, 627–65. Boston: D. C. Heath.

Berthrong, Donald J. 1979. *The Southern Cheyennes*. Norman: University of Oklahoma Press.

Bierhorst, John. 1985. *The Mythology of North America*. New York: William Morrow.

Black, Mary B. 1977. "Ojibwa Power Belief System." In *The Anthropology of Power: Ethnographic Studies from Asia, Oceania, and the New World*. Edited by Raymond D. Fogelson and Richard N. Adams, 141–51. New York: Academic Press.

Bock, Phillip K. 1988. *Rethinking Psychological Anthropology: Continuity and Change in the Study of Human Action*. New York: W. H. Freeman.

Bohannan, Paul, and Mark Glazer. 1988. *High Points in Anthropology*. 2nd ed. Edited by Paul Bohannan and Mark Glazer. New York: McGraw-Hill.

Bourke, John Gregory. 1894. "Capt. Bourke on the Sun-Dance." In *11th Annual Report of the Bureau of [American] Ethnology [for] 1889–'90*, 351–544. Washington DC: Smithsonian Institution.

Bowers, Alfred W. 1950. *Mandan Social and Ceremonial Organization*. Chicago: University of Chicago Press.

———. 1965. *Hidatsa Social and Ceremonial Organization*. Washington DC: Government Printing Office.

Boyd, Maurice. 1981. *Kiowa Voices: Ceremonial Dance, Ritual and Song*. Vol. 1. Fort Worth: Texas Christian University Press.

———. 1983. *Kiowa Voices: Myths, Legends and Folktales*. Vol. 2. Fort Worth: Texas University Press.

Brant, Charles S. 1951. "The Kiowa Apache Indians: A Study in Ethnology and Acculturation." PhD diss., Cornell University.

———. 1953. "Kiowa Apache Culture History: Some Further Observations." *Southwestern Journal of Anthropology* 9, no. 2: 195–202.

———. 1969. *The Autobiography of a Kiowa Apache Indian*. Edited by Charles S. Brant. New York: Dover.

Brown, Donald N., and Lee Irwin. 2001. "Ponca." In *Handbook of North American Indians*. Vol. 13, *Plains*. Edited by Raymond J. DeMallie, 416–31. Washington DC: Smithsonian Institution.

Brown, Jennifer S. H., and Robert Brightman. 1988. *"The Orders of the Dreamed": George Nelson on Cree and Northern Ojibwa Religion and Myth, 1823*. Winnipeg: University of Manitoba Press.

Brown, Joseph Epes. 1953. *The Sacred Pipe: Black Elk's Account of the Seven Sacred Rites of the Oglala Sioux*. New York: Penguin Books.

———. 1989. "Sun Dance." In *Native Religions: North America*, edited by Lawrence E. Sullivan, 193–99. New York: Macmillan.

Bruner, Edward M. 1961. "The Mandan Community." In *Perspectives in American Indian Culture Change*. Edited by Edward H. Spicer, 187–277. Chicago: University of Chicago Press.

Bucko, Raymond A. 1998. *The Lakota Ritual of the Sweat Lodge: History and Contemporary Practice*. Studies in the Anthropology of North American Indians. Lincoln: University of Nebraska Press.

———. 2004. "Religion." In *A Companion to the Anthropology of American Indians*, edited by Thomas Biolsi, 171–95. Malden MA: Blackwell.

Buntin, Martha. 1932. "The Quaker Indian Agents of the Kiowa, Comanche, and Wichita Indian Reservation." *Chronicles of Oklahoma* 10:204–18.

Catlin, George. 1841. *Letters and Notes on the Manners, Customs, and Condition of the*

North American Indians. 2 vols. London: Published by the author, printed by Tosswill and Myers.

———. 1867. *O-Kee-Pa: A Religious Ceremony, and Other Customs of the Mandans*. London: Trübner.

Chamberlain, Von Del. 1982. *When Stars Came Down to Earth: Cosmology of the Skidi Pawnee Indians of North America*. Ballena Press Anthropological Papers 26. Edited by Thomas C. Blackburn. Los Altos CA: Ballena.

Clark, William P. 1885. *The Indian Sign Language*. Philadelphia: L. R. Hamersly.

Collier, Donald. 1936. "Kiowa Social Organization." Master's thesis, University of Chicago.

———. 1944. "Conjuring among the Kiowa." *Primitive Man* 17:45–49.

Cooper, John Montgomery. 1957. *The Gros Ventres of Montana*. Pt. 2, *Religion and Ritual*. Edited by Regina Flannery. The Catholic University of America Anthropological Series 16. Washington DC: Catholic University of America Press.

Corwin, Hugh D. 1958a. *The Kiowa Indians: Their History and Life Stories*. Lawton OK: Privately printed.

———. 1958b. "Saddle Mountain Mission and Church." *Chronicles of Oklahoma* 36:118–30.

———. 1959. *Comanche and Kiowa Captives in Oklahoma and Texas*. Guthrie OK: Cooperative Publishing.

———. 1961–62. "Delos K. Lonewolf." *Chronicles of Oklahoma* 39:433–36.

———. 1962. "Fifty Years with the Kiowa Indians, 1850–1900." Typewritten manuscript. D'Arcy McNickle Center for the History of the American Indian, Newberry Library, Chicago.

———. 1968. "Protestant Missionary Work among the Comanches and Kiowas." *Chronicles of Oklahoma* 46:41–57.

Crawford, Isabel. 1915. *Kiowa: The History of a Blanket Indian Mission*. New York: Fleming H. Revell.

———. n.d. *From Tent to Chapel at Saddle Mountain*. Edited by Mary G. Burdette. Chicago: The Woman's Baptist Home Mission Society.

Curtis, Edward S. 1907–30. *The North American Indian: Being a Series of Volumes Picturing and Describing the Indians of the United States, the Dominion of Canada, and Alaska*. 20 vols. Edited by Frederick W. Hodge. Norwood MA: Plimpton Press.

Deloria, Ella Cara. 1929. "The Sun Dance of the Oglala Sioux." *Journal of American Folk-lore* 42:354–413.

Deloria, Vine. 2006. *The World We Used to Live in: Remembering the Powers of the Medicine Men*. Golden CO: Fulcrum.

DeMallie, Raymond J. 1984. *The Sixth Grandfather: Black Elk's Teachings Given to John G. Neihardt*. Lincoln: University of Nebraska Press.

———. 1987. "Lakota Belief and Ritual in the Nineteenth Century." In *Sioux Indian Religion: Tradition and Innovation*. Edited by Raymond J. DeMallie and Douglas R. Parks, 25–43. Norman: University of Oklahoma Press.

———. 1994. "Introduction: Fred Eggan and American Indian Anthropology." In *North American Indian Anthropology: Essays on Society and Culture*. Edited by Raymond J. DeMallie and Alfonso Ortiz, 3–22. Norman: University of Oklahoma Press.

———. 2001. "Teton." In *Handbook of North American Indians*. Vol. 13, *Plains*. Edited by Raymond J. DeMallie, 794–820. Washington DC: Smithsonian Institution Press.

DeMallie, Raymond J., and John C. Ewers. 2001. "History of Ethnological and Ethnohistorical Research." In *Handbook of North American Indians*. Vol. 13, *Plains*. Edited by Raymond J. DeMallie, 23–43. Washington DC: Smithsonian Institution Press.

DeMallie, Raymond J., and Robert H. Lavenda. 1977. "*Wakan*: Plains Siouan Concepts of Power." In *The Anthropology of Power: Ethnographic Studies from Asia, Oceania, and the New World*. Edited by Raymond D. Fogelson and Richard N. Adams, 153–65. New York: Academic Press.

DeMallie, Raymond J., and David Reed Miller. 2001. "Assiniboine." In *Handbook of North American Indians*. Vol. 13, *Plains*. Edited by Raymond J. DeMallie, 572–95. Washington DC: Smithsonian Institution Press.

DeMallie, Raymond J., and Douglas R. Parks, eds. 1987. *Sioux Indian Religion: Tradition and Innovation*. Norman: University of Oklahoma Press.

DeMallie, Raymond J., and Douglas R. Parks. 2001. "Tribal Traditions and Records." In *Handbook of North American Indians*. Vol. 13, *Plains*. Edited by Raymond J. DeMallie, 1062–73. Washington DC: Smithsonian Institution Press.

Dempsey, Hugh A. 2001. "Blackfoot." In *Handbook of North American Indians*. Vol. 13, *Plains*. Edited by Raymond J. DeMallie, 604–28. Washington DC: Smithsonian Institution.

Denig, Edwin Thompson. 1930. "Indian Tribes of the Upper Missouri." In *46th Annual Report of the Bureau of American Ethnology [for] 1928–1929*. Edited with notes and biographical sketch by J. N. B. Hewitt, 375–628. Washington DC: Smithsonian Institution.

———. 1961. *Five Indian Tribes of the Upper Missouri: Sioux, Arikaras, Assiniboines, Crees, Crows*. Edited by John C. Ewers. Norman: University of Oklahoma Press.

Densmore, Frances. 1918. "Teton Sioux Music." *Bureau of American Ethnology Bulletin* 61. Washington DC: Smithsonian Institution Press.

Denton, Joan Frederick. 1987. "The Kiowa Murals." *Southwest Art* 17, no. 2: 68–75.

Dorsey, George A. 1903a. *Traditions of the Arapaho: Collected under the Auspices of the Field Columbian Museum and the American Museum of Natural History*. Field Columbian Museum Publication 81, Anthropological Series, vol. 5. Chicago: Field Museum of Natural History.

———. 1903b. *The Arapaho Sun Dance: The Ceremony of the Offerings Lodge*. Field Columbian Museum Publication 75, Anthropological Series, vol. 4. Chicago: Field Museum of Natural History.

———. 1904a. *Traditions of the Arikara*. Carnegie Institution of Washington Publication 17. Washington DC: Carnegie Institution of Washington.

———. 1904b. *The Mythology of the Wichita*. Carnegie Institution of Washing Publication 21. Washington DC: Carnegie Institution of Washington.

———. 1904c. "Traditions of the Skidi Pawnee." *Memoirs of the American Folk-Lore Society* 8. Boston: Houghton Mifflin.

———. 1904d. *Traditions of the Osage*. Field Columbian Museum Publication 88, Anthropological Series, vol. 7. Chicago: Field Museum of History.

———. 1905a. *The Ponca Sun Dance*. Field Columbian Museum Publication 102, Anthropological Series, vol. 7. Chicago: Field Museum of History.

———. 1905b. *The Cheyenne I: Ceremonial Organization*. Field Columbian Museum Publication 99, Anthropological Series, vol. 9. Chicago: Field Museum of History.

———. 1905c. *The Cheyenne II: The Sun Dance*. Field Columbian Museum Publication 101, Anthropological Series, vol. 9. Chicago: Field Museum of History.

———. 1905d. *Traditions of the Caddo*. Carnegie Institution of Washington Publication 41. Washington DC: Carnegie Institution of Washington.

———. 1906. *The Pawnee: Mythology: Part I*. Carnegie Institution of Washington Publication 59. Washington DC: Carnegie Institution of Washington.

Dorsey, George A., and Alfred L. Kroeber. 1903. *Traditions of the Arapaho*. Field Columbian Museum Publication 81, Anthropological Series, vol. 5. Chicago: Field Museum of History.

Dorsey, George A., and James R. Murie. 1907. "The Pawnee: Society and Religion of the Skidi Pawnee." Unpublished manuscript. In Douglas R. Park's possession.

Dorsey, James Owen. 1884. "Omaha Sociology." In *3d Annual Report of the Bureau of [American] Ethnography [for] 1881–'82*, 205–370. Washington DC: Smithsonian Institution.

———. 1885a. "Siouan Folk-lore and Mythologic Notes." *American Antiquarian and Oriental Journal* 7:105–8.

———. 1885b. "Mourning and War Customs of the Kansas." *American Naturalist* 19:670–80.

———. 1894. "A Study of Siouan Cults." In *11th Annual Report of the Bureau of [American] Ethnology [for] 1889–'90*, 545–53. Washington DC: Smithsonian Institution Press.

Dunbar, John B. 1880. "The Pawnee Indians: Their History and Ethnology." *Magazine of American History* 4:241–81.

Eggan, Fred. 1955. "The Cheyenne and Arapaho Kinship System." In *Social Organization of North American Tribes*. 2nd ed. Edited by Fred Eggan, 32–95. Chicago: University of Chicago Press.

Ellenbrook, Edward Charles. 1991. *Outdoor and Trail Guide to the Wichita Mountains of Southwest Oklahoma*. 4th printing. Lawton OK: In-The-Valley-of-the-Wichitas House.

Ellis, Clyde. 1990. "'Truly Dancing Their Own Way': Modern Revival and Diffusion of the Gourd Dance." *American Indian Quarterly* 14, no. 1: 19–33.

———. 1993. "'A Gathering of Life Itself': The Kiowa Gourd Dance." In *Native American Values: Survival and Renewal*. Edited by Thomas E. Schirer and Susan M. Branstner, 365–74. Sault Ste. Marie MI: Lake Superior State University Press.

———. 1996. *To Change Them Forever: Indian Education at the Rainy Mountain Boarding School, 1893–1920*. Norman: University of Oklahoma Press.

———. 1999. "'We Don't Want Your Rations, We Want This Dance': The Changing Use of Song and Dance on the Southern Plains." *Western Historical Quarterly* 30, no. 2: 133–54.

———. 2003. *A Dancing People: Powwow Culture on the Southern Plains*. Lawrence: University of Kansas Press.

Evans-Pritchard, E. E. 1937. *Witchcraft, Oracles and Magic among the Azande*. Oxford: Clarendon Press.

Ewers, John C. 1958. *The Blackfeet: Raiders on the Northwestern Plains*. Norman: University of Oklahoma Press.

———. 1978. *Murals in the Round: Painted Tipis of the Kiowa and Kiowa-Apache Indians*. Washington DC: Renwich Gallery of the National Collection of Fine Arts.

———. 1979. "Introduction." In *Calendar History of the Kiowa Indians*, vii–xiii. Washington DC: Smithsonian Institution Press.

———. 1980. *The Horse in Blackfoot Indian Culture*. Washington DC: Smithsonian Institution Press.

———. 1992. "Introduction." In *Changing Military Patterns of the Great Plains Indians*, ix–xvii. Lincoln: University of Nebraska Press.

Fletcher, Alice C. 1883. "The Sun Dance of the Ogalalla Sioux." In *Proceedings of the American Association for the Advancement of Science, 31st Meeting, Held at Montreal, Canada, August, 1882*, 580–84. Salem MA.

———. 1885. "Observations upon the Usage, Symbolism and Influence of the Sacred Pipes of Fellowship among the Omahas." In *Proceedings of the American Association for the Advancement of Science, 33d Meeting, Held at Philadelphia, Penn., September, 1884*, 615–17. Salem MA.

———. 1887a. "[Indian Ceremonies]: The White Buffalo Festival of the Uncpapas. The Religious Ceremony of the Four Winds or Quarters, as Observed by the Santee Sioux." In *16th Report of the Peabody Museum of American Archaeology and Ethnology, Harvard University [for] 1882*. Vol. 3, 260–75. Cambridge MA.

———. 1887b. "[Indian Ceremonies]: The Elk Mystery Festival. Oglala Sioux." In *16th Report of the Peabody Museum of American Archaeology and Ethnology, Harvard University [for] 1882*. Vol. 3, 276–88. Cambridge MA.

———. 1887c. "[Indian Ceremonies]: The Shadow or Ghost Lodge: A Ceremony of the Ogallala Sioux." In *16th Report of the Peabody Museum of American Archaeology and Ethnology, Harvard University [for] 1882*. Vol. 3, 296–307. Cambridge MA.

———. 1887d. "The 'Wawan,' or Pipe Dance of the Omahas." In *16th Report of the*

Peabody Museum of American Archaeology and Ethnology, Harvard University [for] 1882. Vol. 3, 308–33. Cambridge MA.

———. 1892. "Hae-Thu-Ska Society of the Omaha Tribe." *Journal of American Folk-Lore* 5:135–44.

———. 1896. "The Sacred Pole of the Omaha Tribe." In *Proceedings of the American Association for the Advancement of Science, 44th Meeting, Held at Springfield, Mass., August–September, 1895,* 270–80. Salem MA.

———. 1899. "A Pawnee Ritual Used When Changing a Man's Name." *American Anthropologist,* n.s., 1:82–97.

———. 1900. "Giving Thanks: A Pawnee Ceremony." *Journal of American Folk-Lore* 13:261–66.

———. 1902. "Star Cult among the Pawnee: A Preliminary Report." *American Anthropologist,* n.s., 4:730–36.

———. 1903. "Pawnee Star Lore." *Journal of American Folk-Lore* 16:10–15.

Fletcher, Alice C., and Francis La Flesche. 1911. "The Omaha Tribe." In *27th Annual Report of the Bureau of [American] Ethnology [for] 1905–'06,* 17–672. Washington DC: Smithsonian Institution Press.

Fletcher, Alice C., and James R. Murie. 1904. "The Hako: A Pawnee Ceremony." Assisted by James R. Murie. Music transcribed by Edwin S. Tracy. In *22d Annual Report of the Bureau of American Ethnology [for] 1900–'02.* Pt. 2, 1–368. Washington DC: Smithsonian Institution Press.

Forbes, Bruce D. 1985. "John Jasper Methvin: Methodist 'Missionary to the Western Tribes' (Oklahoma)." In *Churchmen and the Western Indians 1820–1920.* Edited by Clyde A. Milner II and Floyd A. O'Neil, 41–73. Norman: University of Oklahoma Press.

Foreman, Grant. 1941. "Historical Background of the Kiowa-Comanche Reservation." *Chronicles of Oklahoma* 19: 129–40.

Fortune, Rio F. 1932. "Omaha Secret Societies." *Columbia University Contributions to Anthropology* 14. New York.

Foster, George M., and Barbara Gallatin Anderson. 1978. *Medical Anthropology.* New York: John Wiley.

Foster, Morris W. 1992. "Introduction." In *Rank and Warfare among the Plains Indians,* v–xv. Lincoln: University of Nebraska Press.

Foster, Morris, and Martha McCollough. 2001. "Plains Apache." In *Handbook of North American Indians.* Vol. 13, *Plains.* Edited by Raymond J. DeMallie, 926–40. Washington DC: Smithsonian Institution Press.

Fowler, Loretta. 1982. *Arapahoe Politics, 1851–1978: Symbols in Crisis of Authority.* Lincoln: University of Nebraska Press.

———. 1987. *Shared Symbols, Contested Meanings: Gros Ventre Culture and History, 1778–1984.* Ithaca NY: Cornell University Press.

———. 1996. "The Great Plains from the Arrival of the Horse to 1885." In *The Cambridge History of the Native Peoples of the Americas.* Vol. 1, *North America.* Pt.

2. Edited by Bruce G. Trigger and Wilcomb E. Washburn, 1–55. Cambridge: Cambridge University Press.

———. 2001. "Arapaho." In *Handbook of North American Indians*. Vol. 13, *Plains*. Edited by Raymond J. DeMallie, 840–62. Washington DC: Smithsonian Institution Press.

Frederickson, Vera-Mae, Albert E. Elasser, Alex Nicoloff, and Martha Nicoloff. n.d. "A Chronicle of the Kiowa Indians." Pamphlet for exhibit "Treasures of the Lowie Museum." R. H. Lowie Museum of Anthropology, University of California, Berkeley.

Frey, Rodney. 1987. *The World of the Crow Indians: As Driftwood Lodges*. Norman: University of Oklahoma Press.

Gatschet, Albert S. 1884. "Tonkawe Language: Collected at Fort Griffin. Shackleford Co., Texas, Sept.–Oct. 1884." Manuscript 1008. National Anthropological Archives, Smithsonian Institution Press.

Gelo, Daniel J. 1986. "Comanche Belief and Ritual." PhD diss., Rutgers University.

Gilette, J. M. 1906. "Medicine Society of the Dakota Indians." In *Collections of the State Historical Society of North Dakota* 1, 459–74. Bismarck.

Gilmore, Melvin R. 1926. "An Hidatsa Shrine and the Beliefs Respecting It." *American Anthropologist*, n.s., 28:572–73.

———. 1932. "Sacred Bundles of the Arikara." *Papers of the Michigan Academy of Science, Arts, and Letters* 16 (for 1931): 33–50.

Goddard, Pliny Earle. 1919a. "Notes on the Sun Dance of the Sarsi." *American Museum of Natural History Anthropological Papers* 16:271–81.

———. 1919b. "Notes on the Sun Dance of the Cree in Alberta." *American Museum of Natural History Anthropological Papers* 16:295–310.

———. 1919c. "Plains Ojibwa Sun Dance." *American Museum of Natural History Anthropological Papers* 16:453–522.

Greene, Candace S. 1996. "Exploring the Three 'Little Bluffs' of the Kiowa." *Plains Anthropologist* 41, no. 157: 221–42.

———. 2001. *Silver Horn: Master Illustrator of the Kiowas*. Norman: University of Oklahoma Press.

———. 2009. *One Hundred Summers: A Calendar Record*. Lincoln: University of Nebraska Press.

Grim, John A. 2005a. "Power, Plains." In *American Indian Religious Traditions: An Encyclopedia*. Edited by Suzanne J. Crawford and Dennis F. Kelley, 759–65. Santa Barbara CA: ABC-CLIO.

———. 2005b. "Sun Dance." In *American Indian Religious Traditions: An Encyclopedia*. Edited by Suzanne J. Crawford and Dennis F. Kelley, 1051–59. Santa Barbara CA: ABC-CLIO.

Grinnell, George Bird. 1889. *Pawnee Hero Stories and Folk-tales: With Notes on the Origin, Customs, and Character of the Pawnee People*. New York: Forest and Stream.

———. 1890. *Pawnee Hero Stories and Folk-tales: With Notes on the Origin, Customs,* and Character of the Pawnee People, to Which Is Added a Chapter on the Pawnee Language by John B. Dunbar. New York: Scribner.

———. 1892. *Blackfoot Lodge Tales: The Story of a Prairie People*. New York: Charles Scribner's Sons.

———. 1910. "Great Mysteries of the Cheyenne." *American Anthropologist*, n.s., 12:542–57.

———. 1914. "The Cheyenne Medicine Lodge." *American Anthropologist*, n.s., 16:245–56.

———. 1915. *The Fighting Cheyennes*. New York: Charles Scribner's Sons.

———. 1923. *The Cheyenne Indians: Their History and Ways of Life*. 2 Vols. New Haven CT: Yale University Press.

———. 1926. *By Cheyenne Campfires*. New Haven CT: Yale University Press.

Griswold, Gillett. 1958. "Old Fort Sill: The First Seven Years." *Chronicles of Oklahoma* 36:2–14.

Gulliford, Andrew. 2005. "Sacred Sites and Sacred Mountains." In *American Indian Religious Traditions: An Encyclopedia*. Edited by Suzanne J. Crawford and Dennis F. Kelley, 945–61. Santa Barbara CA: ABC-CLIO.

Haines, Francis. 1976. *The Plains Indians: Their Origins, Migrations, and Cultural Development*. New York: Thomas Y. Crowell Company.

Hall, Harland (Tõćákút). 2000. *Remember, We Are Kiowas: 101 Kiowa Indian Stories*. 1st Books Library.

Hallowell, A. Irving. 1960. "Ojibwa Ontology, Behavior, and World View." In *Culture in History: Essays in Honor of Paul Radin*. Edited by Stanley Diamond, 19–52. New York: Columbia University Press.

Hamilton, Allen L. 1988. *Sentinel of the Southern Plains: Fort Richardson and the Northwest Texas Frontier, 1866–1878*. Fort Worth: Texas Christian University Press.

Hanks, Lucien M., Jr., and Jane Richardson Hanks. 1950. *Tribe Under Trust: A Study of the Blackfoot Reserve of Alberta*. Toronto: University of Toronto Press.

Harrington, John P. 1928. "Vocabulary of the Kiowa Language." *Bureau of American Ethnology Bulletin* 84:1–255.

Harrod, Howard L. 1987. *Renewing the World: Northern Plains Indian Religion*. Tucson: University of Arizona Press.

———. 1995. *Becoming and Remaining a People: Native American Religion on the Northern Plains*. Tucson: University of Arizona Press.

———. 2000. *The Animals Came Dancing: Native American Sacred Ecology and Animal Kinship*. Tucson: University of Arizona Press.

———. 2005. "Bundles, Sacred Bundle Traditions." In *American Indian Religious Traditions: An Encyclopedia*. Edited by Suzanne J. Crawford and Dennis F. Kelley, 93–101. Santa Barbara CA: ABC-CLIO.

Harvey, Graham. 2006. *Animism: Respecting the Living World*. New York: Columbia University Press.

Hassrick, Royal B. 1964. *The Sioux: Life and Customs of a Warrior Society*. In collaboration with Dorothy Maxwell and Cile M. Bach. Norman: University of Oklahoma Press.

Heidenreich, C. Adrian. 2005. "Oral Traditions, Western Plains." In *American Indian Religious Traditions: An Encyclopedia*. Edited by Suzanne J. Crawford and Dennis F. Kelley, 707–17. Santa Barbara CA: ABC-CLIO.

Henderson, J. Neil, and Kedar K. Adour. 1981. "Comanche Ghost Sickness: A Biocultural Perspective." *Medical Anthropology* 5, no. 2: 195–205.

Hewitt, J. N. B. 1902. "Orenda and a Definition of Religion." *American Anthropologist*, n.s., 4:33–46.

Hinsley, Curtis M. 1981. *Savages and Scientists: The Smithsonian Institution Press and the Development of American Anthropology, 1846–1910*. Washington DC: Smithsonian Institution.

Hoebel, E. Adamson. 1941. "The Comanche Sun Dance and Messianic Outbreak of 1873." *American Anthropologist*, n.s., 43:301–3.

———. 1960. *The Cheyennes: Indians of the Great Plains*. New York: Holt, Rinehart and Winston.

Hoig, Stan. 1979. *The Battle of the Washita: The Sheridan-Custer Indian Campaign of 1867–69*. Garden City NY: Doubleday.

Holder, Preston. 1974. *The Hoe and the Horse on the Plains: A Study of Cultural Development among North American Indians*. 2nd ed. Lincoln: University of Nebraska Press.

Holm, Tom. 2005. "Warfare, Religious Aspects." In *American Indian Religious Traditions: An Encyclopedia*. Edited by Suzanne J. Crawford and Dennis F. Kelley, 1135–41. Santa Barbara CA: ABC-CLIO.

Horse Capture, George P. 1980. *The Seven Visions of Bull Lodge: As Told by His Daughter, Garter Snake*. Gathered by Fred P. Gone. Ann Arbor: Bear Claw.

Howard, James H. 1955. "The Tree Dweller Cults of the Dakota." *Journal of American Folk-lore* 68, no. 268: 169–74.

———. 1965. "The Ponca Tribe." In collaboration with Peter Le Claire, Tribal Historian, and other members of the tribe. *Bureau of American Ethnology Bulletin* 195. Washington DC: Smithsonian Institution Press.

———. 1984. *The Canadian Sioux*. Studies in the Anthropology of North American Indians. Raymond J. DeMallie and Douglas R. Parks, eds. Lincoln: University of Nebraska Press.

Irving, John Treat. 1835. *Indian Sketches: Taken during an Expedition to the Pawnee Tribes*. 2 vols. Philadelphia: Carey, Lea and Blanchard.

Irving, Washington. 1868. *Astoria: or, Anecdotes of an Enterprise beyond the Rocky Mountains*. New York: G. P. Putnam and Son.

Irwin, Lee. 1994. *The Dream Seekers: Native American Visionary Traditions*. Norman: University of Oklahoma Press.

———. 2005. "Vision Quest Rites." In *American Indian Religious Traditions: An Encyclopedia*. Edited by Suzanne J. Crawford and Dennis F. Kelley, 1127–33. Santa Barbara CA: ABC-CLIO.

Isaacs, Hope L. 1977. "*Orenda* and the Concept of Power among the Tonawanda Seneca." In *The Anthropology of Power: Ethnographic Studies from Asia, Oceania, and the New World*. Edited by Raymond D. Fogelson and Richard N. Adams, 167–84. New York: Academic Press.

Jenness, Diamond. 1932. "The Indians of Canada." Anthropological Series 15. *National Museum of Canada Bulletin* 65. Ottawa.

Jones, David E. 1972. *Sanapia: Comanche Medicine Woman*. New York: Holt, Rinehart and Winston.

Jordan, Michael Paul. 2011. "Reclaiming the Past: Descendants' Organizations, Historical Consciousness, and Intellectual Property in Kiowa Society." PhD diss., University of Oklahoma.

Kavanagh, Thomas W. 1986. "Political Power and Political Organization: Comanche Politics, 1786–1875." PhD diss., University of New Mexico.

———. 1996. *The Comanches: A History, 1706–1875*. Lincoln: University of Nebraska Press.

———. 2001. "Comanche." In *Handbook of North American Indians*. Vol. 13, *Plains*. Edited by Raymond J. DeMallie, 886–906. Washington DC: Smithsonian Institution Press.

———. 2008. *Comanche Ethnography: Field Notes of E. Adamson Hoebel, Waldo R. Wedel, Gustav G. Carlson, and Robert H. Lowie*. Compiled and edited by Thomas W. Kavanagh. Studies in the Anthropology of North American Indians Series. Lincoln: University of Nebraska Press.

Keesing, Roger M. 1975. *Kin Groups and Social Structure*. New York: Holt, Rinehart and Winston.

Kemnitzer, Luis S. 1968. "Yuwipi: A Modern Dakota Healing Ritual." PhD diss., University of Pennsylvania, Philadelphia.

———. 1970. "The Cultural Provenience of Objects Used in Yuwipi: A Modern Teton Dakota Healing Ritual." *Ethnos* 35:40–75.

———. 1976. "Structure, Content, and Cultural Meaning of *yuwipi*: A Modern Lakota Healing Ritual." *American Ethnologist* 3, no. 2: 261–80.

Kennedy, Michael Stephen. 1961. *The Assiniboines: From the Accounts of the Old Ones Told to First Boy (James Larpenteur Long)*. Edited by Michael Stephen Kennedy. Norman: University of Oklahoma Press.

Klein, Alan M. 1993. "Political Economy of the Buffalo Hide Trade." In *The Political Economy of North American Indians*. Edited by John H. Moore, 133–60. Norman: University of Oklahoma Press.

Kracht, Benjamin R. 1982. "The Effects of Disease and Warfare on Pawnee Social Organization, 1830–1859: An Ethnohistorical Analysis." Master's thesis, University of Nebraska.

———. 1989. "Kiowa Religion: An Ethnohistorical Analysis of Ritual Symbolism, 1832–1987." PhD diss., Southern Methodist University.

———. 2000. "Kiowa Religion in Historical Perspective." In *Native American Spir-*

ituality: A Critical Reader. Edited by Lee Irwin, 236–55. Lincoln: University of Nebraska Press.

———. 2005a. "Spiritual and Ceremonial Practitioners." In *American Indian Religious Traditions: An Encyclopedia.* Edited by Suzanne J. Crawford and Dennis F. Kelley, 1025–35. Santa Barbara CA: ABC-CLIO.

———. 2005b. "Sacred Societies, Plains." In *American Indian Religious Traditions: An Encyclopedia.* Suzanne J. Crawford and Dennis F. Kelley, 974–84. Santa Barbara CA: ABC-CLIO.

———. 2005c. "Dance, Plains." In *American Indian Religious Traditions: An Encyclopedia.* Edited by Suzanne J. Crawford and Dennis F. Kelley, 206–13. Santa Barbara CA: ABC-CLIO.

———. 2012. "'It Would Break Our Hearts Not to Have Out Kiowas': War Dancing, Tourism, and the Rise of Powwows in the Early Twentieth Century." *Chronicles of Oklahoma* 90:286–309.

Kroeber, Alfred L. 1902–7. "The Arapaho." 4 pts. 1: General Description; 2: Decorative Art and Symbolism; 3: Ceremonial Organization; 4: Religion. *Bulletin of the American Museum of Natural History* 18, no. 1: 3–35; 18, no. 1: 36–150; 18, no. 2: 151–229; 18, no. 4: 279–454.

———. 1907. "Gros Ventre Myths and Tales." *American Museum of Natural History Anthropological Papers* 1:55–139.

LaBarre, R. Weston. 1938. *The Peyote Cult.* Yale University Publications in Anthropology 19. New Haven CT: Yale University Press.

———. 1957. "Autobiography of a Kiowa Indian." Unpublished manuscript. *Publications of Primary Records in Culture and Personality* 2, no. 14. Reproduced in microcard. Madison WI: The Microcard Foundation.

———. 1980. *Culture in Context: Selected Writings of Weston LaBarre.* Durham NC: Duke University Press.

LaBarre, R. Weston, Jane Richardson, William Bascom, Donald Collier, Bernard Mishkin, and Alexander Lesser. 1935. "Notes on Kiowa Ethnography." Typewritten manuscript. National Anthropological Archives, Smithsonian Institution Press.

La Flesche, Francis. 1889. "Death and Funeral Customs among the Omaha." *Journal of American Folk-Lore* 2:3–11.

———. 1890. "The Omaha Buffalo Medicine-Men." *Journal of American Folk-Lore* 3:215–21.

———. 1919. "Researches among the Osage." *Smithsonian Miscellaneous Collections* 70:110–13. Washington DC: Smithsonian Institution Press.

———. 1920. "The Symbolic Man of the Osage Tribe." *Art and Archaeology* 9:68–72.

———. 1921. "The Osage Tribe: Rite of the Chiefs: Sayings of the Ancient Men." In *36th Annual Report of the Bureau of American Ethnology [for] 1914–1915,* 37–640. Washington DC: Smithsonian Institution Press.

———. 1930. "The Osage Tribe: Rite of the Wa-xo'Be." In *45th Annual Report of the*

Bureau of American Ethnology [for] 1927-'28, 529-833. Washington DC: Smithsonian Institution.

———. 1939. "War Ceremony and Peace Ceremony of the Osage Indians." *Bureau of American Ethnology Bulletin* 101. Washington DC: Smithsonian Institution Press.

———. 1995. *The Osage and the Invisible World: From the Works of Francis La Flesche.* Edited by Garrick Bailey. Norman: University of Oklahoma Press.

Landes, Ruth. 1968. *The Mystic Lake Sioux: Sociology of the Mdewakantonwan Santee.* Madison: University of Wisconsin Press.

Lassiter, Luke Eric. 1993. "'They Left Us These Songs . . . That's All We Got Now': The Significance of Music in the Kiowa Gourd Dance and Its Relation to Native American Cultural Continuity." In *Native American Values: Survival and Renewal.* Edited by Thomas E. Schirer and Susan M. Branstner, 375-84. Sault Ste. Marie MI: Lake Superior State University Press.

———. 1997. "'Charley Brown': Not Just Another Essay on the Gourd Dance." *American Indian Culture and Research Journal* 21, no. 4: 75-103.

———. 1998. *The Power of Kiowa Song: A Collaborative Ethnography.* Tucson: University of Arizona Press.

Lassiter, Luke Eric, Clyde Ellis, and Ralph Kotay. 2002. *The Jesus Road: Kiowas, Christianity, and Indian Hymns.* Lincoln: University of Nebraska Press.

Lesser, Alexander. 1930. "Levirate and Fraternal Polyandry among the Pawnee." *Man* 30:98-101.

———. 1933a. "Cultural Significance of the Ghost Dance." *American Anthropologist* 35:108-15.

———. 1933b. "The Pawnee Ghost Dance Hand Game: Ghost Dance Revival and Ethnic Identity." *Contributions to Anthropology* 16. New York: Columbia University Press.

———. 1958. "Siouan Kinship." Ann Arbor: University Microfilms International.

———. 1979. "Caddoan Kinship Systems." *Nebraska History* 60, no. 2: 260-71.

Levy, Jerrold E. 1958. "Kiowa and Comanche: A Report from the Field." *Anthropology Tomorrow* 6, no. 2: 30-44.

———. 1959. "After Custer: Kiowa Political and Social Organization from the Reservation Period to the Present." PhD diss., University of Chicago.

———. 1961. "Ecology of the South Plains." In *American Ethnological Society Proceedings of the Annual Spring Meetings,* 18-25.

———. 2001. "Kiowa." In *Handbook of North American Indians.* Vol. 13, *Plains.* Edited by Raymond J. DeMallie, 907-25. Washington DC: Smithsonian Institution Press.

Lewis, Thomas H. 1968. "The Oglala Sun Dance 1968." *Pine Ridge (SD) Research Bulletin* 5:52-64.

———. 1972. "The Oglala (Teton Dakota) Sun Dance: Vicissitudes of Its Structure and Function." *Plains Anthropologist* 17, no. 55: 44-49.

Liberty, Margot. 1965. "Suppression and Survival of the Northern Cheyenne Sun Dance." *Minnesota Archaeologist* 27, no. 4: 120–44.

———. 1967. "The Northern Cheyenne Sun Dance and the Opening of the Sacred Medicine Hat 1959." *Plains Anthropologist*, n.s., 12, no. 38: 67–85.

———. 1968. "A Priest's Account of the Northern Cheyenne Sun Dance." *University of South Dakota: W. H. Over Museum Notes* 29:1–32.

———. 1980. "The Sun Dance." In *Anthropology on the Great Plains*. Edited by W. Raymond Wood and Margot Liberty, 164–78. Lincoln: University of Nebraska Press.

Linderman, Frank B. 1930. *American: The Life Story of a Great Indian. Plenty-Coups, Chief of the Crows*. New York: John Day.

Linton, Ralph. 1922a. "The Thunder Ceremony of the Pawnee." *Department of Anthropology Leaflet 5*. Chicago: Field Museum of Natural History.

———. 1922b. "The Sacrifice to the Morning Star by the Skidi Pawnee." *Department of Anthropology Leaflet 6*. Chicago: Field Museum of Natural History.

———. 1923a. "Purification of the Sacred Bundles: A Ceremony of the Pawnee." *Department of Anthropology Leaflet 7*. Chicago: Field Museum of Natural History.

———. 1923b. "The Annual Ceremony of the Pawnee Medicine Men." *Department of Anthropology Leaflet 8*. Chicago: Field Museum of Natural History.

———. 1926. "The Origin of the Skidi Pawnee Sacrifice to the Morning Star." *American Anthropologist*, n.s., 28:457–66.

———. 1935. "The Comanche Sun Dance." *American Anthropologist*, n.s., 37:420–28.

Llewellyn, Karl N., and E. Adamson Hoebel. 1941. *The Cheyenne Way: Conflict and Case Law in Primitive Jurisprudence*. Norman: University of Oklahoma Press.

Loughlin, Patricia. 2005. *Hidden Treasures of the American West: Muriel H. Wright, Angie Debo, and Alice Marriott*. Albuquerque: University of New Mexico Press.

Lowie, Robert H. 1909. "The Assiniboine." *American Museum of Natural History Anthropological Papers* 4:1–270.

———. 1912. "Comanche Fieldnotes." Manuscript in Department of Anthropology Archives. American Museum of Natural History, New York.

———. 1913a. "Dance Associations of the Eastern Dakota." *American Museum of Natural History Anthropological Papers* 11:101–42.

———. 1913b. "Societies of the Crow, Hidatsa and Mandan Indians." *American Museum of Natural History Anthropological Papers* 11:143–358.

———. 1913c. "Military Societies of the Crow Indians." *American Museum of Natural History Anthropological Papers* 11:143–218.

———. 1914. "The Crow Sun Dance." *Journal of American Folk-lore* 27:94–96.

———. 1915a. "The Sun Dance of the Crow Indians." *American Museum of Natural History Anthropological Papers* 16:1–50.

———. 1915b. "Societies of the Arikara Indians." *American Museum of Natural History Anthropological Papers* 11:645–78.

———. 1915c. "Dances and Societies of the Plains Shoshone." *American Museum of Natural History Anthropological Papers* 11:803–35.

———. 1916a. "Plains Indian Age-Societies: Historical and Comparative Summary." *American Museum of Natural History Anthropological Papers* 11:877–992.

———. 1916b. "Societies of the Kiowa." *American Museum of Natural History Anthropological Papers* 11:837–51.

———. 1918. "Myths and Traditions of the Crow Indians." *American Museum of Natural History Anthropological Papers* 25:1–308.

———. 1919a. "The Hidatsa Sun Dance." *American Museum of Natural History Anthropological Papers* 16:411–31.

———. 1919b. "The Tobacco Society of the Crow Indians." *American Museum of Natural History Anthropological Papers* 21:101–200.

———. 1919c. "The Sun Dance of the Shoshone, Ute, and Hidatsa." *American Museum of Natural History Anthropological Papers* 16:387–431.

———. 1919d. "The Sun Dance of the Wind River Shoshone, and Ute." *American Museum of Natural History Anthropological Papers* 16:387–431.

———. 1922. "The Religion of the Crow Indians." *American Museum of Natural History Anthropological Papers* 25:309–444.

———. 1923. "A Note on Kiowa Kinship Terms and Usages." *American Anthropologist*, n.s., 25:279–81.

———. 1924. "Minor Ceremonies of the Crow Indians." *American Museum of Natural History Anthropological Papers* 21:323–65.

———. 1935. *The Crow Indians*. New York: Rinehart.

Lyon, William S. 2012. *Spirit Talkers: North American Indian Medicine Powers*. Kansas City: Prayer Efficacy Publishing.

Marett, Robert R. 1914. *The Threshold of Religion*. 2nd ed. London: Methuen.

Marriott, Alice. 1945. *The Ten Grandmothers*. Norman: University of Oklahoma Press.

———. 1947. *Winter-telling Stories*. New York: Thomas Y. Crowell.

———. 1948. *Maria: The Potter of San Illdefonso*. Norman: University of Oklahoma Press.

———. 1952. *Greener Fields*. New York: Greenwood Press.

———. 1957. *The Black Stone Knife*. New York: Thomas Y. Crowell.

———. 1963. *Saynday's People: The Kiowa Indians and the Stories They Told*. Lincoln: University of Nebraska Press.

———. 1968. *Kiowa Years: A Study in Culture Impact*. New York: Macmillan.

Marriott, Alice, and Carol K. Rachlin. 1975. *Plains Indian Mythology*. New York: Thomas Y. Crowell.

Maximilian, Alexander Phillip Prinz zu Wied. 2008–12. *The North American Journals of Prince Maximilian of Wied*. 3 vols. Translated by Stephen S. Witte, Marsha V. Gallagher, and Dieter Karch. Norman: University of Oklahoma Press.

Mayhall, Mildred. 1984. *The Kiowas*. 2nd ed. Norman: University of Oklahoma Press.

McAllister, J. Gilbert. 1949. "Kiowa-Apache Tales." In *The Sky Is My Tipi*. Edited by Mody C. Boatright, 1–141. Publications of the Texas Folklore Society 22. Dallas: University of North Texas Press.

———. 1955. "Kiowa-Apache Social Organization." In *Social Anthropology of North American Tribes*. 2nd ed. Edited by Fred Eggan, 99–169. Chicago: University of Chicago Press.

———. 1965. "The Four Quarts Rocks Medicine Bundle of the Kiowa-Apache." *Ethnology* 4, no. 2: 210–24.

———. 1970. "Dävéko: Kiowa-Apache Medicine Man." *Bulletin of the Texas Memorial Museum* 17. Austin TX.

McHugh, Tom. 1972. *The Time of the Buffalo*. New York: Alfred A. Knopf.

Meadows, William C. 1999. *Kiowa, Apache, and Comanche Military Societies: Enduring Veterans, 1800 to the Present*. Austin: University of Texas Press.

———. 2008. *Kiowa Ethnogeography*. Austin: University of Texas Press.

———. 2010. *Kiowa Military Societies: Ethnohistory and Ritual*. Civilization of the American Indian. Norman: University of Oklahoma Press.

Merrill, William L., Marian Kaulaity Hansson, Candace S. Greene, and Frederick J. Reuss. 1997. *A Guide to the Kiowa Collections at the Smithsonian Institution Press*. Smithsonian Contributions to Anthropology 40. Washington DC: Smithsonian Institution Press.

Methvin, John Jasper. 1899. *Andele: or, the Mexican-Kiowa Captive*. Louisville: Pentecostal Herald Press.

———. 1927. "Reminiscences of Life among the Indians." *Chronicles of Oklahoma* 5:166–79.

———. n.d. *In the Limelight: or, History of Anadarko [Caddo County] and Vicinity from the Earliest Days*. Anadarko OK: N.T. Plummer.

Mikkanen, Arvo Quoetone. 1987. "'Skaw-tow': The Centennial Commemoration of the Last Kiowa Sun Dance, 1887–1987." Privately printed.

Miller, Jay. 1983. "Basin Religion and Theology: A Comparative Study of Power (Puha)." *Journal of California and Great Basin Anthropology* 5: 66–86.

Milligan, Edward A. 1969. "Sun Dance of the Sioux." Bottineau ND: Privately printed.

Mishkin, Bernard. 1940. "Rank and Warfare among the Plains Indians." *Monographs of the American Ethnological Society* 3. New York: J. J. Augustin.

Momaday, N. Scott. 1969. *The Way to Rainy Mountain*. Albuquerque: University of New Mexico Press.

Monahan, Forrest D. 1971–72. "Kiowa-Federal Relations in Kansas, 1865–1868." *Chronicles of Oklahoma* 49:477–91.

Mooney, James. 1891–1904. "Kiowa Heraldry Notebook: Descriptions of Kiowa Tipis and Shields." Manuscript 2531. National Anthropological Archives, Smithsonian Institution.

———. 1896. "The Ghost-dance Religion and the Sioux Outbreak of 1890." In *14th Annual Report of the Bureau of American Ethnology [for] 1892–'93*. Pt. 2, 641–1136. Washington DC: Smithsonian Institution Press.

———. 1898. "Calendar History of the Kiowa Indians." In *17th Annual Report of* the Bureau of American Ethnology [for] 1895-'96, Pt. 1, 129–468. Washington DC: Smithsonian Institution Press.

———. 1907. "The Cheyenne Indians." Bound with sketch of the Cheyenne grammar by Rodolphe Petter. *Memoirs of the American Anthropological Association* 1, pt. 6: 357–442.

Moore, John H. 1974. "A Study of Religious Symbolism among the Cheyenne Indians." PhD diss., New York University.

———. 1987. *The Cheyenne Nation: A Social and Demographic History*. Lincoln: University of Nebraska Press.

———. 1996. *The Cheyenne*. Oxford: Blackwell.

Moore, John H., Margot P. Liberty, and Terry Strauss. 2001. "Cheyenne." In *Handbook of North American Indians*. Vol. 13, *Plains*. Edited by Raymond J. DeMallie, 863–85. Washington DC: Smithsonian Institution Press.

Murie, James R. 1914. "Pawnee Indian Societies." *American Museum of Natural History Anthropological Papers* 11:543–644.

———. 1981. "Ceremonies of the Pawnee." 2 pts. 1: The Skiri; 2: The South Bands. Edited by Douglas R. Parks. *Smithsonian Contributions to Anthropology* 27.

Neighbors, Robert S. 1852. "The NA-ü-ni, or Comanches of Texas: Their Traits and Beliefs, and Their Divisions and Intertribal Relations." In *Historical and Statistical Information Respecting the History, Condition and Prospects of the Indian Tribes of the United States*. Vol. 2. Compiled and edited by Henry Rowe Schoolcraft, 125–34. Philadelphia: Lippincott, Grambo.

Neihardt, John G. 1932. *Black Elk Speaks: Being the Life Story of a Holy Man of the Oglala Sioux*. New York: William Morrow.

Newcomb, William W. 1978. *The Indians of Texas: From Prehistoric to Modern Times*. 4th ed. Austin: University of Texas Press.

———. 2001. "Wichita." In *Handbook of North American Indians*. Vol. 13, *Plains*. Edited by Raymond J. DeMallie, 548–66. Washington DC: Smithsonian Institution Press.

Nieberding, Velma S. 1976. *The Quapaws: Those Who Went Downstream*. Quapaw OK: Quapaw Tribal Council.

Nye, Wilbur S. 1934. "The Annual Sun Dance of the Kiowa Indians: As Related by George Hunt." *Chronicles of Oklahoma* 12:340–58.

———. 1937. *Carbine and Lance: The Story of Old Fort Sill*. Norman: University of Oklahoma Press.

———. 1962. *Bad Medicine and Good: Tales of the Kiowas*. Norman: University of Oklahoma Press.

Opler, Morris E., and William E. Bittle. 1961. "The Death Practices and Eschatology of the Kiowa Apache." *Southwestern Journal of Anthropology* 27, no. 4: 383–94.

Osborn, Alan J. 1983. "Ecological Aspects of Equestrian Adaptations in Aboriginal North America." *American Anthropologist* 85, no. 4: 563–91.

Ottaway, Harold N. 1970. "The Cheyenne Arrow Ceremony, 1968." *Oklahoma Anthropological Society Bulletin* 19.

Palmer, Gus, Jr. 2003. *Telling Stories the Kiowa Way*. Tucson: University of Arizona Press.

Paper, Jordan. 2005. "Tobacco, Sacred Use of." In *American Indian Religious Traditions: An Encyclopedia*. Edited by Suzanne J. Crawford and Dennis F. Kelley, 1099–1102. Santa Barbara CA: ABC-CLIO.

Parks, Douglas R. 1984. *Arikara Coyote Tales: A Bilingual Reader: Naa'iikawiš Sahniš*. Roseglen ND: White Shield School District 89, Bilingual Education Program.

———. 1985. "Alexander Lesser 1902–1982." *Plains Anthropologist* 30, no. 107: 65–71.

———. 1991. *Traditional Narratives of the Arikara Indians*. 4 vols. Studies in the Anthropology of North American Indians. Lincoln: University of Nebraska Press.

———. 2001. "Arikara." In *Handbook of North American Indians*. Vol. 13, *Plains*. Edited by Raymond J. DeMallie, 365–90. Washington DC: Smithsonian Institution Press.

Parks, Douglas R., and Waldo R. Wedel. 1985. "Pawnee Geography: Historical and Sacred." *Great Plains Quarterly* 5, no. 3: 143–76.

Parsons, Elsie Clews. 1929. "Kiowa Tales." *Memoirs of the American Folk-Lore Society* 22. New York.

Pepper, George H., and Gilbert L. Wilson. 1908. "An Hidatsa Shrine and the Beliefs Respecting It." *Memoirs of the American Anthropological Association* 2:275–328.

Peterson, Karen Daniels. 1964. "Cheyenne Soldier Societies." *Plains Anthropologist* 9, no. 25: 146–72.

Pond, Gideon H. 1854. "Power and Influence of Dakota Medicine-men." In *Historical and Statistical Information Respecting the History, Condition and Prospects of the Indian Tribes of the United States*. Vol. 4. Compiled and edited by Henry Rowe Schoolcraft, 641–51. Philadelphia: Lippincott, Grambo.

———. 1867. "Dakota Superstitions and Gods." *Collections of the Minnesota Historical Society* 2:32–62.

Pond, Samuel W. 1908. "The Dakotas or Sioux in Minnesota As They Were in 1834." *Minnesota Historical Society Collections* 12:320–501.

Powell, Peter J. 1958. "Mahuts, the Sacred Arrows of the Cheyenne." *Westerners Brand Book* 15:35–40.

———. 1960. "Issiwun: Sacred Buffalo Hat of the Northern Cheyenne." *Montana: The Magazine of Western History* 10:24–40.

———. 1969. *Sweet Medicine: The Continuing Role of the Sacred Arrows, the Sun Dance, and the Sacred Buffalo Hat in Northern Cheyenne History*. 2 vols. Norman: University of Oklahoma Press.

———. 1980. *The Cheyennes, Ma'he'o's People: A Critical Bibliography*. Bloomington: Indiana University Press.

Powers, William K. 1977. *Oglala Religion*. Lincoln: University of Nebraska Press.

———. 1982. *Yuwipi: Vision and Experience in Oglala Ritual*. Lincoln: University of Nebraska Press.

———. 1989. "The Plains." In *Native Religions: North America*, edited by Lawrence E. Sullivan, 19–33. New York: Macmillan.

Provinse, John H. 1955. "The Underlying Sanctions of Plains Indian Culture." In *Social Anthropology of North American Tribes*. Edited by Fred Eggan, 341–74. Chicago: University of Chicago Press.

Rand, Jackie Thompson. 2008. *Kiowa Humanity and the Invasion of the State*. Lincoln: University of Nebraska Press.

Randolph, Richard W. 1937. *Sweet Medicine and Other Stories of the Cheyenne Indians, as Told to Richard W. Randolph*. Caldwell ID: Caxton.

Richardson, Jane Hanks. 1940. "Law and Status among the Kiowa Indians." *Monographs of the American Ethnological Society* 1. New York: J.J. Augustin.

Ridington, Robin, and Dennis Hastings. 1997. *Blessing for a Long Time: The Sacred Pole of the Omaha Tribe*. Lincoln: University of Nebraska Press.

Sandoz, Mari. 1942. *Crazy Horse: The Strange Man of the Oglalas*. New York: Alfred A. Knopf.

Sanford, Margaret S. 1971. "Present Day Death Practices and Eschatology of the Kiowa Apache." *University of Oklahoma Papers in Anthropology* 12:81–134.

Schlesier, Karl H. 1987. *The Wolves of Heaven: Cheyenne Shamanism, Ceremonies, and Prehistoric Origins*. Norman: University of Oklahoma Press.

Schultes, Richard Evans. 1937. "Peyote and Plants Used in the Peyote Ceremony." *Botanical Museum Leaflets, Harvard University* 4, no. 8: 129–52.

Schweinfurth, Kay Parker. 2002. *Prayer on Top of the Earth: The Spiritual Universe of the Plains Apache*. Boulder: University Press of Colorado.

Scott, Hugh L. 1911. "Notes on the Kado, or Sun Dance of the Kiowa." *American Anthropologist*, n.s., 13:345–79.

Secoy, Frank C. 1953. "Changing Military Patterns on the Plains (17th Century through Early 19th Century)." *Monographs of the American Ethnological Society* 21. Locust Valley NY: J.J. Augustin.

Skinner, Alanson B. 1914a. "Political Organizations, Cults and Ceremonies of the Plains-Cree." *American Museum of Natural History Anthropological Papers* 11:513–42.

———. 1914b. "Political and Ceremonial Organization of the Plains-Ojibway." *American Museum of Natural History Anthropological Papers* 11:475–511.

———. 1915a. "Societies of the Iowa, Kansa, and Ponca Indians." *American Museum of Natural History Anthropological Papers* 11:679–801.

———. 1915b. "Ponca Societies and Dances." *American Museum of Natural History Anthropological Papers* 11:777–801.

———. 1919a. "The Sun Dance of the Plains-Cree." *American Museum of Natural History Anthropological Papers* 16:283–93.

———. 1919b. "The Sun Dance of the Plains-Ojibway." *American Museum of Natural History Anthropological Papers* 16:311–15.

———. 1919c. "Notes on the Sun Dance of the Sisseton Dakota." *American Museum of Natural History Anthropological Papers* 16:381–85. New York.

Snow, Chief John. 1977. *These Mountains Are Our Sacred Places: The Story of the Stoney Indians*. Toronto: Samuel Stevens.

Spencer, Joab. 1908. "The Kaw or Kansas Indians: Their Customs, Manners and Folklore." *Transactions of the Kansas State Historical Society for 1907–1908* 10:373–82.

Spier, Leslie. 1921a. "Notes on the Kiowa Sun Dance." *American Museum of Natural History Anthropological Papers* 16:433–50.

———. 1921b. "The Sun Dance of the Plains Indians: Its Development and Diffusion." *American Museum of Natural History Anthropological Papers* 16:451–527.

Stahl, Robert. 1983. "Kiowa Voices: Echoes and Reverberations." In *Reviews in Anthropology*, Summer, 43–54.

Standing Bear, Luther. 1928. *My People the Sioux*. Edited by Earl A. Brininstool. Boston: Houghton Mifflin.

———. 1933. *Land of the Spotted Eagle*. Boston: Houghton Mifflin.

Stands in Timber, John, and Margot Pringle Liberty. 1967. *Cheyenne Memories*. New Haven CT: Yale University Press.

Steele, Aubrey L. 1939. "The Beginning of Quaker Administration of Indian Affairs in Oklahoma." *Chronicles of Oklahoma* 17:364–92.

Stewart, Frank Henderson. 2001. "Hidatsa." In *Handbook of North American Indians*. Vol. 13, *Plains*. Edited by Raymond J. DeMallie, 329–48. Washington DC: Smithsonian Institution Press.

Stewart, Omer C. 1987. *Peyote Religion. A History*. Norman: University of Oklahoma Press.

Stover, Dale. 2005. "Symbolism in American Indian Ritual and Ceremony." In *American Indian Religious Traditions: An Encyclopedia*. Edited by Suzanne J. Crawford and Dennis F. Kelley, 1084–92. Santa Barbara CA: ABC-CLIO.

Swagerty, William R. 1988. "Indian Trade in the Trans-Mississippi West to 1870." In *Handbook of North American Indians*. Vol. 4, *History of Indian-White Relations*. Edited by Wilcomb E. Washburn, 335–50. Washington DC: Smithsonian Institution Press.

Swan, Daniel C., and Michael P. Jordan. 2011. "Tipis and the Warrior Tradition." In *Tipi: Heritage of the Great Plains*. Edited by Nancy B. Kosoff and Susan K. Zeller, 145–63. Seattle: University of Washington Press.

Szabo, Joyce M. 2007. *Art from Fort Marion: The Silberman Collection*. Norman: University of Oklahoma Press.

Thompson, Stith. 1929. *Tales of the North American Indians*. Bloomington: Indiana University Press.

Twohatchet, Delores. 1996. "Choosing the Jesus Road: To Build a Church." In *Eagle Flights: Native Americans and the Christian Faith*, 8–10. Nashville: Cokesbury.

Vennum, Thomas, Jr. 1982. *The Ojibwa Dance Drum: Its History and Construction*. Smithsonian Folklife Series 2. Washington DC: Smithsonian Institution Press.

Voget, Fred W. 1950. "The Diffusion of the Wind River Sundance to the Crow Indians of Montana." PhD diss., Yale University.

———. 1984. *The Shoshoni-Crow Sun Dance*. Norman: University of Oklahoma Press.

Wahrhaftig, Albert L., and Jane Lukens-Wahrhaftig. 1977. "The Thrice Powerless: Cherokee Indians in Oklahoma." In *The Anthropology of Power: Ethnographic Studies from Asia, Oceania, and the New World*. Edited by Raymond D. Fogelson and Richard N. Adams, 225–36. New York: Academic Press.

Walker, James R. 1917. "The Sun Dance and Other Ceremonies of the Oglala Division of the Teton Dakota." *American Museum of Natural History Anthropological Papers* 16:51–221.

———. 1980. *Lakota Belief and Ritual*. Edited by Raymond J. DeMallie and Elaine A. Jahner. Lincoln: University of Nebraska Press.

Wallace, Ernest, and E. Adamson Hoebel. 1952. "The Comanche: Lords of the Southern Plains. Based on Field Work 1933–1945." *Human Relations Area Files* 6, vol. 3. Norman: University of Oklahoma Press.

Wallis, Wilson D. 1919. "The Sun Dance of the Canadian Dakota." *American Museum of Natural History Anthropological Papers* 16:317–80.

Waters, William T. 1984. "Otoe-Missouria Oral Narratives." Master's thesis, University of Nebraska.

Watkins, Laurel J. 1984. *A Grammar of Kiowa*. Edited by Raymond J. DeMallie and Douglas R. Parks. Studies in the Anthropology of North American Indians. Lincoln: University of Nebraska Press.

Wedel, Mildred Mott. 2001. "Iowa." In *Handbook of North American Indians*. Vol. 13, *Plains*. Edited by Raymond J. DeMallie, 432–46. Washington DC: Smithsonian Institution Press.

Wedel, Waldo R. 1933. "Comanche Notes, Drafts, Photos, and Negatives, Field Notebooks, Maps, Specimen Catalog: Fieldnotes of San Francisco Bay." Waldo R. Wedel Collection, box 108. National Anthropological Archives, Smithsonian Institution.

Weltfish, Gene. 1965. *The Lost Universe: Pawnee Life and Culture*. Lincoln: University of Nebraska Press.

Whitewolf, Jim. 1969. *Jim Whitewolf: The Life of a Kiowa Apache Indian*. Edited by Charles S. Brant. New York: Dover.

Whitman, William. 1937. "The Oto." *Columbia University Contributions to Anthropology* 28. New York.

Wishart, David J. 2004. "Grinnell, George Bird (1849–1938)." In *Encyclopedia of the Great Plains: A Project of the Center for Great Plains Studies*. Edited by David J. Wishart, 303–4. Lincoln: University of Nebraska Press.

Wissler, Clark. 1912a. "Societies and Ceremonial Associations in the Oglala Division of the Teton-Dakota." *American Museum of Natural History Anthropological Papers* 11:1–99.

———. 1912b. "Ceremonial Bundles of the Blackfoot Indians." *American Museum of Natural History Anthropological Papers* 7:65–284.

————. 1912–16. "Societies of the Plains Indians." Edited by Clark Wissler. *American Museum of Natural History Anthropological Papers* 11.

————. 1913. "Societies and Dance Associations of the Blackfoot Indians." *American Museum of Natural History Anthropological Papers* 11:359–460.

————. 1915–21. "Sun Dance of the Plains Indians." Edited by Clark Wissler. *American Museum of Natural History Anthropological Papers* 16.

————. 1916. "General Discussion of Shamanistic and Dancing Societies." *American Museum of Natural History Anthropological Papers* 11:853–76.

————. 1918. "The Sun Dance of the Blackfoot Indians." American *Museum of Natural History Anthropological Papers* 16:223–70.

Wissler, Clark, and David C. Duvall. 1908. "Mythology of the Blackfoot Indians." *American Museum of Natural History Anthropological Papers* 2, pt. 1: 1–163.

Wissler, Clark, and Herbert J. Spinden. 1916. "The Pawnee Human Sacrifice to the Morning Star." *American Museum Journal* 16:49–55.

Witherspoon, Gary. 2005. "Emergence Narratives." In *American Indian Religious Traditions: An Encyclopedia.* Edited by Suzanne J. Crawford and Dennis F. Kelley, 258–65. Santa Barbara CA: ABC-CLIO.

Wood, W. Raymond, and Lee Irwin. 2001. "Mandan." In *Handbook of North American Indians.* Vol. 13, *Plains.* Edited by Raymond J. DeMallie, 349–64. Washington DC: Smithsonian Institution Press.

Wright, Muriel H. 1956. "A History of Fort Cobb." *Chronicles of Oklahoma* 34:53–71.

————. 1986. *A Guide to the Indian Tribes of Oklahoma.* 9th printing. Norman: University of Oklahoma Press.

Young, Gloria A. 2001. "Music." In *Handbook of North American Indians.* Vol. 13, *Plains.* Edited by Raymond J. DeMallie, 1026–38. Washington DC: Smithsonian Institution Press.

Zwink, T. Ashley. 1978–79. "On the White Man's Road: Lawrie Tatum and the Formative Years of the Kiowa Agency." *Chronicles of Oklahoma* 56:431–41.

Index

songs for, 86, 97; status of owners of, 59, 87; taboos around, 139–40, 141, 191; women and, 89. *See also specific medicine bundles*

Medicine Hat bundle, 11

Medicine Horse, T. Larson, Sr., 248

Medicine Lodge Treaty (1867), xiv, 52, 220, 251–52, 256, 272–73

medicine men, 74; Buffalo Society and, 115–26; contests between, 105; fear of, 103; *gietso* of, 96, 105, 107; gifts to, 98, 101, 131, 132; and peyote-based power, 98–100; reduced numbers of, 131, 133, 151; requesting help from, 97–98, 120–21; shields of, 91

"medicine teepee ceremony," 197

memory, 19

meteor showers, 63

Methvin, John Jasper, 15, 199, 214, 240, 264–65, 273

Mexico raids, 49–52, 165–66, 258, 270

middle-world powers, 64–71; visions and, 61

migration, 35, 36–37

Mikkanen, Arvo Quoetone, 18, 201

Miles, Nelson, 259–60

military societies, 15

Milky Way, 63

Milligan, Edward, 4

mining, 128–29

Mishkin, Bernard, xiv, xvii, 19, 275; background of, 21; collaborators with, 26, 53, 86; on Kiowa warfare, 164, 168; *Rank and Warfare among the Plains Indians*, 164, 275; on shields, 180; on social organization, 42, 87, 277

missionaries, 130, 272–73

Mo-keen, 16, 43, 162, 182, 185; conversion of, to Christianity, 267; descendants of, 190; at the Sun Dance,

205, 215, 223, 266; and the Taime, 265, 267

Mole power, 78, 107

Momaday, N. Scott, 54, 75, 261

Monographs of the American Ethnological Society, 275

Moon, 62–63; prayer to, 63

Mooney, James, xiv, 13–14, 16, 279, 297n97; antelope drive described by, 78; on Bear taboo, 76; on Buffalo power, 87–88, 116; Buffalo shield bought by, 118; *Calendar History of the Kiowa Indians*, xvi, 13–14, 15, 45, 155, 279; and collaborators, 25, 115; fieldnotes of, 278; on Ghost Dance, 5, 271; heraldry notes of, 175; on horse and buffalo culture declining, 251; inheritance patterns studied by, 115; "Kiowa Heraldry Notebook," 115; on meteor showers, 63; origin stories documented by, 54, 57; on the Red River War, 258; on smoking, 167–68; on societies, 187; on the Sun Dance, 199, 203, 245, 264, 265; Sun Dance camp reconstruction of, 220–21; on Taime, 153–54, 157, 158, 159, 160; on Ten Medicines, 139; on tipi designs, 79; on war, 167–68

Moore, John, 8, 43, 251

Morgan, Gabriel Po-Kei-Tay, 248

Morgan, Thomas, 262, 264

Morning Star, 63

Moth Woman (Old Lady Kintadl), 28–29, 39, 77; on the Bear Society, 75, 188, 189; on Botadli, 93; on Deer, 77, 78; on Earth, 71; on geographical distribution, 44; on ghost sickness, 66; on grave looting, 192; on the Guhale, 254, 255; on medicine men, fear of, 103, 114–15; on Milky Way, 63; on Mole, 78; on Moon, 63; on the Old Women's Society, 189–90; on

Smokey, Enoch, 22, 24–25
snakes, 79, 86, 105
Snapping Turtle, 79
Snyder Act (1924), 24
social class, power and, 87
social organization, 21, 39–45; geography and, 44; giveaways and, 243; groups and bands, 41–45; horses changing, 36; kinship, 39–41; leadership and, 42–44; rank and, 36–37, 41–42, 206, 243; seasonality of, 44–45
societies, 3–5, 11, 15, 33, 186–95; after 1935, 190–95; blood-brothers in, 187; collapse of, 183, 190; collective power of, 114–15; functions of, 187–88; non-age-graded, 186; policing hunts, 187–88, 216, 268; power and, 114; in the reservation era, 266–67; shield, 175–80, 183, 266–67; Sun Dance and, 138, 206, 219, 227–28; types of, 114, 137–38, 163; war, 163–64, 186–88, 190–95; women's, 75, 114, 140, 188–90. *See also specific societies*
songs, 101, 119, 121, 122; bundles activated by, 86; Ghost Dance, 271, 273; learned in dreams, 58–59; Native American Church, 82; for protection in war, 83; Sun Dance, 213, 227–28, 229–30, 231, 247
Son of the Sun, 61, 185–86
Soondeton (Tail Of An Industrious Bird), 255
sorcery, 69, 78, 107; descriptions of, 103–4; disease caused by, 103; and identifying sorcerers, 104–5; killing by, 107, 112–13, 261; in modern times, 134–35; protection against, 110–11, 134; rebounding on practitioner, 107, 134; vs. witchcraft, 296n62
souls: owls as, 68; sickness and, 119
Spear Lake WY, 139
Spencer, Joab, 6

spiders, 79, 100, 102
Spider Woman (Spider Grandmother, Spider Old Woman), 38, 57
Spier, Leslie, 4, 15–16, 200
Spinden, Herbert, 6
spirits: animal, 74; Bear Society as intermediaries with, 189; communing with, 108–9, 110; dream, 58, 59, 60–61, 86, 88, 95, 138; earth, 71–73; owls as, 68, 69, 70, 108
Split Boys, 56, 57, 139, 140
Spotted Wing (Tsodlte, Tsodltoi), 105
springtime, 44, 64, 67, 82–83
Standing Bear, Luther, 11–12
Stands in Timber, John, 11
Star Boy, 56–57
Star Girls, 75
"Star-girl-tree-river," 263, 284
Star Husband/Star Rope tale, 56
stars, 63
Starting Song of the Sun Dance, 234, 238, 243
Star Woman ceremony, 75
Stinking Creek, 26, 30
"Stone-necklace Sun Dance," 282
stone symbolism, 237
Stumbling Bear. *See* Setĭmkía (Stumbling Bear)
Stumbling Bear, Andrew, 46, 53, 76; on the Ghost Dance, 270; on the Sun Dance, 202, 207, 209, 230; on the Sun People, 269
Stumblingbear, Trina, 126–27
Stumbling Bear, Virginia, 26
Stumbling Bear/Kicking Bird band, 26
sucking technique, 79, 99–103, 121, 124, 131–33; *gietso* and, 96; methods of, 98; peyote and, 98–99; sorcery and, 76, 103–4, 105
Sugar Creek, 26
Sun, 61–62, 198; Buffalo and, 61–62, 74, 198; as creator, 218; designs, 62, 173,

decline in, 126; on mountains, 71–72, 88–90; multiple, 88, 97; power acquired through, 86; preparing for, 96–97; reconstructing, 91–95; ritual of, 89–90; seasonality of, 74; women engaging in, 89

visions: age and, 88; conversations as part of, 94–95; dream shields and, 172, 173; elevation and, 71–72; at home vs. on quest, 88; modern experiences of, 128, 129–30; mourning and, 73; occurring in middle world, 61; power and, 58, 59; as ritual, 86–87; songs and, 101

Voget, Fred, 4

wakanda, wahką́da, 58, 60

Waldo, Jim (Kogaitadl, Lean Elk), 22, 23, 24, 140, 151

Walker, Francis, 257

Walker, James, 11

walking, symbolism of, 218

war, 48; cessation of, in reservation era, 262, 266; chiefs, 167–68, 224; cries, 120; dancing, 134, 168, 171; decreasing territory leading to, 49; Eagle shields in, 177; general expeditions, 165–66; honors, 87, 163–64, 165–66, 171–72; horses in, 77, 163; intertribal, 37, 38, 46–47, 68, 166, 255; Kiowas at, 164–67; paint, 170, 171, 172–73; parties, organization of, 167; parties, return of, 170–71; protective medicines and, 169–70; religious motivations for, 114, 163–64; of revenge, 165, 166–67, 168, 169, 170; ritual smoking and, 167–68; stories, 171, 172; treaties preventing, 47, 48, 51–52; with U.S. troops, 166–67, 258–60; victory in, 170, 171–72; weapons of, taken by U.S., 175–76, 180, 185, 186, 260–61; women's role

in, 186, 189–90; wounds, treating, 118–19, 120. *See also* Red River War

Ware, James, 190

Ware, Lewis, 247

Ware, Lynn, 28, 29; descendants of, 32

Ware, Patricia, 78, 128

war factions, 253–61

war powers, 64, 74, 83, 162–95; animals conferring, 66–67, 69; horses sharing, 77; obtaining, 85, 163; protective, 137; proving, 90–91; rites related to, 167–72, 175; Sun connected to, 62

Warren Wagon-Train Massacre, 256

the War Twins, 38

Wasson, R. Gordon, 274

water creatures, 79

Waters, William, 3

The Way to Rainy Mountain (Momaday), 54, 75, 261

wealth, 41–42

weather, 64–66, 67–68; controlling, 107–8

Wedel, Waldo, 9

Weltfish, Gene, 6, 11, 20, 275

whistles, 209

Whitaker, Rachel, 70

White Bear, 77, 220, 252; as "hostile," 166, 256, 257, 265; in the Red River War, 258, 259; release of, 257, 258; Sun Dance and, 220, 284; war regalia of, 174. *See also* Set'aide

White Buffalo, 104, 139, 153; on the buffalo-calling ceremony, 231–32; on the Sun Dance, 201, 202, 244; on the Sun Dance camp, 213–14, 215; on the Sun Dance dancers, 206, 207, 208, 209; on the Sun Dance, day one, 228, 230, 231, 232, 233–34; on the Sun Dance, day two, 237, 238, 239, 240; on the Sun Dance, day three, 241; on the Sun Dance,

In the Studies in the Anthropology of North American Indians Series

CPSIA information can be obtained
at www.ICGtesting.com
Printed in the USA
LVHW040157150723
752404LV00001B/96